MINERVA AND THE ARTS

This mural portrays Minerva protecting Architecture, Sculpture, and Painting from the
ravages of Time.

CLASSICAL MYTHS

BY

MAX J. HERZBERG

PRINCIPAL, WEEQUAHIC HIGH SCHOOL
NEWARK, NEW JERSEY

ALLYN AND BACON

BOSTON NEW YORK CHICAGO
ATLANTA SAN FRANCISCO DALLAS

DTF

Norwood Press

J. S. Cushing Co. — Berwick & Smith Co.

Norwood, Mass., U.S.A.

PREFACE

Specifically, this volume is intended to furnish a necessary background of myth and legend for the student of Latin, but it is hoped that the book will prove equally useful to readers of English and American literature, in which these ancient stories play so large a part, and as a reference work. In order to be of such general assistance Northern and Celtic stories have been included, although the chief emphasis has been placed, as the title indicates, on our classical heritage.

Experience has shown that young people of today, despite a widely held educational theory that they enjoy only events and persons that occur in the passing moment, are deeply interested in these antique tales and will read them voluntarily if given the opportunity to do so. It is, on examination, natural enough that this should be so, inasmuch as these myths are, after all, entrancing merely as stories and represent in addition the quintessence of a people's thought and poetry. Their striking plots, the strange and remarkable characters who appear in them, the frequent allegory of the occurrences, the rich imagination shown in the details, the constant and familiar use of them made in literature and in ordinary conversation, these are sufficient reasons for the enduring popularity of the myths retold in this volume, especially those garnered from Greek and Latin literature.

Attention may be called to the special features of *Classical Myths*. Because the point of view is that of the student of Latin, Roman names are used instead of Greek, although the Greek equivalent is supplied when a name is first introduced.

There are full accounts of the Roman gods, the early Roman kings, the special aspects of Roman religion, the Roman festivals, and the mythological subjects treated by Virgil, Ovid, and other writers of Latin literature.

While a great mass of factual material may be found in these pages, the endeavor is always to make this material as entertaining as possible. For the most part facts are presented in story form. At the end of each chapter the employment of the myths in literature is analyzed, and a wide and varied series of quotations is presented for the student's explanation. Much stress is laid on word study, and from the sections under this heading at the ends of chapters students will gain a comprehensive idea of the great role that myth has played in the enrichment of our English vocabulary. There is also a rapid quiz at the end of each chapter, as a provision for a brief review; and to this has been added a special quiz for students of Latin. In the list of books at chapter ends students will find much material for additional reading in fiction, non-fiction, drama, and poetry. Many projects and subjects for composition are likewise suggested.

It may be noted, too, that the relations of mythology to art and music have by no means been neglected. A glance at the numerous and carefully selected illustrations will indicate the care that has been taken in connection with painting and sculpture, and in the bibliographies many musical compositions have been included; there are likewise frequent references to music in the text proper. The relations of mythology to science, to advertising, and to other subjects have likewise been considered. The full index makes the book, it is believed, a reference volume of unusual value.

In the miscellaneous material at the back of the book may

be found some amusing games, additional quotations for explanation and additional exercises, a reading list for teachers, an extensive glossary, and some recent college-entrance and Regents examinations in which a knowledge of mythology is called for.

For help in connection with the preparation of this volume grateful acknowledgment is due William Lewin, Christopher Morley, Seumas O'Brien, Beatrice Winser, William H. Powell of the Atlantic Terra Cotta Company, Murray Martin of the Public Relations Committee of Rockefeller Center, Edna N. Herzberg, and Richard Arnold Herzberg.

M. J. H.

CONTENTS

PAGE

MYTHS AS A CLASSICAL HERITAGE 1

MYTHS OF GREECE AND ROME

I.	HOW THE WORLD BEGAN	16
II.	THE GODS OF THE SKY	31
III.	STORIES OF JUPITER AND MINERVA	58
IV.	STORIES OF VENUS	78
V.	STORIES OF APOLLO	104
VI.	STORIES OF DIANA	128
VII.	THE GODS OF NATURE	144
VIII.	STORIES OF THE GODS OF NATURE	160
IX.	IN THE UNDERWORLD	189
X.	THREE HEROES AND TWO FRIENDS	207
XI.	THE ADVENTURES OF HERCULES	232
XII.	THE GOLDEN FLEECE	250
XIII.	THE TROJAN WAR	267
XIV.	AFTER THE TROJAN WAR	295
XV.	THE ADVENTURES OF AENEAS	320
XVI.	THE DIVINITIES OF ROME	348
XVII.	MYTHS IN HOMER, VIRGIL, AND OVID . . .	377

NORTHERN AND CELTIC MYTHS

XVIII.	GODS OF THE NORTHLAND	395
XIX.	HEROES OF THE NORTH	418
XX.	THE CELTIC FAIRYLAND	435
XXI.	SOME ASPECTS OF MYTHOLOGY	467

PAGE

APPENDIX:

REVIEW REFERENCES TO MYTHOLOGY IN LITERATURE . . 485

BRIEF DESCRIPTIONS 489

SOME QUESTIONS AS TO MATTERS OF FACT AND FANCY . . 490

SUGGESTIONS FOR COMPOSITIONS, ORAL AND WRITTEN . . 491

DRAMA PROJECTS 493

SOME MISCELLANEOUS EXERCISES 494

READING LIST FOR TEACHERS 498

A TRUE-FALSE TEST 498

A MULTIPLE-CHOICE TEST 499

QUESTIONS INVOLVING MYTHOLOGICAL REFERENCES IN RECENT
   COLLEGE BOARD AND REGENTS ENGLISH EXAMINATIONS . 500

QUESTIONS FROM COLLEGE ENTRANCE BOARD EXAMINATIONS IN
   LATIN 502

ILLUSTRATIVE MATERIAL 505

SOURCES FOR PICTORIAL MATERIAL DEALING WITH MYTHOLOGY 505

GLOSSARY 509

INDEX OF AUTHORS, ARTISTS, AND COMPOSERS . . . I

GENERAL INDEX 9

ILLUSTRATIONS

Minerva and the Arts (*colored*) . . . . . . *Frontispiece*

PAGE

Apollo and the Muses 1
Jupiter 3
Music 5
Orpheus and Eurydice 6
Siegfried and Kriemhild 7
Peter Pan 10
Prometheus 16
Sphinx and Chimera 19
Atlas 20
The Creation of Man by Prometheus : Minerva Gives Him a Soul 23
Pandora 25
The Hours Taking Horses from Juno's Car 31
Council of Jupiter, Mercury, and Minerva 32
Juno 34
Mars 36
Vulcan Forging Arrows for Cupid 37
Ganymede and the Eagle 38
Apollo in His Chariot, with the Hours 40
Mount Parnassus 41
Diana 42
Venus of Capua with Cupid 44
Minerva 46
Mercury Inventing the Caduceus 47
The Three Fates 49
Victory (Nike) of Samothrace 50
The Temple of Zeus, Athens 58
Europa and the Bull 59
Daedalus and Icarus 61
Oedipus and the Sphinx 63
Baucis and Philemon Entertaining Jupiter and Mercury . . 67

PAGE

Athens 69
Transformation of Arachne into a Spider 71
Minerva of Poitiers 73
Venus and Cupid 78
Venus de Milo 79
Cupid Weeping over Adonis 81
Cupid Awakening Psyche 83
Psyche at Nature's Mirror 85
Charon and Psyche 88
Cupid and Psyche Are Welcomed to Mount Olympus . . . 89
Atalanta's Race 90
Cybele 92
Hero and Leander 95
Thisbe 97
Apollo and Diana Discharging Arrows 104
Latona with Infants Apollo and Diana 105
The Fall of Phaëthon 111
Battle of the Lapiths and Centaurs 113
Aesculapius 114
Lecythus (Vase for Oil) Showing King Admetus with Chariot of
    Wild Beasts 115
Apollo Slays the Python 119
Olympic Games 120
Runners 121
Discobolus 122
Diana in Chariot 128
Diana Beholds the Sleeping Endymion 129
The Sleeping Endymion 131
The Pleiades 132
A Daughter of Niobe 134
Meleager 137
A Mythological Map of the Ancient World . . . 142–143
The Winds 144
Ceres 145
Silenus with the Infant Bacchus 147
Seated Faun 148
Aurora 150

PAGE

Nereid on a Fish 151
Neptune 152
Triton 153
Pan and Bear 160
Abduction of Proserpina 161
Isle of the Dead 162
The Return of Persephone (*colored*) . . . . *facing* 162
Demeter and Persephone 164
The Judgment of Midas 166
Arion and the Dolphins 168
Mercury Plays Argus to Sleep 170
Eros with Bow 172
Apollo and Daphne 174
Echo 176
Narcissus 177
Aurora 179
The Nymph Transformed into a Fountain 183
Danaïdes 189
Mercury Consigns the Soul of a Woman to Charon . . 190
Cerberus and the Furies 191
Tantalus, Ixion, and Sisyphus in Tartarus 194
Orpheus and Eurydice 197
Eurydice Bids Farewell to Orpheus as Mercury Leads Her Away 199
Orpheus Pursued by the Maenads 200
Sacrifice for the Freeing of Andromeda 207
Danaë and the Shower of Gold 208
Perseus and the Gray Sisters 210
Perseus on Pegasus Slays Medusa 211
Atlas and Perseus 212
Perseus Rescuing Andromeda 214
Perseus and Andromeda 215
Head of Medusa 217
Theseus Lifting the Rock 219
The Minotaur 221
Ariadne 222
Mounted Amazon 224
Bellerophon 226

PAGE

Hercules in the Garments of a Woman Spinning Wool . . 232
Infant Hercules Strangling Snakes 233
Hercules with Lion Skin 234
Hercules and the Hydra 237
Hercules and the Cretan Bull 239
Amazon 240
Hercules at the Feet of Omphale 243
Hebe 245
Jason 250
Building of the "Argo" 253
Hylas and the Nymphs 255
Phineas and the Harpies 257
Medea 261
Jason and Medea Seize the Golden Fleece 263
Juno and Minerva Assist Greeks 267
Judgment of Paris 268
Venus Persuading Helen to Elope with Paris 271
The Abduction of Helen 273
Ulysses Feigning Madness 274
Achilles' Education by Chiron 275
Sacrifice of Iphigenia 276
Hector's Farewell to Andromache 279
Vulcan and Thetis 280
The Horses of Achilles 283
The Wooden Horse 285
Laocoön 286
Trojan Fugitives 287
Ulysses and His Companions Give Wine to Polyphemus . . 295
Ajax and Cassandra 296
Orestes Pursued by the Furies 297
Orestes and Pylades before Iphigenia 298
An Island Supposed to Be That of the Cyclopes . . . 301
Polyphemus 303
Circe and Ulysses' Companions 306
The Sirens 307
Nausicaä and Her Maids Playing Ball 309
Penelope and Her Suitors 311

PAGE

Ulysses Recognized by His Dog 312
Penelope 313
The Slaying of the Suitors 314
Aeneas at the Court of Dido 320
Aeneas and Anchises 321
Wanderings of Ulysses and Aeneas (*map*) . . . *following* 322
Neptune Calming the Sea 323
Mercury Notifies Aeneas that Jupiter Commands Him to Leave
    Carthage 325
Parting of Dido and Aeneas 326
Dido on Funeral Pyre 328
Aeneas' Landing at Latium 330
Romulus and Remus Nursed by the Wolf 334
The Vestal Virgins 335
Rome Today 336
Oath of the Horatii 337
Chariot Race 339
The Cumaean Sibyl 340
Horatius at the Bridge 342
A Sacrifice 348
A Prayer to the Gods 349
Janus 351
Saturn 352
Vesta 353
Fortuna 355
Fama 356
Roma 357
Pomona 359
The Genius of Augustus 360
Father Tiber 361
The Apotheosis of the Empress of Marcus Aurelius . . . 363
Council of the Gods 365
Gladiatorial Combat 368
Temple of Vesta, Rome 370
Spring — An Ancient Festival (*colored*) . . . *facing* 370
Vintage Festival 371
Homer Singing to the People 377

PAGE

Homer Receives Inspiration from the Muse 379
Homer 381
Virgil 384
Venus Giving Advice to Aeneas 386
Aeneas and the Golden Bough 389
Ovid 390
On to Valhalla 395
Odin 397
The Norns 399
One of the Valkyries 401
Thor 403
Freya and Frey 404
Thor Chaining Fenrir 406
Odin's Battle with the Frost Giants 409
Balder 413
Siegfried and the Dwarf at the Forge 418
Siegfried 419
Siegfried and the Dragon 422
Siegfried Bathing in the Blood of the Dragon . . . 423
Siegfried Is Slain 426
Beowulf Is Welcomed at the Court of Hrothgar . . 429
The Druids' Circle 435
Stonehenge 438
An Archdruid in Full Judicial Robes 439
Isle of Man 443
Cuchulain (Setanta) Sets Out 446
Fingal Listens to the Bard Ossian 450
A Knight Riding Forth on a Quest 455
Leprechaun 459
The Prometheus Fountain in the Sunken Plaza, Rockefeller
    Center, New York City 467
A Totem Pole 469
Rip Van Winkle Arrives Home after Twenty Years . . 472
The Constellation Orion 475
The Milky Way 476
Neptune 478
Mercury 479

CLASSICAL MYTHS

APOLLO AND THE MUSES

Whom all the Muses loved, not one alone ;
Into his hands they put the lyre of gold. — LONGFELLOW

MYTHS AS A CLASSICAL HERITAGE

That large utterance of the early gods.
— JOHN KEATS

THE IMPORTANCE OF MYTHS

WITHOUT a knowledge of the ancient Greek and Roman myths, one cannot understand literature — neither the classical literature of the Romans that is still a cornerstone of education in our secondary schools nor our own great American and English literature.

For into these myths went the genius of the old Greeks and Romans. In them are expressed the yearnings, the fears, the hopes, and the dreams that are an essential part of human nature, yesterday and today. Myths are by no means stories created at random, mere idle fancies without particular significance and easily replaced by other idle fancies. They are, on the contrary, in the nature of an *essence*. Generation after generation, innumerable minds have sifted them and altered them, until they express many ideas and ideals deep in our hearts.

An ancient myth was rarely the creation of a single person. Possibly some individual first created the germ of a particular myth. But his fellows, then and later, cherished his idea, polished it, perfected it, so that in the end it was the work of a clan rather than of one person. Those who study older English literature know that the famous ballads went through a similar process, and that even today, in some regions of our own country where old ways are preserved, ballads are still being made and handed down from generation to generation, with changes as they are handed down that alter and smooth them as a pebble is polished by the eternal flowing of a stream.

Moreover, although the myths are often lovely and entrancing stories, they were originally much more than stories. To those that first made them they were science too. That is, myths were explanations.

If we hear thunder today, we explain it — so far as we can — by saying that the thunder was produced by that form of electricity we call lightning. Of course, as a matter of fact, true scientists know that our explanation is not really a deep or complete explanation, since electricity itself is still a very mysterious force.

But the ancient, in the darkness of a forest, or on a plain suddenly made black by gathering clouds, or in a cave where he hid in terror, heard in the thunder the anger of the great god Jove, sitting in majesty on Mount Olympus. His thunder signified one thing or another, according to the direction from which it came, — it was a personal message from a high god.

The sun was a chariot moving across the sky, driven by a noble deity named Apollo; and the moon was another chariot driven by his sis- ter, Diana. (Note how in some languages the names for these heavenly bodies differ in gender: *sol* (sun) is masculine in Latin, *luna* (moon) is feminine, whereas in German *die Sonne* (sun) is feminine, *der Mond* (moon) mascu- line.) To other races, the sun or the moon was a boat rather than a chariot; and fanciful persons today have often seen the moon as a huge face — the man in the moon, who peers down on the strange earth.

JUPITER

And all Olympus trembled at his nod.

— HOMER

How did fire originate? A Greek myth tells how a kindly god, pitying poor mankind, stole some from high heaven and gave it to the mortal creatures that were his friends, and how he was punished for doing so. What caused storms? Everyone can see that in storm a sea is *angry*, as we still say, but to the Greeks and the Romans the anger was that of a definite person, the blue-haired god Neptune, who ruled the waves with a trident, or three-tined fish spear, as his scepter. What caused the grain to grow and beautiful flowers to cover the earth? It was the Earth-Mother, Ceres, who poured the harvests and the blossoms from her Horn of Plenty. It was Somnus that brought sleep, Bacchus who made the grapes to grow, Mars who ruled the nations at war, Venus and her mischievous son Cupid that presided over the affairs of lovers, Mors that brought death.

All nations have their myths, and we all love to *mythologize*. But these Greek and Roman creations still walk the pages of our finest literature and are immortalized in our art and are referred to in our daily writing and conversation.

WHY MYTHS ARE STUDIED

Why do we study myths? For at least five reasons.

These stories are still studied because they have had such a deep influence on all great literatures. It is especially true that the myths of the Greeks and Romans have profoundly affected English and American literature. The great writers in our language have been fascinated by the stories that these ancient peoples told. We can hardly understand Shakespeare or Milton or Keats or Lowell without being familiar with the myths of Greece and Rome. They also provide modern drama with themes and spectacles.

The gods, the demigods, and the heroes of myth play, too, their part in music. The very word *music* pays tribute to the Muses, and many of the myths tell how musical instruments were first invented. Numerous compositions for instrumental or vocal performance have been inspired by the ancient figures whose stories are told in this book.

The story of Orpheus and Eurydice was the theme of the first opera ever written, and it has since then been a favorite subject of musical composers. Perhaps the most famous

MUSIC

By its very name Music pays tribute to the inspiring Muses.

treatment of this story is that by Gluck, with its famous solo and duet: *I have lost my Eurydice* and *Orpheus and Eurydice*. Other tales that have attracted musicians are those of Medea and Jason and of Iphigenia. Among composers who have handled themes from mythology are Massenet, Offenbach, and Purcell.

Poussin   *Metropolitan Museum of Art*

ORPHEUS AND EURYDICE

Orpheus with his lute made trees,
And the mountain-tops that freeze,
    Bow themselves, when he did sing. — SHAKESPEARE

But perhaps the greatest of all musical geniuses who have turned to the treasure house of mythology for material is Richard Wagner, who in many of his operas employs the myths of his native land — particularly the story of Siegfried. The second half of the cycle of four operas, *The Ring of the Nibelung*, tells the adventures of that great hero.

SIEGFRIED AND KRIEMHILD

To believe in the heroic makes heroes. — DISRAELI

Moreover, myths have had a potent influence on the other arts. The great painters and sculptors of all ages, like the great musicians, have found in these ancient legends inspiration for their finest achievements. To this inspiration the illustrations in this volume testify eloquently.

Then, these stories are in themselves often both beautiful and entertaining. They are fables such as still appeal to our imagination today. Often there may be found in them a kernel of allegorical truth, but they may be read for amusement, for their striking plots and remarkable characters.

Finally, they are an important link with the past. They are often our only source of knowledge as to how our distant forefathers regarded the world around them and how they explained its innumerable phenomena. Often, too, we may be surprised to find that because the ancients used a certain idea to explain some puzzle in nature, we today may still have a word that preserves that idea. Our language is full of terms that go back to these old myths, and that can be explained only by learning the myths. Thus, for example, so common a word as *janitor* goes back to *Janus*, the two-headed god of gates whom the Romans worshiped. The name of *June* is derived from *Juno*, queen of the gods among the Romans; while *Thursday* comes from *Thor*, god of war among the old Germanic tribes. We praise food by saying it "tastes like ambrosia," which was the food of the deities on Mount Olympus; and our ideas of the underworld are very much like those of Homer and Virgil. We are bound to the past in innumerable ways, and it is well to know the old myths in order that we may understand our own times.

WHERE MYTHS MAY BE FOUND

Myths are found in many kinds of writings.

There are, first, the ancient documents in which they first occur. In reading Homer or Virgil or Ovid one may see the myths in the form in which they crystallized among the peoples that devised them. Similarly, the *Eddas* of the Scandinavians, the *Sacred Books of the East*, and similar productions give the myths of other nations and races.

In later times scholars have often collected old stories. Geoffrey of Monmouth, an English writer of the twelfth century, told some of the legends which the Celts related concerning their ruler, King Arthur, and his famous knights. At the present time scholars are collecting stories of the Indians, of the Eskimos, of the African tribes, and of the Bushmen of Australia.

Poets and storytellers of all nations use myths for many purposes. They retell them in their own language — in prose and verse, in short story and epic and play. Dante has Ulysses, the Greek hero, tell part of his story in the *Inferno*. Shakespeare reworks certain episodes of the Trojan War in *Troilus and Cressida*. Goethe tells the story of *Iphigenia in Tauris* and Racine that of *Andromache*. William Morris recounts in a long poem the adventures of Jason in search of the Golden Fleece, and several novels have been written about Helen of Troy and about the adventures of King Arthur's knights.

But the poets make even greater use of myths in their references and allusions, in their similes and other figures of speech. Hundreds of lines are quoted in the course of these pages to make clear this fact, but one can prove it by turning to almost any of the English poets and to prose

PETER PAN

Peter escaped from being a human when he was seven days old; he flew
back to the Kensington gardens. — BARRIE

writers like Charles Lamb and John Ruskin. Their pages are starred with the names of characters in Greek and Roman myths. One may take a novel, placed by many critics among the best America has produced, Thomas Wolfe's *Of Time and the River*, and note that six of its eight parts have these titles: "Orestes," "Telemachus," "Proteus," "Jason's Voyage," "Antaeus," and "Kronos and Rhea," all from Greek mythology.

In everyday life, as has already been suggested, we employ a great many words based on these same myths. Later on we shall study such words as *martial, volcano, cereal, mercurial, Wednesday, Saturday, museum, labyrinth,* and many others. Two other points may be made here. Rather oddly, some persons still *swear* by the Greek and Roman gods. For we still hear people say, "By Jove!" — and Jove, or Jupiter, was the chief god of the Romans; and we occasionally hear someone say "Gemini!" — the Latin word for *twins*, referring to the twin gods, Castor and Pollux, rulers of boxing and wrestling.

In advertising, also, there is frequent recourse to mythology. An automobile may be named after a Roman goddess, or the figure of a swift runner in Greek myth may be placed on the radiator. A motor may take its name from an ancient giant, a pencil from the graceful goddess of love, a process for treating a tire from the god of the forge. It is interesting to observe in how many different ways the writers of advertisements recall these old stories.

Moreover, mythmaking still fascinates modern writers. They may not believe, as the ancient mythmakers did, in the tales they tell, but they are delighted with their creations, and their readers are often delighted too. Joel Chandler Harris put myths into the mouth of his Uncle Remus; Lord

Dunsany has told tales of the gods of Pegana — a heaven of his own invention; and Sir James M. Barrie's Peter Pan is familiar to everybody — the name recalling quaintly Pan, the Greek god of nature.

SOME DEFINITIONS

A *myth* is an account of the deeds of a god or of a supernatural being. It relates a supposed historical event, or it serves " to explain some practice, belief, institution, or natural phenomenon" (Webster). Races, nations, tribes, or localities often have their own myths.

Mythology is an interwoven series of myths told by a given race. The word also means the study of myths in general.

Polytheism is the belief in many gods, such as is found in all mythologies. These gods may be thought of as human in form (as among the Greeks and Romans), as animal in form (as among many Indian tribes), or as combining animal and human forms (as among the Egyptians); or they may be creatures of fantasy (like the Chinese dragons).

STUDY APPLICATION

A PROJECT

Begin today to make an *Album of Mythology*. Collect as many references to the myths of ancient times as you can. Where the reference occurs in a magazine or a newspaper and *it is permissible for you to do so*, clip the article or the advertisement containing the reference. Underline the exact words neatly in black or red ink. Where it is not feasible for you to cut out the clipping, copy the reference neatly on a slip of blank paper.

Gather these references, and when you have a dozen or twenty, paste them carefully in a blank book (if possible, one with unruled pages). Arrange your references in groups; for example, put together all references to Jupiter, to Siegfried, and so on. Add to them from time to time.

Your *Album of Mythology* can be made still more attractive if you also make a collection of pictures to use as illustrations of the references.

Some pictures you can find in newspapers and magazines. Others you can purchase inexpensively.[1] Still others may be had by asking your friends who are traveling to send you picture post cards showing scenes from mythology or figures of the gods. Or, perhaps, you may be fortunate enough to do your own traveling and make your own collection of pictures.

At intervals through your album insert appropriate quotations, either taken from your own reading or selected from the numerous quotations that you will find scattered throughout this volume. Prepare a dedication page, on which you inscribe the book to someone of whom you are fond or who has helped you in your work.

Often the most practical way of preparing this *Album* is to secure a loose-leaf notebook binder, preferably one that will hold pages $8\frac{1}{2}$ by 11 inches. You can then use ordinary typewriting paper of a good quality on which to paste your clippings and illustrations and to write your quotations and inscriptions.

EXERCISE

William Wordsworth, in his poem *The Excursion*, has a famous passage, quoted below, in which he endeavors to explain how myths arose in ancient Greece. He imagines the shepherd listening to a distant strain of music and in awe inventing a beardless god who played a lute; he imagines the hunter turning the moon into a goddess, accompanied by her nymphs, the stars; he imagines the traveler thanking the naiad, deity of the fountain. Similarly he explains the origin of the oreads, nymphs of the mountains; the zephyrs, rulers of the west wind, wooing their favorites with gentle breezes; and the satyrs, gods half goat and half man, with their monarch, Pan himself. Read his account carefully, and tell whether you agree with him.

> Once more to distant ages of the world
> Let us revert, and place before our thoughts
> The face which rural solitude might wear
> To the unenlightened swains of pagan Greece.
> — In that fair clime, the lonely herdsman, stretched
> On the soft grass through half a summer's day,
> With music lulled his indolent repose:

[1] See list of sources on pages 505 f.; also suggestions on page 505.

And, in some fit of weariness, if he,
When his own breath was silent, chanced to hear
A distant strain, far sweeter than the sounds
Which his poor skill could make, his fancy fetched,
Even from the blazing chariot of the sun,
A beardless youth, who touched a golden lute,
And filled the illumined groves with ravishment.

The nightly hunter, lifting a bright eye
Up towards the crescent moon, with grateful heart
Called on the lovely wanderer who bestowed
That timely light, to share his joyous sport:
And hence, a beaming goddess with her nymphs,
Across the lawn and through the darksome grove,
Not unaccompanied with tuneful notes
By echo multiplied from rock or cave,
Swept in the storm of chase; as moon and stars
Glance rapidly along the clouded heaven,
When winds are blowing strong.
                              The traveler slaked
His thirst from rill or gushing fount, and thanked
The naiad.   Sunbeams, upon distant hills
Gliding apace, with shadows in their train,
Might, with small help from fancy, be transformed
Into fleet oreads sporting visibly.

The zephyrs fanning, as they passed, their wings,
Lacked not, for love, fair objects whom they wooed
With gentle whisper.
                     Withered boughs grotesque,
Stripped of their leaves and twigs by hoary age,
From depth of shaggy covert peeping forth
In the low vale, or on steep mountain side;
And, sometimes, intermixed with stirring horns
Of the live deer, or goat's depending beard —
These were the lurking satyrs, a wild brood
Of gamesome deities; or Pan himself,
The simple shepherd's awe-inspiring god!

A Second Project

Show, by reference to some of Mr. Disney's films, that this statement from the magazine *Fortune* is true: "Walt Disney's rambling Spanish studio at Hollywood is a factory for making myths."

Word Study

1. Show how a knowledge of mythology will help you to understand the following words: janitor, June, Thursday, ambrosia, Gemini.

2. Give a definition of *myth, mythology, polytheism.*

3. Look up in the dictionary all words beginning with *myth-*. What does *mythomania* mean?

Rapid Quiz

How did myths originate? What facts did they help to explain? How were myths handed down? Are myths confined to any one nation or race? Why do we study myths? What poets have been influenced by them? How do myths help us to understand the past? Where may myths be found? Are myths still referred to today? What are some words that are explained by myths? How does advertising employ mythology? Do modern writers ever invent myths?

For Students of Latin

In what ways is the study of mythology especially important for Latin students? Mention some myths referred to in recent Latin lessons.

I

HOW THE WORLD BEGAN

The horde of Titans, Earth-sons born in ancient days.
— VIRGIL

THE COMING OF THE GODS

At first there was *Chaos* — a vast, seething confusion. There were no limits or bounds in the world, there was no plan or outline. It was all a tremendous disorder, but in it were hidden all things that now exist.

Gradually, after a long lapse of ages, Chaos ceased to be mere darkness and confusion. It resolved itself into two great beings, two majestic deities — *Gaea* (Latin name: *Tellus*), or Mother Earth, and *Uranus*, or the Overhanging Heavens. But a constant memory of Chaos remained and still remains in *Night*, the mysterious darkness in which Chaos lived.

From the marriage of Gaea and Uranus many children were born. Some of the children were very beautiful; others were terrifying monsters. The former were called *Titans*. They were twelve in number and of great size and strength; like men, only much grander. Among the most famous of them were *Oceanus* and *Tethys*, who ruled the sea; *Hyperion* and *Thea*, deities of the sun and moon; *Rhea*, later known as the "Great Mother"; *Themis*, guardian of universal law, shown blindfolded and holding a pair of scales; *Mnemosyne*, goddess of memory, and *Cronus*, youngest and most powerful of them all. The monsters born to Gaea and Uranus were of two kinds. Three of them had each a hundred hands. Three others had each only one eye. The former were called *Hecatoncheires*, the latter *Cyclopes*. Most famous of the former was *Briareus*.

Now Uranus hated all his children, but above all he hated the six monsters, and he therefore confined them in the lower regions of the earth, called *Tartarus*. Mother Earth, to whom none of her brood was hateful, was angry at the imprisonment of six of her children, and she called upon the Titans to help her against their father. None would help her except Cronus (whom the Romans held to be the same as their *Saturn*). He took a sharp sickle and slew his father. From the blood of Uranus sprang the *giants*, more like men than gods, who wore the skins of wild beasts, and who were fierce fighters.

From his blood sprang, too, the terrifying *Furies*, whose hair was writhing serpents. These were called *Erinyes* (Latin : *Dirae*), or dread avengers, but to avoid offense to them, they were referred to usually as *Eumenides*, "the Kindly Ones." One was Tisophone, the Avenger of Blood; the second, Alecto, the Implacable; and the third, Megaera, the Disputatious.

Having overthrown his father, Cronus seized the rule of the world. He took Rhea to be his wife, and divided his empire among his fellow Titans. But his own reign came in time to an end. He feared that a fate similar to that of his father would overtake him, and so he swallowed his children as they were born — three daughters, *Vesta, Ceres*, and *Juno;* and three sons, *Pluto, Neptune*, and *Jupiter*. At least, he thought he had swallowed Jupiter, but when it came to the turn of their youngest born Rhea cunningly substituted a stone in place of the infant.

Jupiter was secretly conveyed to the island of Crete, and there the nymphs Ida and Adrastea fed him on the milk of the goat Amalthaea. When Jupiter attained full growth and strength, he resolved to conquer Cronus. With the aid of his grandmother Gaea, he managed to make Cronus disgorge the five deities he had swallowed; and then with the help of these he made war on the ancient god. On the side of Cronus were ranged almost all the Titans; on the side of Jupiter were not only his brothers and sisters, but also the hundred-handed and the one-eyed monsters, whom Cronus, like Uranus, had confined in Tartarus. The Cyclopes, in gratitude for their release by Jupiter, forged for him the thunderbolt and the lightning. The Hecatoncheires, on the other hand, provided him with the shock of earthquakes as a weapon.

On Mount Ossa stood the old gods, on Olympus the young gods. For ages the war lasted, and every time a battle took place the whole earth shook with the tread of the divine warriors and the air resounded with their tremendous battle cries. Once the Titans even piled Mount Pelion on Mount Ossa, in a vain attempt to get at the Olympians.

SPHINX AND CHIMERA

What the sage poets, taught by the heavenly Muse.
Storied of old in high immortal verse,
Of dire chimeras and enchanted isles. — MILTON

Jupiter hurled thunderbolt on thunderbolt. The forests burst into flames, the rivers boiled, the very skies were scorched. At last the Titans could withstand the might of Jupiter no longer. They were hurled in fire from their mountain stronghold. The young gods pursued and overcame them.

National Museum, Naples

ATLAS

There Atlas,
With head inclined and ever-during arms,
Sustains the spacious heavens. — HESIOD

Most of the Titans and their allies were confined in Tartarus. There, for example, was imprisoned *Typhoeus*, whose hundred heads gave forth fearful voices, and who was supposed to be the father of all dangerous winds. Among his descendants were Cerberus, the Sphinx, the Chimera, and other dread monsters. The son of one of the Titans, *Atlas*, was assigned the task of bearing the world on his shoulders forever. Another Titan's two sons, *Prometheus* and *Epimetheus*, who had refused to take arms against Jupiter, escaped imprisonment; and for a time Prometheus was the chief adviser of Jupiter.

Now the gods divided the world among themselves. To Jupiter (Greek: *Zeus;* also called *Jove* by the Romans) was given the overlordship of gods and men, and he was to rule as king on their mountain stronghold, Mount Olympus. As his queen Jupiter chose Juno (Greek: *Hera*). Neptune (Greek: *Poseidon*) was assigned the government of the ocean. To Pluto (sometimes called *Hades*) went the sway of the underworld. Vesta (Greek: *Hestia*) became goddess of hearth and home, Ceres (Greek: *Demeter*) goddess of agriculture.

THE FOUR AGES OF MAN

Meanwhile, on the face of the earth, the races of mankind had already come into being. As ancient stories tell, several races of men succeeded one another. In the *Golden Age* of Cronus life was an eternal springtime. The soil brought forth so profusely that all toil was unnecessary. Men were both happy and good; old age came slowly. They dwelt always in a kindly out-of-doors, and knew neither strife nor poverty. When death at length came to them, it was like a peaceful sleep into which they fell.

Next came the *Silver Age*. Jupiter created the seasons and made labor necessary. Hunger and cold prevailed, and houses had to be built. Man in that age showed courage, but he was often overbearing and forgot to pay due reverence to the gods.

The Age of Silver was followed by the *Age of Bronze*, in which men learned the use of arms and made war upon one another. Last was the *Age of Iron* — an era of crime and dishonor, when the gifts of the gods were misused and mankind sank into utter degradation.

Bound up with the history of mankind in these early ages is the wonderful story of Prometheus. The name of this Titan means "forethought" or "foresight," just as that of his brother, Epimetheus, means "afterthought" or "hind-sight." In other words, Prometheus by the powers of his mind could tell beforehand what was going to happen. For a time Prometheus was the chosen counselor of Jupiter, who relied upon him for help in all things. Yet between them in time a quarrel arose; and all because of mankind. For when Jupiter beheld how men fell away from their former glory in the Silver Age, he swept them off the face of the earth, and resolved to create a new race. He called upon Prometheus for assistance, and the Titan took clay from the banks of a river in Arcadia and molded it into the likeness of the gods and breathed the breath of life into the images that he made. So a new race was born, and ever since the name Arcadia (sometimes called Arcady) has sig-nified a region of simple pleasure, rustic contentment, and fragrant peace.

Yet these men were feebler than the men of the two pre-ceding ages, and they came into a world that demanded more of them than had ever before been demanded of men. They had to struggle against the changes of the weather. The earth would not bear food for them unless they first tilled the soil, and around them were dangerous wild beasts. It seemed as if this race would perish unless help came.

Prometheus, looking down upon them, saw what was happening.

"Come," he said to Jupiter, "let us give these poor crea-tures the blessed gift of fire. With fire they will not need to fear the cold. With fire they can make themselves tools and weapons."

But Jupiter feared that if he gave this great boon to men, they would think themselves the equals of the gods, and he refused to grant the request of Prometheus.

The Creation of Man by Prometheus: Minerva Gives Him a Soul

Thy godlike crime was to be kind,
To render with thy precepts less
The sum of human wretchedness,
And strengthen man with his own mind. — Byron

The Titan, since then revered as the champion of mankind
and defier of tyranny, was deeply grieved, and at length
he resolved that he would no longer dwell with Jupiter but
would make his abode with men.   So he left Olympus, and
carried with him, hidden in a reed, the gift of fire.   Prometheus taught men how with fire they might make weapons
to fight wild beasts and to contend with their enemies, how
with fire they might contrive tools for all handicrafts and
trades.   It was in this age that tin and copper were first
mixed in the furnace to make bronze.   Prometheus likewise
taught men how to subdue the ox, the ass, and the horse;
he showed them how to build ships and to reckon the course
of the year and to write and reckon and to cure diseases.

THE DOWRY OF PANDORA AND THE PUNISHMENT OF PROMETHEUS

So men prospered.   And as they prospered Jupiter was
more and more displeased.   He finally settled on a cunning
stratagem to overcome Prometheus.   With the help of his
son Vulcan (Greek : *Hephaestus*), lord of the forge, and of
the other gods, he devised a most beautiful woman, named
Pandora (a word in Greek that means "all gifts ").   Upon
her each of the deities bestowed some grace or beauty.   Her
he sent to Prometheus, and with her went the so-called
"Pandora's Box," which was a great jar, such as men use
for storing oil; and the jar was carefully sealed.   Prometheus, suspecting a trick on the part of Jupiter, refused
to accept either the woman or the jar; and Jupiter sent
her to Epimetheus, who had been warned by his brother
against the wiles of Jupiter.   But Epimetheus, won by the
beauty of Pandora, accepted her as his wife.

"This is my dowry," she explained, when Epimetheus inquired what was in the jar; and together they broke the seal and opened it. Immediately a cloud of evils flew forth — all the diseases and troubles and worries that still afflict mankind. Too late, they tried to put the lid back again. But only one spirit remained in the jar: *Hope*.

Jupiter was, of course, discontented with the result of his stratagem. He had, to be sure, inflicted upon mankind many ailments and cares, but Prometheus was still unpunished. So he commanded two giants to seize Prometheus, and he bade Vulcan, who obeyed unwillingly, to bind the Titan fast to a great crag in the Caucasus Mountains. There Prometheus was left, and there each morning came a fierce

Fred Bates

PANDORA

Pandora, whom the gods
Endowed with all their gifts.
— MILTON

eagle (some say a vulture) and consumed part of his body, which each night grew whole again.

"Yield to me," commanded Jupiter, "and you shall be released."

But never would Prometheus yield to Jupiter or give up his devotion to mankind. He gazed, moreover, into the future, and saw that one day a deliverer would come to him, and that this deliverer would be a descendant of Jupiter himself. He saw, too, that on another day Jupiter himself would be overthrown, and the ultimate God, the true God, worshiped as ruler of the universe. So he bore his torments unflinchingly.

Jupiter, in the meantime, had made up his mind to get rid of men by wiping them all out through a great flood. Prometheus warned his son Deucalion that this flood was coming, and he with his wife Pyrrha took refuge on Mount Parnassus. When the surging floods overwhelmed the earth and all its inhabitants, this pair was saved, for Jupiter at last took pity on them and remembered their blameless lives.

When the waters receded, Deucalion and Pyrrha sought a temple of the gods. There a mysterious voice spoke to them and said, "Repeople the earth with the bones of your mother." Deucalion interpreted this to mean stones. He and his wife veiled their heads and, as they walked along, they cast stones behind them. The stones that Deucalion cast became men, and those that fell from his wife's hand became women; and these, according to the ancient legends, were the ancestors of all the beings that people the earth today. Of those that lived first, Deucalion was the king, and he taught them many useful arts.

STUDY APPLICATION

THE MYTHS IN LITERATURE

From the earliest times poets and other writers have especially delighted to tell the story of Prometheus and Pandora.

Prometheus was the subject of many ancient dramas, one of which, the *Prometheus Bound* of Aeschylus, has come down to us. In more modern times he has been treated in poems by Byron, Longfellow, Lowell, and others, and in plays by Shelley and William Vaughn Moody. To our imagination Prometheus has appealed particularly as the great benefactor of mankind — he who first brought fire from the heavens; and also as the great rebel — he who dared to outface the tyranny of Jove and who was willing to suffer endless torments for having done so.

Similarly, the story of Pandora appeals to us because it gives an ingenious explanation for the presence on earth of evils and diseases, and because the figure of Pandora herself, despite the troubles she brought, is an attractive one. Milton, wishing to praise Eve, describes her as even "more lovely than Pandora, whom the gods endowed with all their gifts."

The fall of the old gods and their replacement by the younger dynasty of Jupiter and his fellows have been treated by no poet more magnificently than by John Keats in his *Hyperion*, which pictures Saturn, after his overthrow, sitting quiet as a stone,

> Deep in the shady sadness of a vale
> Far sunken from the healthy breath of morn,
> Far from the fiery noon, and eve's one star.

From the numerous references in literature to these and other myths a group of lines has been selected, in the exercise that follows, for you to examine and explain. As you study the famous masterpieces of literature, as you read stories and novels for pleasure, as you examine advertisements and listen to intelligent conversation, you will come across many similar references, which the myths in this and later chapters will help you to understand.

REFERENCES TO MYTHOLOGY IN LITERATURE

What do the following references mean? Where a word or phrase is italicized, explain only the word or phrase.

1. Unveil thine eyes, O Themis! stand, unveil thine eyes!
   From the high zenith hang thy balance in the skies! — *Bridges*
2. The rock, the vulture, and the chain. — *Byron*
3. It was the Titans warring with Olympus. — *Carlyle*
4. To whom the *Golden Age*
   Still nature's laws doth give. — *Drayton*
5. Upon Ossa they strove to set leafy Pelion, that so the heavens might be scaled. — *Homer*

6. Even the *Titanic* strength of Valerie's car was hard put to it not to falter on the heavier grades. — *Hughes*
7. Or lacks she the Promethean fire? — *Lamb*
8. Prometheus, beautiful, rebellious one! — *Mackaye*
9.   Who first taught
   In the beginning how the heavens and earth
   Rose out of Chaos. — *Milton*
10.   *Chaos*, that reigns here
    In double night of darkness and of shades. — *Milton*
11. When went there by an age, since the *Great Flood*,
    But it was famed with more than with one man?
                               — *Shakespeare*
12. Deucalion and chaste Pyrrha, to restore
    The race of mankind drowned, before the shrine
    Of *Themis* stood devout. — *Milton*
13. Even the blood of giants, which were slain
    By thund'ring Jove. — *Spenser*
14. And next told he of stones by Pyrrha cast. — *Virgil*
15.   The horde
    Of Titans, Earth-sons born in ancient days. — *Virgil*

EXERCISES IN COMPOSITION, ORAL AND WRITTEN

1. Give a talk on the myth of Prometheus, in such a way as to prove what Byron says of him, that his "only crime was to be kind."

2. A motion picture is about to be prepared, called "The Four Ages, in Four Scenes." Mention some of the facts that would go into each scene.

3. Write a playlet, entitled "The Coming of Pandora." The first scene shows Prometheus warning his brother against the gifts of the gods. The next scene shows the coming of Pandora and the opening of the box. (How will you show the escape of the evils that torment mankind?) The final scene shows Epimetheus and Pandora, living in the happiness that Hope gives them. In their conversation they tell what has happened to Prometheus.

4. Why has Thomas A. Edison been called "the Prometheus of our times"? Give a talk comparing the Titan and the modern inventor.

5. Among the evils that flew out of the box that Pandora brought along as her dowry were, undoubtedly, evils of language: mistakes in grammar, spelling, punctuation, and the like. Make a drawing showing Pandora opening the box and allowing these evils to fly away. For example, one sees *ain't* on the wing. (Suggested by Wolfarth-Mahoney's *Self-Help English Lessons*.)

WORD STUDY

1. The words and phrases we use in everyday speech still bear many traces of the ancient myths studied in this chapter. See if you can tell how the following words came to have their present meaning:

> chaotic — shapeless, disordered, confused
> Titanic — enormous, very large
> geology — the science of the earth
> Cyclopean — huge, massive
> cereal — a grass yielding grain
> Olympian — heavenly, godlike

2. Pronounce the following words correctly: (The pronunciation of many of these words is given in the index.)
Chaos, Gaea, Uranus, Titan, Tethys, Hyperion, Themis, Mnemosyne, Hecatoncheires, Cyclopes, Ceres, Adrastea, Amalthaea, Prometheus, Epimetheus, Poseidon, Demeter, Hephaestus, Pandora, Deucalion.

3. What does *Dora*, the common name for a girl, mean? What does the expression *Golden Age* signify? What do the names *Prometheus* and *Epimetheus* signify? What is meant by the expression "to pile Pelion on Ossa"? What does Whittier mean when he says of Daniel Webster: "In port and speech Olympian "?

4. Give the Greek form for *Jupiter, Neptune, Vulcan*. Give the Latin form for *Demeter, Hera, Hestia*. What was Pluto's other name?

5. The name of Gaea, Mother Earth, is sometimes given as *Ge*. What is the science called that treats the history of the earth?

6. Look up *euphemism* in Webster's *Dictionary*. Show how the word *Eumenides* illustrates the definition.

7. Has *typhoon* any connection with the Greek monster Typhoeus? See Webster.

Rapid Quiz

What was Chaos? Who were the first gods? What name was given to their beautiful children? to the monsters that were born to them? What happened to Uranus? Who became the chief of the gods? What did he do to his children? How was he overthrown? Who then became the ruler of the gods? Who were his brothers and sisters? What Titans helped the new gods? What were the Four Ages? How did Prometheus help mankind? How did Jupiter punish him? How did Jupiter seek to wipe out the human race? How was the earth repopulated?

For Students of Latin

1. What are some Latin proper names used in this chapter?
2. Retell briefly in Latin a story narrated in this chapter; or answer in Latin some of the questions in the Rapid Quiz.

Reading List

Poems, Plays, and Music

Byron, Lord: *Prometheus — The Isles of Greece*
Henderson, Daniel: *Prometheus in New Jersey*
Keats, John: *Ode on a Grecian Urn*
Longfellow, Henry Wadsworth: *Epimetheus — Masque of Pandora — Prometheus*
Moody, William Vaughn: *The Firebringer — The Masque of Judgment*
Rossetti, D. G.: *Pandora*
Scriabine, Alexander: *Prometheus* [symphony]
Taylor, Bayard: *Prince Deukalion*

Novels and Descriptive Works

Church, A. J.: *Three Greek Children*
Davis, W. S.: *A Day in Old Athens — A Victor at Salamis*
Hall, Jennie: *Buried Cities*
Lamprey, Louise: *Children of Ancient Greece*
Mills, Dorothy: *The Book of the Ancient Greeks*
Mitchison, Naomi: *Cloud Cuckoo Land*
Sheepshanks, Richard: *Hector and Achilles*
Snedecker, Caroline D.: *The Spartan*
White, Edward Lucas: *Helen*

THE HOURS TAKING HORSES FROM JUNO'S CAR

The rosy-bosom'd Hours. — MILTON

II

THE GODS OF THE SKY

Hence! Wilt thou lift up Olympus! — SHAKESPEARE

ON MOUNT OLYMPUS

In the northern part of Greece lies a mountain range, separating the regions called Macedonia and Thessaly. At the eastern end of the chain looms *Mount Olympus*. Its height is about 10,000 feet, and its summit is covered with perpetual snow. Near by is Mount Ossa, and the valley between was called Tempe, through which flowed the River Peneus to the sea. Tempe was famous for its rural beauty and cool shades, and the gods loved to wander there.

On Olympus, the ancient Greeks believed, Jupiter had fought against the power of Cronus; and when his reign was established, it was on Mount Olympus that he held court and conducted the councils of the gods. He lived in a magnificent palace, and near by were the mansions of the other important gods. Daily they came to Jupiter and sat around him in solemn conclave; or else the younger gods danced before him and entertained him with song. Their food was *ambrosia*, their drink *nectar*. They were shut off from the view of men by a wall of clouds, at the gates of which sat the *Hours* as guardians.

Flaxman   *Gramstorff Bros.*

COUNCIL OF JUPITER, MERCURY, AND MINERVA

For not even Jupiter can please all. — THEOGNIS

Some of the gods were constantly thought of as living in this home in *the sky*. Others, again, were thought of as the gods of *nature or the earth* proper; and still others were associated with *the underworld*. Of each of these three groups of gods we may speak in turn.

JUPITER, JUNO, VESTA [1]

Three children of Cronus dwelt ever on Mount Olympus, although errands brought them on visits to mankind.

[1] See the table of gods on pages 366–367.

Jupiter, called the father of gods and men, was the founder of kingly power, the patron of rulers, the establisher of law and order and justice. All good and all evil sprang alike from him. To every mortal he assigned his earthly share of sorrow and of prosperity. He was armed with the thunder and the lightning; the shaking of his shield produced the storm. He was the god of weather, especially of rain, and Homer said of him: "He lightens, fashioning either a mighty rain, or hail, or snow, when the flakes sprinkle all the plowed lands." Waiting to be his messenger, a great eagle crouched before him. The oak, monarch of trees, was sacred to him; and some believed that by listening to the whispering of its leaves, one might guess the mind of Jove.

Among the Romans Jupiter was greatly revered, and many special *epithets* were added to his name to indicate particular offices or duties assigned to him. Thus he was called Jupiter Stator, or "the stayer of flight," and to him soldiers prayed in battle. Again he was called Jupiter Fulminator, "the lightning hurler"; Jupiter Tonans, "the thunderer"; and Jupiter Pluvius, "the one who gives rains." He was worshiped as Jupiter Optimus Maximus (often written as "Jupiter O. M."), meaning "best and greatest." He even reached out and took over the powers of other gods, as when the Romans called him Jupiter Ammon, identifying him with the supreme god of the Egyptians. Jove's eagle was, too, the sacred symbol of the fighting Roman legions.

Beside him sat his wife and consort Juno. When she spoke her mind, Jupiter listened to her with respect, and she knew all his secrets. Yet she was inferior to him in power and had to obey him. She was the goddess of marriage, and her appearance was that of a beautiful and majestic woman of middle age, with a wide forehead, large and

JUNO

Vatican Museum, Rome

The ox-eyed, awful Juno. — HOMER

attractive eyes, and a grave expression commanding reverence. Her head was adorned with a crown, and a veil hung behind her head. The peacock, in its gorgeous array, and the cuckoo, herald of the springtime, were sacred to her. Her constant attendant was *Iris*, goddess of the rainbow. Juno was not very amiable, and she was inclined to be jealous of Jupiter, whose favorites she sometimes persecuted and punished.

The Romans had an odd belief that every woman had an individual *juno*, as a guardian spirit of her sex; and the goddess herself was believed especially to favor the virtuous and faithful. She was often called Juno Moneta, " she that warns," and a temple was dedicated to her under this name. In this temple money was coined for the Roman treasury, and hence the Latin *moneta*, meaning "a mint," and the English word *money*.

Vesta, the sister of Jove, was the goddess of the home fire and of the hearth; she was the guardian of family life. She was wooed by several of the gods, but Jupiter decreed that she must forever remain unmarried. Her sacred fire burned on every hearthstone; and inasmuch as a town or a village was only an extended family, there was in every ancient Roman and Greek community a public hearth, blazing with the holy flames of Vesta and tended by her priestesses, the Vestal Virgins.

These priestesses of Vesta, always garbed in white, were appointed before they were ten years old and served for thirty years. They were then free to leave their duties in the temple and to marry, if they wished to do so. But they usually continued to serve the goddess. In public the Vestal Virgins were attended by a lictor, as a sign of honor; and the highest magistrates lowered their *fasces* before them.

MARS

Mars approaches, and approaching gives the signs of war. — OVID

They were given seats of honor at the public games, and their persons were sacred.

When emigrants set forth to found a new settlement, they took with them part of the sacred home fire and used it to kindle the hearth flames in their new homes.

CHILDREN OF JUPITER AND JUNO

One of the most important of the gods was a son of Jupiter and Juno — *Mars* (Greek: *Ares*), the god of war. He reveled in battle and slaughter. He appeared in full armor, a long plume floating from his helmet. Often he rode at high speed in his war chariot, drawn by four fiery steeds.

Gramstorff Bros.

VULCAN FORGING ARROWS FOR CUPID

Some Cupid kills with arrows, some with traps. — SHAKESPEARE

Dogs of prey and vultures accompanied him; his symbols were a spear and a burning torch. His sons were known as Terror, Trembling, Panic, and Fear. He was a favorite deity of the Romans, who named the month of *March* after him.

GANYMEDE AND THE EAGLE

Or else flush'd Ganymede, his rosy thigh
Half buried in the Eagle's down. — TENNYSON

Another son of the royal gods was *Vulcan*, already mentioned as god of the forge. He presided over fire in many of its manifestations, from the smithy to the volcano, but especially over fire in its practical uses. He was himself a skilled workman and the patron of artisans; all the palaces on Mount Olympus were his handiwork. The workshop of Vulcan was usually on some volcanic island — Etna, for example; and when the volcano was in eruption, the people near by would say in awe that Vulcan was at work. One legend related that he attempted once to interfere in a quarrel between Jupiter and Juno, and that the former in wrath hurled him from the high heavens. All day he plunged through the air, and at sunset fell in the island of Lemnos. Ever after he was lame. He was represented as a vigorous, bearded man, holding in his hand a hammer or some other tool. He wore an oval cap, and his right shoulder and arm were uncovered.

Another child of Jupiter and Juno was *Hebe*, goddess of youth and cupbearer to the other gods. In later ages she was married to the great hero Hercules. Against Juno's wishes her place as cupbearer was taken by the youth Ganymede, snatched by the eagle of Jove from the plains of Troy over which his brother, King Priam, ruled. Thereafter he served the divinities at their fragrant banquets.

OTHER CHILDREN OF JUPITER

Jupiter had numerous other children, some of whom were assigned important duties to perform.

Latona (Greek: *Leto*) bore to Jupiter twin children, Apollo and Diana; and to them their father assigned the charge of the sun and the moon.

Phoebus Apollo, god of the sun, was pictured as driving the flaming chariot of the luminary of the day across the sky. He was, too, the god of song and music and prophecy. He led the choir of the *Muses* — nine maidens, themselves the daughters of Jupiter and of Mnemosyne, the Titaness who presided over memory. To Apollo was attributed the invention of the flute and the lyre. From the bow that he carried went forth flaming arrows of plague and pestilence,

Sargent   *Boston Museum of Fine Arts*

APOLLO IN HIS CHARIOT, WITH THE HOURS

The sleepless Hours
Waken me when their Mother, the gray Dawn,
Tells them that dreams and that the moon is gone.
— SHELLEY *(Hymn of Apollo)*

and sometimes he was called the god of vengeance. Yet he was, too, *Apollo Paean*, the god of healing, and the father of Aesculapius, the first of physicians.

With the fame of Apollo Mount Parnassus was particularly connected. This mountain was regarded as the home of poetry and music, and "to climb Parnassus" (meaning to write poetry) is still a common phrase. Still another mountain associated with Apollo and poetry was Helicon. On its slopes two fountains, Aganippe and Hippocrene, joined to make "Helicon's harmonious stream," from which those

who seek poetic inspiration are still supposed to drink.
Near by wandered the winged horse Pegasus, a fiery steed
that only the most daring poets dared mount.

Apollo's sister *Diana* (Greek: *Artemis*), goddess of the
moon, guided her silvery chariot over the sky at night. She
had three aspects: Diana in the heavens, Luna on earth,

Claude Lorrain   *Boston Museum of Fine Arts*

Mount Parnassus

My palate is parch'd with Pierian thirst —
Away to Parnassus I'm beckon'd. — Horatio Smith

and Hecate, goddess of witchcraft, in the underworld. Like
Apollo she was armed with a bow, a quiver, and arrows.
The sudden deaths of women were attributed to her shafts.
But she was, likewise, a goddess of healing, and also of the
chase. She was often represented as a huntress, with hunting
dogs and a boar's head at her side. Several huntresses are
remembered for their devotion to Diana: for example,

Correggio

DIANA

Fair silver-shafted queen, for ever chaste. — MILTON

Atalanta, heroine of the hunt in which the Calydonian boar was slain. Sometimes she was shown in her chariot, drawn by four stags with golden horns. She was the patron of purity in women, and at her festivals little girls dressed in yellow danced and sang. As goddess of the moon she appeared with a robe that reached to her feet, a white veil on her head, and a crescent moon rising above her forehead.

Dione was the daughter of Oceanus and Tethys, the Titans who preceded Neptune in the rulership of the ocean. She bore to Jupiter the goddess of beauty, *Venus* (Greek: *Aphrodite*). Some fables related that Venus was born of the foam of the sea, and that the waves carried her first to the island of Cythera. She is therefore sometimes called "the foam-born" and sometimes "the Cytherean." Sometimes, again, she was named Acidalia, from the fountain Acidalius sacred to her.

She surpassed all gods and all mortals in beauty, and she had moreover the power of granting beauty to others. She possessed a magic girdle, and if she granted the use of this girdle to another goddess or woman, immediately that person became an object of love and desire. Her husband was, oddly enough, the lame god Vulcan. The myrtle and the rose were sacred to her; her chariot was drawn by doves. Often she was represented with her son *Cupid* (Greek: *Eros*), who carried arrows of two sorts: some tipped with lead to produce hatred, some tipped with gold to incite love.

Minerva (Greek: *Pallas Athena*) was said by the Greeks to have sprung full-armed and full-grown from the head of Jupiter. Perhaps the legend is an allegory that explains the realm over which Minerva ruled, for she was the goddess of wisdom. She was the preserver, too, of states and governments. Rulers who displayed wisdom were particularly

VENUS OF CAPUA WITH CUPID

Thereupon she called to her that winged, bold boy. — APULEIUS

under her care. She was a patron of the fine arts, and was especially interested in weaving. She was usually represented as carrying a staff and wearing a breastplate called the *aegis*. On this aegis hung the head of a monster called the *Gorgon*, a woman with locks of snakes who had the power to freeze to stone those that gazed at her. Her image appeared on the Roman coin *triens*. Like Diana, Minerva watched over maidens. But she was the protectress, too, of heroes like Hercules, Ulysses, and Perseus, as we shall see later.

Atlas, the Titan on whose shoulders Jove placed the burden of the heavens, had seven daughters called the *Pleiades*, who, according to Greek legend, were transported to the sky as stars. The eldest of them was named *Maia*, and to her and Jupiter was born a son *Mercury* (Greek: *Hermes*). He had a most curious mixture of qualities. His chief duty was to act as the messenger of the gods, and he was spoken of as "fleet-footed Mercury." Even as a child, however, he had a tendency toward thievishness, and he was the patron of thieves and other rascals. It was said that on the very day of his birth he stole the oxen of Apollo, driving them backwards into a cave to conceal their hiding-place. Even while Apollo was accusing the infant god of the theft, Mercury slyly robbed him of his quiver. When the elder god found how cleverly he had been tricked, he burst into a roar of laughter.

As the messenger of the gods, Mercury was the guardian of travelers; and as the herald of the gods, he became the god of oratory. He it was that conducted the shades of the dead to the underworld. All gymnasiums were under his control, and little heads of the god, called *hermae*, were erected on posts alongside roads and at doors and gates.

Elihu Vedder

Congressional Library, Washington

MINERVA

Whom Jove brought forth, golden, all radiant. — SHELLEY

He was represented as a graceful youth. Among his symbols were a hat with small wings, that enabled him to go invisible; a staff (the *caduceus*) intertwined with snakes that was the sign of his authority; and winged sandals. Mercury appeared on a Roman coin called *sextans*.

Idrac   *Luxembourg Museum*

MERCURY INVENTING THE CADUCEUS

Thus glib-tongued Mercury in his hand
Stretched forth the sleep-compelling wand.
— JOHN TRUMBULL

Homer tells how the gods of high Olympus took pity on some orphaned girls and brought them gifts. Venus gave them curds and honey and pleasant drink. Juno made them fair beyond other women and endowed them with understanding. Holy Diana endowed them with noble growth, and Minerva bestowed on them skill in handiwork. Such was the kindness of the gods in gracious mood.

To keep them kind the ancients not only prayed fervently to their deities, but poured libations to them as they drank (letting part of the liquid drop on the ground) and brought sacrifices to them in their temples. Flowers and fruits were laid on the altar, a lamb or a kid or an ox was slain as an offering to the gods.

MINOR DEITIES OF OLYMPUS

The Muses, who have already been mentioned, each presided over a distinct realm: *Clio*, over history; *Euterpe*, over music and lyric poetry; *Thalia*, over comedy; *Melpomene*, over tragedy; *Terpsichore*, over dancing; *Erato*, over love poetry; *Polyhymnia*, over religious poetry; *Urania*, over astronomy; and *Calliope*, over epic poetry. To them, called by the poet Pindar "the black-haired Nine," would pray poets and others who wished inspiration.

To the three *Fates* even Jupiter himself was obedient, for their decrees ruled both gods and men. They were represented as spinning at a great web, and in their hands were shears, with which they cut the thread of a man's life where they pleased. *Clotho* did the spinning, *Lachesis* assigned to each man his fate, and in the hands of *Atropos* moved the fatal shears.

On Mount Olympus likewise dwelt *Dike*, goddess of justice; the three *Graces*, and the four *Seasons;* and here was the abode of *Nemesis*, the spirit of just anger and punishment, and of *Victoria* (Greek: *Nike*), goddess of victory.

The Greeks believed that in certain places and by certain means the gods made known their will to mankind through *oracles*. The most famous of these oracles was at Delphi, which was on the slope of Mount Parnassus. Here was located a temple of Apollo, and at the center of the temple was the oracle — a fissure in the earth, from which came volcanic vapors. A priestess or sibyl (called Pythia) sat on a tripod over the fissure, and the words that she spoke

Thumann   Gramstorff Bros.

THE THREE FATES

Conciliate the Fates and the Gods. — LUCAN

after inhaling the vapor were regarded as the revelations of Apollo. Apparently, she went off into a trance. But her answers were often hard to understand, and "the thrilling Delphic oracle" was sometimes obscure or dubious in meaning. Thus once Pythia told King Croesus that if he went to war with King Cyrus, "he would destroy a mighty kingdom." He did, but it was his own. Many great treasures were to be found in this great temple, the gifts of those who had consulted the oracle. An altar in the temple was supposed to mark the exact center of the earth (flat, of course, in the Greek mind). Over the door of the temple were inscribed two words believed to sum up all Greek wisdom: "Know thyself."

Louvre Museum

VICTORY (NIKE) OF SAMOTHRACE

Nikë, dispenser of sweet gifts, allots to mortals and immortals the prize of valor.
— BACCHYLIDES

Another oracle, sacred to Jupiter, was the grove of oaks at Dodona. Here questions might be asked of the ruler of gods and men, and the rustling of the leaves, as interpreted by the priests, would be his reply.

An ancient writer mentions an image of Hermes that was regarded as an oracle. He who would consult it came at nightfall, burnt incense on a hearth in front of the image, lit the bronze lamps clamped to the hearth, placed a coin to the right of the image, and whispered a question into the ear of the god. Then he stopped up his ears and walked away. When he had gone a little distance, he uncovered his ears, and whatever word he heard first, he took for an oracle and answer to his question.

STUDY APPLICATION

THE MYTHS IN LITERATURE

To the gods of high Olympus due honor has been paid in our literature and our language, but some of these deities have, naturally, been greater favorites than others.

Undoubtedly more poems have been written about Apollo and about Venus than about any other ancient gods. The shining god of poetry and light and the lovely goddess of beauty have won constant allegiance throughout the history of literature. There is, for example, Shelley's *Hymn of Apollo*, in which the god himself speaks:

> Then I arise, and climbing heaven's blue dome,
>   I walk over the mountains and the waves;
> Leaving my robe upon the ocean foam;
>   My footsteps pave the clouds with fire; the caves
> Are filled with my bright presence, and the air
> Leaves the green earth to my embraces bare.

Others who have written about Apollo are Jonathan Swift and Keats. Poems in which Venus appears have been written by Chaucer, Shakespeare, and Swinburne. Her son Cupid is likewise a favorite of the bards.

Juno, prominent in Homer and in Virgil, has not attracted modern poets, but her name occurs in a fine passage in Shakespeare, where it is coupled with that of Venus:

>   Violets dim,
>   But sweeter than the lids of Juno's eyes,
>   Or Cytherea's breath.

Jupiter is the subject of few poems, but he is referred to many times, as are also Mars, Pallas Athena, the Muses, Vulcan, and other inhabitants of Olympus. A celebrated discussion in prose of Pallas Athena is Ruskin's *Queen of the Air*. The moon goddess Diana, on the other hand, has proved very attractive to many writers; for example, to Keats in *Endymion*, to Maurice Hewlett in *Artemision*, and to Ben Jonson in the *Hymn to Diana* —

> Queen and huntress, chaste and fair,
>   Now the sun is laid to sleep,
> Seated in thy silver chair
>   State in wonted manner keep:
>   Hesperus entreats thy light,
>   Goddess excellently bright.

If one leaves the realm of pure literature, one will still find many references to these gods. Newspaper articles and editorials make much use of these ancient gods; there are many references, for example, to something which is born in full strength or maturity, "like Minerva out of the head of Jove." In cartoons the figure of Mars may often be seen. In daily speech, too, we make constant use of the ancient gods, and we speak of some man as an Apollo and some woman as equal in beauty to Venus or one of the Graces; or we remark playfully that so-and-so is a victim of Cupid. Science, likewise, makes use of the gods, particularly in naming the planets — Venus, Mercury, Mars, Jupiter, Neptune, and others. In advertising, the names of deities are employed both in naming products and in the text of advertisements; for example, the *Venus* pencil. Painters delight to employ their imagination in representations of the gods and of scenes from the stories that deal with them, as the illustrations in this volume indicate; and many musical compositions go back to these mythical persons and stories for their inspiration.

In the passages that follow a selection has been made of references to the deities of Olympus. See if you can explain them.

REFERENCES TO MYTHOLOGY IN LITERATURE

What do the following references mean? Where a word or phrase is italicized, explain only the word or phrase.

A. References to the Major Gods

    1. Let us send Hermes forth, the Speedy-Comer. — *Homer*
    2. The ox-eyed, awful Juno. — *Homer*

3. So saying, the goddess spread a table, loading it with *ambrosia* and mixing ruddy *nectar*. — *Homer*

4.   Apollo's upward fire
Made every eastern cloud a silvery pyre
Of brightness. — *Keats*

5. And, just beyond, on light tiptoe divine,
A quiver'd Dian. — *Keats*

6. *Jove* heard his vows, and better'd his desire. — *Keats*

7. Juno's proud birds are pecking pearly grain. — *Keats*

8. Turn to some level plain where haughty Mars
Has legion'd all his battle. — *Keats*

9. Foot-feather'd Mercury appear'd. — *Keats*

10.   Her hovering feet,
More bluely veined, more soft, more whitely sweet
Than those of sea-born Venus, when she rose
From out her cradle shell. — *Keats*

11. His Minerva is *born in panoply*. — *Lamb*

12. Jupiter himself cannot please all, whether sending rain or withholding it. — *Latin proverb*

13. Hence had the huntress Dian her dread bow,
Fair silver-shafted queen for ever chaste,
Wherewith she tam'd the brinded lioness
And spotted mountain pard. — *Milton*

14. Were it a draught for *Juno* when she banquets,
I would not taste thy treasonous offer. — *Milton*

15. Offering to every weary traveler,
His orient liquor in a crystal glass,
To quench the drouth of *Phoebus*. — *Milton*

16. On high her mighty horses *Luna* drives. — *Ovid*

17. You will find that *Minerva* roams the woods quite as much as *Diana*. — *Pliny the Younger* [to explain and justify his love of the country and its solitudes]

18. Wedding is great Juno's crown. — *Shakespeare*

19. We Americans are a race of *lightning-shod Mercuries*, and proud of it; instead of being, like our ancestors, a race of plodding crabs, and proud of that. — *Mark Twain*

20. Juno, within whose care are marriage bonds. — *Virgil*

B. References to Lesser Deities and Mythical Ideas

  1. Not from the lips of cunning fell
      The thrilling *Delphic oracle.* — *Emerson*
  2. The matchless Ganymede, divinely fair. — *Homer*
  3. And joined with the nymphs the lovely *Graces.* — *Horace*
  4. *Tempe* with the west wind stirred. — *Horace*
  5. But might I of Jove's *nectar* sup. — *Ben Jonson*
  6.   Hebe bring
      A full-brimm'd goblet. — *Keats*
  7. As large, as bright, as color'd as the bow
      Of Iris. — *Keats*
  8. For when the Muse's wings are airward spread,
      Who shall delay her flight? — *Keats*
  9.   The Seasons four
      Join dance with shadowy Hours. — *Keats*
 10. Spin, spin, Clotho, spin!
      Lachesis, twist! and Atropos, sever! — *Lowell*
 11. But the fair guerdon when we come to find,
      And think to burst out into sudden blaze,
      Comes the blind Fury with *the abhorred shears*,
      And slits the thin-spun life. — *Milton*
 12. The Graces and the rosy-bosomed Hours. — *Milton*
 13. Nods and becks and wreathéd smiles,
      Such as hang on *Hebe's* cheek. — *Milton*
 14. And hears the Muses in a ring
      Aye round about Jove's altar sing. — *Milton*
 15. I'll have no worse a name than Jove's own page,
      And therefore look you call me Ganymede. — *Shakespeare*
 16. O for a *Muse* of fire that would ascend
      The brightest heaven of invention! — *Shakespeare*
 17. Begin, O *Clio*, and recount from hence
      My glorious sovereign's goodly ancestry. — *Spenser*
 18. All the charm of all the *Muses* often flowering in a lonely word.
      — *Tennyson*
 19. They furnish matter for *the tragic Muse.* — *Thomson*
 20. She dished out the potpie with *Olympian* impartiality. — *Wylie*

Exercises in Composition, Oral and Written

1. Give a brief description of the geography of Greece. Is the country mountainous? Are there many seaports? Does the country naturally fall into sections, or is it unified? What are the chief cities? Where is Mount Olympus located? How high is it? Where is Macedonia? Thessaly?

2. Imagine yourself transported in a dream to Mount Olympus. You wander to and fro and gaze in awe on the palaces of the gods and on the gods. Give an account of what you behold.

3. You are (let us suppose) composing a novel of ancient Greece. One of your characters writes a hymn in prose to one of the high gods of Olympus, a deity to whom he is particularly devoted. What would he say? Introduce into this hymn some of the god's qualities as mentioned in this chapter. Select for the subject of the hymn any god you please.

4. In this same supposed novel another character pays a visit to the oracle at Delphi. Find out as much as you can about this oracle, and then have your character write a letter to a friend, in which he tells what happened to him and what he saw. Head your composition, "Iras to Charmian."

5. Which of the gods of Olympus do you personally like best? Why does this deity attract you? Give an account of the god or the goddess you select, including both the details in the text and any others you can find in an encyclopedia or other book of reference.

6. Address a prayer (twenty or thirty words) to the god or goddess whom you selected, asking for some boon. (Perhaps it would be well to make your language a little old-fashioned, using *thou* and *thee* instead of *you*.)

7. "The Muses were uncomfortable goddesses, I think," says Maggie Tulliver in George Eliot's *The Mill on the Floss*, "obliged always to carry rolls and musical instruments about with them." Would musicians agree with this assertion?

Word Study

1. How did the following words come to have their present meanings?

martial — of a warlike disposition

iris — of an appearance resembling the rainbow; a play of prismatic colors

vulcanization — the application of heat to rubber or other
 substances
museum — a collection of works of art or other objects of interest
nemesis — a just or deserved fate
nectar — a delicious or inspiring beverage
Parnassians — a group of butterflies that inhabit, for the most
 part, mountain regions.

2. What is the correct pronunciation of the following words? See
the index to this book.

Iris, Hippocrene, Hebe, Ganymede, Artemis, Dione, Aphrodite,
Cythera, Cytherean, aegis, Pleiades, caduceus, Maia, Clio, Euterpe,
Thalia, Melpomene, Terpsichore, Erato, Lachesis, Atropos, Dike,
Nemesis, Dodona.

3. The names of what three months are derived from persons mentioned in this chapter?

4. Explain the origin of the following words: jovial, vestal, volcano,
mercury, calliope, money.

5. The name "kewpie" has recently been devised for a certain kind
of doll. The name of what deity suggested the term?

6. Can you think of any other names used for advertising that are
derived from persons mentioned in this chapter? Or can you find
symbols used in advertisements that recall the old gods and goddesses?

7. What is an *epithet?* Mention some epithets applied to the gods.

8. Explain: "to climb Parnassus," "to mount Pegasus," "to drink
the waters of Helicon."

9. The Greeks named certain three-legged tables "Delphic tables."
Why? Why does "a Delphic utterance" mean something obscure or
difficult to understand?

Rapid Quiz

Where was Mount Olympus situated? What children of Cronus
dwelt there? What was the realm of each? What were the symbols
of each? Who were some children of Jupiter and Juno? What were
their realms and symbols? Who were some other children of Jupiter?
What were their realms and symbols? How many Muses were there?
Name one of them. How great was the power of the three Fates?

Who were some other inhabitants of Mount Olympus? What were oracles? Where were two famous oracles situated?

FOR STUDENTS OF LATIN

1. What are some of the special qualities in Jupiter that the Romans worshiped? in Juno?
2. What belief in a juno for every woman did the Romans have?
3. How did the Romans pay honor to Vesta?
4. What were *fasces*? How is the idea preserved in a modern word?
5. How did the Romans honor Mars?
6. What deities appeared on the Roman coins *triens* and *sextans*?
7. Answer in Latin two or three questions in the Rapid Quiz.

READING LIST

Poems, Plays, and Music

Arnold, Matthew: *Euphrosyne*
Benet, William Rose: *The Horse Thief* [about Pegasus]
Blake, William: *To the Muses*
Doolittle, Hilda ("H. D."): *Hermes of the Ways*
Keats, John: *Ode to Maia*
Lowell, James Russell: *Hebe*
Mozart, W. A.: *Jupiter* [symphony]
Schiller, Friedrich von: *The Gods of Greece*
Shelley, Percy Bysshe: Homer's *Hymn to Mercury*
Taylor, Bayard: *Masque of the Gods*
Tennyson, Lord: *The Talking Oak*

Publishers' Photo

THE TEMPLE OF ZEUS, ATHENS

What trace remaineth of the Thunderer's shrine? — BYRON

III

STORIES OF JUPITER AND MINERVA

Jupiter is wheresoever you look, wheresoever you move. — LUCAN

EUROPA AND HER KIN

Jupiter was the chief figure in one romantic episode, which brought in its train a number of important events and consequences.

Europa was a princess of Asia, the daughter of the king of Phoenicia. She shone pre-eminent among her attendant maidens as Venus did among the Graces. The son of Cronus beheld her, and he fell in love with her. He wooed Europa in the fashion of a bull, lovely and mighty to behold. He came into the flowering meadow where Europa disported herself with her maidens, and when the rest fled, he cast his spell on the princess so that she was not afraid. She

58

approached him and he lowed gently, and he bowed himself before her feet and showed her his broad back. She, smiling, was tempted, and sat down upon the back of the bull; and scarcely was she seated, when he rose from the ground, moved towards the neighboring seashore, and leaped easily into the waves.

Lorraine   Gramstorff Bros.

EUROPA AND THE BULL

And he stood before the feet of fair Europa, and cast his spell over the maiden. — MOSCHUS

In vain she called to her companions, in vain she implored the seemingly gentle bull to return to dry land and to permit her to escape. Over the sea, suddenly smooth before him, he swam with powerful strokes, and never a wavelet wet the hem of the maiden's garments. Around him gamboled the monsters of the sea, and bevies of sea nymphs rose from the waves and greeted him joyously.

"Whither do you bear me?" at last the maiden cried in awe; and the bull answered her in deep, immortal tones, bidding her to be courageous.

"Behold, I am Jupiter," he said, "and love of you has compelled me to wear this semblance. But Crete shall presently receive us and shall be our bridal chamber — Crete where I myself was born."

So he said, and so it was; and from this Princess Europa it was that the whole continent received its name. Three sons were born to Europa — Minos, later king of Crete, Rhadamanthus, and Sarpedon. The two former sons after their death became judges of the shades in the underworld.

An interesting story is told of Minos while he was still a ruler of Crete. He had as one of his servants a man named Daedalus, who was a skilled mechanic and worker in metals and an ingenious inventor — the forefather, so to speak, of all inventors. It was Daedalus who devised for Minos a complicated series of tunnels and windings, called the *labyrinth*, in which was confined the Minotaur, a monster half man, half bull.

Later Daedalus lost the favor of Minos, who imprisoned him and his son, Icarus. But Daedalus set his mind to work on finding means to escape. Finally he devised a pair of wings for himself and a pair for Icarus. He fastened them to his own shoulders and to those of the boy, using wax as the binding material. Then both triumphantly flew away. Swiftly they skimmed through the air, and closer and closer they came to the mainland. But Icarus, flushed with excitement and exhilaration, soared ever higher towards the sun — despite the cries and warnings of his father. At last he flew so high that the heat of the sun melted the wax, and off dropped the wings. The lad plunged downward into

DAEDALUS AND ICARUS

Wings fastened with wax by Daedalean craft. — HORACE

the sea and was drowned. The sea into which he fell was later called the Icarian Sea. Daedalus escaped, and for a long time lived in Sicily.

When Europa was carried off by the bull, her father commanded her brother, Cadmus by name, to go in search of her and not to return until he had found her. But Cadmus sought for months and years in vain. Then an oracle of Apollo bade him follow a certain cow wherever she wandered, and to build a city at the point where the cow finally rested. Cadmus obeyed, and at last on the plain of Panope the cow stood still. Cadmus, wishing to offer a libation to his patron goddess Minerva, sought near by for water. Soon he came to a spring from which gushed a crystal-pure stream. But a dragon guarded the fountain, and no sooner had Cadmus's servants dipped their pitchers into the water than it darted upon them and killed some with its fangs, while it crushed others in its folds.

Then Cadmus himself gave battle to the dragon and finally slew it, not knowing that it was sacred to Mars. The god of war was angry with Cadmus, and the latter was obliged to serve him for eight years. From the dragon's teeth, sown over the ground by the command of Minerva, sprang armed men, who became the subjects of Cadmus. He built the city of Thebes, and to him was ascribed the introduction of the alphabet. When he grew old, he and his wife Harmonia were changed into serpents. But he never saw Europa again.

THE STORY OF OEDIPUS

The descendants of Cadmus continued to suffer from the hatred of Mars, even though that god had forgiven Cadmus

Ingres   The Louvre

OEDIPUS AND THE SPHINX

Every man's own reason is his best Oedipus. — SIR THOMAS BROWNE

himself for slaying his dragon.   But of all these descendants the greatest misfortunes afflicted Oedipus.

An oracle warned Laius, king of Thebes, on the birth of a son, that the infant, if allowed to grow up, would endanger his throne and his life.   So Laius ordered a herdsman to kill the child.   But the herdsman, in pity, merely pierced the infant's feet and left him upon a mountain side.   There another herdsman found the child and took him to King Polybus of Corinth.   He adopted him as his son and called him Oedipus, or Swollen-Foot.

When Oedipus became older, he too consulted an oracle and learned, to his horror, that he was destined to kill his father, Polybus as he supposed.   To avoid the decree of the gods he hastily left Corinth and in a chariot with a single servant, set off on wanderings over Greece.   Once, on a narrow road, he met a man in another chariot who haughtily ordered him to give way.   When Oedipus refused, an attendant leaped out of the other chariot, and killed one of Oedipus' horses.   Then Oedipus, in great anger, slew the man in the chariot.   It was Laius, and unwittingly Oedipus had killed his father.

When Oedipus came to Thebes itself, he found the city in deep distress.   A monster called the Sphinx, half lion and half woman, stopped all travelers and set them a riddle. If they could not give the right answer, the Sphinx killed them.   But Oedipus fearlessly approached the Sphinx. "What creature is it," inquired the Sphinx, "that in the morning goes on four feet, at noon on two, and at night on three?"   "Man," replied Oedipus, "who creeps on hands and feet in childhood, stands erect on two feet when full grown, and in old age needs the help of a crutch."   The Sphinx, chagrined, threw herself off a cliff and was killed.

In gratitude the Thebans had Oedipus marry their queen Jocasta, widow of Laius. Only when a plague afflicted the city did Oedipus and Jocasta learn through an oracle of the crimes he had committed. In horror Jocasta committed suicide and Oedipus blinded himself. For many months Oedipus, accompanied by his faithful daughter Antigone, went begging through Greece. At last the gods released him from life.

Even with the death of Oedipus the misfortunes of Thebes did not cease. His sons, Eteocles and Polynices, agreed to reign alternate years, but when it came the turn of the latter, his brother refused to give up the throne. Polynices induced six other heroes to espouse his cause, and they undertook an expedition that was called "The Seven against Thebes." The war proved indecisive, and finally the two brothers met in single combat to determine who should be king — and slew each other. All but one, Adrastus, of the seven heroes perished; and to punish Thebes seven sons of these chieftains similarly marched against the city, captured it, and placed one of their number, Terpander, on the throne.

CALLISTO AND HER SON

In Arcadia lived a beautiful maiden named Callisto with whom Jupiter fell in love. She bore to him a son named Arcas. When Juno saw how happy Callisto was in the love of Jove and in the growing handsomeness of her boy, she felt bitterly jealous. At last her anger and envy went beyond all bounds, and she changed Callisto into a bear.

Disconsolately through the woods of Arcadia roamed Callisto in her new and awkward form. She dared not mingle with the other bears, for her fear of them was as

great as when she had been a human being; and yet she
fled from the hunters, since naturally they would pursue
her at sight and slay her if they could.

One day, however, she caught a glimpse in the distance
of her own son Arcas, grown now to splendid manhood. Her
love and yearning overcame her, and approaching him with
clumsy gait, she stood on her hind legs and sought to embrace
him. But he drew back in mingled wonderment and alarm;
and as the bear persisted in following him, he raised up his
spear and would have killed the strange but terrifying animal.
As the spear-point was about to enter Callisto's breast,
Jupiter, looking down from the heavens, saw what was happening and in pity stayed the spear of Arcas. Then he
snatched both of them from the earth and placed them as
constellations in the heavens. One is the group of stars
that we call the Great Bear; and near by is the group we
know as the Little Bear.

It is said, in the ancient legends, that Juno complained
bitterly to the gods of the sea at the way Jupiter had treated
her rival and her rival's son; and these gods granted to her
as a special boon that the Great Bear and the Little Bear
should never come into their waters. Hence it is that these
constellations constantly circle the pole, but do not sink
into the ocean, as do the other stars.

BAUCIS AND PHILEMON

Sometimes Jupiter, although first of all a god of the wide
heavens and usually thought of as abiding always in his
wonderful palace on Mount Olympus, visited the earth and
mingled with its inhabitants in human guise. His purpose
in such visits was to discover whether men truly observed

the dictates of hospitality, for not only was Jupiter the Thunderer and the king of gods and men; he was also particularly the god of hospitality, and those who were cruel or unkind to strangers incurred his wrath.

Rubens

BAUCIS AND PHILEMON ENTERTAINING JUPITER AND MERCURY

On hospitable thoughts intent. — MILTON

Once Jupiter, disguised as a humble traveler and accompanied only by Mercury, visited the land of Phrygia. They sought shelter for the night at one house after another, but everywhere they were driven away with harsh words and contemptuous remarks.

Darkness had long since fallen, and the two immortals were on the point of giving up their quest in despair, when they came to the house of an aged couple named Baucis and Philemon. It was a lowly cottage, thatched with straw and with reeds from a near-by marsh, but here Baucis and her husband had dwelt together since they were wedded, and in it they had found content.

When Baucis and Philemon heard the knocking at their door they quickly opened it and bade the strangers welcome. Gladly they granted the request of the two travelers that they be allowed to remain for the night. They hurried around their humble home, gathered sticks to replenish the fire, brought forth such homely fare as they possessed, and prepared it for the strangers.

As the strangers stretched forth their hands for the food, a strange thing happened. Suddenly there was much more of it, and it exhaled a wonderful fragrance. Then, suddenly, the gods revealed themselves in all their splendor, and the aged couple fell on their knees and begged forgiveness for the wretched food they had laid before them. Jupiter, however, bade Baucis and Philemon arise, and he led them to the summit of a neighboring hill. When they looked back at the valley in which they had lived, the old people saw to their astonishment that it was now a great lake. Even as they wept at the fate of their neighbors, another miracle happened — a great temple rose beside them out of the ground. The care of this temple Jupiter entrusted to them.

When many years later Baucis and Philemon died at a ripe old age, their deaths occurred at the same time. Jupiter transformed them into trees, an oak and a linden, which the peasants worshiped as symbols of the duties of hospitality.

TWO CONTESTS OF MINERVA

Pallas Athena (called by the Romans Minerva) once engaged in a contest with Neptune as to which should have the honor of naming a newly founded city in Attica. Each was so eager to win this honor that a bitter quarrel seemed likely. To avert it the gods decided that each deity must produce some gift for the benefit of mankind, and that to the one that produced the more useful gift should go the honor of naming the new city.

ATHENS

Athens, the eye of Greece, mother of arts and eloquence. — MILTON

Neptune struck the earth with his trident and from it in a moment sprang a beautiful horse, struggling with its hind legs to throw off the encumbering earth. As it stood before the gods tossing its proud head and pawing the ground with its hoofs, the gods exclaimed in wonder. Then Pallas Athena struck the earth with her spear, and hardly had the point of the spear left the ground when up from the soil sprang a noble tree, laden with glossy black fruit, the olive.

Silent sat the gods, and gazing into the future they saw to how many uses the tree and its produce would be put by mankind. With one accord they acclaimed Athena victor, and the city was named ATHENS.

On another occasion Athena contested for honors with a mortal. This mortal was Arachne. Her father was Idmon, skilled in the art of dyeing in purple, and from infancy the girl had been taught her father's art, joined with that of weaving. In all the land there was none that surpassed her. So conceited did she become that, lifting her head proudly to the skies, she challenged Athena herself, patron of the arts of the household, to compete with her.

Pallas Athena had watched with kindly interest the progress that Arachne was making, and when she heard the presumptuous challenge, she was not offended. She assumed the guise of an old woman and made her way into Idmon's home. There she came to the spindle at which Arachne was weaving and admired the girl's skill.

"I am," she said, "a woman old in experience, and I have seen much in this wide world. To me has come the knowledge of your challenge to Athena. Let me counsel you to withdraw your words. You surpass and shall surpass all other mortals, but how vain and foolish it is to contend with the immortal gods, from whom comes all skill!"

"Be silent, foolish old woman," replied Arachne scornfully. "I fear not Athena, but shall put her to shame with my skill. Let her appear and put me to the test."

Even as she spoke, Athena threw off her disguise and in solemn majesty stood before the girl.

"Athena is here," she said; and at her words Arachne trembled and realized too late how insane had been her challenge. But she summoned up her courage and began

R. T. Pusch

TRANSFORMATION OF ARACHNE INTO A SPIDER

Poor Arachne's silver tapestry. — WILDE

to weave her most skillful web.   On a wide woof she pictured
some of the love affairs of the gods.   In all colors she wove
the web, but mostly in that royal purple of which her father
was the master.   At last her work was complete.

Then Athena began to weave, and she depicted wondrous
scenes in high Olympus, and from her very web floated
forth divine fragrance of nectar and ambrosia.   An unearthly beauty hovered over the design.   In the corner
Athena pictured the fate that had come to mortals who had
defied the gods, and as she went from one to the other
Arachne began to feel doom stealing closer and closer.   As
the last corner was completed, Athena turned to her, touched
her with her magic spindle, and said :

"Punished shall you be for your presumption, but the
gods will not let die such skill as you have shown.   Change
to an insect, that other mortals may take warning from you,
but ever weave a web of marvelous design."

At the words of Athena Arachne began to shrink and
shrivel.   Shortly she was completely transformed.   Where
a girl had stood an insect crawled — the spider ; and before
the eyes of the terrified beholders it scuttled off to a corner
and immediately began weaving a web of shimmering threads.
So to this day the Greeks call the spider "arachne."

STUDY APPLICATION

THE MYTHS IN LITERATURE

Of all the stories related in this chapter, the most profound effect has
been exercised by that of Oedipus.   In it both the ancients and the
moderns have found a powerful illustration of the doctrine that it is
impossible to escape one's fate, and that to run away from a dreaded
event often helps to bring it on.   The greatest of ancient dramatists,
Sophocles, followed the strange fortunes of Oedipus in three plays, all
of which have fortunately come down to us.   The Sphinx who appears

Museum of Poitiers, France

MINERVA OF POITIERS

I sing the glorious power with azure eyes,
Athenian Pallas, timeless, chaste, and wise. — SHELLEY

in the story has become identified with the mysterious object in the Egyptian desert, although archaeologists now believe that the latter is intended as an allegorical portrait of an Egyptian king.

Europa may have been an actual princess carried off by ancient Hellenes or Greeks to their own land; and a long tradition which ascribes the introduction of the alphabet into Greece by the Phoenician Cadmus may be based on fact. Byron refers to this tradition when, in a poem addressed to the Greek still enslaved by the Turk, he exclaims:

> You have the letters Cadmus gave —
> Think you he meant them for a slave?

Europa's abduction has been treated by Walter Savage Landor, Edward Dowden, and other poets. Tennyson, in *The Palace of Art*, paints a series of pictures, among which is one of the Phoenician princess:

> Or sweet Europa's mantle blew unclasp'd —
>   From off her shoulder backward borne:
> From one hand droop'd a crocus; one hand grasp'd
>   The mild bull's golden horn.

Swift has taken the tale of Baucis and Philemon, transposed it to modern times, and furnished it with modern details, in a poem which burlesques the old story. References to the contest between Arachne and Minerva and between the latter and Neptune occur in the poets, who have not, however, been inspired to any long flights of fancy on these subjects.

References to Mythology in Literature

What do the following references mean? Where a word or phrase is italicized, explain only the word or phrase.

1. And there, they say, two bright and aged snakes,
   Who once were Cadmus and Harmonia,
   Bask in the glens or on the warm seashore. — *Arnold*
2. Fear is the fire that melts *Icarian* wings. — *Coates*
3. Your *Icarian* flight melts into a groveling existence. — *Disraeli*
4. And angry Juno's unrelenting hate. — *Dryden*
5. Cadmus by sowing dragon's teeth, we read,
   Raised a vast army from the poisonous seed. — *Gay*

6. For in the charge of Zeus all strangers and beggars stand.

— Homer

7.   By this gloom,
And by old *Rhadamanthus'* tongue of doom. — *Keats*

8.   Heeding Zeus,
Who holds the guest-right sacred. — *Ledoux*

9. Next she placed on the board some olives, green and ripe, truthful Minerva's berries. — *Ovid*

10. Play unto this riddle the Oedipus. — *Poe*

11. I am no Oedipus! [spoken by a character who is not good at conundrums]. — *Terence*

EXERCISES IN COMPOSITION, ORAL AND WRITTEN

1. To a nymph who becomes her companion in Crete the princess Europa relates her adventures. What would she tell her?

2. Prepare a talk on "Ancient Inventions." What were some early tools? How old is the wheel? How was time measured at the beginning? Who first, like Daedalus, attempted to fly? Find the answers to these questions and to others that will occur to you in such books as George Iles's *Inventors at Work* and S. E. Forman's *Stories of Useful Inventions*, or from the section on "Inventions" in *The New Larned History*.

3. Put the story of Baucis and Philemon into the form of a brief drama Only two scenes will be necessary: one in the homely cottage, and in this the travelers relate their experiences; and one on the summit of the hill.

4. When Neptune produced the horse and Pallas Athena produced the olive, each addressed the assembly of deities and predicted to them the future of the horse and of the tree, praising the value of their gifts. What might each of them have said? Have two sections in your sketch: the first Neptune's speech, the second Athena's speech. At the close the assemblage hails Athena and cries out, "Name the city Athens!"

WORD STUDY

1. Explain the origin of the following geographical and astronomical terms:

Europe — one of the continents
Icarian Sea — part of the Aegean Sea

Europa — a satellite of the planet Jupiter
The Great and the Little Bear — also called the Big and the Little Dipper
Athens — the capital of Greece

2. How are the following names pronounced? See the index for many of these words.

Europa, Phoenicia, Minos, Rhadamanthus, Sarpedon, Daedalus, Icarus, Icarian, Callisto, Baucis, Philemon, Arachne, Laius, Oedipus, Jocasta, Antigone.

3. Explain the origin of the following words: *labyrinth* and the Greek word for "spider." Why is a library or a learned society sometimes called an "Athenaeum"?

4. Who, according to the Greeks, introduced the alphabet into their land? Bring to class a few facts as to the spread of the alphabet. (Use an encyclopedia or Clodd's *Story of the Alphabet.*)

5. Repeat the "riddle of the Sphinx."

Rapid Quiz

In what part of the world was the father of Europa a ruler? In what guise did Jupiter carry off this princess? To what land did he carry her? Which one of her sons later ruled this land? Which two became judges in the underworld? Who was the forefather of inventors? What was the *labyrinth?* What other device did this inventor prepare? How was it used? What command did the father of Europa lay upon her brother? How did he carry it out? How did he offend Mars? What service to Greece is credited to this brother? What finally became of him and his wife? What oracles did the father of Oedipus and Oedipus himself seek to evade? What were the consequences? What was the riddle of the Sphinx? What caused Juno to become the enemy of Callisto? What fate did she visit on her? What became of Callisto and her son? How did Jupiter test the hospitality of the inhabitants of Phrygia? What couple was successful in the test? What was their reward? In what two contests did Minerva engage? Who was her opponent in each instance?

For Students of Latin

1. When did Greece, including Crete, come under the rule of the Romans?

2. Is the Latin the same as the Greek alphabet? Which have later ages preferred? Why?

3. Retell briefly in Latin one of the myths in this chapter, or answer in Latin two or three questions in the Rapid Quiz.

READING LIST

Poems, Plays, and Music

Arnold, Matthew: Fragment of an *Antigone*
De Vere, Aubrey: *The Rape of Europa*
Emerson, Ralph Waldo: *The Sphinx*
Garrick, David: *Upon a Lady's Embroidery*
Landor, Walter Savage: *Europa and Her Mother*
Sophocles: *Oedipus the King*
Sophocles: *Oedipus Coloneus*
Sophocles: *Antigone*
Stravinsky, Igor: *Oedipus Rex* [opera-oratorio]
Taylor, Bayard: *Icarus*

VENUS AND CUPID

Cupid, boy of a hundred tricks. — HORACE

IV

STORIES OF VENUS

Creator Venus, genial power of love,
The bliss of men below and gods above! — DRYDEN

VENUS AND ADONIS[1]

Venus had, of course, many love affairs, but the most famous of them is that which took place between her and Adonis. Adonis was a youth of a country in Asia Minor. He was so handsome that even today we call a man of exceptional attractiveness an "Adonis." One day Venus was idly toying with the arrows of her son Cupid and accidentally scratched herself with one of them. Before the

---

[1] In some versions of this story Venus is given the name of the Assyrian goddess of love — Astarte or Ishtar.

78

VENUS DE MILO

Lo, this is she that was the world's delight. — SWINBURNE

wound was healed and the dangerous venom out of her veins, she beheld Adonis and immediately fell deeply in love with him.

Then she neglected all her ordinary pursuits and was seen no more in the haunts that she usually visited. Her only joy was to be with Adonis and to accompany him wherever he went. Adonis, despite his beauty, was of a very manly character, and loved hunting above all things. With him, then, in his pursuit of dangerous game of all kinds went Venus, and daily they roamed the woods together. No longer did Venus adorn herself with all her charms, nor did she spend, as once she was wont, hours in heightening her attractions. Rather she went roughly clad, bearing a bow and quiver like the huntress goddess, Diana. She, too, learned to follow and to kill the deer, but she left to Adonis the slaying of wolves and bears, of panthers and boars.

Yet Venus warned Adonis and urged him not to be too bold. She feared that sooner or later some ferocious beast would turn against him and harm him. So indeed it happened. For one day Venus left Adonis and flew to Olympus in her chariot drawn by doves. Her last word to Adonis was a caution. But Adonis would not heed any counsel to cultivate cowardice. He was always first in the chase, the first to come up to the animal to be killed; and he scorned to let others bear the brunt of the danger. On this day a wild boar, huge and ferocious, had been roused by the dogs and had fled before them. With eagerness in his heart and spear ready for the thrust Adonis rushed forward. He managed to wound the animal, but the spear point went in only a little way, and then the beast rushed headlong at Adonis. He buried his tusks savagely in the sides of the fair youth, who fell dying upon the plain.

Long and bitterly did Venus lament for Adonis, and every springtide the inhabitants of his native region mourned for him in a sacred festival. From his blood sprang, it was

Gramstorff Bros.

CUPID WEEPING OVER ADONIS

The rivers weep the sorrows of Aphrodite, the wells of the mountains shed tears for Adonis: the beauteous Adonis is dead. — BION

said, the anemone, and it was said, too, that Jupiter, in pity for his daughter, allowed Adonis to ascend from the lower world for six months of every year to dwell with Venus as her husband, and during these six months summer likewise dwelt on the earth.

CUPID AND PSYCHE

One of the most beautiful of ancient stories was told by a Latin writer named Apuleius concerning Cupid and Psyche. There was once a king, he told, who had three daughters, of whom the youngest, named Psyche (which in the Greek means either "soul" or "butterfly"), was the most beautiful.

So fair was she that when she walked in the streets, people strewed flowers before her, and so much admiration was paid her that the altars of Venus were neglected.

The goddess of love was enraged when she saw how Psyche had supplanted her in the affections of the people, and she resolved to punish the maiden whose beauty was so presumptuous. She therefore called her son Cupid to her and bade him prepare the means of her revenge. He was ordered to go to Psyche with certain waters from a fountain in the garden of Venus and inspire her by means of them with love for a low and mean person. Cupid flew away on his mission, but when he beheld Psyche lying in lovely sleep he almost repented of his mission. Yet he performed his errand. As he bent over her, he accidentally wounded himself with one of his own arrows. Paying no attention to his own hurt, he sought to counteract the effect of the magical waters. From another vial he poured over her a sweet, medicinal draft and flew away.

Frowned upon by Venus, from that time forth Psyche, despite her beauty, won no favor. Her two sisters were married to powerful princes, but no one came to sue for the hand of Psyche. At last her parents consulted an oracle, which told them that they must send Psyche to the top of a mountain, where in a house appointed for her a monster, of immortal birth, awaited her as a husband. With lamentations and tears they dressed Psyche as a bride and took her to a lonely cliff whereon stood a mean house, and there abandoned her to her fate.

But suddenly the west wind, Zephyrus, lifted Psyche gently up, and bore her to a fragrant valley, and there, in the midst of flowers, stood a noble palace, its roof supported by pillars of pure gold. Psyche in amazement entered the

CUPID AWAKENING PSYCHE

Surely I dreamt today, or did I see
The winged Psyche with awakened eyes? — KEATS

palace, and at every step new wonders met her eye. As she paced through the high halls a voice of a maiden met her ear, and she learned that she had at her service many invisible servitors, ready to do whatever she commanded. A delicious meal was prepared for her, and, as she ate, sweet strains of music fell upon her ears. When she retired it was to a chamber gorgeously decorated with many scenes from the adventures of the gods, and still in deep wonder she fell asleep.

At midnight a melodious voice awakened her.

"I am your husband," it said. "This house and all that is in it are yours, but on one condition — that you must never attempt to see my face."

So only at night were Psyche and her husband united, and although she heard his voice, never did she catch a glimpse of his face.

For a long time Psyche was very happy, but as the months rolled by she was filled with a desire to see her parents and sisters again. Her desire made her pine away, and at last her husband realized that something was amiss. He questioned her, and reluctantly then she told him how much she longed to see her sisters again, if only for a little while. For a time her husband was silent, but at length he agreed to let them visit her for a short time.

"But do not let them persuade you," he warned her, "into asking to see my face."

Joyfully Psyche prepared for their visit, getting ready many beautiful gifts. Word was sent to them, and at the appointed time Zephyrus bore them gently to the palace in which Psyche dwelt. In amazement, her sisters gazed on its marvels, and before long they were filled with jealousy. They cast suspicion upon Psyche's story, and tried to

Thumann   *Gramstorff Bros.*

PSYCHE AT NATURE'S MIRROR

O latest born and loveliest vision far
Of all Olympus' faded hierarchy! — KEATS (*Ode to Psyche*)

persuade her that she was indeed married to a monster. They advised her that she must provide herself with a lamp to enable her to see what her husband really was like and with a knife to slay him if he turned out to be a monster.

Psyche at first refused to credit their suspicions, but finally they had their effect upon her, and she made up her mind to do as they counseled. When her sisters had gone home, she resolved to learn the truth. Her husband returned as usual to the palace. When she knew that he was plunged in slumber, Psyche silently lit her lamp and bent over him. To her wonder and joy she saw before her a most beautiful youth, and immediately her love for him was as great as his for her. But before she could withdraw the lamp from over him, a drop of oil from the vessel fell upon his shoulder and awakened the sleeping god. Cupid saw immediately what had happened, and without a word spread his white wings and flew away from the palace.

When Psyche knew that Cupid had left her, she was filled with despair and reproached herself so much for her base suspicions that she cast herself into a river and wished to die. But the river god refused to slay anything so beautiful and cast her up on the shore. Then for a long time Psyche wandered disconsolate over the earth, and took no heed how rough the ways were or how ill she fared. At last she came to a temple of Venus, and resolved to enter the service of the goddess. Venus knew that her son had married Psyche, but she was still filled with anger against the girl. Through the mouth of the priestess she told her that if she wished to deserve love, certain hard tasks would have to be performed by her, and she believed that Psyche would never perform these tasks. But Psyche accepted the undertaking eagerly and asked what it was she had to do.

Then Venus gave her the first of the tasks. In an enormous storehouse of the temple lay heaped together seeds of all kinds — wheat, beans, lentils, poppy, barley, millet, and many others, as food for the guardians of the temple and for the doves of Venus.

"Separate these grains, each in a heap by itself," ordered Venus. "The task must be accomplished by nightfall."

Not in ten days could Psyche have finished this task. But Cupid, who still secretly watched over her, stirred up the ants to do the work. The whole nation of them labored eagerly together, and by nightfall each kind of seed was in a heap by itself.

When Venus returned and saw that Psyche had carried out her first command, she was indignant, for she knew that not by herself could the girl have accomplished it. Then she set the second task :

"Gather from the golden-shining sheep in yonder field three tufts of wool."

Psyche set out for the field, walking slowly along the side of a river. There the reeds whispered to her and bade her wait, for the sheep were very fierce.

"Wait," they urged, "until midday has passed, and then look at the bushes."

She obeyed this counsel, and in the afternoon found tufts of golden wool hanging upon the bushes against which the sheep had rubbed in passing. Joyfully she returned with these to Venus.

Grimly the next morning Venus assigned the third task.

"Go to Proserpina, the queen of Hades," she bade the girl, "and bring me a box of the ointment wherewith she preserves her divine beauty."

Terrible was this task, but she accomplished it, entering the underworld through a cave, prevailing on Charon to ferry her across the Styx, and winning Proserpina by pity to give her the precious ointment. But on the way back Psyche could not resist opening the box. Immediately she fell to the ground in a deadly sleep. Then Cupid could

Neide   *Gramstorff Bros.*

CHARON AND PSYCHE

Charon, in that crazy bark he hath, will put thee over upon the further side of Styx. — APULEIUS

no longer resist flying to her aid. He awakened her from her insensibility and begged the king of heaven to favor his cause. Jove interceded with Venus and persuaded her to accept the girl as Cupid's wife. Mercury then conveyed Psyche to Olympus, and there the girl ate of the divine ambrosia and became immortal. To Cupid and Psyche was born in time a daughter, and her name was Pleasure.

CUPID AND PSYCHE ARE WELCOMED TO MOUNT OLYMPUS

Till free consent, the gods among,
Makes her his eternal bride. — MILTON

THE GOLDEN APPLES: ATALANTA AND
HIPPOMENES

A contest of another kind was that in which Atalanta, a maiden of Boeotia, engaged. While she was still a child, it was prophesied of her that her marriage would be fatal to her. So she made up her mind never to marry. She avoided all communication with men and lived in the woods as a follower of Diana, devoted to hunting and other wood-

Poynter

ATALANTA'S RACE

Hippomenes turns her astray
By the golden illusions he flings on her way. — MOORE

land sports. Yet because she was so beautiful and because outdoor life had given her such health and vigor, many men approached her as suitors. They troubled her constantly and would not be denied.

At last Atalanta hit upon a stratagem. She called her suitors together and announced that she would become the bride of the one who could conquer her in a foot race. But on those who failed would be imposed the penalty of death. For a time there was silence among the suitors, but then a number of them announced their readiness to engage in the contest. All of them failed, for never was there maiden who ran with such swiftness as Atalanta, and no man could approach her in speed. Upon all those who were beaten was imposed the cruel penalty.

In one race in which she engaged, a certain youth, Hippomenes, acted as a judge. He had spoken with scorn of those foolish enough to engage in the contest, and had boasted that no maiden was so beautiful or so desirable as to be worth the hazard of death.

Yet when he saw the graceful form of Atalanta skimming over the ground as lightly as a bird, when at the rope that she touched as victor he gazed upon her face as lovely as that of a goddess, he changed his mind, and was as eager as the rest to win her hand.

She came forward flushed with the contest, and Hippomenes eagerly approached her and challenged her to another race on the morrow.

"These are only laggards," he exclaimed. "It shall be another story with me who am of the divine lineage of Neptune."

Atalanta looked at him and was sorry, for of all the youths who had contended with her none pleased her better than Hippomenes, and she felt a pang in her heart that he must suffer death. But Hippomenes forthwith sought the aid of the goddess most likely to help him. He prayed to Venus, and bade her consider how a victory of Atalanta would be contrary to her rule of love. Venus heard him, and listened to his prayer. Going to the Garden of the Hesperides, far to the west of the world, she gathered three of the wonderful apples that grew on the great tree in the center of the garden, and gave them to Hippomenes with instructions as to how to act.

The next day the race took place, before a great concourse

of people. Both contestants flashed from the starting place
like arrows from a bow, but shortly, despite his best efforts,
Hippomenes saw the girl take the lead. Then from his
hand he whirled directly into the path of Atalanta one of
the golden apples. Its beauty dazzled her eyes, and without realizing what she was doing she stooped and snatched
it from the ground. As she did so, Hippomenes overtook
and passed her. But again she hastened and passed him,

CYBELE

The towered Cybele,
Mother of a hundred gods. — MILTON

and again a golden apple fluttered into her path. Again
she paused to pick it up and once more gave Hippomenes
the advantage. But her speed was so great that even these
handicaps were not enough for Hippomenes, and in a few
moments she led the way again. Now the end of the course
was near, and in desperation Hippomenes threw forward
the last of the golden apples. It rolled to the side of the
track, and Atalanta hesitated as to whether or not to stop
to pick it up. But the wonder of the apple was so great
that perforce she turned aside and stooped and lifted it

from the ground. As she did so, a great shout thundered in the air. Hippomenes had won.

Atalanta was not altogether sorry to become the wife of Hippomenes, but her doom was yet to be fulfilled. Both lovers failed to give due gratitude to Venus, from whom the victory of Hippomenes had come. Angered at their forgetfulness the goddess changed them to beasts — Hippomenes to a lion, Atalanta to a lioness, and harnessed them to the chariot of the Titaness Rhea. Rhea was also called Cybele and the Great Mother, since she was the mother of Jove and other great gods. She was often represented as wearing a crown in the form of a city wall with towers.

PYGMALION AND GALATEA

Once there lived a king of the island of Cyprus named Pygmalion, who was not only a wise ruler but also an excellent sculptor. He had, however, one peculiarity: he distrusted women, and announced that he intended forever to remain unmarried.

At one time Pygmalion was working on a statue of ivory, in the semblance of a maiden. Day by day he worked, and ever the statue became more beautiful. Into it Pygmalion wove all his dreams, in it he expressed his sincerest ideals. He was himself delighted with the statue, and when nightfall came he continued to give it little touches here and there to add to the beauty, until his eyes ached and deep darkness lay over his studio. He called the statue Galatea.

At last the statue was completed, and then, to his own surprise, Pygmalion found that he could not rest in quiet away from his masterpiece. Sooner or later he found his way back to the fine chamber in which he had placed it, and constantly his eyes gazed in delight at his work. Only one day did he awake to a realization of the truth — he was in love with the statue.

Not long afterwards there was celebrated in Cyprus a festival of Venus. Standing solemnly before the altar of the goddess Pygmalion addressed her, reminded her of his respect and devotion to her temple, and begged a boon; namely, that his statue might take flesh and live.

When he returned home that night, Pygmalion went with slow steps to the room where the statue stood. To his amazement a garland of fragrant flowers hung around her neck, and he knew that this was a favorable sign, for none was allowed to enter the room except himself. As he stood there in wonder, he saw how a delicate flush of red began to run over the marble whiteness of the statue. Then came a tender pulsing on the forehead and at the wrists, then a slow moving of the knees and of the head. Hesitatingly, Pygmalion moved forward and touched Galatea's hand, and as he did so, her fingers were clasped around his. Slowly her foot moved forward, and she stepped from the pedestal.

"Galatea!" cried Pygmalion, as she moved smilingly to his embrace.

Venus blessed the wedding of Pygmalion and Galatea. From their union was born Paphos, who founded a city — Paphos in Cyprus — sacred to the goddess of love.

HERO AND LEANDER

On the Hellespont, almost directly opposite each other, lived a youth named Leander, whose home was in Abydos, and a maiden named Hero, who dwelt at Sestos. Hero's beauty was such that it was said that both Apollo and Cupid sued for her hand, but in vain.

Bodenhausen   *Gramstorff Bros.*

HERO AND LEANDER

The winds are high on Hellë's wave,
  As on that night of stormy water
When Love, who sent, forgot to save
The young, the beautiful, the brave,
  The lonely hope of Sestos' daughter. — BYRON

Now Hero served Venus as a priestess, and one day it happened that Leander came to Sestos to do honor to the goddess. There he beheld Hero, and she at the same moment saw him, and both fell in love at first sight. But Hero's parents would not listen to the suit of Leander, and they even forbade the young people to see each other.

Not so easily were they thwarted, however. They managed to arrange a code of signals, and whenever Hero at night hung a lantern upon the tower of the temple, Leander would swim the Hellespont and join her for a brief hour or two. But one night a storm arose after Leander had set out on his dangerous journey. Shortly the winds blew out the guiding lantern, and Leander instead of swimming to safety directed his course toward a treacherous patch of sea. In vain he struggled; the storm was too much for him, and he perished. Next morning the waves washed his body ashore at the very feet of Hero, who was anxiously looking out to sea, dreading lest harm might have overtaken Leander. In deep grief she threw herself into the ocean and was drowned.

PYRAMUS AND THISBE

In Babylon, in those days when Queen Semiramis reigned there, lived Pyramus, a youth noted for his handsome appearance, and Thisbe, often regarded as the most beautiful maiden in all the city. They lived in adjoining houses, and as childhood passed into youth, their friendship deepened into love.

But to their marriage their parents objected. All communication between them was forbidden, and they were able to converse only by signs and glances. One day, however, they discovered a crack in the wall that separated their houses, and through this crack they were able, at times, to whisper their undying devotion.

At length they could endure separation no longer, and they arranged to meet, one evening at dusk, under a white mulberry tree that stood just outside the city walls. Thisbe arrived first at the place agreed upon, but as she approached she saw a terrifying lioness before her. She screamed and fled in haste, dropping her veil as she ran. The beast made no attempt to pursue Thisbe, but picked up the veil in her blood-streaked mouth and then dropped it. Not long afterward she turned away to the near-by woods.

At this very moment Pyramus came to the rendezvous.

Burne-Jones

THISBE

In such a night
Did Thisbe fearfully o'er-trip the dew.
— SHAKESPEARE

He saw the veil on the ground, and marked the spots of blood upon it; and deadly fear seized him.

"Thisbe has been slain!" he exclaimed. "But she does not die alone!" With the words he plunged his sword into his side. As he lay dying upon the ground, Thisbe came back. She had conquered her dread, and she wished to warn Pyramus of the danger that awaited him. But she was too late, and when she saw what had happened, she too sought an escape from a life that no longer held any joy for her. The same sword that had slain her lover was the means of her death; and the commingled blood from the youth and the maiden mounted up the trunk of the mulberry tree and stained its fruit a deep purple. So it has remained ever since, in memory of the hapless lovers.

STUDY APPLICATION

The Myths in Literature

The love stories narrated in this chapter have offered an inexhaustible mine of material to the poet; and the writers of our day are making just as much use of this material as did those of Shakespeare's age.

Naturally Cupid has been a favorite subject. Every good poet apparently considers it his duty to write at least one poem about the little god of love. Many poets have endeavored, moreover, to retell what has been called "the last great myth" — that of Cupid and Psyche, originally told by the Latin writer Apuleius, in his novel, *The Golden Ass*. The best English version of this story is to be found in Walter Pater's *Marius the Epicurean*.

About Hero and Leander Musaeus wrote in ancient times, and his poem was ably rendered into English by two contemporaries of Shakespeare — Marlowe and Chapman. The story of Pygmalion has been told excellently by William Morris (teller of so many ancient tales), and done into an effective play by Sir William S. Gilbert; Morris wrote, too, on Atalanta's race. Shakespeare wrote a long, languorous poem on *Venus and Adonis*, and to this love story occur many references in English poetry. Shakespeare also made use of the story of Pyramus and Thisbe, in an amusing burlesque form, in *A Midsummer Night's Dream*. Thisbe laments:

> Asleep, my love?
> What, dead, my dove?

O Pyramus, arise!
   Speak, speak! Quite dumb?
   Dead, dead? A tomb
Must cover they sweet eyes.
   Those lily lips,
   This cherry nose,
These yellow cowslip cheeks,
   Are gone, are gone!
   Lovers, make moan.
His eyes were green as leeks.

REFERENCES TO MYTHOLOGY IN LITERATURE

What do the following references mean? Where a word or phrase is italicized, explain only the word or phrase.

1. Woe, woe for *Adonis*, he hath perished, the lovely Adonis!
                           — *Bion*

2. The winds are high on Hellë's wave,
As on that night of stormy water,
When Love, who sent, forgot to save
The young, the beautiful, the brave,
The lonely hope of Sestos' daughter. — *Byron*

3. She [Venice] looks a sea-Cybele, fresh from ocean,
Rising with her tiara of proud towers. — *Byron*

4.   The silver flow
Of Hero's tears. — *Keats*

5. Sinking bewilder'd 'mid the dreary sea:
'Tis young Leander toiling to his death. — *Keats*

6.   From his hand now dropt
A golden apple. — *Landor*

7. They show us an Alexander in the shades cobbling shoes, or a
Semiramis getting up foul linen. — *Lamb*

8. O Aphrodite, kind and fair,
That what thou wilt canst give,
O listen to a sculptor's prayer,
And bid mine image live! — *Lang*

9. At Sestos *Hero* dwelt, Hero the fair,
Whom young Apollo courted for her hair. — *Marlowe*

10. Beds of hyacinths and roses,
    Where young *Adonis* oft reposes,
    Waxing well of his deep wound,
    In slumber soft, and on the ground
    Sadly sits th' Assyrian queen. — *Milton*

11. But far above in spangled sheen
    Celestial Cupid, her fam'd son, advanc'd;
    Holds her dear *Psyche*, sweet entranc'd
    After her wandering labors long. — *Milton*

12.   With these in troop
    Came Astoreth, whom the Phoenicians called
    Astarte, Queen of Heav'n, with crescent horn. — *Milton*

13.   Set at naught
    The frivolous bolt of *Cupid*. — *Milton*

14. The treacherous flame cast on his shoulder fair
    A burning drop; he woke. — *Morris*

15. Rose-cheek'd *Adonis* hied him to the chase. — *Shakespeare*

16. The senior-junior, giant-dwarf, Dan Cupid,
    Regent of love-rhymes, lord of folded arms. — *Shakespeare*

17. Lo! where beyond he lieth languishing,
    Deadly engor'd of a great wild boar;
    And by his side the goddess groveling
    Makes for him endless moan. — *Spenser*

18.   That same pair
    Which through the sky draw *Venus' silver team*. — *Spenser*

19. And let fair Venus, that is queen of love,
    With her *heart-quelling son* upon you smile. — *Spenser*

20. A hoarse voice spoke through the letter-box. "Has he gone,
    laddie?" I put my mouth to the slit, and we talked together
    like *Pyramus and Thisbe*. — *P. G. Wodehouse*

Exercises in Composition, Oral and Written

1. Write a supposed dialogue between Venus and Adonis, in which the goddess, just before she sets out for a visit to Mount Olympus, warns him against being too reckless and bold in the chase; and he replies to her.

2. When Cupid awakens and sees that Psyche has disregarded his warning, he prepares to fly away. But Psyche holds him back by the

hand and tries to apologize and explain. Naturally she would speak in broken phrases and before she can say very much, Cupid disengages her hand and leaves her — without a word. Describe the scene and give the plea of Psyche.

3. Can you think of any other stories in which someone is set a task that no one, apparently, can fulfill? Remember, for example, some of the fairy stories you have read. Retell one of these stories.

4. Which of the stories in this chapter would be best suited to motion-picture reproduction? Describe the way in which the story you select would be given in photoplay form.

5. With the help of several other students, give to your class a presentation of Shakespeare's burlesque of the Pyramus and Thisbe story (see *A Midsummer Night's Dream*, act v, scene 1).

6. Compare the love story of Pyramus and Thisbe with that of Romeo and Juliet, as you find it in Shakespeare's play or in Lamb's *Tales from Shakespeare*.

Word Study

1. Give the correct pronunciation of the following words.

Adonis, Astarte, Psyche, Proserpina, Boeotia, Hippomenes, Hesperides, Pygmalion, Galatea, Cyprus, Abydos, Thisbe, Semiramis.

2. What does "an Adonis" mean? What does "psyche" mean in Greek? Give an English derivative from this word. What does "zephyr" mean? What is its origin?

3. Give the Greek forms for *Venus, Jupiter, Jove, Diana, Cupid, Neptune*.

4. Look up in Webster's *Dictionary* the plant called *Adonis* and bring the class some facts concerning it.

5. Why does Shakespeare speak of "*Dan* Cupid"? Look up *Dan* in Webster's *Dictionary*.

Rapid Quiz

Who was Adonis? How did Venus's love for him change her character? What was the cause of his death? How did Venus show her devotion to him? Why was Venus angry with Psyche? What command did she give Cupid concerning Psyche? What effect did Psyche have on Cupid? By what means did she become his wife? What warning did he give her? What caused her to disregard it? What was the result? What penances were laid on Psyche? How did she carry them out? Was Venus finally reconciled to her? Why did Atalanta of Boeotia wish to avoid marriage? What condition did she impose on her suitors? What means did Hippomenes devise to win her? Why were both punished? What was the attitude of Pygmalion toward women? How did he fall in love? What prayer did he address to Venus? How was the prayer granted? What obstacle did Hero and Leander meet in their love affair? What obstacle did Pyramus and Thisbe meet? How did the first pair evade opposition? What was the result? What happened to Pyramus and Thisbe? Who was Semiramis? What was the origin of the purple fruit of the mulberry tree?

FOR STUDENTS OF LATIN

1. In the work of what Latin author does the myth of Cupid and Psyche first occur?

2. Why would the Romans be especially interested in stories of Venus? (See page 333.)

3. Answer briefly in Latin two or three of the questions in the Rapid Quiz.

READING LIST

Poems, Plays, and Music

Anonymous: *The Vigil of Venus* (*Pervigilium Veneris*)
Browning, Elizabeth Barrett: *Psyche*
Browning, Robert: *Pheidippides*
Bunner, H. C.: *A Lost Child*
Byron, Lord: *Stanzas Written after Swimming from Sestos to Abydos*
Chapman, George: *Sequel to Marlowe's "Hero and Leander"*
Doolittle, Hilda ("H. D."): *Pygmalion*
Franck, César: *Psyche* [musical suite]
Herrick, Robert: *The Cheat of Cupid*
Hunt, Leigh: *Cupid Drowned*
Jonson, Ben: *Venus' Runaway*
Keats, John: *Ode to Psyche*
Kilmer, Aline: *To Aphrodite, with a Mirror*
Landor, Walter Savage: *Hippomenes and Atalanta*
Lang, Andrew: Bion's *Lament for Adonis*

Lazarus, Emma: *Venus of the Louvre*
Lyly, John: *Cupid and My Campaspe Played*
Marlowe, Christopher: Musaeus's *Hero and Leander*
Moore, Thomas: *Cupid and Psyche*
Morris, William: *Atalanta's Race — Pygmalion and the Image — The Story of Cupid*
Moulton, Louise Chandler: *Laus Veneris*
Noyes, Alfred: *The Venus of Milo*
Ovid: *Leander to Hero* (in *Heroines*) — *Hero to Leander* (in *Heroines*)
Sappho: *Hymn to Aphrodite*
Shakespeare, William: *A Midsummer Night's Dream*
Sill, Edward: *The Two Aphrodites*
Tennyson, Lord: *Hero to Leander*
Wilde, Oscar: *The Garden of Eros*

In Prose

Pater, Walter: Apuleius's "Cupid and Psyche" (in *Marius the Epicurean*)

APOLLO AND DIANA DISCHARGING ARROWS

Call it not revenge! 'Tis duty, 'tis devotion! — SOUTHEY

V

STORIES OF APOLLO

God of the golden bow,
And of the golden lyre,
And of the golden hair,
And of the golden fire. — KEATS

THE WANDERINGS OF LATONA

Among the daughters of the Titans was Latona, goddess of darkness. Her beauty was very great, and Jupiter fell in love with her and thereby incurred the anger of Juno. Juno, indeed, never forgave Latona, and whenever she had an opportunity she visited some form of punishment upon her.

To Jupiter Latona bore twin children, the sun god Apollo and the moon goddess Diana. With her infants in her arms she wandered from land to land, followed everywhere by the jealousy of Juno, who foresaw the future greatness of Latona's two children and was enraged that the offspring of her rival should attain such splendor.

In her wanderings Latona endured many hardships. Once, in Lycia, she saw ahead of her a pleasant, tree-shaded pool.

Metropolitan Museum

LATONA WITH INFANTS APOLLO AND DIANA

Latona's twin-born progeny. — MILTON

Joyfully she hastened toward it with her children, for she was weary and thirsty. But as she approached and stooped down to the cool waters, a number of rude country folk jostled her out of the way and forbade her to drink. In vain she implored them. She pointed to the infants who were with her, and reminded them in the name of Jove that hospitality was sacred to the gods. But they merely jeered at her and would not allow her to come near the pool. Some of them even waded through the water so as to make it too muddy to drink.

Then at last Latona lost her patience and remembered that she, too, was a goddess. Pointing her hand in wrath she cried: "Never leave the pool! Let it be your place of habitation forever!" Even as she spoke, the rustics were strangely transformed. Their hands and bodies turned green, their heads became flat, their voices became harsh. Their descendants the frogs still live today in many a muddy pool.

For a time Latona and her children dwelt in the mountain glens of Pieria, a favorite haunt of the Muses. There the nine sisters taught Apollo the art of music and song, until in time, instead of being their pupil, he became their master. But he did not as yet have the lyre, which Mercury later presented to him. Diana was brought up in a cave of Mount Cynthus (she was therefore sometimes called *Cynthia*), and her guardian was Hecate, the queen of witches. In the glades of Cynthus Diana roamed freely and fearlessly, and there she learned to know and understand the wild creatures. When both Apollo and Diana were full grown, they went to Mount Olympus, and took their places among the high gods.

HYACINTHUS

Apollo was the god most beloved by the Greeks, and around him they wove many legends. He was a protector of men — especially when in the vigor of their youth they engaged in sports and contests. It was told of him, among other stories, that he gave his friendship to a fair lad named Hyacinthus, son of the king of Sparta. The boy loved all kinds of games, and Apollo accompanied him on his fishing expeditions and in hunting trips, and he participated in all the sports in which Hyacinthus took part. Zephyrus, god of the west wind, was equally fond of Hyacinthus and tried to win his favor, but the lad cared only for Apollo.

One day Apollo and Hyacinthus began a game of quoits. Both were skillful players, and now one, now the other, made the farther throw. Unnoticed by either of them, Zephyrus crept up and observed them. He was filled with jealous anger that Hyacinthus preferred Apollo to him. Suddenly he could endure it no longer. Apollo was casting a quoit, and as it whizzed through the air the West Wind seized it in his invisible grasp, changed its course, and sent it with deadly force toward Hyacinthus. The heavy missile struck the boy on the head, and he fell senseless to the ground. Not all the efforts of Apollo could revive him, and the god mourned for him bitterly, as he lay dying. But taking the boy's lifeless body in his arms, Apollo gave him promise of immortal life.

"You die," he exclaimed to the boy, "but from your blood shall spring a flower that all shall love."

As he spoke a delicate blossom, in shape like the lily, but of a delicate purple hue, sprang from the ground. On its petals were marked the letters, "Ai, Ai," meaning "Woe, Woe." This flower the Greeks called the hyacinth, but today it is called the iris, in honor of the goddess of the rainbow.

APOLLO AND MARPESSA

A mortal maiden who rejected the love of Apollo was Marpessa. She was the daughter of a king named Evenus, who selfishly thought he could keep her with him forever and wanted her never to marry. But she was very beautiful, and had many suitors. Among them the contest narrowed down finally to two — Idas, a brave and handsome nobleman, and the great god Apollo. Of these Marpessa favored Idas, who urged her father to let him marry her. But Evenus angrily denied his request, ordered him out of his sight, and threatened to kill him if he returned.

Idas was in despair, but at this moment Neptune came to his rescue. The sea god presented Idas with a wonderful chariot, to which were attached not only some of the swiftest horses that ever lived, but also a pair of wings that still further hastened the progress of the car. With this chariot Idas waited for Marpessa at a well where she was accustomed to draw water for her household. He persuaded her to elope with him, and hardly had she mounted to his side, when the chariot sped away, fast as the wind. Word came to Evenus as to what had happened, and in high anger he mounted his own chariot and set off in immediate pursuit. But it was all in vain. Marpessa and Idas were beyond his reach.

But Apollo was not willing that Idas should so easily win Marpessa in marriage. Suddenly he appeared in front of the speeding chariot, and seized the horses by the bridles. Haughtily he commanded Idas to give up the maiden to him. Although Idas knew that his doom was certain, he prepared to fight till death. Again, however, Neptune came to his aid. Sitting on high Olympus beside Jupiter, he pleaded with the king of gods and men to do justice in the unequal contest. So, even as Apollo spoke, there was heard in the air the great rumble of thunder.

Apollo heard and bowed to the ground and trembled, for he knew the sign of Jupiter. Then came the voice of Jupiter himself, commanding: "Let the maiden decide whom she will wed."

So before the maiden in her chariot pleaded her two lovers,

the mortal and the god. Apollo promised her endless felicity, a knowledge of all things past and to come. He told her that she should have it within her power to bring bliss or bane to men, to lift up and to cast down. Then Idas spoke, in deep humility. He could offer her nothing but love, he could appeal to nothing but her pity for one to whom her beauty was the light of the world.

As he spoke she stretched out her hand to Idas and said: "Idas is my choice. For he and I shall grow old together, and old still shall I love him and he shall love me. But Apollo in time would tire of me, faded and mortal."

Apollo bowed his head to her decree and returned, without anger but grieving, to the haunts of Olympus, while Idas and Marpessa continued their journey happily together.

PHAËTHON AND AESCULAPIUS

Apollo had two sons who perished by the thunderbolts of Jove. Phaëthon was the son of Apollo and the nymph Clymene. He was brought up as a mortal, but often his mother would point to the sky and tell him that the sun god was his father. When Phaëthon told this story to his playmates, they scoffed at him and refused to believe that he was of divine parentage. In tears he came to his mother, and she consoled him. She told him that if he visited the sun god, Apollo would accept him as his son and prove to all the world that he was divine.

So Phaëthon set off for the palace of Apollo. Far off, where the stream Oceanus winds its way around the edge of the earth, he came upon the house of his father. There stood the god, in his shining and fragrant garments, and around him hovered the Days and the Hours, the Seasons and the Years. Awed by the splendor he saw before him, the youth could not speak. But the sun god, in kindly tones, bade him tell what was in his mind.

"Am I truly your son?" stammered the boy.

Then Apollo gazed more closely upon him and recognized his son. He kissed him and made much of him.

"But what brings you on such a far journey?" he asked Phaëthon.

Phaëthon told him then what had occurred, and asked a boon of his father.

"Let me have the fulfillment of one wish," he pleaded, "and all shall be well with me. Just grant me one wish."

At the sight of the tears and distress of his son, Apollo at once granted his request.

"By the head of Jupiter, you shall have whatever you ask," he swore.

Phaëthon was overjoyed. Quickly he cried out:

"Let me drive your sun chariot over the sky for a single day."

When he heard the lad's words, Apollo was terrified at his boldness. But in vain he warned the boy of the dangers through which he must pass, of the dreadful perils of such a journey, of the fierceness of the steeds which he must drive, of the overpowering heat that would surround him. Phaëthon insisted, and since his father's word had been given, nothing could be done to save Phaëthon.

So next morning the great steeds of the sun, blowing flame from their nostrils and champing fiercely at their bits, were brought forth and harnessed. Sorrowfully Apollo bade farewell to his son and helped him seat himself in the chariot. Scarcely were the reins in the boy's hands when the steeds leaped out across the sky. Almost at once the sun horses

THE FALL OF PHAËTHON

Though he did not succeed, his enterprise
Was greatly daring. — OVID

recognized an unfamiliar and weak hand on the reins, and in a short time they were uncontrollable. Amazing were the antics of the sun that day. Sometimes the chariot swung too high in the sky, and bitter cold assailed the human beings below. In Africa, however, it came too close, and everybody was scorched — hence the dusky skins of the Ethiopians.

At last it looked as if the whole earth would be shriveled with heat and destroyed. All mankind prayed to Jupiter for aid. Reluctantly he laid his hand on a thunderbolt, reluctantly he hurled it forth, and Phaëthon, blazing like a falling star, fell headlong to the earth. The steeds of the sun, left riderless, returned panting to their stables. Apollo was so filled with grief at the death of his son that for days he refused to come forth, and left the sky covered with black clouds. The sisters of Phaëthon mourned bitterly for him, and they were changed into poplars.

The doom of Aesculapius came about in a different way. He was the son of Apollo and of the Thessalian princess Coronis. His mother died at his birth, and Apollo entrusted his education to Chiron, one of an odd race of divinities, called *centaurs*. They were represented as half horses and half men, and were said to have been the offspring of a mortal named Ixion and a cloud. On one occasion the centaurs were invited to a wedding feast by a tribe called the Lapithae, but became so disorderly that the other guests attacked them, and they were driven out of their home in Thessaly. Ancient artists loved to represent this battle.

Chiron was the wisest and noblest of all the centaurs, and had received instruction from Apollo and from Diana in hunting, medicine, music, gymnastics, and the art of prophecy. He was the teacher of many of the great heroes of Greece

Even in later ages Leonardo da Vinci, one of the greatest geniuses that ever lived, had at times a most vivid hallucination — that he saw and spoke with Chiron.

For no pupil did Chiron do more than for Aesculapius. The child grew wiser and wiser; and when he reached

Michelangelo *Casa Buonarroti, Florence*

BATTLE OF THE LAPITHS AND CENTAURS

They see the centaurs,
Reared proudly. — ARNOLD

maturity, he became a great physician. He not only cured the sick, but in one instance so wondrous was his skill that he recalled a dead man to life. Then Jove feared that if Aesculapius continued to grow in his command of the healing art, he would help men to escape death altogether. So he hurled a bolt at him and slew him, but placed him afterward among the stars. Aesculapius had two sons who became

AESCULAPIUS

Then Jove
The leech that wrought such healing hurled
With lightning down to Pluto's world. — VIRGIL

physicians too, but were never so great as their father.   He
became the god of medicine, with serpents as his symbols.

THE SHEPHERD OF KING ADMETUS

The death of Phaëthon had filled Apollo with great dis-
pleasure toward Jupiter, and the slaying of Aesculapius
increased his anger.   This time he was not content merely
with thoughts and words of anger.
In a most ungodlike fashion he
resolved to wreak his wrath on the
innocent forgers of the thunderbolts of Jove — the one-eyed Cyclopes who worked in Vulcan's
forge underneath the volcano of
Mount Etna. So he shot his
potent shafts at them and slew
them.   Jupiter was furious at this
unjust act and determined to ban-
ish Apollo to the darkness of the
underworld.   But the mother of
Apollo interceded for him, and
finally Jupiter decreed that as
punishment for his wicked deed
Apollo must serve a mortal for the
space of a year.

Yale Gallery of Fine Arts

LECYTHUS [VASE FOR
OIL] SHOWING KING AD-
METUS WITH CHARIOT OF
WILD BEASTS

Fortune and Love befriend the
bold. — OVID

Admetus, king of Pherae in
Thessaly, was selected for the
honor of being the master of the
sun god.   Apollo was placed in
charge of the flocks of Admetus,
and for a twelvemonth he wan-

dered faithfully with the browsing sheep in the pastures of the king. Then it was, according to the legend, that Apollo, to amuse himself, learned to play the lyre, and with it charmed all who heard its sweet music.

So honorably and kindly was Apollo treated by King Admetus that he conceived a great fondness for his mortal master, and tried to aid him in all things. While Apollo tended the flocks of Admetus, they were extraordinarily fruitful and increased in number beyond all measure. Apollo also aided Admetus in another way. Admetus wished to have as his bride a beautiful maiden named Alcestis, the daughter of Pelias, who was a son of Neptune. But Pelias announced that he would give his daughter in marriage only to the man who should come for her in a chariot drawn by lions and boars. Admetus despaired of ever being able to perform this task. Apollo, when he heard what conditions Pelias had imposed, came to his aid. With his help Admetus harnessed to his chariot both lions and boars, and drove triumphantly to the palace of Pelias. Pelias was then obliged to carry out his promise, and Alcestis became the happy bride of Admetus.

ADMETUS AND ALCESTIS

Concerning the later life of this pair is told one of the most beautiful of Greek legends.

After several years of wedded happiness it befell that Admetus became seriously ill. Soon it was evident that his death hour was approaching and all the skill of his physicians availed him nothing. Not even Apollo, who was anxious to repay him for his justice and kindness to him when he had been his herdsman, could help him. But Apollo approached Jupiter and obtained one favor for Admetus.

"If there be anyone," declared Jupiter, "who is willing to die in place of Admetus, then his life will be accepted in place of that of the king, and the years of Admetus will be prolonged by as many years as his savior still has to live."

Joyously Apollo returned to the palace of Admetus with the tidings of this decree of the king of gods and men. As he came within the palace he found the king's family and friends, his retainers and soldiers, clustered in tears around him. Silence fell upon them as Apollo approached and raised his hand. Eagerly the sun god announced in what fashion the life of Admetus might yet be spared, and he thought to himself, "Surely all these mourners will be glad to die for the king."

But as Apollo concluded not a voice answered him. He turned to the aged parents of Admetus, and implored them to give their lives for Admetus. But they refused, saying that they wished to enjoy what few days remained to them. He turned then to the followers whom Admetus had often led into battle; to the courtiers who had often assured the king in flattering tones that they would willingly die for his slightest whim. All remained deaf to Apollo's pleading.

But even as he argued with them, there broke in upon him a clear and brave voice. It was that of Alcestis, the wife of the king.

"I will gladly die for my husband," she said.

Apollo was horrified.

"What!" he cried. "You will give your young life for his! Think too of your little children and how they will be left motherless without you — left to the care of an unpitying world. Better that Admetus should die than that your life should be offered in place of his."

And Apollo turned to go. But Alcestis ran to him and held him and told him he must fulfill the command of Jupiter.

So in sorrow he agreed, and Alcestis reclined on a couch. Slowly, then, her face grew pale, strength left her limbs, her breath faltered. While life ebbed from her body, it returned in increasing strength to Admetus. The blood returned to his visage, he felt the vigor of renewed vitality course through him from head to foot, and in a few minutes he sprang from the bed on which he had been lying — as well and healthy as ever he had been.

But on her couch Alcestis lay dying.

Just at this moment a strange diversion occurred. A great hero named Hercules (about whom many stories will be told you in a later chapter) happened to be passing through Thessaly, and he stopped to pay his respects to Admetus. As he approached the palace gates he wondered at the strange silence that prevailed, and he was amazed that no sentry sprang up to bid him halt, that no attendant came to greet him. As he came nearer, he heard the wails and lamentations that issued from the chamber in which Admetus lay. He turned towards this chamber, and unnoticed stood at the portal and heard all that took place within.

As he listened to the magnanimous offer of Alcestis and as he watched the pallor of death steal over her, he was filled with pity that so brave a woman must die. Just then he heard a rustle. He turned around and there, at his very side, was Death — a shadowy, black-robed figure. Stealthily Death stole forward, ready to bear Alcestis away in his grasp. But Hercules, who was daunted by no terrors of either heaven or earth or the depths underneath the earth, made a sudden resolve.

"Never," he cried to himself, "shall Death take this noble soul!"

So saying he rushed forward and seized Death. Almost impalpable was the substance of the Ill-Omened One, but

Hercules used every cunning of the wrestler's art, and try as Death would, he could not escape from the hero's grasp. Finally Death gave up the struggle and resigned Alcestis to Hercules. The hero placed her again in the arms of her husband, and the great mourning of the Thessalians, the bitter wails of the little children of Alcestis, were changed to rejoicing and thanksgiving. Alcestis, so miraculously restored to life, lived with her husband in happiness and prosperity for many years. Both men and gods were glad to do honor to her noble spirit. When, full of age, at last she died, Admetus did not long survive her.

Keystone View Co.

APOLLO SLAYS THE PYTHON

When by a thousand darts the Python slain
With orbs unroll'd lay cov'ring all the plain. — POPE

THE SLAYING OF THE PYTHON

A fierce monster was slain by Apollo, and because of this deed men venerated him and paid him great honor.

On the sides of Mount Parnassus there dwelt a terrible dragon, named the Python, which not only molested human beings who came by, but even opposed the passage of the gods. Once it lifted its head in wrath against Latona, mother of Apollo and Diana, and she called on her son for assistance. Apollo sped to the mountain and sought out the dragon. A great battle took place, but soon the snake lay dead on the ground, pierced by the arrows of the god.

Gramstorff Bros.

OLYMPIC GAMES

Time in ancient Greece was reckoned in Olympiads of four years each, beginning with the first Olympic Games, 776 B.C.

ATHLETIC GAMES

The Greeks were very fond of contests and greatly admired athletic prowess. After Apollo had slain the Python, therefore, they established the Pythian Games, which took place at regular intervals at Delphi in honor of Apollo's victory. Even more important were the Olympic Games, held in honor of Jupiter every four years. The Greeks thought so highly of these games that they reckoned their calendar by them, speaking of an event as taking place in the seventh or the seventy-ninth Olympiad — that is, in the four-year space between the games. The Nemean Games also were celebrated in honor of Jupiter.

Sargent   *Boston Museum of Fine Arts*

RUNNERS

Push on, pursue, in no wise faint of foot! — AESCHYLUS

At these and other games the Greeks, who might otherwise be engaged in war with one another, came together in friendly rivalry and paid homage to the gods in common. One day would be given up to sacrifices and processions. Then would come three days of contests — foot races, varying in length from two hundred yards to three miles; the pentathlon, which included five kinds of skill — throwing the discus, throwing the spear, running, jumping, and wrestling; chariot racing, accompanied by much excitement and often described by the poets; boxing and wrestling matches. Besides these, there were usually contests in poetry and music. On the last day of the festival the prizes would be awarded — beautiful wreaths that varied according to the god. At the Olympic Games the wreaths were of olive leaves, at the Pythian Games of laurel, at the Nemean Games of parsley.

DISCOBOLUS

Toil-mastering Strength the muscle strains. — PINDAR

Following the games would come new sacrifices and much feasting. Great honors would be paid to the victors in the various contests, not only then but after the crowds had dispersed. Poets wrote odes about them, sculptors designed their forms in bronze and marble, and their native cities received them on their return home with delegations of welcome and choral songs. An athlete who won three victories at Olympia was awarded the honor of having his statue erected in the open space outside the temple of Jupiter.

STUDY APPLICATION

The Myths in Literature

Apollo has inspired many poets to sing his praise. All the adventures of Apollo have been told again and again in rhyme and story.

Perhaps the most beautiful of all treatments of the Apollo legends is Stephen Phillips's narrative poem called *Marpessa*. Unforgettably the poet has told the story of a mortal's rejection of an immortal in favor of another mortal: the story is the complement of that of Aurora and Tithonus, told on page 178. He pictures the scene when the three met, the god and the man ready to plead each his cause:

> They three together met; on the one side,
> Fresh from diffusing light on all the world,
> Apollo; on the other without sleep
> Idas, and in the midst Marpessa stood.
> Just as a flower after drenching rain,
> So from the falling of felicity
> Her human beauty glowed, and it was new;
> The bee too near her bosom drowsed and dropped.

Many poets have been won by the nobility of the Admetus-Alcestis story. One of the most moving of ancient plays is the *Alcestis* of Euripides. Browning turned this play into a narrative of his own, *Balaustion's Adventure;* and the story has been excellently treated by poets as diverse as Emma Lazarus, James Russell Lowell, Walter Savage Landor, and William Morris.

Among the Greeks a fruitful theme for poetry was the victor in an athletic contest. Greatest of the poets who celebrated such contests and their heroes was Pindar; and in his poems he introduced many mythological references and connected the family history of the winner at some game with ancient gods and demigods.

REFERENCES TO MYTHOLOGY IN LITERATURE

What do the following references mean? Where a word or phrase is italicized, explain only the word or phrase.

A

1. Who drives the horses of the sun,
   Shall lord it but a day. — *Cheney*
2.   Pitying the sad death,
   Of Hyacinthus, when the cruel breath
   Of Zephyr slew him. — *Keats*
3. Methought I saw my late espoused saint
   Brought to me like *Alcestis* from the grave. — *Milton*
4. How charming is divine philosophy!
   Not harsh and crabbed, as dull fools suppose,
   But musical as is *Apollo's* lute. — *Milton*
5. As when those hinds that were transformed to frogs
   Railed at Latona's twinborn progeny. — *Milton*
6. When she had spoken, *Idas* with one cry
   Held her, and there was silence. — *Phillips*
7. Why, Phaëthon,
   Wilt thou aspire to guide the heavenly car,
   And with thy daring folly burn the world? — *Shakespeare*
8.   The blue bells
   Of hyacinth tell Apollo's written grief. — *Shelley*

B

1. And lie thou there,
   My laurel bough,
   Scornful *Apollo's ensign*, lie thou there! — *Arnold*
2. I will go lie in wait for Death, black-stoled
   King of the corpses. I shall find him sure. . . .
   Confident I shall bring Alcestis back. — *Browning*

3. Or view the lord of the unerring bow,
   The god of life and poetry and light. — *Byron*
4. Who fears nor Fate, nor Time, nor what Time brings,
   May drive Apollo's steeds, or wield the thunderbolt. — *Coates*
5. Son of Latona! hear my vow!
     Apollo, grant my prayer!
   Health to enjoy the blessings sent
     From heaven; a mind unclouded, strong;
   A cheerful heart; a wise content;
     And honored age; and song. — *Horace*
6. Like to that sanguine flower *inscribed with woe*. — *Milton*
7. This snake the god of the glittering bow destroyed. — *Ovid*
8. It was then as men think, that the people of Ethiopia became
   black-skinned, since the blood was drawn to the surface of
   their bodies by the heat. — *Ovid*
9. When, like *Apollo*, from his golden bow
   The Pythian of the age one arrow sped
   And smiled. — *Shelley*

Exercises in Composition, Oral and Written

1. Imagine that you, like Latona, were a wayfarer in ancient times
and that you, too, were approaching the pool in Lycia — just behind
her and her children. Describe the scene you witnessed.

2. In a gentle breeze that moves its petals the iris speaks. It relates
how once it was a mortal youth, beloved of Apollo, and goes on to tell
of the sudden death and strange transformation. Give the words of
the flower.

3. Prepare a pantomime in two scenes, showing the story of Marpessa. In one Idas appears before King Evenus and is angrily ordered
away. In the second Apollo confronts Marpessa and Idas, and the
two suitors make their plea to the maiden, who chooses the mortal.
Write stage directions describing actions and gestures.

4. Describe a scene in the schoolhouse of Chiron as he is about to
give a lesson in hunting or the use of herbs to Aesculapius.

5. Give an account of the modern Olympic Games. How do they
resemble and how do they differ from those of ancient times? Do
you know personally some victor in the Olympic Games? If so, interview him, and obtain from him details as to how they are conducted.

Word Study

1. Explain the origin, according to the Greeks, of the word *hyacinth*. What name does the flower bear today?

2. What does the word *phaeton* mean in English? Explain its origin. How is it pronounced? What is a *python* in modern usage? What is meant by "the Aesculapian art"?

3. How are the following words pronounced?

Latona, Lycia, Zephyrus, Cynthus, Pieria, Marpessa, Evenus, Clymene, Aesculapius, Phaëthon, centaur, Chiron, Coronis, Admetus, Alcestis, Pherae, Pelias, Python, Nemean, pentathlon.

4. The *centaury* (by some believed to be the cornflower) was an herb the usefulness of which in medicine was discovered by Chiron, according to legend. What was his connection with the art of healing?

5. Give the Greek names of the following deities: Latona, Juno, Diana, Neptune, Jupiter. *Lito   Hera*
Artemis   Jove

Rapid Quiz

Who was Latona? Over what realms did her two children rule? Who was jealous of her? How did Latona punish the boors of Lycia? What youth was the friend of Apollo? By whose jealousy did this youth die? For the favor of what maiden were Apollo and a mortal rivals? Who was successful? What were the names of two sons of Apollo? What ambition did the one of them cherish? How was it gratified, and what was his fate? By whom was the other educated? In what art did he attain great skill? How did he die? What revenge did Apollo take? How did Jupiter punish Apollo? What master did he serve? What doom threatened this master? What sacrifice did Alcestis make? How was she saved? What monster did Apollo slay? What games were established in commemoration of his deed? What other athletic contests were held in ancient Greece?

For Students of Latin

1. Did the Romans favor Apollo as much as Mars? Explain.
2. Which of these myths would a Roman lad like best? Why?
3. Answer briefly in Latin two or three questions in the Rapid Quiz.

READING LIST

Poems, Plays, Novels, and Music

Doolittle, Hilda ("H. D."): *Centaur Song*
Drummond, William: *Song to Phoebus*
Euripides: *Alcestis*
Gluck, C. W.: *Alceste* [opera]
Hood, Thomas: *Lycus the Centaur*
Keats, John: *Hymn to Apollo*
Landor, Walter Savage: *Hercules, Pluto, Alcestis and Admetus*
Lazarus, Emma: *Admetus*
Lowell, James Russell: *The Shepherd of King Admetus*
Lulli, G. B.: *Alceste* [opera]
Morris, William: *The Love of Alcestis*
Noyes, Alfred: *The Inn of Apollo*
Phillips, Stephen: *Marpessa*
Saint-Saëns, Camille: *Phaëton* [symphonic poem]
Saxe, John G.: *Phaëthon*
Shelley, Percy Bysshe: Homer's *Hymn to Apollo — Hymn of Apollo*
Snedeker, Caroline D.: *The Perilous Seat*
Stephens, James: *The Centaurs*
Wordsworth, William: *The Power of Music*

DIANA IN CHARIOT

Huntress of the silver bow. — HOOD

VI

STORIES OF DIANA

Queen and huntress, chaste and fair. — BEN JONSON

THE STORY OF ENDYMION

Diana, goddess of the moon, was usually as cold and withdrawn as the orb over which she ruled; and she was regarded as the particular patron of unyielding maidenhood. Sometimes she was pursued by lovers, but never would she surrender to them, and for some of them she prepared a cruel fate. But once she fell in love — with Endymion.

Endymion was a young shepherd who tended his flocks on the green slopes of Mount Latmos. So beautiful a youth was he and so noble in his demeanor that the people of the

Vatican Museum, Rome

DIANA BEHOLDS THE SLEEPING ENDYMION

Queen of the wide air: thou most lovely queen! — KEATS

vicinity regarded him with awe, and said of him that he must surely be the son of Jupiter. One summer night Endymion, after he had taken care of his flocks, lay down to sleep under an oak. When he fell asleep, the deep darkness was unlighted save by the stars, but in a little while Diana came riding over the skies in her silver chariot and illumined mountain and valley. Slowly Diana drove her milky steeds, and as she drove she gazed upon the earth beneath. Suddenly she caught sight of Endymion, and as suddenly fell deeply in love with the handsome shepherd lad.

She gazed on him with ecstasy, and would gladly have awakened him to tell him her love, but she dared not do so. For she had often reproached the other gods with their admiration for mortals, she had often boasted that she herself was immune to such weakness, that she was the goddess of eternal maidenhood — and now she was in love.

So she stole softly from her chariot, and seated herself beside Endymion, and gently kissed him, but took care not to awaken him. Upon his sleep she cast lovely dreams, in the midst of which often moved the figure of the goddess of the moon, and Endymion sighed happily in his slumbers. So Diana passed night after night.

But the other gods began to remark that Diana was often absent from the skies, that her chariot moved with no regular speed over the heavens. Then they began to spy on her, and shortly her secret was revealed to all on high Olympus. The others, particularly Venus, would have mocked Diana, but Jupiter checked them. The father of gods and men feared that in time Diana, because of the shepherd lad, would entirely neglect her duties as luminary of the sky at night.

He resolved, therefore, that to Endymion must be given a difficult choice. He called the youth to him and bade him

Guercino   Gramstorff Bros.

THE SLEEPING ENDYMION

Soon was he quieted to slumbrous rest. — KEATS

elect which he would take: a death in any manner he chose, or perpetual youth plunged in perpetual sleep. Endymion chose the latter fate, and still he sleeps in a cave on Mount Latmos, where, when her course leads her to a certain point in the sky, Diana may still peep at him.

Gramstorff Bros.

THE PLEIADES

Sisters of the sky! — FELICIA HEMANS

HOW ORION BECAME AN INHABITANT OF THE SKIES

The magnificent constellation called Orion was supposed by the Greeks to have been originally the body of a great giant, the son of Neptune. He was a handsome man and an eager hunter, and very vain of his personal appearance and of his skill in the chase. He was a great favorite of Diana, and some even suspected the moon goddess of being in love with him. Apollo sometimes chid her for her attentions to Orion, but to no avail.

Once Apollo pointed out to his sister a black spot far off in the waters and challenged her to hit it with her arrow. She did so, and too late discovered that she had killed Orion. But she placed him in the stars, where his dog Sirius follows him, the Hare flies before him, and the Pleiades are frightened at his coming.

The Pleiades, according to the Greeks, were seven maidens, daughters of Atlas, who had been pursued by Orion until in desperation they called on Jupiter for help. He changed them into doves, then into stars.

THE VENGEANCE OF DIANA AND APOLLO

That vindictiveness which Apollo shows in some episodes appears again in the story of Niobe. Niobe was the daughter of King Tantalus. She was married to Amphion, a son of Jupiter, and in the course of time she became so proud of her descent, her husband, and her fine family of seven brave sons and seven beautiful daughters, that she boasted unduly about them.

Once in particular she went too far. It was on the occasion of a feast day of Latona, the mother of Apollo and Diana. In her overweening conceit Niobe bade the people cease worshiping Latona, with her two children, and to pay reverence to her instead, with seven times as many.

Latona heard, and she addressed her son and her daughter reproachfully. They were just as indignant as she was at Niobe's irreverent boastfulness; and they resolved to punish the foolish woman at once.

Swiftly they approached the city in which Niobe dwelt. Swiftly they surveyed the scene before them and took heed how among the youths who exercised proudly on the plain —

A DAUGHTER OF NIOBE

One eyes the coming woe
And shudders. — MELEAGER OF GADARA

engaging in athletic sports of various kinds — were the seven sons of Niobe. Swiftly the two children of Latona drew their bows to their shoulders and the arrows flew. All seven sons of Niobe fell.

Yet even so her pride was not humbled, and still she defied Latona.

"My daughters still are better and greater than your two children!" she exclaimed; and scarcely had the words left her lips, when the daughters, too, dropped to the ground even as they mourned their brothers. At the sight Niobe was turned to stone with grief. But her tears continued to flow; and the gods, in pity, changed her into a fountain.

THE CALYDONIAN HUNT

A maiden named Atalanta (but not the one who raced with Hippomenes) was renowned for her skill in hunting and in games. Her father had abandoned her in the woods of Arcadia as an infant, and she had been found by a she-bear, who brought her up as she might have done a cub. Under the special protection of Diana, Atalanta grew up into a bold huntress.

Now it happened in the region called Calydon that the ruler, Oeneus, failed to pay certain honors to Diana, and she in anger sent an enormous boar to punish him. The beast laid waste all the land and spread terror everywhere.

The wife of Oeneus was named Althaea, and among their children was a son named Meleager. At his birth his mother had dreamed that she saw the three Fates spinning the web of his life, and that she heard snatches of their conversation.

"As soon," said one of them, "as the brand now burning on

the hearth of his mother shall be consumed, so soon shall the span of his life be ended."

Hastily awakening from her dream, Althaea had run to the hearth and snatched forth the burning brand. She quenched it in water, and laid it aside carefully among her most precious possessions.

Meleager grew up into a manly and courageous young man, liked by all who knew him. When word of the boar came to him, he resolved that he would make the slaying of it a great festival. So he sent messengers into every part of Greece and summoned all the heroes of the land to take part in the hunting of the boar. To his call they willingly responded. Among others came Atalanta, eager to be the one to slay the monster. As she approached she and Meleager came face to face, and immediately the young hero fell in love with her.

As the hunt progressed he was ever at her side. To win her approval he performed deeds of great valor, and when at last the boar was driven to bay, it was Meleager who delivered the fatal blow that stretched the monster out dead before them.

Now the monster was skinned, and his huge hide, a marvelous trophy of the chase, was handed to Meleager. But he gave it to Atalanta — as a gift from him. At this act of chivalry two brothers of Althaea, men of low minds, began to murmur.

"What!" they cried. "Shall it be said that this great prize went to a mere girl? It ought to hang forever in the king's halls."

With the words they strode angrily towards Atalanta and rudely snatched the hide from her hands. When Meleager saw what was happening, he did not pause for reflection, but

MELEAGER

Gramstorff Bros.

Grave, and with gathered sinews, like a god. — SWINBURNE

drawing his bow to his shoulder, dispatched two shafts at his uncles. They fell to the ground, mortally wounded.

In horror the others gazed on their bodies, and immediately messengers, bearers of evil tidings, hastened back to the court, filling the air with their lamentations. Althaea heard them, and came to meet them. When she heard what had happened, a senseless anger fell upon her. She hurried to the place where she kept her treasures, seized the brand that she had hidden at Meleager's birth, and without allowing herself time for thought, she cast it into the blazing hearth. Eagerly the flames seized it and shortly it was consumed.

Meanwhile on the hunting ground Meleager stood talking sorrowfully to Atalanta. Suddenly burning pains seized him. He fell to the ground, and in a few minutes lay dead.

When Althaea heard how her dream had been fulfilled, and that the brand had truly concealed the life of her son, in deep despair she killed herself.

STUDY APPLICATION

THE MYTHS IN LITERATURE

Most magnificent of all the works which the myths included in this chapter have evoked is Algernon Charles Swinburne's *Atalanta in Calydon*. This great English poet was saturated in the spirit of the Greeks, and in this drama he produced his masterpiece. The Greeks themselves never wrote finer poetry about their gods and their wonderful adventures than did Swinburne in *Atalanta in Calydon*. The greatest passage in the poem is the chorus addressed to Diana, of which part reads:

> Come with bows bent and with emptying of quivers,
>   Maiden most perfect, lady of light,
> With a noise of winds and many rivers,
>   With a clamor of waters, and with might;

Bind on thy sandals, O thou most fleet,
Over the splendor and speed of thy feet;
For the faint east quickens, the wan west shivers,
Round the feet of the day and the feet of the night.

Endymion, too, has been a favorite subject; and John Keats made his entrance into English poetry with a long poem called by the name of the beloved of Diana, of whom he says:

Therefore 'tis with full happiness that I
Will trace the story of Endymion.
The very music of the name has gone
Into my being.

Byron made splendid use of the Niobe story when, in his *Childe Harold*, he referred thus to the then desolate and ruined city of Rome:

The Niobe of nations! there she stands,
Childless and crownless, in her voiceless woe.

REFERENCES TO MYTHOLOGY IN LITERATURE

What do the following references mean? When a word or phrase is italicized, explain only the word or phrase.

1. Maid *Artemis* is near!
   For up Cithaeron with a flying throng
   Of nymphs and dogs I saw her go. — *Hewlett*
2.   Alas, no charm
   Could lift *Endymion's* head. — *Keats*
3. Poor, lonely Niobe! when her lovely young
   Were dead and gone. — *Keats*
4. And of those highly favor'd ones, *Endymion* and Adonis.
                                   — *Langhorne*
5. On such a tranquil night as this,
   She woke Endymion with a kiss. — *Longfellow*
6. Amid her daughters slain by Artemis
   Stood Niobe. — *Ovid*
7. Like Niobe, all tears. — *Shakespeare*
8.   Then all abode save one,
   The Arcadian *Atalanta:* from her side
   Sprang her hounds. — *Swinburne*

9. Many a night, from yonder ivied casement, ere I went to rest,
Did I look on great *Orion*, sloping slowly to the West.

— *Tennyson*

10. *Endymion* would have passed across the mead
Moonstruck with love. — *Wilde*

EXERCISES IN COMPOSITION, ORAL AND WRITTEN

1. Write a brief play, giving the dialogue between Jupiter and
Endymion, when the latter is summoned before the ruler of gods and
men to make a choice of dooms.

2. Come to class prepared to chart out on the blackboard the appearance of the constellation called Orion. Indicate also the position
of Sirius, and show by dots the grouping of the Pleiades.

3. Were the children of Latona justified in taking such extreme
vengeance on Niobe? Give reasons for your answer.

4. When Althaea hears how Meleager has slain her brothers, she
is faced by a terrible dilemma — whether or not to end the life of her
son. What arguments would she address to herself? Tell what she
might say.

WORD STUDY

1. How are the following words pronounced?
Endymion, Orion, Sirius, Niobe, Amphion, Oeneus, Althaea,
Meleager.

2. Give the Greek names of the following deities: Diana, Vulcan,
Venus, Jupiter, Jove, Latona.

3. Explain the following phrases: "a mighty hunter, like Orion";
"melting away in tears, like Niobe."

RAPID QUIZ

Did Diana ever fall in love? What choice of fates was offered to
Endymion? Which did he choose? What was the character of Orion?
How did he come to his death? Where may he still be seen? Who
were the Pleiades? In what way did Niobe incur the wrath of Latona?
On whom did Latona call for help? What doom overtook the sons of
Niobe? Why were her daughters slain? What was the fate of Niobe
herself? Who was Atalanta of Arcadia? Why did a monster ravage
the fields of Calydon? Who was Meleager? What strange dream

did his mother have when he was born? What action did Meleager take to get rid of the monster? Who came to the Calydonian hunt? Why did Meleager's uncles quarrel with him? What was the outcome? How did his mother punish Meleager? What was her own fate?

For Students of Latin

1. What group of women in Rome took vows of maidenhood for a term of years? Were they followers of Diana?
2. What weapons did the Greeks and Romans employ in hunting?
3. Answer briefly in Latin two or three questions in the Rapid Quiz.

Reading List

Poems and Plays

Catullus: *A Hymn to Diana*
Gosse, Edmund: *The Praise of Artemis*
Jonson, Ben: *Hymn to Diana*
Keats, John: *Endymion*
Lang, Andrew: *To Artemis*
Longfellow, Henry Wadsworth: *Endymion — The Occultation of Orion*
Lowell, James Russell: *Endymion*
Lyly, John: *Endymion*
Noyes, Alfred: *Niobe*
Procter, B. W.: *The Worship of Diana*
Swinburne, Algernon Charles: *Atalanta in Calydon*
Wilde, Oscar: *Endymion*

POSEIDON

AVERNUS

The GOLDEN FLEECE

THE SEIZURE OF PROSERPINA

HELLAS

OLYMPUS

THE MIDDLE

Circe's Island

Gorgons

Gray Sisters

Scylla

CHARYBDIS

ITHICA

Hesperian Land

CIRCE'S ~ MAGIC

Mt. ATLAS

Isles of THE BLEST

ULYSSES AND POLYPHEMUS

The ELYSIAN PLAIN

HERCULES

APOLLO

ÆNEAS AND DIDO

OCEANUS

A MYTHOLOGICAL MAP

OCEANUS

LAND OF THE HYPERBOREANS

ZEUS

DÆDALUS AND ICARUS

BOREAS

TROY

MT. IDA

AMAZONS

AEGEAN SEA

CRETE

SEA

The MINOTAUR

PHOENICIA

EUROPA

LOTUS-EATERS

EGYPT

PEGASUS

ANDROMEDA RELEASED

HADES

OF THE ANCIENT WORLD

THE WINDS

Aeolus represses by his authority the struggling winds and the resounding tempests. — VIRGIL

VII

THE GODS OF NATURE

Now Aurora forsakes the ocean and crimsons the orient sky. — CATULLUS

HOW THE ANCIENT GREEKS REGARDED THE EARTH

The Greeks believed for many ages that the earth was flat, with Greece at the very center. Across the center of the disk of the earth flowed the Mediterranean Sea — the middle sea, as its name indicates. Around the edges flowed the River Oceanus. Toward the north dwelt the Hyperboreans, in a land of eternal spring — far beyond the mountains from whose slopes and hollows came the bitter north winds of winter. Toward the south dwelt the Ethiopians, whom the gods, and particularly Neptune, held in great favor. Toward the west lay the Elysian Islands, a kind of paradise.

Out of the stream of Ocean and back into it moved the luminaries of the heaven. Each day the sun and later the

CERES

Peace maintains Ceres, Ceres is the friend of peace. — OVID

moon traveled chariotwise across the heavens; so too did the stars. From the west, where the sun set, the sun god was conveyed in a winged boat back to his starting point.

GODS OF THE EARTH

The sister of Jupiter, *Ceres* (Greek: *Demeter*), was the goddess of the earth and of its crops and fruits. Hidden in her worship was the veneration of the seed of life in all its manifestations. She was the protectress of farmers. She was represented with a garland of corn ears or of simple ribbons; in her hand she held a scepter or a poppy; sometimes also a *cornucopia*, or horn of plenty, grains and fruits tumbling out of it. Her daughter was *Proserpina*, the goddess of springtime.

Chief among the other deities especially associated with the earth were *Bacchus* (Greek: *Dionysus*, sometimes called *Iacchus* and sometimes *Lyaeus*) and *Pan*.

Bacchus was the son of Jupiter and of Semele. Jupiter placed the education of Bacchus in charge of Silenus, a jovial old toper, sometimes shown as having goat feet. Bacchus became the god of wine and, in general, of the fertility and bounty of vegetation. He was a joyous god and with his worship was associated constant merrymaking. His chief festival was celebrated in March of each year, when the wine was ready for drinking; and as at such times in ancient Greece it was customary to give dramatic performances, Bacchus became the god of drama and of the theater. By the Romans he was also given the name *Liber*, and with him was associated *Libera*, goddess of the vine.

Usually Bacchus is shown in a chariot drawn by leopards, his head crowned with vine leaves or with wreaths of ivy and

SILENUS WITH THE INFANT BACCHUS

The immortal splendor of his face he shows. — GOSSE

in his hand a *thyrsus*, a staff entwined with ivy and with a pine cone at the top. Sacred to him were the grapevine, the ivy, and the panther. He had special groups of followers. His female followers were called bacchantes or maenads, and were represented as wild with enthusiasm, their heads thrown backward, their hair disheveled. In their hands they carried thyrsi.

Janet Scudder   Museum of the Brooklyn Institute

SEATED FAUN

Rough Satyrs danced, and fauns with cloven heel
From the glad sound would not be absent long. — MILTON

Pan, whose name means "all," has always fascinated persons of imagination down to our own time. He was the son of Mercury and a wood nymph. God of flocks, shepherds, and of nature, he was described as wandering among the mountains and valleys of Arcadia, either amusing himself with hunting or leading the dances of the nymphs. To him is ascribed the invention of the shepherd's flute. He was usually represented as a bearded man, who had a large hooked nose and the ears and hoofs of a goat, and whose body was covered with hair. In his hand was his shepherd's flute or a shepherd's crook. Inasmuch as Pan was the god of lonely and desolate scenes, especially in mountain countries, he was associated with the sudden and causeless fear that comes on travelers in such wild places; and this fear, first in the outdoor world, later even in the midst of battles, was attributed to Pan, and was called a Panic fear. His followers, the *satyrs*, or *fauns*, had goatlike ears, short tails, and budding horns. Silenus was the chief of the satyrs.

Minor deities associated with nature were the nymphs. There were many kinds of nymphs, but five groups were more important than the others — the *dryads* or *hamadryads*, each of whom lived in a tree and was supposed to die when the tree died; the *Oceanids* and the *Nereids*, who dwelt in the waters of the ocean; the *naiads*, who were the presiding spirits of fresh water — of springs, rivers, brooks, lakes, etc.; and the *oreads*, the nymphs of mountains and grottoes. To individual nymphs the ancient poets often gave most melodious names, as when Virgil mentions Deiopea, a nymph of Juno, and Cymothoe, a nymph of Neptune.

GODS OF THE DAWN, DUSK, AND AIR

Over the coming of the dawn presided each day *Aurora* (Greek: *Eos*), "the rosy-fingered child of the morning." Every morning she left her couch and in a chariot drawn by swift horses ascended to heaven from the River Oceanus, to announce the coming of the sun. She put to flight the morning star; and as she passed a fresh wind sprang up; while behind her flamed brighter and brighter the flush of approaching day. Her special favor was bestowed upon the splendid dawn of life; and young people were under her care, especially as they went forth in the morning to hunt or to fight.

Phosphor, the Morning Star, was the son of Aurora and the hunter Cephalus. *Hesperus* (or Vesper), the Evening Star, was according to some legends the father of the Hesperides,

Guido Reni   *Respigliosi Palace, Rome*

AURORA

Now Morn, her rosy steps in th' eastern clime
Advancing, sow'd the earth with Orient pearl. — MILTON

three maidens who guarded the Tree of the Golden Apples in a wonderful garden far to the west of the known world. Other legends call these guardians daughters of the Titan Atlas.

The king of the winds was *Aeolus*, who dwelt on the steep islands later known as the Aeolian Islands. There he confined the winds in a mountain cavern, letting them out only as they were needed. His son Salmoneus became king of Elis. His pride in his descent and in himself was so great that he ordered his people to offer him sacrifices and strove to imitate the thunder of Jove by driving his bronze chariot over a bridge. But Jove, angered, killed him with a thunderbolt and destroyed Elis. The four wind gods were *Boreas*, the North Wind (also called Aquilo); *Zephyrus*, the West Wind; *Notus*, the South Wind (also called Auster); and *Eurus*, the East Wind. The wife of Zephyrus was *Chloris;*

she was the goddess of flowers, and the Romans called her
Flora.

GODS OF THE WATERS

Just as in the skies there were elder and younger gods, so
in the ocean an older dynasty was displaced — in part at
least — by a younger group, the latter headed by Neptune.

During the reign of
Cronus *Oceanus* and
Tethys ruled the
waters, with the help
of innumerable ocean
nymphs. This mon-
arch and his wife dwelt
in a wonderful palace,
surrounded by gar-
dens. One of their
daughters, Doris, mar-
ried another dweller
in the ocean, *Nereus*,
a wise old man who
had the gift of proph-
ecy and the additional
gift of being able to
assume various forms.
Like the other deni-

Naples National Museum

NEREID ON A FISH

Around her the surge of the sea was sundered.
— HOMER

zens of the deep Nereus is often represented with seaweed
instead of hair. Nereus and Doris had fifty daughters,
known as the *Nereids*, who made up one of the kinds of
sea nymphs. They were all renowned for their loveliness.
They dwelt in various parts of the Mediterranean, and are

NEPTUNE

Great Neptune, with his three-fork'd mace,
That rules the seas, and makes them rise or fall. — SPENSER

sometimes pictured as half maidens and half fish — like mermaids. Among the most famous of them were Thetis, Galatea, and Amphitrite. Amphitrite married Neptune, and so formed a friendly bond between the old dynasty of the ocean and the new. Oceanus and Tethys dwelt undisturbed in their palace, though their power had passed to

TRITON

By scaly Triton's winding shell. — MILTON

Neptune. It has been said of the great sea-deity that he "moved in a kind of rolling splendor."

Neptune dwelt now in his palace in the sea and now on Mount Olympus. In the waters he had many attendants — among whom were the water nymphs. His son *Triton* was his trumpeter and carried a sea shell on which he blew blasts that raised or calmed the waves. Sometimes he was represented as half-man, half-dolphin, and at other times as constantly accompanied by a school of dolphins.

Another attendant of Neptune was *Proteus*, who in many ways — in the power to prophesy and to change his form — resembled Nereus. He had special charge of the seals of Neptune. At midday he rose from the sea and slept in the shade of the rocks on one of his favorite islands, with the monsters of the deep reposing around him. Anyone could seize him while he slept, and could compel him then to reveal what the future would bring. But even after he had been grasped Proteus still had his tricks. He assumed every possible form, wriggling suddenly from one shape into another. Only after he saw that his efforts were of no avail did he resume his usual form and make answer to his captor's questions.

Among others who inhabited the waves were the *sirens*. They were sea nymphs, half bird and half woman, who had the power of charming by their songs all who heard them. Many a luckless mariner, his judgment and caution put to sleep by their wondrous melodies, allowed his ship to drift on the rocks. Too late he saw the wrecks of ships and bones of men lying around the reef where the sirens sang.

Scylla and *Charybdis* were two monsters who dwelt on neighboring rocks. Scylla, once a beautiful maiden, had been transformed into a creature with six necks and heads, each armed with three rows of sharp teeth and each barking like a dog. When her hands could reach a ship, she seized men for food. Near by lay Charybdis, an immense shapeless mass, under a huge fig tree. Thrice each day she swallowed the waters of the sea and thrice she belched them forth again. Only those especially favored of the gods were able to pass in safety between these terrors of the sea. Those who sought to explain them said one was a treacherous reef, one a whirlpool.

STUDY APPLICATION

For the Myths in Literature, see page 182.

References to Mythology in Literature

What do the following references mean?   Where a word or phrase
is italicized, explain only the word or phrase.

A

1. Notice *Neptune*, though,
   Taming a sea-horse, thought a rarity. — *Browning*
2. For I will fly to thee,
   Not charioted by *Bacchus and his pards*.[1] — *Keats*
3. There came a noise of revelers: the rills
   Into the wide stream came of purple hue —
   'Twas *Bacchus* and his crew! — *Keats*
4. And the store thrice-told [2]
   Of *Ceres' horn.* — *Keats*
5. I prayed to *Pan*, half god, half goat;
   He played his pipes. — *Keller*
6. By th' earth-shaking *Neptune's* mace. — *Milton*
7. And with his *trident Neptune* smites the earth. — *Ovid*
8. Blue *Neptune* storms, the bellowing deeps resound. — *Pope*
9. *Ceres*, most bounteous lady. — *Shakespeare*
10. Under the bowers
   Where the Ocean powers
   Sit on their pearléd thrones. — *Shelley*
11. *Demeter*, rich in fruit and rich in grain. — *Theocritus*
12. Wrinkled scolds with hands on hips,
   Girls in bloom of cheek and lips,
   Wild-eyed, free-limbed, such as chase
   Bacchus round some antique vase. — *Whittier*

B

1. Now *Aurora* forsakes the ocean and crimsons the orient sky.
   — *Catullus*
2. No dolphin came, no *Nereid* stirred. — *Gray*

[1] Leopards.   [2] Reckoned or counted three times.

3. See how *Aurora* throws her fair
   Fresh-quilted colors through the air. — *Herrick*
4. From thy dead lips a clearer note is born
   Than ever *Triton* blew from wreathéd horn. — *Holmes*
5. With lucid lilies in her golden hair,
   Eos, sweet Goddess of the Morning, stood. — *Horne*
6. Thou frownest, and old *Aeolus* thy foe
   Skulks to his cavern! 'mid the gruff complaint
   Of all his rebel tempests. — *Keats*
7. The moss-lain *dryads* shall be lulled to sleep. — *Keats*
8. And here is manna, pick'd from Syrian trees,
   In starlight, by the three *Hesperides*. — *Keats*
9. The *naiad* 'mid her reeds
   Press'd her cold finger closer to her lips. — *Keats*
10. A sudden ring
    Of *Nereids* were about him. — *Keats*
11. An arch face peep'd — an *oread* as I guess'd. — *Keats*
12. By the dim echoes of old Triton's horn. — *Keats*
13. Of Hesperus and his daughters three
    That sing about the Golden Tree. — *Milton*
14. Once in this scene I used to rouse the *naiads* with alternate
    stroke [of oars]. — *Petronius*

C

1. Now to Aurora, borne by dappled steeds,
   The sacred gates of orient pearl and gold
   Expanded slow. — *Landor*
2. Old *Silenus*, bloated, drunken,
   Led by his inebriate satyrs. — *Longfellow*
3. The *Nereids* arose out of the salt water. — *Moschus*
4. Seldom has a winter not extremely cold been so hard on the
   furnace-tender. *Boreas* was usually looking in at him through
   the cellar-window. — *New York Times*
5. His usual company, *satyrs* and *bacchantes*, thronged around
   him. — *Ovid*
6. You nymphs, call'd *naiads*, of the winding brooks.
   — *Shakespeare*

7. Blue *Proteus* and his humid nymphs shall mark
   The shadows of fair ships. — *Shelley*
8. *Aeolus*, to whom the father of gods and men has granted the
   power with winds to soothe and lift up the waves. — *Virgil*
9. See, the bright *naiad* plucks wan violets. — *Virgil*
10. Cold streamlets trickle, and at *Zephyr's* breath
    Crumbles and cracks the clod. — *Virgil*
11. Already a huge Triton blows a horn. — *Wilde*
12. Have sight of *Proteus* rising from the sea,
    Or hear old *Triton* blow his wreathèd horn. — *Wordsworth*

Exercises, Oral and Written

1. Contrast our view of nature with that of the Greeks.

2. An artist is about to draw a picture in colors of Ceres. Give
him directions in full.

3. Imagine that in a certain play will appear one of each of the five
kinds of nymphs. As each appears on the stage she explains briefly
who she is and what she does; for example, "I am a hamadryad," etc.
Tell what each would say, but give somewhat fuller details from your
own imagination than are given in this chapter.

4. Prepare a little table showing how Neptune is related to Oceanus
and Tethys and also introducing Triton.

Word Study

1. Explain the origin of the following words:

   panic — extreme or sudden fear
   cereal — grain
   boreal — northern, cold
   auroral — rosy
   aurora borealis — northern lights
   zephyr — a gentle breeze
   protean — changeable, very variable
   Bacchic — jovial or riotous
   siren — a steam whistle or fog signal

2. What is the correct pronunciation of the following words?
Oceanus, Hyperboreans, Elysian, Dionysus, Semele, Silenus, Liber,
thyrsus, bacchantes, maenads, satyrs, dryads, hamadryads, Oceanids,

Nereids, naiads, oreads, Aurora, Eos, Cephalus, Aeolus, Boreas, Nereus, Thetis, Amphitrite, Proteus, Scylla, Charybdis.

3. Give the Greek names of the following deities: Jupiter, Ceres, Neptune, Bacchus, Aurora. What was the name of the staff that Bacchus carried?

4. What does the expression, "between Scylla and Charybdis," mean? What is meant when a man is called a "Silenus"? or a woman a "siren"? What is an "aeolian harp"?

5. Some think that "satire" is connected with "satyr." Do you see any connection?

6. One species of butterfly is called *Nymphalidae*. Is the name appropriate to these bright-winged insects?

7. Is there any connection between Auster, the South Wind, and Australia?

8. Note that the names of two of the classes of nymphs were derived from the names of persons — Oceanus and Nereus. Does this fact influence the spelling? How?

Rapid Quiz

What was the Greek notion of the earth? What was the realm of Ceres? Who was her daughter? What was the character of Bacchus? Over what realms did he rule? How is he generally represented? Who was Pan? Give his characteristics. Who were his followers? Who was the chief of them? Name the five principal kinds of nymphs. Who was the goddess of the dawn? Who was Phosphor? Hesper? the Hesperides? Who was the king of the winds? Name the North Wind and the West Wind. Who were the first rulers of the ocean? How were they related to Neptune, the later ruler? Who was Nereus? What were his daughters called? Who was Triton? Proteus? Who were the sirens? Scylla and Charybdis?

For Students of Latin

1. Give the Latin names of Demeter, Dionysus, Eos, and Chloris.

2. What goddess of the vine did the Romans worship? What does her name mean?

3. What is a *thyrsus*? Give the plural form.

4. What Latin author is mentioned in this chapter? What Latin authors are quoted in the References to Literature?

5. Answer in Latin one or two of the questions in the Rapid Quiz.

READING LIST

Poems, Plays, and Music

Beddoes, T. L.: *Song of the Stygian Naiades*

Binyon, Laurence: *The Sirens*

Browning, Elizabeth Barrett: *The Dead Pan — The Musical Instrument*

Buchanan, Robert: *Pan*

Campion, Thomas: *A Hymn in Praise of Neptune*

Debussy, Claude: *Sirènes* [music]

Doolittle, Hilda ("H. D."): *Oread*

Emerson, Ralph Waldo: *Bacchus*

Fletcher, John: *Song of Pan — Song of the Priest of Pan*

Gosse, Edmund: *The Praise of Dionysus*

Keats, John: *Hymn to Bacchus* (in *Endymion*, book iv) — *Hymn to Pan* (in *Endymion*, book i)

Landor, Walter Savage: *Cupid and Pan* — Sophron's *Hymn to Bacchus*

Longfellow, Henry Wadsworth: *Drinking Song*

Milton, John: *Comus*

Respighi, Ottorino: *The Triton Fountain at Morn* [musical tone-picture]

Shelley, Percy Bysshe: *Hymn of Pan*

Stedman, Edmund C.: *Pan in Wall Street*

Swinburne, Algernon Charles: *The Palace of Pan*

Tietjens, Eunice: *The Bacchante to Her Babe*

Emmanuel Fremiet

PAN AND BEAR

Goatfoot Pan of Arcady. — SIMONIDES

VIII

STORIES OF THE GODS OF NATURE

As frighted Proserpine let fall
Her flowers at the sight of Dis. — HOOD

CERES, PROSERPINA, AND PLUTO

When Jupiter at the beginning of his reign divided the sovereignty of the world, he assigned to his brother Pluto (sometimes called *Dis* and sometimes *Hades*) control of the underworld and the shades of the dead. In later days the land of the dead was itself called Hades.

Pluto was not very well pleased at having been given so gloomy a realm over which to rule, but he protested in vain.

"Be content," urged Jupiter. "Though now you have no people in your kingdom, in time to come it shall be well peopled. All that live shall in the end come under your sway. You have, moreover, in your keeping all the vast wealth that lies hidden in the earth. You shall be the god of wealth, you shall be Pluto the wealthy one."

Gramstorff Bros.

ABDUCTION OF PROSERPINA

Ah, strong were his arms to wrest
slight limbs from the beautiful earth,
young hands that plucked the first
buds of the chill narcissus. — HILDA DOOLITTLE

So Pluto perforce submitted and in time grew contented with his lot. But he craved a wife to share his destiny, and Jupiter promised him *Proserpina* (or *Persephone*), the beautiful daughter of Ceres. But he feared to tell the girl's mother his plan, and not all the urging of Pluto that he fulfill his promise sufficed to make him announce his decision. Pluto then resolved to take the matter into his own hands.

Boecklin

ISLE OF THE DEAD

This is the place of shadows, of sleep, and of drowsy night.

— VIRGIL

One day Proserpina and her maidens were gathering flowers in the sunny fields of Sicily. As they chattered of the joyous days to come, suddenly the earth trembled, a rift opened at their very feet, and out of it sprang a chariot, driven by a man of dark and forbidding visage. He leaped from the seat, and without a word seized Proserpina and carried her to the chariot. Her screams and struggles were of no avail. The chariot disappeared again into the earth.

Lord Leighton, P.R.A.

Leeds Gallery

THE RETURN OF PERSEPHONE

When Ceres missed her child, she was frantic with despair. No one could tell her who it was that had snatched Proserpina away. All over the earth she searched for her in vain. In her sorrow she neglected her duties. The crops withered and died, and famine threatened the race of men. Jupiter tried to persuade the goddess of harvests to resume her care of the fruits of the earth, but Ceres sent back word that not again would she set foot in the house of Jupiter nor yet would she suffer the fields to bear their harvests until her daughter had been returned to her.

Then Jupiter said, "If the maiden Proserpina has not tasted food during the days she has spent in the abode of Hades, she shall be free again, and she shall not be his spouse."

So he sent Mercury, the fleet-foot messenger, to the dark palace of the underworld and bade him command Pluto to release the maiden. And Pluto obeyed, but before Proserpina left he set before her food and drink. Now up to this time Proserpina had refused to let a morsel of food pass her lips, for she knew that he who eats of the fare of Hades becomes his henchman. But in her joy she relaxed the vow she had placed upon herself, and she cut a pomegranate in half and ate six of the seeds.

Then she departed with Mercury, and returned to her dear mother. But because she had broken her fast she was destined to return to Hades six months of every year, one month for each seed she had eaten. So Proserpina, goddess of the spring, disappears when the summer time is over, Ceres in her sorrow once more neglects her duties, and winter reigns over the earth until Proserpina returns. From the heads of those who later died on earth a lock of hair was always cut, as a tribute to Proserpina.

DEMETER AND PERSEPHONE

Ceres' golden reign. — GRAY

The main seat of the worship of Ceres was at Eleusis, near Athens. Here were celebrated what were called "the Eleusinian Mysteries," of which little is known today, but which, it is supposed, commemorated the loss and the return of Proserpina. No one was allowed to attend the ceremonies without a process of initiation and purification, lasting for a whole year. The initiate then entered the Temple of Mystery and read sacred inscriptions from a book of stone. In the temple strange fires appeared, terrifying noises were heard, and mystic messages given. At the close of the exercises the high priest cried, "*Konx Ompax!*" But what the words meant no one now knows. It is believed by some that at Eleusis were taught the belief in one God and perhaps the doctrine of the soul's immortality.

THE WANDERINGS OF BACCHUS

As a child the character of Bacchus was innocent and happy, and he was tended by the nymphs and herdsmen of Nysa. When he grew up, the legends say, he was pursued by Juno, who was jealous of him, and he wandered through many parts of the world establishing the culture of the vine and teaching its use. But he taught, too, the arts of peace and of justice and honorable dealing. He had many adventures and punished severely those who interfered with his rites. One of his most celebrated feats was performed when he hired a ship to carry him from Icaria to Naxos. The mariners were in reality pirates, and they resolved to sell into slavery the beautiful youth whom they were carrying as a passenger. So they turned their vessel toward Asia. Thereupon the god changed the mast and oars into serpents and himself into a lion; ivy grew around the vessel, and the sweet sound of flutes was heard on every side. The mariners, beholding in amazement these miraculous events, were seized with madness, leaped into the sea, and were transformed into dolphins.

Rubens   *Corcoran Art Gallery*

THE JUDGMENT OF MIDAS

The nymphs of the woods and waves
Were silent with love — as you now, Apollo,
With envy of my sweet pipings. — SHELLEY

THE STORY OF MIDAS AND PAN

Pan was so proud of his knowledge of music that once he challenged Apollo to a contest. Apollo agreed to compete with him, and Midas, the king of Phrygia, was selected as the judge. Apollo played beautiful harmonies on the lyre, Pan replied with sweet notes on his flute, and Midas, without much pondering, decided in favor of Pan. Apollo was greatly incensed and, in a most unsportsmanlike way, resolved to punish Midas for showing such bad taste — bad in Apollo's opinion. So he changed the ears of Midas to those of an ass. Midas was very much ashamed of this odd transformation. He contrived, however, to conceal his ass's ears under his Phrygian cap. According to the story, however, his barber discovered the secret when he cut Midas's hair. Midas threatened him with severe punishment if he told anyone about the royal deformity, and for a long time the barber managed to keep quiet. But one day he could hold the secret no longer. He went out into the fields, dug a hole, and whispered into the cavity, "Midas has the ears of an ass!"

Later reeds grew up at the very spot, and by their whisperings betrayed the secret to the whole world.

It was this same Midas to whom another misfortune happened. He once performed a service to Silenus, who was the teacher of Bacchus. The latter told Midas he would grant him any boon for which he asked. In his folly Midas begged, "Let all I touch be changed to gold!" He was already fabulously rich, but he wanted still more. The consequences can be imagined. Everything Midas touched was indeed changed — including, however, his food and water and even his beloved child. Finally in desperation Midas prayed to Bacchus and bade him take his gift back again. Bacchus commanded him to bathe in the sources of the River Pactolus, and when Midas did so, the curse was removed. But ever since that time the Pactolus has had an abundance of gold in its sands.

ARION AND THE DOLPHINS

Another contest appears in the story of *Arion*. He lived in Lesbos and was famous for a hymn to Bacchus. Once he set out from Greece to take part in a poetry contest in

Sicily. He was successful in the competition, and carried considerable money with him on board the ship that was to carry him back to Greece.

Sargent   *Boston Museum of Fine Arts*
ARION AND THE DOLPHINS
And all the raging seas for joy forgot to roar. — SPENSER

The sailors on board, knowing this, made up their minds to murder him and rob him of his wealth. They approached Arion and ordered him to jump overboard. But he begged that he might be allowed to play one song more before he died. As he played, dolphins gathered from every direction about the vessel ; and as Arion finished his song, he flung himself into the sea. He landed on the back of one of the dolphins, and was borne safe to shore. The sailors on reaching land were executed.

THE STORY OF IO

Many stories are told of the beautiful nymphs, and often the gods of Olympus strayed on the earth because of the attractions of some lovely earth-goddess. Jupiter himself fell in love with Io, daughter of the river god Inachus, who was himself a son of the mighty Oceanus. Once, as Jove was talking to the nymph, he suddenly noticed that he had attracted the attention of Juno. So he promptly spread a cloud around himself and Io. But Juno, suspicious and jealous, brushed away the cloud, and saw Jupiter — with a beautiful heifer standing beside him. For Jupiter had changed Io into that form in order to escape the reproaches of Juno.

Juno praised the heifer and asked Jupiter to give it to her. Reluctantly the god acceded to her request, and then Juno turned the heifer over to her servant Argus to watch. Argus was a good watchman, for he had a hundred eyes, which took turns in sleeping. Nothing could throw him off his guard or distract his attention altogether, it seemed. The poor heifer suffered greatly in her new form, and could not even express her distress except in a way that nobody understood. But Jupiter remembered her and sent Mercury to put Argus out of the way.

Mercury approached the hundred-eyed watchman in the guise of a shepherd. He sat down beside him, told stories, and played upon his pipes. Argus was pleased at the shepherd's attention and often seemed on the point of dropping off to sleep, but always some of his eyes remained watchful. At length Mercury told him the tale of the invention of the syrinx, the pipes on which he was playing.

"Once, ages ago," he said softly, "the god Pan fell in love with the nymph Syrinx. But she was a faithful follower of Diana and would have nothing to do with him. 'I shall never marry,' she told him. He paid no heed to her words, but sought to embrace her. She escaped from his arms and fled swiftly toward a near-by river. Closer and closer came Pan, and now seemed on the very point of seizing her. She called for help to the god of the stream, and as Pan threw his arms around her, he found himself embracing not a nymph but a clump of tall reeds. Pan sighed with regret, and as he sighed his breath moved musically through the reeds. The air, as it touched the hollow stems, made a gentle, soothing melody. Pan, pleased with the music, broke off the reeds and fashioned a pipe for himself. Then he sat down on the bank

Salvatore Rosa   *Nelson Gallery of Art, Kansas City*

MERCURY PLAYS ARGUS TO SLEEP

As Argus' eyes, by Hermes' wand oppress'd,
Clos'd one by one to everlasting rest. — POPE

of the river and for a long time played sad, sweet songs, to which the shepherds listened with delight. So was born the syrinx."

As Mercury concluded his story he saw that all of the eyes of Argus were closed in sleep. At once he leaped up softly and slew him, and set Io free. In reward for the faithfulness of her servant, Juno took the eyes of Argus and scattered them in the tail of the peacock, where they may still be seen.

But she continued to pursue Io. She sent a gadfly to torture the poor heifer, who in torment fled into the sea and swam across. It is still called, after her, the Ionian Sea. After many wanderings she reached Egypt, and when Jupiter promised Juno that he would pay her no more attentions, Juno agreed to release her from the bondage of her heifer form.

APOLLO AND DAPHNE

The name of the glorious and beautiful god Apollo is, of course, associated with the names of many nymphs. But not always, handsome as Apollo was, did these nymphs favor him and accept his advances.

There was Daphne. She was the daughter of the river-god Peneus in Thessaly. Apollo fell in love with her by a trick of Cupid. One day Apollo, returning from the hunt, saw the son of Venus playing with his bow and arrows. He taunted the little god and bade him leave such weapons to those that were able to understand and use them.

"You shall see," promised Cupid, "how well I understand my shafts."

Shortly afterward Apollo was straying with the beautiful nymph Daphne. Cupid saw the god in company with the nymph, and immediately let fly two arrows — a leaden shaft at her to excite dislike, a golden shaft at him to produce love.

Apollo's life became one of endless torment. The more skillfully and persuasively he pleaded his cause, the colder grew Daphne toward him. She told him that she abhorred all thoughts of love, that her delight was in hunting and in woodland sports. Desperate at last, Apollo resolved to carry her off and make her his wife in spite of her coldness. He

EROS WITH BOW

And therefore hath the wind-swift Cupid wings.

— SHAKESPEARE

seized her, but she escaped from his grasp and fled through the thickets and the forest. The more rapidly she fled, the more beautiful she seemed to the god. His pursuit became faster. She had more and more difficulty in escaping him. At last her strength failed her, and she sank to the ground, but as she fell she breathed a prayer to her father.

"Help me, O father!" she cried. "Save me from Apollo!"

Peneus heard her, and resorted to a desperate device to save his daughter. Even as Daphne spoke her form began to change, and Apollo cast his arms about her only to find that he was embracing a beautiful laurel tree instead of the nymph. Even so he still loved her; and the laurel became his favorite tree. Since that time those who win the favor of Apollo are crowned with the laurel. Poets in particular have always regarded the laurel wreath as a mark of special honor.

Still another nymph who fled from the attentions of Apollo was Castalia, also daughter of a river-god. To escape him she plunged into a spring on Mount Parnassus near Delphi, and the spring thereafter was called Castalia or Castaly. Those who drank of it were supposed to be immediately inspired.

APOLLO AND CLYTIE

In the case of Clytie, however, the tables were turned, and it was Apollo who proved cold to the advances of this nymph, who was one of the daughters of Oceanus. Timidly she showed her affection to the god, but he became more and more indifferent. So she began to pine away. All her thought was for the sun god, ever her gaze was upon him. She gave no care to herself, taking neither food nor drink, giving no heed to her raiment or her hair or her appearance. So in

Bernini   Borghese Gallery, Rome

APOLLO AND DAPHNE

The god being one day too warm in his wooing,
She took to the tree to escape his pursuing.
— JAMES RUSSELL LOWELL

time she died, but still, even in death, she remained constant to her idol. Her limbs became rooted in the ground, her body changed to a slender trunk, her head became a flower. But, unlike other flowers, Clytie's head moved on the stalk. Ever she turned her gaze toward the sun, looking at the east in the morning, at the west in the evening. For Clytie became the sunflower, who

> turns on her god when he sets
> The same look that she gave when he rose.

ECHO AND NARCISSUS

Most celebrated of the nymphs was Echo, a beautiful oread who was the special favorite of Diana. Juno, too, was fond of her, but one day she discovered that Echo had purposely delayed her with interesting conversation while Jupiter was being entertained by other nymphs. Juno in anger punished Echo by taking from her all power to begin a conversation — Echo could only answer when someone else spoke to her.

This was merely an annoying punishment until a beautiful youth named Narcissus happened to wander into the woods that Echo haunted. Echo immediately fell in love with him, but when Narcissus spoke to her, all she could do was to repeat his last words. Narcissus thought she was making fun of him and did all he could to avoid her. But everywhere that he went Echo followed him; and to all the reproaches of Narcissus she could merely reply by repeating to him what he had just said. In despair Echo faded away until she was no more than a voice — a voice that still haunts caves and cliffs and desolate places, and repeats what you say.

Gramstorff Bros.

ECHO

Sweet Echo, sweetest nymph,
Sweet Queen of Parley. — MILTON

Narcissus, however, not merely repelled Echo — he also repelled all the other nymphs, for he was very conceited and believed nobody quite good enough for him. One maiden finally prayed that he might have the experience of knowing

Gramstorff Bros.

NARCISSUS

On the clear river's marge Narcissus lies,
Wooing that drifting imagery. — WILDE

what it was to love and not to be loved in return; and the prayer was granted — in a most curious way. Narcissus, bending one day over a mountain pool to quaff its cooling waters, caught a glimpse of his own image in the waves. He thought it was some coy water nymph hiding from his advances. He talked to it, made love to it, finally reached over to embrace it — but all in vain. So, like Echo, he too pined away and died. But from his body sprang the flower that bears his name.

AURORA AND TITHONUS

Many legends are associated with Aurora, but the best known is the story of Tithonus. He was the son of the king of Troy, and when Aurora beheld him, she fell in love with him. She stole him away and made him her husband. So deeply in love was she with him that she desired to keep him with her forever. She went to Jupiter, therefore, and begged from him a boon.

"Grant Tithonus," she prayed, "eternal life!"

Jupiter smiled as he answered that her request was granted, for Aurora had forgotten to add to her prayer that he be granted, at the same time, eternal youth. Slowly, then, Tithonus grew old. White hairs began to show, the wrinkles in his face grew deeper and deeper, and he became completely decrepit. Finally, Aurora shut him up in a chamber, from which only his feeble voice could be heard in endless petition. Then, at last, she changed him into an insect — the grasshopper.

AURORA AND CEPHALUS

Aurora also fell in love with Cephalus, a hunter who lived in Attica, and who was already the husband of a beautiful woman named Procris. Cephalus was a favorite of the gods, and to him Diana gave a dog named Laelaps ("Storm") and a spear that never missed its aim.

When Procris learned that Aurora was pursuing her husband, she became violently jealous. But Cephalus managed a reconciliation. Procris, however, could not quite get over her jealousy. One day she followed her husband as he went hunting and watched him from the bushes. Cephalus, thinking he heard some animal stirring in the undergrowth,

AURORA

Meanwhile Aurora had restored her gentle light. — VIRGIL

hurled his spear and killed Procris. When he saw what he had done, he killed himself with the same spear.

CEYX AND HALCYONE

A descendant of Aurora named Ceyx, king of Trachis in Thessaly, married Halcyone, the daughter of King Aeolus, ruler of the winds. For many years they reigned happily, until the brother of Ceyx died and many strange events accompanied his death — long-lasting tempests, darkenings of the sun and moon, the appearance of terrifying monsters. Ceyx thought he had better consult the gods, and he therefore announced that he intended to sail to Claros in Ionia, to ask help of the oracle of Apollo there situated. His wife tried to dissuade him, for it was a season of storms, but he insisted on setting forth. He was almost at his goal when his ship was wrecked and he was drowned. But as he sank beneath the waves, he prayed to Neptune that the waves might carry his body until it reached his native land, and that Halcyone might see it and bury it.

Month after month passed and Halcyone, full of anxiety, awaited her husband's return. She offered prayers and incense and sacrifices to the gods and most of all to Juno; and she implored of them that her husband might return safely. Juno finally was moved at her entreaties; and inasmuch as she could do nothing for a man already dead, she resolved to let Halcyone know that there was no further hope.

She therefore called her messenger Iris and bade her carry a command to Somnus, the god of sleep. Over her bow of many colors Iris hastened to the land of darkness, where dwelt the drowsy god of slumbers. She found him in a cave from which all light was excluded, and to which all sounds and noises of the world penetrated either not at all or dully muffled. Around the gloomy chamber fluttered innumerable dreams; and some sat on the very head of Somnus, who lay on a feathery couch plunged deep in sleep. Iris had much trouble in arousing him, but at last she was able to make her message clear to the heavy-lidded god. He called his son Morpheus and bade him send a dream to Halcyone. Hardly were the indolently spoken words out of the mouth of Somnus than he fell back on his couch fast asleep. Iris hastened out of the cave, brushing dreams away from her face and keeping herself awake with difficulty.

Meanwhile Morpheus himself flew to the palace of Ceyx, and there, assuming the very form of its master, he appeared to Halcyone. But how changed was that form in the dream! He had on him the pallor of death, and the water dripped from his bedraggled robes. He told his wife that a storm on the Aegean had sunk his ship, and that he was dead.

As her dream vanished, Halcyone awoke, and tears rolled down her cheeks. Early the next morning Halcyone went down to the sea, and as she paced the beach, she saw floating toward her an indistinct object. Nearer and nearer it came, and as it touched the shore she saw that it was the body of her husband. She could not endure the sight of the hapless corpse and threw herself into the water. But Jupiter in pity changed her even as she leaped into the waves; and she became a bird that sang dolefully as it flew over the water. Ceyx was likewise transformed, and joined his wife again. From them are descended the kingfishers.

Their devotion so moved King Aeolus, moreover, that because of them he granted a special boon to all mariners. Seven days before the winter solstice begins, seven days after it, no winds blow. It is a season of calm and peace; and then

Halcyone, whose nest floats over the sea, sits on her nest in quiet. This period sailors call "the halcyon days," for then the ruler of the winds forbids all storms to blow that his grandchildren may be born in peace.

THE FOUNTAIN ARETHUSA

In Elis dwelt the Nereid Arethusa, famed for her beauty. The river-god Alpheus fell in love with her, but she would have none of him. When he pursued her too violently with his attentions, she dived into the sea and did not appear again until she reached Ortygia, off the coast of Sicily. But Alpheus had pursued her all the way, and the gods, as at least a partial reward of his devotion, transformed both of them into a fountain — the fountain Arethusa, which may be seen to this day in Syracuse in Sicily. It is said, moreover, that if you throw a cup or some other object into the River Alpheus in Elis, it will in no great time come up in the spring of Arethusa.

STUDY APPLICATION

THE MYTHS IN LITERATURE

Of all the material included in this chapter the story of Pluto and Proserpina has proved most fascinating. Interesting in itself, the story has also the attraction of an allegory and typifies the passing of summer and the coming of spring as no other story does. A whole galaxy of poets has celebrated the divine maiden snatched away to dwell in the underworld — Swinburne, George Edward Woodberry, Lewis Morris, Aubrey De Vere, R. H. Stoddard, Tennyson, and others.

Nowhere did the Greek imagination work more lovingly than on the forces and appearances of nature — as may be seen when Greek myths are compared with those of most other nations.

Poets of all times have therefore regarded these ancient Greek legends with joy and have adopted them as their own in many poems and stories.

THE NYMPH TRANSFORMED INTO A FOUNTAIN

"Oh save me! Oh guide me!
And bid the deep hide me,
For he grasps me now by the hair!" — SHELLEY

To different types of mind, however, different types appeal. The wild revels of Bacchus have often been sung, as by Dryden, Catullus, Longfellow, Edmund Gosse, Thomas Love Peacock, and B. W. Procter.

Pan, as a symbol of nature in its wilder forms, has fascinated some modern minds. Milton called him "universal Pan." Shelley wrote a *Hymn of Pan* full of ecstatic melody. Mrs. Browning in one of the most musical of her poems, *The Musical Instrument*, tells how Pan made the first flute :

> Sweet, sweet, sweet, O Pan !
> Piercing sweet by the river !
> Blinding sweet, O great god Pan !
> The sun on the hill forgot to die,
> And the lilies revived, and the dragon-fly
> Came back to dream on the river.

Mrs. Browning, too, lamented *The Dead Pan*, while Edmund Clarence Stedman quizzically pictured *Pan in Wall Street*.

The water deities have been less fortunate than the land or air gods in winning poets to celebrate them. But the sirens have always had their bards — beginning with Homer and Virgil. Often a poet has tried to imagine what song the sirens sang. William Morris thus repeats what they sang to Jason and the Argonauts, Daniel their song to Ulysses. Rossetti, Andrew Lang, and Lowell have, likewise, written of the sirens. A remarkable story of them, in a modern setting, is Edward Lucas White's prose narrative, *The Song of the Sirens*.

Triton and Proteus appear in Wordsworth's famous sonnet, *The world is too much with us :*

> Have sight of Proteus rising from the sea,
> Or hear old Triton blow his wreathéd horn.

One of Shelley's loveliest poems records the myth of *Arethusa*. It begins :

> Arethusa arose
> From her couch of snows
> In the Acroceraunian mountains, —
> From cloud and from crag,
> With many a jag,
> Shepherding her bright fountains.

James Russell Lowell, at the beginning of his *Fable for Critics*, makes a burlesque use of the story of Daphne:

> Phoebus, sitting one day in a laurel tree's shade,
> Was reminded of Daphne, of whom it was made,
> For the god being one day too warm in his wooing,
> She took to the tree to escape his pursuing. . . .
> "My case is like Dido's," [1] he sometimes remarked,
> "When I last saw my love, she was fairly embarked
> In a laurel, as she thought — but (ah, how Fate mocks!)
> She has found it by this time a very bad box!
> Let hunters from me take this saw when they need it —
> You're not always sure of your game when you've treed it.
> Just conceive such a change taking place in one's mistress!
> What romance would be left? Who can flatter or kiss trees?
> And, for mercy's sake, how could one keep up a dialogue
> With a dull wooden thing that will live and will die a log —
> Not to say that the thought would forever intrude
> That you've less chance to win her the more she is wood?
> Ah! it went to my heart, and the memory still grieves,
> To see those loved graces all taking their leaves;
> Those charms beyond speech, so enchanting but now,
> As they left me forever, each making its bough:
> If her tongue had a tang sometimes more than was right,
> Her new bark is worse than ten times her old bite."

References to Mythology in Literature

What do the following references mean? Where a word or phrase is italicized, explain only the word or phrase.

1. No sane man would demand from the gods the gift of Midas.
                                      — *Blackwood's Magazine*

2. Amidst our arms as quiet you shall be
   As *Halcyons* brooding on a winter sea. — *Dryden*

3. Had I the power to Midas given of old. — *Flecker*

4. You could feel just as certain that he was opulent as if he had exhibited his bank account, or as if you had seen him touching

[1] Who saw Aeneas sail away from her in a *bark* (vessel). (See p. 324.)

the twigs of the Pyncheon Elm, and, *Midas-like*, transmuting them to gold. — *Hawthorne*

5. *Dawn* rose from her couch by high *Tithonus*, to bring light to immortals and to mankind. — *Homer*

6. As frighted *Proserpine* let fall
Her flowers at the sight of *Dis*. — *Hood*

7. Dulcet-eyed as *Ceres' daughter*
Ere the God of Torment taught her
How to frown and how to chide. — *Keats*

8. Sweet *Echo*, sweetest nymph, that liv'st unseen
Within thy airy shell. — *Milton*

9. Till civil-suited Morn appear,
Not tricked and frounced, as she was wont
With the Attic boy [Cephalus] to hunt. — *Milton*

10. That fair field
Of Enna, where Proserpine gathering flowers,
Herself a fairer flower, by gloomy Dis
Was gathered. — *Milton*

11. Let the vile mob valueless things admire.
May golden-locked Apollo grant to me
Full cups from his *Castalian* mountain-spring. — *Ovid*

12. Even when he had been received into the infernal abodes, he kept on gazing on his image in the Stygian pool. — *Ovid*

13. The halcyon days of American shipping. — *Peattie*

14. Therefore, thou gaudy gold,
Hard food for *Midas*, I will none of thee. — *Shakespeare*

15. Arion, when
He forth was thrown into the greedy seas. — *Spenser*

16. Me only cruel immortality
Consumes: I wither slowly in thine arms. — *Tennyson*

17. And I will sing how sad Proserpina
Unto a grave and glowing lord was wed. — *Wilde*

EXERCISES, ORAL AND WRITTEN

1. Show that the myths in this chapter endeavor to explain phenomena of nature. (See page 2 f.)

2. One of the maidens who were gathering flowers with Proserpina in the Sicilian field tells her mother that evening just what occurred

when Pluto appeared. Write down the conversation. Would she know it was Pluto?

3. Imagine a conversation between Narcissus and Echo, in which Echo can do more than repeat the last word or syllable of what Narcissus says.

4. You are a courtier in the service of King Midas. Describe the scene on the day when Midas is given his gift of changing all he touches to gold.

5. Invent a myth to account for some object in the world around us — the rose, for example, or the first automobile, or the coming of twilight. Introduce into your myth the figures of some of the gods about whom you have read.

WORD STUDY

1. What is the correct pronunciation of the following words?
Icaria, Phrygia, heifer, Peneus, Clytie, Narcissus, Tithonus, Ceyx.

2. Give the Greek names of these deities: Pluto, Bacchus, Juno, Mercury, Cupid, Diana, Aurora.

3. What is a heifer? a Phrygian cap? a syrinx? a pomegranate?

4. Explain the title, "poet laureate," given to the official poet of the king of England.

5. What is meant by the expression, "the touch of Midas"? by "halcyon days"? by "plutocrat"? by "argus-eyed"? Why is *Argus* a good name for a newspaper?

6. How did the Greeks explain the origin of the word *echo?* of the name of the Ionian Sea?

RAPID QUIZ

What other names has Pluto? Over what realm did he rule? Who was promised him as his wife? What means did he use to obtain her? What happened when Ceres missed her child? What did Jupiter promise her? What, meanwhile, had happened in Hades? What does the story explain? What punishment did Bacchus visit on the pirates who treated him disrespectfully? What two gods once competed in musical ability? Who was the judge, and what was his decision? What revenge did the defeated god take? What other misfortune happened to Midas? Who was Io? How did she incur the wrath of Juno? Into what form did Jupiter change her? Whom did Juno set to guard her? How did Mercury outwit the watchman? What nymph rejected Apollo's advances? How did she manage to escape him? Whose love did Apollo reject? What was her fate? How did Echo originate? With whom did she fall in love? What fate overtook him? What boon did Aurora ask for Tithonus? What boon did she forget to ask? Why did Ceyx set forth on his journey? What happened to him? Why did Juno intervene? What was the final fate of the husband and wife?

For Students of Latin

1. Locate on a map places mentioned in this chapter. When did they fall under the rule of Rome?

2. What Latin author is mentioned in the References to Literature? Can you translate the quotation back into Latin?

3. Answer in Latin two or three of the questions in the Rapid Quiz.

Reading List

Poems and Plays

Aristophanes: *The Frogs* [see references to Bacchus]

Bridges, Robert: *Demeter*

Doolittle, Hilda ("H. D."): *Demeter*

Fletcher, John: *God Lyaeus*

Frank, Florence Kiper: *The Return of Proserpine* (in *Three Plays for a Children's Theater*)

Ingelow, Jean: *Demeter and Persephone*

Ledoux, Louis V.: *The Story of Eleusis*

Rossetti, Dante Gabriel: *Proserpine*

Shelley, Percy Bysshe: *Song of Proserpine*

Sherman, Frank Dempster: *Bacchus*

Stoddard, R. H.: *The Search of Proserpine*

Story, W. W.: *Clytie*

Swinburne, Algernon Charles: *The Garden of Proserpine — Song to Proserpine*

Taylor, Bayard: *An Epistle from Mount Tmolus*

Tennyson, Frederick: *Daphne*

Tennyson, Lord: *Tithonus*

DANAÏDES

"Danaïd's work" is endless and purposeless labor. — GERWIG

IX

IN THE UNDERWORLD

Easy is the descent to Avernus, but to retrace one's steps and escape to the upper air, that is difficult, that is toilsome. — VIRGIL

THE REGIONS OF THE UNDERWORLD

Hades, the realm of the underworld which Pluto ruled, stretched in many directions and the regions that it embraced were varied. Its entrance was called *Avernus*. Through it flowed five rivers. The first to which the shades of the dead came was called the *Styx*. So dreadful in color and appearance was this river that the gods swore by it, and an oath taken "by the Styx" was never broken. Pluto was sometimes spoken of as "the Stygian Jove." The dead waited on the shore until the ferryman Charon, an old man with a bedraggled beard and a mean dress, approached to carry them to the other side. His pay was an obolus — a Greek coin placed on the mouth of every corpse previous to burial.

(That the ancients could jest occasionally about their gods is evident in the fact, for example, that when Mark Antony, in the period of confusion that followed Caesar's death, created a number of new senators, most of them quite un-

MERCURY CONSIGNS THE SOUL OF A WOMAN TO CHARON

The lot is cast, sooner or later, to send us to Charon's boat for eternal exile. — HORACE

worthy of the honor, the Roman called them "Charonides," implying that Charon had dug them up from the underworld.)

Once on the other side the ghosts wandered on until they came to the River *Lethe*, the river of forgetfulness. Kneeling on its shore they cupped their hands, and drank of its water. Immediately all memory of their past lives disappeared from their minds. Too and fro, like hurried clouds, the bands of ghosts wandered on in the lampless regions of Hades. The other rivers were *Acheron*, river of woe, with its tributaries — *Phlegethon*, the river between whose banks flowed fire instead of water, and *Cocytus*, the river of wailing. These rivers were the boundaries of the underworld, which lay "beneath the secret places of the earth."

Keystone View Co.

CERBERUS AND THE FURIES

The black, infernal Furies. — SPENSER

At the gate of Hades stood a terrifying guardian — *Cerberus*, a monstrous dog, with three heads and the tail of a dragon. He never attempted to molest the shades that entered Hades, but he was ferocious to those who attempted to leave. It was almost impossible for mortals to get past him. When Aeneas visited Hades, as the great Latin poet Virgil tells, he made up a cunning pill that contained a sleeping potion, and threw this sop to Cerberus, who immediately fell unconscious. But this hero and a few others especially favored by the gods were the only ones that ever thwarted Cerberus.

The palace of Pluto himself, where he sat with his cap of darkness, with the key to the underworld in one hand and a magic staff in the other, was dark and gloomy. Around it were groves of dismal trees, and near by stretched meadows of asphodel, the lily of the dead.

Hades, which sometimes was called *Erebus* or *Orcus*, was divided into several regions. The greater part of it was called *Acheron*, after the river; and here, with troubled and vacant faces, moved aimlessly and sadly the majority of those that had died. Far to the west lay *Elysium*, a realm somewhat like our idea of Paradise. Hither came certain favorites of the gods — noted bards and great heroes. Over them reigned Cronus, exiled after his overthrow by Jupiter; and here they lived again a new Golden Age. Quite other was the dire region of *Tartarus*, to which were consigned those whom the gods desired to punish, and who lived in misery and torture.

CHIEF FIGURES OF HADES

Aside from Pluto and Proserpina, from Charon and Cerberus, there were other inhabitants of the underworld. When the souls of the dead had to be submitted to trial and judgment, the king of Hades and his queen acted as judges. Terror-inspiring figures of Hades were the *Furies*, three creatures that attended Proserpina. They were winged maidens, with serpents twined in their hair and blood dripping from their eyes. They pursued those who had escaped punishment for crimes they had committed, and afflicted them with all the horrors of a guilty conscience. The Greeks called the Furies *Eumenides*.

Hecate was a mysterious goddess, a Titaness who retained her power after Jupiter had seized the rule of the world, and who was honored by all the gods. She helped Ceres search for Proserpina, and she remained with the queen of Hades. She it was that sent forth at night all kinds of demons and terrifying phantoms from the underworld to the land of the living. She was the goddess of witchcraft and sorcery; her approach was announced by the weird howling and whining of dogs. She was the personification of the terror of night, just as Diana was the goddess of its bright and beautiful moonlight.

Somnus (Greek: *Hypnos*), whose palace was described in the last chapter, was the god of sleep. He held in his hand a poppy of forgetfulness or else a horn; from the horn trickled the drops of slumber. His twin brother was *Mors* (Greek: *Thanatos*), or Death, often represented as a quiet, pensive youth, with wings, who stood beside a funeral urn decorated with a funeral wreath. Sometimes he held in his hand an extinguished torch. *Morpheus* was the guardian of dreams, which he kept confined in his palace. Idle and deceptive dreams he sent forth from the ivory gate of his palace, prophetic and meaningful dreams he sent forth from the horn gate. *Momus*, god of ridicule, was his brother.

DWELLERS IN TARTARUS

Far down in the uttermost gulfs of Tartarus dwelt those Titans who had made war against Jupiter and had been conquered. Here, too, lived in torment others whom the gods punished — among them Tantalus, Ixion, Sisyphus, and the Danaïdes.

Tantalus had been a monarch while alive, and the gods had bestowed on him many favors. But in spite of this he committed many grave crimes, even killing his own son. When he died, he was condemned to suffer a never-ending punishment. He found himself standing in clear water,

TANTALUS, IXION, AND SISYPHUS IN TARTARUS
This gloom of Tartarus profound. — MILTON

that barely touched his chin; and right above his head there hung branches of all manner of fruit trees, weighed down with the ripe and tempting fruit. Tantalus, constantly tortured with hunger and thirst, sought ever to sip the water and to grasp the fruit. But it was always in vain — always the water receded from his parched lips and the branches moved away from his grasping hands.

Ixion had murdered his father-in-law that he might avoid making the bridal gifts, customary in those days; and later he showed deep disrespect for the gods. In Tartarus he was chained perpetually to a wheel that rolled forever down an endless road.

Sisyphus, the king of Corinth, had promoted trade and navigation, but was a man of avarice and fraud. On his death he was condemned to roll uphill a huge marble block. When, after endless and bitter toil, he reached the top with it, the stone immediately rolled back to the bottom of the hill, and Sisyphus had to begin all over again.

The *Danaïdes* were the daughters of Danaüs, king of Argo. All were guilty of the crime of murdering their husbands, at the instigation of Danaüs. When the women died they were punished in Hades by being compelled to carry water in a sieve. Of course, their labor was in vain and went on forever.

Still another inhabitant of this region was *Tityus*. He was a giant of tremendous size. Once he had dared to insult Latona, mother of Apollo. The sun-god laid him low with his mighty arrows, and then the gods confined the giant in Tartarus. There he sprawled prone on the ground, while a vulture fed perpetually on his liver, which was constantly renewed.

THE ISLANDS OF THE BLEST

Elysium was a kind of Paradise, to which came certain favored mortals. It was a land of perpetual and soothing sunshine. "Here fell not hail or rain or any snow, nor ever winds blew loudly." Upon its eternally blossoming and fragrant meadows heroes and bards reclined in endless bliss, or roamed about in everlasting happiness.

When Aeneas, in his journey through Hades as described by Virgil, came to the Happy Isles, he found that its denizens breathed a freer air than that of the world above, and they saw all things clothed in a purple light. Their land had a sun and stars of its own. Some of the inhabitants indulged in sports on the grassy turf, others engaged in dancing and singing. Sublime bards struck the chords of their lyres; and elsewhere the great warriors whom Aeneas had known rested in peace, their armor rusting, their chariots unused. Here, too, were all the poets and artists and those who in any other way had rendered their memories blessed by serving mankind.

ORPHEUS AND EURYDICE

One of the bards who might be seen in Elysium was a son of Apollo himself, and he had had a singular experience with Death, being one of the few persons who visited Hades while still in the flesh.

This was Orpheus, whom the Muse Calliope bore to the sun-god. He was presented with the lyre by Apollo and given instruction in its use, and he soon won renown as one of the greatest bards of Greece. He enchanted with his music not only men, but even the wild beasts of the field, whose savage breasts were soothed by the tunes he played; and it was said of his playing that the very trees and rocks were affected and tried to move and follow the sound of his strains.

In Thrace lived Eurydice, a lovely maiden, and with her Orpheus fell in love. Their marriage was approved by all, and for a year or two they lived in great happiness. Then, one day, as they were wandering through a flowery meadow, Eurydice was stung by a serpent, and before aid could be summoned, she died in the arms of her husband. He was heartbroken. In constant lamentations and elegies he recounted his grief, and at last made up his mind that he

would follow his wife into the dread regions of Pluto. He
found a cave in the side of a volcano, and passing through
many dark passages and uncanny pits he came at last to the
realm of Hades. There he took up again his divine lyre, and
began to play. As the
strains of wonderful music
sounded through Tartarus,
Sisyphus and Ixion paused
in their endless torments,
and for a moment the tor-
turing thirst and hunger
of Tantalus were allayed.

Orpheus passed on
through the clouds of
ghosts, who followed after
him in enchanted silence.
As he came to the throne
of Pluto and Proserpina
Orpheus bowed before
them, and with magic skill
pleaded his cause to the
music of his lyre. Tears
rolled down the iron cheeks
of Pluto, and Proserpina
remembered the blossom-
strewn fields of Sicily as
she wept.

Gramstorff Bros.

ORPHEUS AND EURYDICE

Or bid the soul of Orpheus sing.
— MILTON

"Grant me my wife
again," Orpheus begged; and the fullness of his sorrow
made the tears roll down his own cheeks.

Such pleading Pluto himself could not resist, and he granted
the prayer of Orpheus. But to the favorable answer was

attached one condition, announced as Eurydice was called before Pluto and restored to the arms of Orpheus.

"As you leave Hades," commanded Pluto, "do not cast a look behind. If you break this commandment, Eurydice shall be snatched from you again, and she shall once more become my subject."

They promised that they would obey, and the pair set out on their happy journey back to the land of the living. Lovingly Orpheus guided his wife on the dangerous path, guided her through gloomy caverns and endless roads, beside dangerous abysses and waters. The hazardous journey was almost ended when they came to a long passageway through which they could go only in single file. Orpheus led the way, stumbling over crags as he went. Now the end was in sight, and before them they could see the blessed light of the sun.

Then, at that fateful moment, anxiety overcame Orpheus. He was seized with terror lest in some way Eurydice might have fallen, or lest some of the terrible creatures of the underworld might have seized and held her. So he gave a swift glance backward. There, quite safe, followed Eurydice; but, even as he gazed, she disappeared from his view and with a terrified scream was drawn back into the realm of Pluto. Orpheus, too, tried to turn back, but he found that his way was barred with solid rock. Never again could he find a way into the underworld.

Thereafter life meant less than nothing to Orpheus. He wandered in deepest gloom from country to country, waiting only to die. Once a band of maenads, followers of Bacchus, sought to entice him to take part in their drunken orgies. He refused, and in rage they hurled rocks at his head. But the music of his lyre charmed the stones, and they fell harmless at his side. Then the maenads yelled so dreadfully and

EURYDICE BIDS FAREWELL TO ORPHEUS AS MERCURY LEADS
HER AWAY

Yet even in death Eurydice he sung,
Eurydice still trembled on his tongue. — POPE

loudly that the noise of his playing was drowned, and the
stones struck him from all sides. Mortally wounded he fell,

Gramstorff Bros.

ORPHEUS PURSUED BY THE MAENADS

What could the Muse herself that Orpheus bore,
The Muse herself for her enchanting son? — MILTON

and for a second time passed to Hades and joined Eurydice
again. His lyre was placed by Jupiter among the stars.
The maenads Bacchus transformed to oak trees.

STUDY APPLICATION

THE MYTHS IN LITERATURE

The regions of darkness and their drear inhabitants have enthralled
poets. Homer and Virgil both pictured these regions, and among
later poets undoubtedly the most wonderful description occurs in
Dante's *Inferno*, the first part of the great Italian poet's *Divine Comedy*.
A very vivid modern description may be found in Stephen Phillips's
Christ in Hades. Swinburne, in *The Garden of Proserpine*, thus pictures the land of the dead:

> No growth of moor or coppice,
>   No heather-flower or vine,
> But bloomless buds of poppies,
>   Green grapes of Proserpine;

> Pale beds of blowing rushes,
> Where no leaf blooms or blushes
> Save this whereout she crushes
>   For dead men deadly wine.

In *Paradise Lost* Milton writes a magnificent description of four of the rivers of Hades:

> Abhorréd Styx, the flood of deadly hate;
> Sad Acheron, of sorrow black and deep;
> Cocytus, named of lamentation loud
> Heard on the rueful stream; fierce Phlegeton,
> Whose waves of torrent fire inflame with rage.

Naturally the story of Orpheus and Eurydice has attracted the poets. Milton reaches the climax of his *L'Allegro* with a detailed reference to Orpheus, and in *Il Penseroso* he uses the same story, thinking of music so sweet,

> That Orpheus' self may heave his head
> From golden slumber on a bed
> Of heaped Elysian flowers, and hear
> Such strains as would have won the ear
> Of Pluto to have quite set free
> His half-regained Eurydice.

In *L'Allegro* he regrets that inspiration is unable to bring back the ancient poet Musaeus,

> Or bid the soul of Orpheus sing
> Such notes as, warbled to the string,
> Drew iron tears down Pluto's cheek,
> And made Hell grant what love did seek.

Shakespeare similarly introduces Orpheus into one of his most famous passages — a paean on the power of music in *The Merchant of Venice:*

> Therefore the poet
> Did feign that Orpheus drew trees, stones, and floods;
> Since naught so stockish, hard, and full of rage,
> But music for the time doth change his nature.

The man that hath no music in himself,
Nor is not mov'd with concord of sweet sounds,
Is fit for treasons, stratagems, and spoils.
The motions of his spirit are dull as night,
And his affections dark as Erebus.
Let no such man be trusted.

REFERENCES TO MYTHOLOGY IN LITERATURE

What do the following references mean? Where a word or phrase is italicized, explain only the word or phrase.

A

1. Under the dripping black Tartarean cliff
   Which Styx's awful waters trickle down. — *Arnold*
2. Lady, when your lovely head
   Sinks to rest among the dead,
   Sleep your fill: but when you wake,
   Dawn shall over *Lethe* break. — *Hilaire Belloc*
3. Come, then, righters of wrong, O vengeful dealers of justice,
   Braided with coil of the serpents! — *Catullus*
4. And 'cross the Styx full many a soul
   Has Charon ferried. — *Austin Dobson*
5.   Like one who dream'd
   Of idleness in groves *Elysian*. — *Keats*
6.   Until the firmament
   Outblacken *Erebus*. — *Keats*
7. Or with a finger stay'd *Ixion's* wheel. — *Keats*
8.   Perhaps, thought I, *Morpheus*,
   In passing here, his owlet pinions shook. — *Keats*
9.   On the verge
   Of light he stood, and on Eurydice
   (Mindless of fate, alas! and soul-subdued)
   Looked back. — *Landor*
10. Like a vapor Eurydice vanished. — *Landor*
11. With useless endeavor,
    Forever, forever,
    Is Sisyphus rolling
    His stone up the mountain! — *Longfellow*

12.   Hence, loathéd Melancholy,
    Of *Cerberus* and blackest Midnight born. — *Milton*
13. Lethe, the river of oblivion. — *Milton*
14. Gloomy Pluto, king of terrors. — *Pope*

B

1. Abhorréd *Styx*, the flood of deadly hate. — *Milton*
2.   Of itself the water flies
    All taste of living wight, as once it fled
    The lip of *Tantalus*. — *Milton*
3. But soon, too soon, the lover turns his eyes;
    Again she falls, again she dies, she dies! — *Pope*
4.   Get you gone,
    And at the pit of *Acheron*
    Meet me i' the morning. — *Shakespeare*
5. Not *Erebus* itself were dim enough
    To hide thee from prevention. — *Shakespeare*
6. With *Hecate's* ban thrice blasted, thrice infected. — *Shakespeare*
7.   Therefore the poet
    Did feign that Orpheus drew trees, stones, floods. — *Shakespeare*
8. *Orpheus* with his lute made trees,
    And the mountain tops that freeze
      Bow themselves when he did sing. — *Shakespeare*
9. Language is a perpetual *Orphic* song. — *Shelley*
10. To Cerberus they give a sop,
    His triple barking mouth to stop. — *Swift*
11. It may be we shall touch the *Happy Isles*. — *Tennyson*
12. *Lethean* poppies thou shalt send to *Orpheus*. — *Virgil*
13. In melancholy moonless *Acheron*. — *Wilde*
14. By reedy *Styx* old *Charon*, leaning on his oar,
    Waits for my coin. — *Wilde*

Exercises in Composition, Oral and Written

1. Draw a map of Hades, as you think that region looked. Put the important characters of Hades at appropriate spots, with their names alongside.

2. The torments of Tantalus, Ixion, Sisyphus, and the Danaïdes have a certain grim humor in them. Can you invent some mild torment, such as would punish appropriately some minor offense? Tell about it.

3. Down in Hades meet, of course, the characters of many ages. Imagine a meeting between two such characters of different eras. What would Homer, for example, say to Shakespeare, or Alexander the Great to Napoleon, or Caesar to Washington? Write the dialogue, as you think it took place.

4. In a dream you visit the Elysian Fields, and there you behold many famous men — great writers, great warriors, great rulers. Give an account of your visit.

5. Orpheus, on his return to earth after losing Eurydice the second time, tells his friend Menander what happened and expresses his own despair. Repeat what it was he said.

Word Study

1. Explain how the following words came to have their present meaning:

Lethean — producing forgetfulness

Elysian — like heaven or paradise

hypnotic — causing sleep

morphine — a drug producing sleep or relief from pain

tantalize — to tease by keeping something desired in view, but just out of reach

Orphic — mystic, used of poetry or prophetic utterances

Cerberus — a vigilant but surly custodian or guardian.

2. What is the correct pronunciation of the following words?

Charon, Lethe, Acheron, Phlegethon, Cocytus, Cerberus, Aeneas, Eurydice, Elysium, Hecate, Morpheus, Sisyphus, Danaïdes, Danaüs, Orpheus, Calliope.

3. Give the Greek names of the following deities: Pluto, Ceres, Somnus, Mors, Bacchus.

4. What is an obolus? asphodel? a lyre?

5. What is meant by the expressions, "to swear by the Styx," "dreams through the ivory gate," "to carry water in a sieve," "a sop to Cerberus," "Stygian darkness," "lethargy"?

6. James Joyce records jokingly in *Ulysses* that a certain policeman on duty " was wrapped in the arms of Murphy, dreaming of fresh fields and pastures new." For whom does *Murphy* stand?

Rapid Quiz

What names were often given the underworld? Who ruled over it? What five rivers flowed through it? Describe two of them. Who was the ferryman of the underworld? Who was its guardian? Into what three parts was it divided? What were the Furies? Who was Hecate? Who was the god of sleep? of death? of dreams? How and why was Tantalus punished? Ixion? Sisyphus? the Danaïdes? What were the characteristics of Elysium? Who was Orpheus? What happened to his wife? What plea did he make to Pluto? What was Pluto's reply? What happened on the journey to the upper world? How did Orpheus die?

For Students of Latin

1. Find, if you can, the original Latin for the quotation from Virgil at the head of this chapter. Where else in the chapter is Virgil referred to?

2. Who were the *Charonides?*

3. Give the Latin name of Hypnos and Thanatos.

4. Answer in Latin two or three of the questions in the Rapid Quiz.

5. Write in Latin a brief description of a character mentioned in this chapter.

Reading List

Poems, Plays, and Music

Buchanan, Robert : *Ades*
Dante : *Inferno*
Dowden, Edward : *Eurydice*
Eliot, George : *Arion*
Fielding, Henry : *Eurydice* [play]
Gluck, Christolph : *Orpheus and Eurydice* [opera]
Gosse, Edmund : *The Island of the Blest — The Waking of Eurydice*
Landor, Walter Savage : *Orpheus and Eurydice*

Lang, Andrew : *The Fortunate Islands*
Lowell, James Russell : *Eurydice*
Morris, Lewis : *Epic of Hades*
Noyes, Alfred : *Orpheus and Eurydice*
Phillips, Stephen : *Christ in Hades*

Humorous Novels

Bangs, John Kendrick : *The House-Boat on the Styx — The Pursuit of the House-Boat*

Cosimo

SACRIFICE FOR THE FREEING OF ANDROMEDA

Who are these coming to the sacrifice? — KEATS

X

THREE HEROES AND TWO FRIENDS

What was that snaky-headed Gorgon shield
That wise Minerva wore, unconquered virgin? — MILTON

THE TRIALS OF PERSEUS

Danaë was a beautiful maiden, whose father, King Acrisius of Argos, was very proud of her. But one day he consulted an oracle of the gods, and was told that the son of his daughter would one day kill him. So, in an attempt to avoid his doom, Acrisius shut Danaë up in a tower and forbade anyone, except her chosen attendants, to have access to her. But not so could Acrisius escape what the gods had in store for him. Jupiter himself, beholding the maiden, fell in love with her and, according to the legend, appeared to her first in a shower of golden rain. In time a son, named Perseus, was born to Danaë.

When Acrisius learned what had happened, he was furiously angry. He had mother and child shut up in a great wooden chest, closed the top, and set it afloat on the sea.

The chest did not sink, but as if guided by some unseen steersman, moved steadily over the waves.

In the course of time the strange boat came to rest on the shore of an island.   A fisherman saw it and when he forced

Veronese   Gramstorff Bros.

DANAË AND THE SHOWER OF GOLD

The brazen tower was storm'd of old,
When Jove descended in almighty gold. — OVID

open the lid, to his astonishment found within the chest a sleeping mother and child, both of surpassing beauty.   He brought them to Polydectes, the king of the land, who received them kindly and gave them every care.

But their troubles were by no means over.   Polydectes fell in love with Danaë and urged her to marry him.   Year after year she refused, for her only thought was to take care of her son.   At last, when Perseus was approaching manhood, Polydectes resolved to get rid of him, hoping that if he were gone, his mother would change her mind. So he commanded the lad to bring him the head of the Gorgon Medusa.

Now Medusa was a fearful creature — one of three sisters whose locks were hissing serpents, who had wings, brazen claws, and enormous teeth, and whose glance turned any beholder to stone. Perseus knew that by himself he could do nothing to conquer Medusa, so he sought the help of Minerva and Mercury. Minerva counseled him to seek out the Three Gray Sisters, who could not only reveal where the Gorgons lived, but could also supply him with three things without which it was useless for him to attempt the quest. She also told him how to get the Three Sisters into his power, since of their own accord they would tell him nothing.

Perseus journeyed far until he came to the lonely land where the Three Sisters dwelt. Quietly he stole up to the cavern where they were wont to come at noon when the sun was hot. Now these Three Sisters, who had been gray since they were born, had a remarkable peculiarity — they had only a single eye among them, and this they passed from one to the other. While the eye was being passed they were all quite blind.

As Perseus lay in wait, one of the three said: "Come, sister, your time has passed. Let me now have the eye."

At the word the sister in whose head the eye was took it out. At that very moment Perseus stretched out his hand and snatched the eye from her.

"Where is the eye?" cried the second of the Three Sisters.

Thereupon Perseus spoke: "I have it."

At the sound of his voice the Three Sisters trembled. They pleaded with Perseus and bade him return the eye.

He told them that he would gladly return vision to them, if they would grant him a boon.   They would not at first grant him his wish.   But when he threatened to go away and leave them blind forever, they realized that they had no choice. So they revealed to Perseus the hiding place of the Gorgons,

Burne-Jones   *Gramstorff Bros.*

PERSEUS AND THE GRAY SISTERS

There sat the crones that had the single eye.
— WILLIAM MORRIS

and they told him where the sea nymphs lived who gave him the three things he needed — the helmet of Pluto, which rendered him invisible; a pair of winged sandals, which enabled him to fly with the speed of the wind; and a pouch in which to place Medusa's head.   (In one version of the story Perseus rides Pegasus on his mission.)

Mercury afforded him additional assistance. He provided him with a sickle of exceeding sharpness to use in

PERSEUS ON PEGASUS SLAYS MEDUSA

Or wingéd Perseus with his flawless sword
Cleaving the snaky tresses of the witch. — WILDE

cutting off Medusa's head, and Perseus was equipped for his battle. He flew quickly until he came to a rocky island in the midst of the stream Oceanus. The ground was thick with evil-smelling and noxious weeds, and everywhere deadly snakes squirmed over the ground. In a cavern at the center of the island lived the Gorgons. When Perseus reached them,

Burne-Jones

ATLAS AND PERSEUS

Supporting on his shoulders the vast pillar
Of Heaven and Earth. — AESCHYLUS

they were asleep. He did not dare look at them directly, but gazed at their reflection in a highly polished shield that he carried. He was able to recognize Medusa by the fact that she was smaller than the others. Holding the shield in front of her, Perseus severed her head with one sweep of his sickle. He thrust it in his pouch and flew away. Hardly had he done so when the two other Gorgons awoke and realized that their sister was dead. Shrieking with wrath they darted out of the cavern and looked for her slayer. The magic helmet of Pluto, however, rendered him invisible, and he escaped in safety.

After killing Medusa, Perseus flew on until he reached the realms of the mighty Atlas who supported the heavens on his shoulders. Here he wished to rest in the Garden of the Hesperides. Atlas, however, remembering the ancient prophecy that a son of Jupiter would come some day and steal some of his cherished golden apples, attempted to keep Perseus out. The latter, enraged at this lack of hospitality, held up the Gorgon's head and changed Atlas to stone.

THE RESCUE OF ANDROMEDA

After flying for many days Perseus at length reached a country in Ethiopia of which Cepheus was king. Now it happened that at that time the whole land was plunged in lamentation. A little before this Cassiopeia, the queen of Cepheus, had become so proud of her great beauty that she boasted that she was more beautiful than the Nereids. They were very angry and they begged Neptune to punish her. He did so by sending a huge sea monster, which laid waste the land and devoured both men and cattle.

The king in despair consulted an oracle and asked what he should do. He was told that nothing would mollify the offended sea deities except the sacrifice of the king's daughter, Andromeda, to the monster.

Now Andromeda was even lovelier than her mother, and her parents were in despair. Yet day by day the monster ascended the shores of the land and did frightful damage.

At last the inhabitants came in great mobs and stormed the gates of the palace.

"Sacrifice Andromeda!" they cried. "She must atone for your impiety!"

So at last a day was set on which Andromeda, chained to a rock, was to await the coming of the monster and by her death free the land from devastation. Weeping and yet brave, she was led to her doom; and her parents and attendants sadly left her to her fate.

PERSEUS RESCUING ANDROMEDA

And Perseus dreadful with Minerva's shield. — POPE

As she lay on the rock, Andromeda prayed that her doom might come quickly. Yet at that very moment her salvation was approaching. For Perseus, flying over Africa, saw below him the great commotion, and sweeping closer he perceived the beautiful maiden chained to the rock. He landed from the sky at her feet and removed the helmet of Pluto that rendered him invisible to her gaze. At first she was frightened at the sudden apparition, but Perseus reassured her and asked her to tell him why she was chained to the rock. When

PERSEUS AND ANDROMEDA

Above them the queen Aphrodite
Poured on their foreheads and limbs, unseen, ambrosial odors.
— CHARLES KINGSLEY

he heard her story, he determined to rescue her.   In silence both awaited the coming of the monster.

Suddenly the water was lashed into mountains of foam, and the monster, huge as a whale, approached.   He plunged his way straight toward the rock on which Andromeda reclined.   But a youth with a shining weapon stood in his way. The monster turned aside to destroy Perseus with one crunch of his massive jaws.   Instead, he received a fierce thrust that brought his heart blood spouting to the surface in great fountains and dyed the water crimson in every direction. As the monster looked again for Perseus, he had disappeared, and even then a blow struck him from above.   In vain the beast contended against the winged hero.   Blow after blow rendered him powerless, until at last his tremendous bulk floated dead on the waves.

From afar the Ethiopians had witnessed the combat, and now they came with rejoicing and freed Andromeda from the rock.   Perseus claimed the maiden as his wife, and her parents were glad to give her to him in marriage.   But her uncle Phineus, to whom she had been promised at an earlier time, now claimed her, although he had made no effort to save her from her deadly peril.   Her parents would not heed him. At the marriage feast, however, he suddenly appeared with a great host of followers, and sought to carry her off.   When it looked as if Perseus would be overcome, he suddenly brought forth the Gorgon's head, and instantly Phineus and his followers were changed to stone.

THE RETURN OF PERSEUS

Cepheus provided Perseus and his bride with a handsome ship, and they set off for the island in which dwelt Danaë.

His mother, he found, had taken refuge in a temple of the gods to escape the attentions of Polydectes, and the king was now trying to starve her into submission.   When Polydectes heard that Perseus had returned, he raised an army and attacked him.   But once more Perseus showed the Gorgon's head and turned his foes to stone.   Thus he freed his mother.   He made the brother of Polydectes king in his stead, and he returned to the sea nymphs the objects he had borrowed from them.   To Minerva he presented the head of Medusa, and ever after the goddess wore it on her breastplate, the aegis. It froze to stone those who gazed at the maiden goddess with disrespect.

Elihu Vedder   *Fine Arts Gallery, San Diego*

HEAD OF MEDUSA

Its horror and its beauty are divine.
— SHELLEY

There remains to be told in the story of Perseus only that event by which was fulfilled the doom of King Acrisius.   Danaë, despite the way in which he had treated her, still loved her father, and as Perseus, too, wished to see his grandfather, both set out to pay him a visit in that ship which Cepheus had given his son-in-law.

Now when word was brought to Acrisius that his daughter and his grandson had not perished, and that they were actually coming to see him, he was filled with fear lest the oracle be at length fulfilled.   So he hurriedly left the country, and when Perseus reached Argos, no one knew where the king had gone.

To while away the time Perseus resolved to attend an athletic contest that was taking place in a neighboring country. He himself took part in the games and carried off many prizes. Nobody knew who he was, and all marveled at his prowess. Toward the end of the games there was a discus-throwing contest. Perseus stepped forward to try his skill, but as he lifted up the heavy stone plate, it slipped out of his hand, flew sideways, and killed an old man who was watching the games. From the dead man's attendants it then became known that the spectator thus unfortunately slain was Acrisius, king of Argos, who had fulfilled his doom by running away from it.

Perseus was deeply grieved at the accident and conveyed the body to Argos for a splendid burial. Then he assumed the crown of Argos and for many years lived in happiness and ruled wisely.

THE EARLY ADVENTURES OF THESEUS

Weary with the cares of state, Aegeus, king of Athens, once retired for a time to the court of his friend, King Pittheus of Troezen. There he met and fell in love with King Pittheus's daughter, the princess Aethra. Aegeus wooed and won Aethra, and when a son named Theseus was born to them, King Aegeus rejoiced that he had an heir to the throne of Athens.

At length, however, Aegeus felt it incumbent on him to return to Athens and resume his responsibilities. But he decided that it would be much better to let Theseus remain in his grandfather's pleasant home than to take him to the too busy city of Athens; and he would be safer, moreover, from the king's many enemies.

"When the lad can lift up the great stone at the entrance

to the wood," he said to Aethra, "and find the sword which
lies underneath, send him to me."

Impatiently Theseus waited for the time when he could
satisfy this test of strength.   At last came a day when, as he

Poussin   *Uffizi Gallery, Florence*

THESEUS LIFTING THE ROCK

A chief who more in feats of arms excell'd
The rising nor the setting sun beheld. — WILLIAM MORRIS

fiercely matched his muscles against the rock, he moved the
obstacle a little.   Once more he tried — and the stone rolled
slowly away.   Underneath it lay a beautifully ornamented
sword and a pair of fine sandals.

"These were left to you by your father," explained Aethra.
"He is king of Athens, but his brother is his enemy, and he
feared that you would be killed if you came to him before
you were strong enough to hold your own.   Now go to him,
and may the gods protect you."

His grandfather advised him to take a short and safe way to Athens, but the boy was eager to prove his manhood, and he deliberately chose a road that was infested by many perils. He ran into these perils almost as soon as he set out.   First he encountered a lame but very strong bandit, named Periphetes, who was supposed to be a son of Vulcan.   This bandit sprang out at Theseus savagely, and aimed a great iron bludgeon at him.   But Theseus evaded the blow, and in a short time managed to kill the fellow.

Another robber was called Procrustes, or the Stretcher. He, too, was of gigantic size, and he had a grim sense of humor.   When he captured a hapless traveler, he slung him over his shoulder and strode off to his den in the woods. There he had an iron bedstead, upon which he threw the traveler.   If the bed was too short, he lopped off the traveler's limbs until he fitted.   If the bed was too long, he stretched the traveler's limbs to equal the bed.   But Theseus proved more than a match for him, and when the hero had vanquished the giant, he punished him by making him fit his own bedstead.

THESEUS AND THE MINOTAUR

When Theseus reached Athens and came into the king's presence, the latter at once recognized the sword he had left for his son and welcomed him joyfully.   He immediately declared him heir to his throne.

At this time there was deep sorrow in Athens.   Some years before, a gang of unruly Athenians had slain the son of Minos, king of Crete, in anger at his superiority in an athletic contest.   As a penalty the city was obliged to send annually as a tribute to Crete seven youths and seven maidens, all selected for their beauty and strength, to be devoured by the Minotaur,[1] a strange monster half bull and half man that had been born to Queen Pasiphaë of Crete.

He lived at the center of a maze called the labyrinth, from which no one who went in without knowing the secret of its construction could make his way out again.

G. F. Watts   Tate Gallery, London

THE MINOTAUR

Two-shaped offspring of Pasiphaë.
— VIRGIL

When Theseus heard about this tribute, he demanded that he be selected as one of the seven youths. Aegeus in vain implored him to change his mind. Theseus was resolved either to slay the Minotaur or to die in the attempt. Aegeus demanded one favor.

"If you return safely," he begged, "change these black sails that your vessel carries to white ones, that I may know you have triumphed over the Minotaur."

Theseus promised to do this, and set out for Crete. There the young men and maidens were brought before King Minos. He marveled at the boldness of Theseus, whose rank he knew, in asking to be included in the tribute, but told him that no more mercy would be shown him than was shown those who were with him.

[1] Some scholars explain the Minotaur as a man who, in certain religious ceremonies or festivals, wore a mask representing a bull's head, just as some Indian tribes today still wear animal heads in their religious dances.

"Tomorrow you must meet your fate," he said.

Now it happened that beside King Minos sat his daughter Ariadne. She was filled with pity as she gazed on the handsome young hero, and she made up her mind to save him, despite her father's decree. That evening she managed to

Capitoline Museum, Rome

ARIADNE

Princess royal of Creta Minoan, tender, sequestered. — CATULLUS

gain access to the room in which the Athenian prisoners were confined. She made known her identity to Theseus. Secretly she passed over to him two objects — a sword and a ball of thread; and she bade him be of good courage.

The next morning the guards took Theseus and his companions to the labyrinth. They left the Athenian victims at the entrance and did not notice that Theseus fastened one end of the thread to the outer gate. Slowly and tearfully the Athenians made their way into the maze, hoping that somehow the monster would not find them. Only Theseus maintained a cheerful mien. At last they heard the fierce bellowings of the monster, which had caught the scent of human flesh. Nearer and nearer it came, until it finally plunged into the room in which the Athenian prisoners stood cowering and lamenting.

But Theseus awaited it with drawn sword, prepared to fight to the death. The monster rushed full at him, seeking to impale Theseus on its horns, but Theseus evaded the blow and severed one of the beast's legs. Then as it lay on the ground, he plunged his sword into its heart.

Quickly then Theseus, attended by the still trembling prisoners, followed the clew of the thread back to the starting point. There Ariadne stood waiting to welcome him, pale with suspense. With a glad cry she hailed his approach, and hurried him and his companions to the ship that had brought them and was still waiting. They hoisted sail immediately and escaped from the Cretan coast before Minos and his men realized what had occurred.

THESEUS'S LATER ADVENTURES

Theseus, unfortunately, was not very grateful to Ariadne, whom he abandoned on the way home upon the island of Naxos. It is said he did this by command of the god Bacchus, who shortly appeared on the island and took Ariadne to be his wife. Moreover, as he approached Athens, Theseus quite forgot the injunction of his father as to the sails. The aged king had watched the horizon day by day, hoping against hope that Theseus might somehow have vanquished the Minotaur. Then at last he caught sight of the sails on the horizon — still black. The sight so grieved him that he threw himself into the sea.

Theseus bitterly regretted his oversight. He was hailed as king of Athens and ruled for many years. His life was rich in adventures. Once, for example, he seized Hippolyta, ruler of the Amazons, a nation of fierce women warriors, and made her his queen. The other women then made

war on him, and when they saw the wife of Theseus help-
ing her husband in battle, they became so angry that
they slew her.   Later Theseus married Phaedra, the sister
of Ariadne.

Gramstorff Bros.

MOUNTED AMAZON

The Amazons array their ranks
In painted arms of radiant sheen
Around Hippolyta the queen. — VIRGIL

He was a close friend of Perithoüs, king of the Lapithae,
and helped to defend him against the Centaurs at his mar-
riage-feast (see page 112).   When the wife of Perithoüs died,
the latter made up his mind that no one but Proserpina
could replace her, and he persuaded Theseus to accompany
him to Hades in an attempt to abduct her.   Both were

seized and doomed to perpetual torture, but Theseus, with
the help of his friend Hercules, managed to escape after a
while.

THE ADVENTURES OF BELLEROPHON

The Chimera was a terrible monster. It was a strange
and awe-inspiring mixture of many beasts — its body part
lion and part goat, its hind legs those of a dragon, its breath
of fire. It lived in Lycia and caused great damage. The
king of the land, Iobates, had sought all over Greece for a
hero able to destroy this monster, when Bellerophon, whose
father was the king of Corinth, came to visit him. When
he heard about the Chimera, he volunteered to try to conquer
it. Iobates accepted his offer, and Bellerophon prepared for
the battle.

Before he set out, however, he consulted an oracle of the
gods, and he was advised to secure as a help in the combat
a winged horse named Pegasus, which had been captured
by Minerva and by her presented to the Muses. Poets
as their inspiration rises are said to ride Pegasus. Bellerophon sought the aid of Minerva, and she presented him
with a golden bridle and led him to the spring at which
Pegasus each morning was accustomed to drink. With the
help of the bridle Bellerophon captured and mastered the
steed. On his back the hero mounted into the air, and when
he found the Chimera he was able to send his arrows into the
monster from every side and to avoid its burning breath.
Thus he overcame it.

It is said that later Bellerophon became overproud of his
mastery of the winged steed and even attempted to fly to
Olympus. But Jupiter sent a gadfly that stung the horse in
mid-flight. He started violently and threw Bellerophon

BELLEROPHON

Bold Bellerophon (so Jove decreed
In wrath) fell headlong from the fields of air. — WORDSWORTH

from the saddle. The young hero was killed, and the horse returned to the service of the Muses.

DAMON AND PYTHIAS

Among the most admired heroes of ancient times were the two friends, Damon and Pythias,[1] who became models of loyalty.

It is likely that these men actually existed. According to the story, they were subjects of the tyrant Dionysius, who ruled over Syracuse in Sicily during the fifth century before the beginning of our era. Both Damon and Pythias were renowned for their wisdom and goodness, but in some manner of which there is no record, Pythias incurred the anger of the tyrant and was condemned by him to death. He bore the sentence bravely, but he asked Dionysius to grant him one favor — permission to go home and settle his affairs. Damon offered to be a hostage for the safe return of his friend.

The tyrant agreed to let Pythias go.

"But you must be here by such and such an hour," he warned him, "or your friend will die for you."

Pythias set out for his home, which was a considerable distance away. He settled his affairs, divided his goods among his kinsfolk, and set out on his way back to Syracuse. Unfortunately, however, he was delayed at every turn. Now it was a river swollen with floods that he had to ford, and now a tremendous storm made the road impassable. He struggled on desperately, and reached Syracuse in the very nick of time, for the executioner was already lifting up his sword to behead Damon. Pythias forced his way through the spectators, and cried out :

[1] Some authorities give the name as *Phintias*.

"Hold your sword! Here I am!" and he knelt down to receive the blow. But Dionysius was so filled with astonishment and admiration at the loyalty of the friends that he pardoned Pythias, and he even asked that he might be admitted to his and Damon's friendship.

STUDY APPLICATION

THE MYTHS IN LITERATURE

Various phases and portions of the story of Perseus have been treated in literature. Undoubtedly the finest poem on the subject is Charles Kingsley's *Andromeda*, in which the meter employed — dactylic hexameter — is the same as that which Homer used in the *Iliad* and the *Odyssey*, and which Virgil later used in the *Aeneid*. As the title indicates, Kingsley has concentrated on that portion of the adventures of Perseus in which Andromeda is concerned. Thus he pictures the sea beast:

Onward it came from the south, as bulky and black as a galley,
Lazily coasting along, as the fish fled leaping before it;
Lazily breasting the ripple, and watching by sand bar and headland,
Listening for laughter of maidens at bleaching or song of the fisher,
Children at play on the pebbles, or cattle that passed on the sand hills.

Bryant has rendered the *Lament of Danaë*, by Simonides, a famous Greek poet. Dowden has written of Andromeda; and William Drummond, Thomas Gordon Hake, and Dante Gabriel Rossetti of the Medusa — to whom in literature there are innumerable references. The story of Perseus has been well told by William Morris in one section of *The Earthly Paradise — The Doom of King Acrisius*.

Theseus and the Amazon queen are important characters in one of Shakespeare's plays — *A Midsummer Night's Dream*, in which the poet has curiously mingled classical mythology with the fairy lore of his own land. Shakespeare followed Chaucer's poetical version of the same story in *The Knight's Tale*.

References to Mythology in Literature

What do the following references mean? Where a word or phrase is italicized, explain only the word or phrase.

1. So was the *Cretan bull* by *Theseus* done to destruction.
   — *Catullus*
2. What was that snaky-headed *Gorgon shield*
   That wise *Minerva* wore? — *Milton*
3. Then whoso will with virtuous wing assay
   To mount to heaven on *Pegasus* must ride. — *Milton*
4. There sat the crones that had the single eye. — *Morris*
5. The star-bright shower
   That came to *Danaë* in her brazen tower. — *Edith Sitwell*
6. Damon and Pythias, whom death could not sever. — *Spenser*
7. Now lies the Earth all *Danaë* to the stars,
   And all thy heart lies open unto me. — *Tennyson*
8. The *labyrinthine* ways of my own mind. — *Thompson*
9. *Pallas*, resplendent with her storm-cloud and grim with her
   Gorgon. — *Virgil*
10. Of lonely *Ariadne* on the wharf
    At Naxos, when she saw the treacherous crew
    Far out at sea. — *Wilde*

Exercises in Composition, Oral and Written

1. After Perseus has slain the monster, Andromeda expresses her gratitude to the hero. She asks his name and then thanks him fervently. What would she say?

2. The Athenian captives appear before King Minos and his court. They are questioned, and the identity of Theseus is revealed. Put the scene into play form.

3. In recent years much interesting and amazing information regarding the ancient Cretans has been brought to light. See if you can find any facts about them in magazine articles or in history textbooks.

4. If newspapers had existed in the time of the ancients, one of them (the Syracuse *Herald*, let us say) might have given an account of the Damon and Pythias episode. Write the story in newspaper style, beginning with the scene at the moment when the one friend was on the point of execution.

Word Study

1. Explain the derivation of the following words:

chimera — an absurd creation of the imagination
labyrinth — a complicated or confused situation

2. What is the correct pronunciation of the following words?

Perseus, Danaë, Acrisius, Polydectes, Andromeda, Cepheus, Cassiopeia, Theseus, Aegeus, Pittheus, Troezen, Aethra, Periphetes, Procrustes, Minotaur, Ariadne, Phaedra, Bellerophon, Iobates, Chimera, Pegasus, Damon, Pythias, Dionysius.

3. Give the Greek equivalents of the following names: Jupiter, Neptune, Mercury, Minerva.

4. Did the tyrant of Syracuse have the same name as the Greek god of wine?

5. What is meant by the following expressions? — "To stretch on a bed of Procrustes," "to mount Pegasus," "to fight a chimera," "as true as Damon and Pythias or David and Jonathan."

6. Has the name of the fraternal order, "The Knights of Pythias," any connection with Pythias?

7. To what plant has the name *Andromeda* been given?

8. A student in a theme wrote that it was his ambition to "be a sculpture." The teacher wrote this comment in the margin: "Page Medusa!" Explain the comment, and correct the word.

Rapid Quiz

What oracle concerning Danaë terrified her father, King Acrisius? How did he try to avert his doom? What happened? When Perseus was born, how did King Acrisius again try to outwit fate? What happened? Why did Polydectes want to get rid of Perseus? On what mission did he send him? Who was Medusa? Whose help did Perseus win? How did he overcome the Gorgon? What maiden did he rescue on his way home? On what two occasions did he have to employ the Gorgon's head? How did he employ it when he returned home? What did Acrisius do when he heard that Perseus was coming? How did Acrisius meet his doom? Of what monarch was Theseus the son? What injunctions did his father give his mother? When did he set out for Athens? What adventures did he meet on the road? What mission did he undertake on his arrival? What was the Minotaur? With whose help and how did Theseus overcome him? Was he grateful? What forgetfulness killed the father of Theseus? What was the Chimera? How did Bellerophon conquer it? How did the hero later meet his death? What two men were devoted friends? How did they prove their friendship?

FOR STUDENTS OF LATIN

1. Which hero in this chapter would Romans admire most? Why?
2. What Latin authors are mentioned in the Myths in Literature and the quotations?
3. Answer in Latin two or three of the questions in the Rapid Quiz.
4. Select one of the quotations and render it into Latin.

READING LIST

Poems, Plays, and a Biography

Bryant, William Cullen: Simonides' *Lament of Danaë*
Chaucer, Geoffrey: *The Knight's Tale*
Corneille, Pierre: *Andromeda*
Dowden, Edward: *Andromeda*
Kingsley, Charles: *Andromeda*
Landor, Walter Savage: *Theseus and Hippolyta*
Longfellow, Henry Wadsworth: *Pegasus in Pound*
Morris, William: *Bellerophon at Argos — Bellerophon in Lycia — The Doom of King Acrisius*
Ovid: *Ariadne to Theseus* (in *Heroines*)
Plutarch: *Life of Theseus*
Rossetti, Dante Gabriel: *Aspecta Medusa*
Shakespeare, William: *A Midsummer Night's Dream*
Shelley, Percy Bysshe: *On the Medusa of Leonardo da Vinci*
Tennyson, Lord: *Parnassus*

HERCULES IN THE GARMENTS OF A WOMAN SPINNING WOOL

His lion spoils the laughing Fair demands,
And gives the distaff to his awkward hands. — DARWIN

XI

THE ADVENTURES OF HERCULES

Do you seek Hercules' equal?
None is, except himself. — SENECA

BIRTH AND EARLY LIFE OF HERCULES

No more celebrated hero lived in ancient times than
Hercules (Greek : Herakles).   He was the son of Jupiter by
Alcmene of Thebes.   Juno was always unfriendly to the
children of Jupiter by other wives than herself, but against
Hercules she cherished a particular hatred.   She managed
before his birth to arrange matters so that he was deprived
of the rulership of a kingdom.   As he lay in his cradle she
sent two serpents to strangle him, but the infant prodigy,
already strong far beyond the ordinary, seized the snakes in
his hands and strangled them.

As a young man Hercules received instruction in all the manly arts and training in character from the best teachers in Greece. Amphitryon, king of Thebes, son of Alcaeus [1] and grandson of Perseus, who was his reputed father, gave him lessons in the art of driving a chariot. Autolycus, a son of Mercury, taught him wrestling. Eurytus, himself a king, was his master in archery. Castor, another son of Jupiter and a great warrior, showed him how to bear himself in heavy fighting. Linus, a son of Apollo, gave him lessons in singing and playing the lyre. Rhadamanthus, later because of his fine character one of the judges of the underworld, trained him in wisdom and virtue. But Hercules as a youth and as a man lacked self-control, and in a fit of sudden rage he killed Linus.

Gramstorff Bros.

INFANT HERCULES STRANGLING SNAKES

Their grasping throats with clenching hands he holds. — DARWIN

For this offense Amphitryon banished him to the country and made him a herdsman. He grew up in the open air, and daily became more powerful. It was at this time that he first began to perform astonishing deeds of strength and courage. He slew the Thespian lion, which had long caused great damage to the flocks near by. He ever afterwards wore the skin of this lion as his ordinary garment, and carried a huge

[1] Hercules is therefore sometimes called "Alcides" — "of the family of Alcaeus."

club, which he cut for himself from a tree in the neighborhood of Nemea.

MARRIAGE AND MADNESS OF HERCULES

The career of Hercules was, on the whole, one of service to his fellow men. It is related of him that, early in his life, there appeared to him in a vision two women who stood at a crossroad.

HERCULES WITH LION SKIN

So from Nemea's den Alcides strode.
— FLACCUS

"I am Pleasure," said one, "and I have many gifts for you. Here are ease and luxury and wealth, grateful friends and a happy home and children that will remember you. You shall want for nothing, you shall endure no toils, you shall never know sorrow. Come with me."

"I am Duty," spoke the other. "Choose me and you shall be ever acquainted with hardship. Rest shall be a stranger to you. Often shall you suffer pain, and grief will often rend your heart. But mankind will remember you with gratitude. You shall become a hero of your people. Your name shall live forever. Come with me."

Unhesitatingly, in his vision, Hercules chose the path of duty; and duty is still sometimes called "Hercules' choice."

What Duty promised him all came true.

When he returned from his exile as a herdsman, he helped

his half brother Iphicles and his foster father Amphitryon in a war which they were waging for the freedom of their city, and although Amphitryon was killed, the enemy, by the prowess of Hercules, was overthrown. As a reward he was given the hand of the princess Megara, and for a time lived happily with her and the children that were born to them.

But Juno, looking down from Olympus, at last could no longer endure the spectacle of the good fortune that had come to Hercules and so she sent madness upon him. In his insanity he slew his own children and two of his brother Iphicles'. Only the intervention of Minerva, who in her pity caused a deep sleep to fall upon him, saved him from further crimes. When he awoke from this sleep, he was in his right mind again, and bitterly grieved over what had occurred.

THE FIRST SIX LABORS OF HERCULES

Hercules knew that mere grief over his act was not enough, and he sought to purify himself in other ways. He consulted wise and holy men and the oracles of the gods. At last he imposed a sentence on himself. He bound himself to serve his cousin, King Eurystheus, and to carry out his commands, no matter what they might be, for the space of twelve years. Eurystheus, meanwhile, inspired by Juno, set himself to devise tasks for Hercules that would cause him the greatest suffering and humiliation.

First, he ordered him to slay the Nemean lion and bring him the skin. In a dangerous ravine lived this huge and monstrous lion, against whom all attacks had been in vain. Dreadful was the combat between Hercules and this beast. The hero found that his mighty arrows and his tremendous club were of no avail against the lion. At last he seized the monster in his hands and strangled it to death.

Second, Hercules was commanded to kill the Lernaean Hydra. This was a water snake. When Hercules came to close quarters with it, he found that it had nine heads. If he struck off one of the heads with a club, two new ones immediately grew in its place; the middle head was immortal and resisted all of his efforts to cut it off. The situation seemed desperate, but with the help of his faithful nephew, Iolaüs, who had accompanied him, he tied up the Hydra, and underneath its mortal heads he built a fire which consumed the new heads as fast as they grew. The ninth head he buried under a huge rock. He even made the Hydra useful, for he dipped his arrows into its blood and made them poisonous.

Third, the capture of the Arcadian stag was imposed upon Hercules. This wonderful animal, of astounding swiftness, had golden antlers and brazen hoofs. For a whole year Hercules pursued it in vain. At last, however, he managed to wound the stag slightly, to seize it, and to carry it to Eurystheus upon his shoulders.

Fourth came the destruction of the Erymanthian boar. Hercules was directed to bring this animal, which had been ravaging the countryside, alive to Eurystheus. He pursued the boar through the deep snow up the mountain where it lived, caught it in a huge net, and carried it to his master.

Fifth was the task of cleansing the Augean stables. Augeas, king of Elis, had a herd of three thousand oxen, whose stalls had not been cleansed for thirty years. Hercules managed to dam the rivers Alpheus and Peneus and to turn them aside into the stables. As soon as the stalls had been thoroughly washed out, he allowed the rivers to go back to their courses once more.

HERCULES AND THE HYDRA

The monster of Lerna. — VIRGIL

Sixth of the labors was the destruction of the Stymphalian birds. These birds, which were under the special care of Mars, had brazen claws, wings, and beaks. They used their feathers as arrows, were very greedy, and preferred human flesh to all other food. They lived on a lake near Stymphalus, in Arcadia, and Hercules was ordered by Eurystheus to expel them. Hercules secured the help of Minerva, who provided him with a great rattle. The noise of this rattle startled the birds into flight, and thereupon Hercules slew them with his arrows.

THE LAST SIX LABORS OF HERCULES

Seventh in the series of the hero's toils was the capture of the Cretan bull. This was a beautiful animal which had been presented by Neptune to Minos, king of Crete. Later it became very ferocious. Hercules was ordered to capture it. He did so, and brought it to Eurystheus on his mighty shoulders.

Eighth of the labors was the capture of the mares of Diomedes. Diomedes was a cruel king who fed his horses on human flesh. With the help of a few friends Hercules seized the horses and set out on his homeward journey. Diomedes and his followers pursued them, and a fight took place in which Hercules was victorious. He killed Diomedes and threw his body to the horses. When they had devoured the flesh of their master, they immediately became tame and thereafter refused human flesh.

Ninth came an unusually difficult task — that of securing the girdle of Hippolyta, the queen of the Amazons. The Amazons were a race of women warriors, who had founded a city in Asia Minor. Hippolyta had received from Mars a

HERCULES AND THE CRETAN BULL

You leave that labor to great Hercules. — SHAKESPEARE

girdle of wonderful beauty. Admeta, the daughter of Eurystheus, longed to possess this girdle. She persuaded her father to command Hercules to get it. After various adventures he at last reached the kingdom of the Amazons. There he was received with friendship by Hippolyta, who even promised to give him the girdle as a gift. But Juno took the form of an Amazon and persuaded the followers of Hippolyta that Hercules was carrying off their queen as a captive. They attacked Hercules, and because he thought Hippolyta had been guilty of treachery, he killed her, seized the girdle, and set out for home.[1]

Vatican Museum, Rome

AMAZON

She towered, fit person for a queen
To lead those ancient Amazonian files.
— WORDSWORTH

Tenth of the labors was the capture of the oxen of Geryon. Geryon was a three-headed monster who lived on the little-known island of Erythea. He was gigantic, enormously powerful, and armed with mighty weapons. To assist him in guarding his immense herds of cattle he had another giant named Eurytion and a two-headed dog. It took Hercules a long time to find Erythea. Among the places he passed was the frontier of Europe. To mark his progress he

[1] See the different version of Hippolyta's death on page 224.

put up two mountains as pillars.   Called by the ancients the
Pillars of Hercules, these now form the sides of the Strait of
Gibraltar.   Annoyed by the heat of the sun in this region,
Hercules shot some of his arrows against the Sun, who so
much admired his boldness that he gave him a golden boat
that guided itself in which to find Erythea.   There Hercules
slew Geryon, Eurytion, and the two-headed dog, loaded the
cattle on his magic boat, and returned to the coast of Greece,
where he gave the boat back to the Sun.

Eleventh of the labors imposed upon him was to fetch the
golden apples of the Hesperides.   Hercules did not know
where this divine garden lay, but he knew that the tree on
which the apples grew was guarded by a dragon, whose
vigilance would allow no one to pass, and who could not be
wounded.   But Hercules also knew that near the garden
lived Atlas, the mighty Titan who bore the weight of the
heavens upon his shoulders, and that this Titan's daughters,
the Hesperides, danced forever around the tree that bore the
wonderful apples.   Hercules after long wanderings at last
found Atlas and persuaded him to go and bring back some of
the apples.   In the meantime Hercules consented to bear in
his stead the weight of the sky.   So Atlas went and shortly
returned with several golden apples.   Now, however, he
refused to take back his ancient burden.   He rejoiced in his
freedom and was quite content to let Hercules take his place
forever.

"I will take back the apples to Eurystheus for you," he
said, chuckling, "and I'll tell him you are unable to bring
them yourself."

Hercules pretended to be content to do as Atlas wished.

"But the burden of the sky isn't quite easy on my
shoulders," he remarked, shifting the weight in pretended

discomfort. "Just hold the sky a moment again while I place my lion's skin as a pad on my back."

Unsuspectingly, Atlas took back the load. No sooner had he done so than Hercules snatched up the golden apples and smilingly bade him farewell.

The *twelfth* and last task was by no means least difficult — to bring Cerberus up from the underworld. Here, once more, Hercules had the help of the gods, for Minerva and Mercury accompanied him on his terrifying journey into the realm of Hades. Pluto granted his request that he be allowed to take Cerberus into the upper world, on condition that no weapons be used against his three-headed watchdog. Hercules struggled with the dog and by sheer strength at last subdued him. He carried him up to Eurystheus for inspection and later returned him to his station in the lower regions.

LATER CAREER OF HERCULES

Many other stories are told of Hercules, who became the national hero of Greece. Once again his madness returned upon him, and he slew his friend Iphitus. For a penance he bound himself to serve three years as a slave. This time he placed himself under the orders of a woman, Queen Omphale, and it is related that to show her power over him, she commanded Hercules to put on the garments of a woman and to spin wool, while she wore his lion's skin.

When Prometheus had been chained to the crag in the Caucasus by Jupiter, one consolation cherished by him in secret was that in time a descendant of Jove himself would come to free him. This event destined by the Fates was fulfilled when Hercules, in the course of one of his journeys, beheld Prometheus and was filled with compassion for the

Gramstorff Bros.

HERCULES AT THE FEET OF OMPHALE

Subjection, but required with gentle sway. — MILTON

Titan who suffered such torments because of his services to mankind. He therefore slew the bird of prey which fed upon Prometheus and freed the Fire-Giver from his chains. On another journey he encountered Antaeus, a son of Neptune, who challenged him to combat. Hercules found that every time he threw Antaeus to the ground, the latter, after contact with Mother Earth, rose with redoubled strength. So he lifted him up into the air and strangled him into submission.

Like many of the Greek heroes, Hercules seems to have been a sort of super-policeman — called on for help when people were in trouble. At one time the king of Troy offended Apollo and Neptune. To appease them he decided to sacrifice his daughter Hesione to a neighboring sea-monster. But Hercules happened to come along at about that time, accompanied by his friend Telamon. On the appeal of the Trojan king and with the promise of a fee of six horses, Hercules engaged the monster in battle and killed it.

But the king refused to pay the reward. So Hercules, in anger, besieged Troy, slew the king, and seizing Hesione, gave her in marriage to Telamon. All three traveled back to Greece, where Hesione became the mother of Teucer, a famous archer in the Trojan War, and step-brother of Ajax who fought in the same war.

Hercules married Deianira, the daughter of Oeneus and a sister of Meleager. It was through her that death came to him. Once Hercules and Deianira came to the ford of a river. Here a centaur, Nessus, carried travelers across for a fee. Hercules himself was able to cross the stream without assistance, but he placed Deianira upon the back of Nessus to be carried across. Deianira was very beautiful, and instead of bearing her to the other bank of the stream, Nessus turned around and started off with her for the cavern in which he lived. Hercules, from the other shore, drew his bow and launched an arrow into the heart of Nessus. The centaur, in the moment before he died, whispered to Deianira that his blood was a love potion, which would enable her to retain the love of Hercules.

Foolishly she believed him; and when some time later she became jealous of the attentions which Hercules was paying to a captive maiden, she steeped a robe that Hercules was to wear in the supposed love potion. But it was, in reality, a deadly poison, and when the hero put it on, the evil of it tore into his flesh with excruciating agony. Hercules ascended a mountain, raised a pile of wood, placed himself on this as a funeral pyre, and ordered it to be set on fire. But Jupiter at the last moment intervened, and snatched him up to Olympus, where he was reconciled to Juno and given her daughter Hebe in marriage.

Thorwaldsen

HEBE

Hebe, honored of them all,
Ministered nectar. — HOMER

STUDY APPLICATION

THE MYTHS IN LITERATURE

Hercules was accorded the admiration not only of the Greeks but of all the ancient world — for his manliness, his strength, his willingness to serve, his achievements in ridding the world of evil monsters, and his athletic prowess. He appears in the tales of the poets and the representations of painters and sculptors. The Romans made a great favorite of him; one of their most familiar oaths was "Me herculë!" and his image appeared on their coin called *quadrans*.

Mark Antony claimed to be a direct descendant of Hercules, and sometimes, to enforce this claim, he would harness lions to his carriage. At the height of his power he even struck off a coin showing an image of himself driving such a chariot.

Among those in ancient times who told the story of this great hero in dramatic form were Euripides and Sophocles among the Greeks, Seneca among the Latins. In modern times George Cabot Lodge's *Herakles* makes striking use of the old story. Perhaps the most effective dramatic use of Hercules is that of Euripides in his drama, *Alcestis*, when the hero enters at a crucial moment to save Alcestis from Death.

The name *Herakles* or, occasionally, the form *Alcides* or, more frequently, its Latin form *Hercules* has of course become a synonym through the ages for great physical strength and courage. Shakespeare, for example, often uses the name in this way. Thus he says:

> How many cowards, whose hearts are all as false
> As stairs of sand, wear yet upon their chins
> The beards of Hercules and frowning Mars.

The Amazons who appear in the story of Hercules are familiar in reference and allusion; and romances and even scientific treatises have played with the idea of a race of women who rule powerfully without the help of men. To the Amazons the poets and others have often turned in thought; Shakespeare, for example:

> For your own ladies and pale-visag'd maids
> Like Amazons come tripping after drums,
> Their thimbles into armed gauntlets changed,
> Their needles to lances, and their gentle hearts
> To fierce and bloody inclination.

REFERENCES TO MYTHOLOGY IN LITERATURE

What do the following references mean? Where a word or phrase is italicized, explain only the word or phrase.

1.   A violent heart hath been
Fatal to all the race of *Herakles.* — *Arnold*

2. Though comparatively weak, opposed to Johnson's *Herculean*
vigor, let us not call his style positively feeble. — *Boswell*

3. The diver, a Hercules named Kendrick, was unscrewing the
valve of his helmet. — *Freeman Wills Crofts*

4. By her in stature the tall *Amazon*
Had stood a pigmy's height. — *Keats*

5. He seemed earth-born, an *Antaeus*, sucking in fresh vigor from
the soil which he neighbored. — *Lamb*

6. Suddenly he sprouts out an entirely new set of features, like
Hydra. — *Lamb*

7.   Or pierce Avernus' darksome vaults,
To pull the triple-headed dog from hell. — *Marlowe*

8.   As when *Alcides* . . .
Felt th' envenom'd robe, and tore
Through pain up by the root Thessalian pines. — *Milton*

9. And Beauty, like the fair *Hesperian tree,*
Laden with blooming gold, had need the guard
Of dragon watch with unenchanted eye. — *Milton*

10. Voyage over dreamful seas
To lost *Hesperides.* — *Peabody*

11.   My fate cries out,
And makes each petty artery in this body
As hardy as the *Nemean lion's* nerve. — *Shakespeare*

EXERCISES IN COMPOSITION, ORAL AND WRITTEN

1. Select *six* scenes from the twelve labors of Hercules and present
them in tableau form. See if your classmates can recognize each scene
as you give it.

2. On his return from one of his labors Hercules is interviewed by a
reporter from the *Theban Courier* (supposing such a paper to have
existed). He gives an account of his adventure.

3. Compare the career of Hercules with that of Samson in the Bible.
How did these heroes resemble each other?

4. Compare the exploits of Hercules with those of the legendary
American lumberjack, Paul Bunyan.

5. What other "strong men" have you ever heard of who could be compared to Hercules? Give an account of them.

6. Hercules, let us suppose, suddenly finds himself in a city of today. What would he say about the sights and sounds around him?

WORD STUDY

1. Explain how the following words came to have their present meaning:

Herculean — of great strength
Amazonian — warlike or masculine, as applied to women
Hesperian — western
atlas — (1) a globe of the earth; (2) a collection of maps; (3) the first vertebra, sustaining the head.

2. Give the correct pronunciation of the following words:

Herakles, Alcmene, Amphitryon, Alcaeus, Alcides, Autolycus, Eurytus, Nemea, Iphicles, Eurystheus, Lernaean, Iolaüs, Erymanthian, Augean, Diomedes, Hippolyta, Geryon, Erythea, Eurytion, Iphitus, Omphale, Antaeus, Deianira, Herculean.

3. How does the story of Hercules account for the ancient name for Gibraltar? Where, according to your map of Africa, did Atlas probably live?

4. Explain the meaning of the following phrases: "great as a labor of Hercules," "a Herculean task," "as bad as cleansing the Augean stables," "the choice of Hercules," "to gain renewed strength from Mother Earth," "an infant Hercules," "hydra-headed evils."

5. According to one account some Spanish explorers, moving up a great river of South America, encountered a race of female warriors. What river was it?

RAPID QUIZ

Who was, throughout his life, the constant enemy of Hercules? How did she show her hatred while he was still an infant? Why is Hercules sometimes called "Alcides"? Who were some of his teachers? What was the great fault of the character of Hercules? The skin of what lion did he wear as his garment? What was "the choice of Hercules"? Who was his first wife? Why did he impose a sentence of penance on himself? What was it? How many tasks did Eurystheus set him? Name them. Describe each in a sentence. When, later in his life, did madness return on him? What penance did he set himself? What great martyr did Hercules free? Who was Antaeus, and what remarkable faculty did he have? How did Hercules overcome him? Who was Deianira? How did Hercules through her come to his death? What boon did Jupiter bestow on him?

For Students of Latin

1. Which is the Latin form: *Hercules* or *Herakles?*
2. Why was Hercules such a favorite with the Romans? Would his choice of roads appeal to those of true Roman character? Mention some examples of the affection they had for him.
3. What was the supposed connection between Mark Antony and Hercules? How did Antony show his pride in this connection?
4. Answer in Latin two or three of the questions in the Rapid Quiz.

Reading List

Plays, Poems, and Music

Euripides: *The Mad Hercules*
Handel, G. F.: *Heracles* [oratorio]
Lang, Andrew: Theocritus' *Idyl XIII*
Lodge, George Cabot: *Herakles*
Morris, William: *The Golden Apples*
Ovid: *Deianira to Hercules* (in *Heroines*)
Saint-Saëns, Camille: *Le Rouet d'Omphale* [symphonic poem]

JASON

"From the cave of Chiron I am come home," said Jason. — PINDAR

XII

THE GOLDEN FLEECE

And her sunny locks
Hung on her temples like a golden fleece.
— SHAKESPEARE

HOW JASON SOUGHT A KINGDOM

There lived in Iolcus in Thessaly a king named Aeson, who grew tired of ruling. His son Jason was still too young to wear the crown and so Aeson appointed his half brother Pelias as regent, with the understanding that when Jason came of age, Pelias would surrender the reins of government into his hands. Meanwhile, Aeson entrusted the education of Jason to the centaur Chiron; and he himself retired to a distant village.

The years went by, and Pelias grew ever more secure in his power. He thought but carelessly of his promise to

Aeson and of the lad Jason, and to himself and to his powerful army of followers he was the king of Iolcus.   Nor was his
rule a kindly one.   Yet at moments there came doubts into
his mind.   To still his half-formed misgivings Pelias resolved
to consult an oracle.   This strange answer was given to him :
   "Fear a man wearing only one sandal !"
   Pelias was mystified by this reply, but resolved to wait and
see what time brought forth.   Now it happened that on the
occasion of a great feast to Neptune, Pelias sent out invitations far and wide, urging everyone to participate.   At the
very time when preparations for the feast were being made,
Jason, grown into a strong and clever young man, had made
up his mind to seek out his uncle and claim the throne that
was his due.   He traveled many days and just before he
came to Iolcus, he saw before him a swift and dangerous
stream.
   Undaunted, he started to cross it and had almost come to
the other side when his foot caught in a projecting rock.
He managed to free himself, but when he reached dry land,
he saw that one of his sandals was missing.   Shrugging his
shoulders, he made the rest of the journey toward the city
without stopping to obtain another sandal.
   It was thus, then, that he came into the presence of King
Pelias, who sat on his throne in the public square in the midst
of revelers.   Straight toward him walked Jason and bowed
respectfully.
   "Hail, king !" he cried.   As he spoke he stretched toward
Pelias his right hand, on one finger of which blazed a magnificent ruby ring that Aeson had bidden Chiron keep for his
son as a sign of his kingly authority.
   Pelias started as he saw and recognized the king's jewel,
but his mind was even more troubled as he glanced downward

and saw that Jason wore but a single sandal. Yet he dissembled his fears and pretended to welcome his nephew with joy. Day after day went by, however, and Pelias made no attempt to surrender his crown to Jason. At last Jason boldly reminded him that by right of inheritance he, not Pelias, was the ruler of Iolcus.

"When will you give up your authority, good uncle?" he asked.

For a time Pelias was silent, pondering what means he could use to get rid of this dangerous youth. He dared not slay him, for already the citizens of the city welcomed the idea of having the son of the kindly Aeson as king, in place of the unscrupulous Pelias.

"Nephew," replied Pelias at length, "it has not seemed to me fitting that a youth without experience, one untested in the ways and wiles of the world, should take over this great rule. Would it not be better, think you, to seek first an apprenticeship in danger and hardship? Then shall you be indeed a wise and noble king."

Now Jason was only too anxious to go forth adventuring before he settled down to the humdrum cares of government. This idea appealed to him very much, and he cried eagerly:

"Set me a task, then, to prove me! I will do whatever you bid!"

Pelias smiled to himself as he saw how Jason, with the overeagerness of youth, had delivered himself into his hands. He replied smoothly:

"Only one quest is fitting for so bold a youth as you — the quest of the Golden Fleece. Bring me that shining trophy, and I shall know you are destined to rule over Iolcus in my stead."

Pelias thought he had rid himself of Jason forever by sending him on this quest.   The Golden Fleece was the skin of a
wonderful ram which Mercury, many years before, had given
to Queen Nephele to carry her two children, Phrixus and
Helle, to safety, when they were threatened with death.   The
two children were placed upon this ram, which, vaulting into

British Museum

BUILDING OF THE "ARGO" UNDER THE SUPERVISION OF
MINERVA

Whose keel of wondrous length the skillful hand
Of Argus fashioned. — DYER

the air, immediately began to travel magically through the
air toward the east.   But while over the strait that separates
Europe from Asia, Helle lost her hold and fell off; and for
many ages after, this stream was called the Hellespont (now
it is the Dardanelles).   The ram landed Phrixus safely in
Colchis, where he was received kindly by the king.   The boy

later sacrificed the ram to Jupiter, but he gave the Golden Fleece to the king, who placed it in a sacred grove, under the care of a sleepless dragon.

It was this treasure that Jason now started out to win; and he went ahead with eager joy in his great adventure. He employed Argus, the best shipbuilder of the time, to fashion for him a vessel with places for fifty rowers. Minerva sent Jason a beam made of the wood of a sacred oak; and from it was fashioned a marvelous figurehead that had the power of speech. When the vessel was finished, it was named the *Argo* and those who sailed in it were called *Argonauts*. No common crew would Jason take with him on his voyage. He sent invitations to all the heroes of Greece to join him, and when they learned what hazards he had undertaken to face, they came forward eagerly.

So upon his quest there went with him Castor and Pollux, those twins who later became the gods of boxing and wrestling;[1] Orpheus, divine bard, not yet descended to Hades; Zetes and Calaïs, speedy runners; Hercules; the hunter Arcas and the huntress Atalanta; Nestor, wise in council; Peleus and Telamon, youthful warriors; Admetus, later a king and master of Apollo; Theseus, and many others.

THE VOYAGE OF THE *ARGO*

It was on a fair day that Jason set sail from Iolcus, and on the shore stood many who shouted farewell and good luck to him. Swift as birds they sailed on, and after many days came to Lemnos, where only women dwelt and did all the work. Leaving this land, they came at length to the nation

---

[1] Sacred to Castor and Pollux was that strange electric glow sometimes seen on the spars of a ship, today called *St. Elmo's Fire* or *corposant*. The twins were often called *Dioscuri*, "sons of Zeus."

of the Doliones, who at first received them suspiciously but later treated them as friends.

It is said that in the region of the Black Sea they lost Hercules and another of the crew by a strange chance. Some of the oars of the vessel had in one way or another been broken, and Hercules went ashore to find wood out of which

Thorvaldsen   *Copenhagen Museum*

HILAS AND THE NYMPHS

The nymphs all clung to his hand, for love of the lad had fluttered the soft hearts of all of them. — THEOCRITUS

to make new oars. With him went a lad named Hylas, who was his squire and whom he loved as if he were his own son. Hercules became thirsty, and he bade Hylas go to the nearest stream and draw water for him.

Hylas came to a little woodland pool, shaded by tall trees and fringed by delicate and fragrant flowers. As he bent down to draw water for his pitcher the nymphs who lived in the stream saw him, and were at once fascinated by his beauty, for there never lived a boy handsomer than Hylas. Swiftly they rose from the pool, and gently they took him by the hand, and soothingly they invited him to their under-water grottoes. Their voices like waters murmuring and leaves rustling lulled Hylas into a will-less slumber, and slowly pulled him down into the embracing waves, which gave him up no more.

But Hercules, when Hylas failed to return, sought for him frantically through the woods, and would not cease from his searching for all the remonstrances of the other heroes. At last they had to leave Hercules behind, and he after many days of vain questing for Hylas made his way back sorrow-fully to Greece.

Soon the heroes came to another country, the king of which took a cruel delight in his great skill in boxing. He made it a condition of his hospitality that every stranger who came to his land must engage in a boxing bout with him. Usually the match ended in the death of the stranger, for the king was both strong and skillful. Now he imposed this condition on the Argonauts, and bade them choose a champion among themselves.

"Perhaps later," he boasted, "you will need to choose still another."

But the Argonauts did not have to debate whom to send against this king. Pollux had a skill in boxing that came to him from the gods. The bout between him and the king did not last long, and in a short time the royal bully had suffered the fate he had meted out to so many others. The people of his land, however, did not like the outcome very much, and immediately attacked the Argonauts, who were obliged to slay a great many of them before they could get back to their ship.

Soon the voyagers came to a country where lived a seer named Phineus. Phineus had been cruel to his own family, and the gods had punished him by blinding him and trans-

PHINEAS AND THE HARPIES

'Tis here the filthy Harpies make their nest;
Broad wings have they, and necks and faces human.

— DANTE

porting him to a barren land inhabited by two monsters. These creatures were called Harpies — their bodies and heads were like those of women, but their feet and wings were like those of ravens; and their names were Storm-Foot and Swift-Wing. These Harpies waited until a meal was spread before Phineus by invisible hands. Then they seized the best part of the food and gobbled it up, and Phineus lived in perpetual hunger. He promised the Argonauts that he would give them advice concerning their voyage that would save them many hardships and dangers, if only they would free him from these fierce and noxious Harpies.

Now Zetes and Calaïs of the crew were sons of Boreas, the North Wind, and they could move as swiftly as the wind because they truly had the wind's wings. They promised Phineus their help if he would swear kindness forever after to his own kin. He swore most solemnly. So they, when next the Harpies appeared, attacked them in the air, and after a lengthy battle drove them away. In gratitude Phineus told the Argonauts that they would soon come to two dangerous rocks, called the Symplegades or the Clashing Islands, and he advised them how they might pass them; and he gave them other wise counsel.

In half a day the Argonauts came to the rocks of which Phineus had warned them, and indeed they were very wonderful and very dangerous. For these rocks were not fastened to the bottom of the sea, but ever moved about and ever crashed together; and no one could tell when their dread meeting would take place. But Jason, as Phineus had bidden him, released a dove as the rocks began to move toward each other; and the dove just barely managed to get through as the rocks crashed. As the rocks rebounded swiftly the heroes urged the *Argo* onward; and with speed equal to that of the dove the vessel passed between. As the heroes looked back, they saw that the rocks no longer moved apart and no longer sailed over the face of the ocean. For it had been prophesied that if ever a ship should pass in safety between the rocks, the rocks would thereafter become rooted to the bottom of the sea.

WINNING THE GOLDEN FLEECE

Not long after this event the *Argo* reached Colchis. Jason threw out anchors of stone and then landed among the wondering crowds on the shore, who never had beheld so great a ship. He commanded that he be taken to the king, Aeëtes. The monarch welcomed him, and bade him state his reason for coming to the land of Colchis.

"I have come for the Golden Fleece," said Jason, "for without it I cannot become ruler of my own land."

Then he explained to the king how Pelias had made it a condition for the surrender of his power to Jason that the latter must bring him the Golden Fleece.

Aeëtes was a man of craft, and he had no wish to deny bluntly Jason's request and so bring about an attack on his people by the heroes of the *Argo*. But he had not the slightest intention of giving it to him. He pondered awhile and replied thus to Jason's story :

"Young hero, do not think the Golden Fleece may be won by any one for the asking. Indeed, I do not believe that such is your thought, for you know that this trophy of the gods is surrounded by many perils. Listen then to the conditions on which you may win the fleece. Tomorrow you must harness the two bulls which Mars keeps in his temple, and you must then sow the dragon's teeth."

Jason agreed to undertake these two tasks, knowing in his heart that deadly danger probably accompanied both. That night, as he lay sleepless on the *Argo*, there appeared suddenly before him a slim maiden veiled in black. For a startled moment he thought that Minerva or another of the divine inhabitants of Olympus stood before him, but shortly a soft voice reassured him:

"I am Medea," said the veiled maiden, "daughter of King Aeëtes. I saw with compassion today how my father led you into a cunning trap, for never, without help, can you harness the bulls or sow the dragon's teeth. Yet I will help you, if you will accept my aid."

"Only help me," cried Jason eagerly, "and then escape with me to my country, and there you shall become my queen."

This thought, indeed, had been in the mind of Medea when she approached Jason, and now she assented gladly to his proposal.

"Here," she whispered to him, "is a magic ointment with which you must smear yourself. For a day you shall then be impervious to fire and invulnerable. The terrible bulls of Mars will, therefore, not be able to scorch you with the flames that they spout from their nostrils, nor able to hurt you with their brazen hoofs. As to the dragon's teeth, know you that from them will spring armed men, fierce with the lust of murder, and on them you must practice this stratagem."

And bending over Jason, she told him in low tones just what he must do to avoid the peril of the dragon's teeth.

Next day, then, the king and the people of the land assembled to see Jason undertake his two tasks. To the marvel and bewilderment of Aeëtes, the young Greek hero

Sichel

Gramstorff Bros.

MEDEA

Thrice she applies the power of magic prayer;
Thrice, hellward bending, mutters charms in air.
— APOLLONIUS RHODUS

went confidently into the grove of Mars and without difficulty harnessed the terrifying bulls to a plow, nor did he seem to heed the spouts of fire that played upon him from their nostrils.

From the king's trembling hand he took next a helmet full of dragon's teeth, and walking up and down sowed them in the furrows that he had made. Hardly were the teeth upon the earth when they took root, and out of the soil sprang fifty mighty warriors, each completely clad in steel and brandishing a sword. Their violent shouts made the heavens and the watching throngs tremble.

But, unseen by the warriors and by Aeëtes, Jason hurled a stone into their very midst. It fell with a loud clangor on the shield of the tallest warrior. Furious with anger he turned and glared at his neighbor, and before a word could be said, he went at him with his sword. All the others, eager for the combat, took sides, and in a few moments the earth shook with the blows given and received. But Jason, wherever he saw his opportunity, plunged into the combat with his sword, and it was not long before all the warriors lay dead upon the ground; and a sudden quiet reigned.

The king saw that Jason had defeated him in this first encounter and by some mysterious means had avoided the deadly trap he had planned for him. But he resolved that rather than see Jason secure the Golden Fleece he would kill him and his followers; and he devised an attack against the *Argo* at early dawn.

Medea guessed what was in her father's mind and had already laid plans to defeat him once more. In the dead of night the pair stole to the sacred grove where the Golden Fleece hung on a tree. Underneath slept the formidable dragon. Go as silently as they might, their light footsteps on the grass awakened him, and in a moment he was on guard, his ferocious head thrust forward with gaping rows of fangs. But when he heard the soothing voice of Medea, who was wont to feed him, he became fiercely attentive.

"Here," she said to him, "is a sop for you,' and she threw him some of his usual food, which he ate greedily.   Mixed

Gramstorff Bros.

JASON AND MEDEA SEIZE THE GOLDEN FLEECE

Slow from the groaning branch the Fleece was rent. — FLACCUS

with it was a sleeping potion and hardly had he gulped down the sweet morsel when he fell on the ground asleep.

Hastily then Jason seized the precious fleece, and with Medea fled to the ship, where the heroes already awaited him at the oars.   The ship slid over the waves and out of the harbor, and by great efforts escaped the pursuing Aeëtes.

It is related of Jason and the Argonauts that on their return voyage they experienced other adventures, in one of which only the wondrous melodies of Orpheus saved them from the enchantments of the sirens.

When Jason returned to Iolcus and displayed the Golden Fleece to Pelias, his uncle still, on one pretext or another, refused to give up the throne to his nephew. The daughters of Pelias, knowing the great powers of Medea and deeming her a witch who had command over life and death, begged her to compound a magic potion that would make their father young again, a feat she had already accomplished with Jason's father, Aeson. She pretended to agree, but gave them instead a deadly poison which killed Pelias. Jason thereupon became king. He offered up the *Argo* to Neptune as a sacrifice, but the Golden Fleece he hung in a temple of Minerva, that young men might come forever and gaze upon it and be inspired to adventures as brave as his had been.

STUDY APPLICATION

The Myths in Literature

The quest of Jason in search of the Golden Fleece makes such a unified, well-balanced subject that it has attracted several epic poets. In ancient times Apollonius of Rhodes wrote the *Argonautica*. In the eighteenth century John Dyer wrote *The Fleece*. But best of all the poems on the Golden Fleece is William Morris's *The Life and Death of Jason*.

The figure of Medea, often conceived of as a sort of witch or wonder-worker, has always attracted much attention; and Euripides wrote a famous play about her, and in her behalf Ovid wrote a letter in the *Heroines*, supposedly from her to Jason.

An interesting modern treatment in prose of the Jason story is that of the Irish writer Padraic Colum in *The Golden Fleece*.

References to Mythology in Literature

1. In such a glen, on such a day,
   On Pelion, on the grassy ground,
   Chiron, the aged centaur, lay. — *Arnold*

2. He could, perhaps, have passed the *Hellespont.* — *Byron*
3. In quest of golden cargo brave Jason and his band
   Upon the good ship *Argo* sailed to the Colchian strand. — *Graves*
4. "This boy rows us as well without learning, as if he could sing
   the song of Orpheus to the *Argonauts.*"
   — *Dr. Johnson in Boswell's "Life of Dr. Johnson."*
5.   The *Argonauts,* in blind amaze,
   Tossing about in Neptune's restless ways. — *Keats*
6. The sight of sleek, well-fed blue-coat boys in pictures was little
   consolatory to us, who saw the better part of our provisions
   carried away before our eyes by *harpies.* — *Lamb.*
7. And the ram that bore unsafely the burden of Helle. — *Longfellow*
8. Never was Hercules apart from *Hylas.* — *Theocritus*
9. These are the flowers which mourning Herakles
   Strewed on the tomb of *Hylas.* — *Wilde*

Exercises in Composition, Oral and Written

1. Give a talk on the geography of the story of the quest of the
Golden Fleece. Illustrate your remarks by pointing out on a map
the places mentioned — a map drawn by yourself, if possible.
2. Medea keeps a diary. Write a half-dozen brief passages that
she might have written in this, after the coming of Jason.
3. Invent another adventure that the Argonauts might have had
before reaching Colchis (150 words).
4. On his way home Hercules had some interesting experiences.
After he reaches home, have him tell a friend about one of them.
5. Give a talk or prepare an essay on "Shipbuilding among the
Ancient Greeks." Your school or community librarian will refer you
to useful books. There is some interesting information in the article
on warships in *The New Larned History,* volume xi, pages 9558 f.

Word Study

1. The word *Argonaut* has, as one meaning, this definition: "one
who went gold-seeking in California in 1849." Explain how this
meaning originated. What does *naut* mean?
2. We sometimes speak of a wise man as a "Nestor." Why?

3. Give the correct pronunciation of the following words:

Iolcus, Aeson, Nephele, Phrixus, Helle, Colchis, Zetes, Calaïs, Peleus, Doliones, Phineus, Symplegades, Aeëtes, Medea.

4. What is a Hellene? What is the meaning of *Hellenic*? Where is the Hellespont? How did the Greeks explain the origin of these words?

RAPID QUIZ

Who was the father of Jason? What trust did his father give to Jason's uncle? What happened when Jason came of age? How did Pelias try to get rid of Jason? What quest did Jason undertake? What preparations did he made? What was the name of his vessel? Who were some of his companions? What mischance removed Hercules from the crew? How did Pollux show his prowess? How did the sons of the North Wind serve Phineus, and what help did he give in return? How did the Argonauts get past the Symplegades? What conditions did King Aeëtes lay on Jason before he could take the Golden Fleece? Who offered Jason her help? How did Jason escape the danger of the bulls of Mars? How did he overcome the armed men that sprang from the dragon's teeth? How did he overcome the guardian of the fleece? What happened to Pelias on the return of Jason with Medea? What did Jason do with the *Argo?*

FOR STUDENTS OF LATIN

1. Why, in your judgment, would the Romans of the Republic have less admiration for Jason than they had for Hercules? Would the Romans of the Empire like him better?

2. Retell briefly in Latin one episode in Jason's career.

3. Answer in Latin one or two questions in the Rapid Quiz.

READING LIST

Poems and Plays

Colum, Padraic: *The Golden Fleece* (in prose)
Euripides: *Medea*
Morris, William: *The Life and Death of Jason*
Ovid: *Medea to Jason* (in *Heroines*)
Taylor, Bayard: *Hylas.*

JUNO AND MINERVA ASSIST GREEKS

Now when the white-armed goddess Hera marked the Trojans making havoc
of the Greeks, she spake winged words to Athena. — HOMER

XIII

THE TROJAN WAR

Was this the face that launch'd a thousand ships,
And burnt the topless towers of Ilium? — MARLOWE

THE JUDGMENT OF PARIS

One of the most beautiful of the Nereids was the silvery-
footed Thetis, who dwelt with her sisters in the depths of the
sea, but was a favorite of Juno and often visited the heights of
Olympus. So lovely was she that both Jupiter and Neptune
wished to marry her, but the oracles declared that her son
would be greater than his father, and neither of the deities
dared risk being overthrown. She was therefore given in
marriage to a mortal, Peleus, king of the Myrmidons of
Phthia in Thessaly.

To the marriage festival of Peleus and Thetis came the gods, bringing many lovely gifts. But one deity had not been invited to the celebrations — *Eris*, or *Atë*, the goddess of discord. She was greatly enraged at the oversight, and resolved that she would take revenge. While the merry-making was at its height, therefore, she suddenly appeared in

JUDGMENT OF PARIS

Ere yet her speech was finished, he consign'd
To her soft hand the fruit of burnish'd rind. — COLUTHUS

the midst of the revelers and threw upon the ground a wonder-ful apple, brought from the Garden of the Hesperides, and labeled "For the Fairest."

Immediately a contention arose as to who should have the apple. All the contestants, finally, withdrew, except three: Juno, Venus, and Minerva. They appealed to Jupiter to settle the dispute and award the apple, but he wisely declined to do so. He agreed, nevertheless, to appoint an arbitrator, and told the three goddesses that Paris of Troy would make the decision.[1]

To Paris then the goddesses repaired. Troy was a city in Asia Minor founded by Dardanus; it was sometimes called Ilion or Ilium. Near by flowed the River Simois. Priam reigned over Troy. He had been twice married, the second time to Hecuba, and had fifty sons, two of whom were of particular note: Hector, one of the noblest heroes of ancient times, and Paris, who was destined to cause the destruction of his people. Another Trojan hero equal to these in renown was Aeneas, son of Venus and a mortal, Anchises.

At the birth of Paris it had been prophesied that he would bring disaster to Troy, and he had consequently been exposed on a mountain side. But some shepherds had found him and had brought him up, and he was at this time a very handsome and attractive youth.

The three goddesses came to him as he tended his sheep. They told him that he must decide which of them was the fairest, to which of them should go the Golden Apple. Each whispered secretly how she would reward him if he gave her the apple. Juno promised him great power and happiness in his domestic life. Minerva assured him of wisdom and of respect from everyone. But Venus promised him the most beautiful woman in the world for his wife, and Paris handed the Golden Apple to Venus. He gained her favor, but won for himself and the Trojans the undying hatred of Juno and Minerva.

There was no doubt as to who was the most beautiful woman then living. She was Helen, daughter of Leda and of

---

[1] This was what the Greeks called a *kallisteion*, or beauty contest. But some ancients interpreted the episode as rather a choice of gifts offered to Paris. The three goddesses were gift-givers; among them Paris had to choose, just as Hercules, in the story already related, had to make a choice of roads.

Jupiter, who had appeared to Leda in the form of a swan, and sister of the great athletes, Castor and Pollux. Even as a child she had inspired almost awe-struck admiration because of her surpassing loveliness. When she passed into girlhood the foremost chieftains of Greece sought her in marriage, and for a time it seemed as if the rivalry for her hand would bring about a deadly war. Among these chieftains, however, there was one very wise man, Ulysses (Greek : Odysseus).

Ulysses proposed that all the suitors of Helen take a solemn oath, not only pledging themselves to abide peacefully by whatever decision she made, but also agreeing that if ever anyone attempted to molest either Helen or her husband, all the others would help him and punish the aggressor. To this oath all the chieftains agreed, and thereupon Helen chose as her husband Menelaus, king of Sparta, whose brother was Agamemnon, king of Mycenae and the most powerful ruler in Greece.

For a time matters rested as they were. Then Paris reminded Venus of her promise, and she bade him go to Greece and visit Sparta. There, with the help of the goddess, Paris induced Helen to elope with him, and the pair returned hastily to Troy. Before this Priam had acknowledged Paris as his son; and now when he returned with Helen, he received them in his home, but reluctantly, for he guessed what troubles were in store for him and his people.

GATHERING OF THE HOSTS

As soon as the abduction of Helen took place, Menelaus sent hasty word to all the heroes who had wooed Helen and called on them for a fulfillment of their pledge. He told them

von Deutsch

THE ABDUCTION OF HELEN

Such Helen was! and who can blame the boy
That in so bright a flame consumed his Troy?

— WALLER

she held him.   He had spent his boyhood receiving a manly
education from the centaur Chiron.

To keep her son out of the Greek army Thetis sent the
young hero to stay with his uncle, who was bidden to disguise
him in women's clothes.   Ulysses learned where he was hiding, and went to the palace as a peddler.   On his trays were
many articles such as appeal to women, but mingled with

Gramstorff Bros.

ULYSSES FEIGNING MADNESS

Ulysses, skilled in every form of shrewd device. — HOMER

them were a sword and a buckler.   As he spread out his
wares before the royal maidens, he noticed that one of them
disregarded the ribbons and the linens and fingered the sword
eagerly.   So he penetrated the disguise of Achilles, and soon
he persuaded the lad to accompany him back to Aulis.

Finally, the Greek army was delayed by an impiety committed unwittingly by Agamemnon.   While out hunting he
slew a stag that was sacred to Diana.   In revenge she afflicted
the Greek army with a plague.   Oracles declared the cause

ACHILLES' EDUCATION BY CHIRON

He is the sea-woman's child
Chiron instructed. — H. D.

of the plague and said that Diana would not be satisfied until Agamemnon's daughter, Iphigenia, was sacrificed upon her

SACRIFICE OF IPHIGENIA

The bright death quiver'd at the victim's throat.
— TENNYSON

altar. Much against his will and in deep sorrow Agamemnon sent for his daughter. He knew that his wife, Clytemnestra, would never let her come to Aulis if she were told that her daughter was to die, and so he bade the messengers tell her that Iphigenia was about to be married to Achilles. When Iphigenia arrived, the bitter tidings were told her, but she bore her fate bravely. On the appointed day she was placed on the altar, and the priest of Diana approached to slay her. Without letting anyone see what was happening, however, Diana substituted a hart for the maiden, and transported her swiftly to the land of the Tauri, where she became a priestess of the goddess. Here in later years she saved her brother Orestes from death and fled with him back to Greece.

THE WAR AGAINST TROY

Now the army sailed in an endless fleet. The Trojans opposed their landing, but in vain, for the Greek numbers were overwhelming. At the very outset a noble Greek made a patriotic sacrifice. There was an oracle that the side that lost the first man would win the war. Protesilaüs, a Greek leader, threw himself into the thick of the fighting and was almost at once killed. When the news of his death reached his wife Laodamia, she asked the gods for permission to converse with him if only for three hours. The gods, in pity, allowed her husband, in charge of Mercury, to visit the upper world again, but when Protesilaüs died, the second time, Laodamia died with him.

The Trojans finally withdrew behind the city walls, and prepared to stand siege, a siege that lasted for ten years. For the first nine years the war was indecisive, victory coming sometimes to the Greeks and sometimes to the Trojans. The gods and goddesses were as much interested in the matter as the actual combatants, and some of them espoused the Greek, some the Trojan side. Venus, as we know, favored the Trojans, and so too did Mars. Juno and Minerva of course favored the Greeks, and with them sided Neptune. Apollo sometimes helped one, sometimes the other. Jupiter tried to be neutral, but for various reasons was sometimes obliged to intervene.

The chief Trojan heroes were Hector and Aeneas, but among those that came to aid Priam was Prince Memnon, son of Aurora and Tithonus, who was ruler of the Ethiopians. He was regarded as the handsomest of all living men, but he, in no great time, was slain by Achilles. It was said that his mother was inconsolable, and wept for him every morning.

In the tenth year the Trojan War approached a climax; and it is a part of this year that the greatest of ancient poets, Homer, describes in the first of his two masterpieces, the *Iliad*. For the most part Homer deals with an episode that caused a great deal of trouble to the Greeks, but ultimately brought about the downfall of the mainstay of the Trojans, the hero Hector.

It all began with a quarrel between Agamemnon and Achilles over a division of the spoils of war. Achilles retired to his tent and sulked, and absolutely refused to come and fight for the Greeks. His mother, meanwhile, went to Jupiter and implored him to allow the Trojans to win for a while, as a punishment for the insult offered to her son. Jupiter consented, despite the anger of Juno; and the Greeks, although Menelaus defeated Paris in personal combat and the Trojan was saved from death only by the intervention of Venus, were soon defeated by the prowess of Hector. For he left his noble wife Andromache and his dearly beloved infant son, Astyanax, and went forth to battle. So hard did he press the Greeks that Agamemnon even proposed that they should all re-embark and return to Greece. Nestor, however, suggested that an embassy should be sent to Achilles, bearing gifts and imploring him to return to help them. This was done, but Achilles refused to fight.

Now the Greeks were obliged to build ramparts to protect themselves against the onslaughts of the Trojans. Dolon, a Trojan spy who managed to get within the Greek lines, was discovered by Ulysses and slain. Hector, wounded by a huge stone hurled at him by Ajax, was stretched senseless on the field but not even this setback sufficed to stay the Trojans. At this critical moment Nestor was able to persuade Patroclus, the dearest friend of Achilles, to borrow the armor of his friend.

Achilles, moved by the defeats that the Greeks were suffering, even consented to let him lead his own Myrmidons into battle.

Patroclus and the Myrmidons at once plunged into the contest. The Trojans, beholding the famous armor of Achilles,

Maignan

HECTOR'S FAREWELL TO ANDROMACHE

So spake glorious Hector, and stretched out his arm to his boy.

— HOMER

thought that the great hero had returned to help the Greeks and fled in terror. The Greek soldiers, inspired by the turn of events, performed mighty deeds of valor. Hector himself had to turn and flee.

In the course of the battle Patroclus at last came face to face with Sarpedon, grandson of Bellerophon and son of Jupiter himself. Jupiter could not intervene, and in the combat that ensued Sarpedon was slain, and a furious battle arose for the possession of his body. The king of the gods, however, snatched the body from the field, and conveyed it to the hero's native land, where it was given honorable burial.

But now the tide of battle turned. Patroclus had swept onward in his victorious course, when suddenly Hector confronted him. Both heroes at first fought from their chariots, but shortly they contended on the level ground, giving and taking fierce blows. Not against the greatest of the Trojans, however, could Patroclus contend, and in a little while he fell, mortally wounded by the spear of Hector. Even greater than the combat over the body of Sarpedon was that over the body of Patroclus. Hector managed to secure the magnificent armor, and he retired immediately to a little distance and put it on in place of his own. The Greeks fought desperately to retain the body, and at last succeeded in bearing it away to their ships.

Detail from a vase

VULCAN AND THETIS

Thetis found him there
Sweating and toiling, and with busy hand
Plying the bellows. — HOMER

When Achilles heard what had happened to Patroclus, he was desperate with grief. His groans reached the ears of Thetis, who came hastily to him and tried to console him. He wished to go at once in search of Hector, but his mother persuaded him that he must have suitable armor, and she promised to bring it to him by the morrow. Hastening to Vulcan, she begged him to make for her son an armor such as no man had ever worn before, and to do it before dawn broke. Vulcan laid aside all his other labors and turned to the fashioning of the armor. When it was completed, it was a miracle of craftsmanship, contrived to serve all purposes of war and yet ornamented with beautiful art. This armor Thetis conveyed to her son.

Arrayed in this armor, Achilles left his tent and called the chiefs to council. He made peace with Agamemnon, and arranged to lead the Greek hosts out to battle immediately. The Trojans fled in fear before him, and even Hector, cautioned by Apollo, avoided an encounter with him. But Aeneas, the Trojan hero, was willing to undertake a duel to the death with Achilles, and had already lifted up a huge stone to hurl at him, when Neptune in pity intervened and spread a cloud between the two warriors. All the followers of Priam hastily returned to the gates of the city, barely in time to escape the avenging blows of Achilles.

Hector awaited Achilles on the wind-swept plain outside the city. From the walls his father and mother called to him, and begged him to seek safety. But he felt that upon him more than upon any other rested the welfare in war of his people. Yet when Achilles approached, terrible as Mars in his shining armor, even Hector was filled with terror and fled. Round the walls of Troy, Greek pursued Trojan, but at last Hector stayed his flight and hurled a spear at Achilles. Harmless it fell from the shield of the Greek hero, and Hector lifted his falchion and rushed at Achilles. As he came nearer Achilles measured with his eye a spot where the armor left Hector's neck uncovered, and there he delivered the fatal blow. Hector fell lifeless on the plains of Troy, before the eyes of his people.

For a time Achilles vented his rage on the body of the Trojan hero. He attached the corpse to his chariot and dragged it in triumph around the walls of Troy. But when Priam in secret embassy approached Achilles and reminded him of his aged father Peleus, he at last consented to allow the body of Hector to be taken to Troy for burial. Meanwhile for Patroclus splendid funeral rites were held, accompanied by funeral games that continued for many days, in accordance with the custom of the Greeks.

THE STRATAGEM OF THE WOODEN HORSE

Not even then did Troy fall. Among those who at this time came to the assistance of the Trojans was Penthesilea, queen of the Amazons and noted for her youth and beauty. It was her fate to be slain by Achilles, but the Greek hero, gazing on her dead body, sincerely mourned for her. Thersites, a deformed and disagreeable leader of the Greeks who made a habit of sneering at his fellows, mocked at the grief of Achilles. The latter, in wrath, felled him with a blow that killed him.

For weary weeks the siege of the city continued, and it was not long before Achilles himself was killed. Paris, who somehow had learned of the vulnerable heel of the hero, discharged at him a poisoned arrow, from the effects of which he died.

When Achilles fell, his body was rescued by Ulysses and Ajax. Thetis directed the Greeks to give her son's armor to the hero thought by the rest to deserve it most. Ulysses and Ajax were the only contenders, and the decision was that the former should have the wonderful armor. When he heard what had happened, Ajax went mad, and sought everywhere for Ulysses, that he might slay him. But Minerva protected the Ithacan hero, and turned the insane rage of Ajax against some cattle and sheep, a number of whom Ajax killed; others he led captive to his tent. When

THE HORSES OF ACHILLES

Then terribly Achilles called upon his horses: "Xanthos and Balios, take heed to bring your charioteer safe back." But Xanthos of the glancing feet made answer: "Yea verily for this hour we will bear thee safe, yet is thy death nigh at hand." — HOMER

he recovered from his fit of insanity and saw what he had done, he committed suicide by falling on his sword.

The example having been given, the Greeks now used poisoned arrows against the Trojans, especially some that Hercules himself had given to Philoctetes, a Greek leader; and one of the first victims was Paris himself. Not long after his death Helen married his brother Deiphobus. Among the innumerable prophecies relating to the fall of Troy was one that proclaimed the city invulnerable so long as a certain statue of Minerva remained in Troy. So, one night, Ulysses and Diomedes entered the city in disguise and carried off this "Palladium."

And still Troy was not captured. Then in desperation the Greeks resolved to adopt a stratagem suggested by the crafty Ulysses. Looking out from the walls of their city, the Trojans saw with wonder one day how the Greeks were making busy preparations to leave. Everywhere the tents were struck, the ships made ready, supplies gathered together. Shortly not a Greek was left on the plains of Troy.

For a time the Trojans hesitated. Then with cries of joy they ran out of the gates of the city. The foremost paused, however, in bewilderment as they saw before them a great wooden horse. They gazed at it from every side and wondered what its purpose could be. But a priest of Neptune, named Laocoön, angrily addressed them and urged them to burn the wooden horse at once.

"It surely is some trick of the foe," he said. "I fear the Greeks even when they come bearing gifts."

At his very words there came from the sea two immense serpents. The people fled to left and right, but the serpents paid no heed to them. Straight for Laocoön they made, and cast their folds not only around him, but around his two children who stood beside him.   Shortly all lay dead upon the ground, and the snakes wound their way back to the sea and disappeared.

Of course the Trojans took this as a significant sign that the gods were punishing Laocoön for impiety.   Just then some in

Motte   *Corcoran Art Gallery*

THE WOODEN HORSE

The Greeks, with the help of Pallas Athena's divine skill, erected a Horse, huge as a mountain. — VIRGIL

the crowd dragged forward a captive — obviously a Greek. He told them that his name was Sinon, that he had been left behind by accident, that the wooden horse (built, he said, by the artificer Epeus) was an offering to Minerva, and that it had been made so monstrous in size especially in order to prevent the Trojans from carrying it within the city and so regaining the favor of the goddess.   To make his tale more plausible, he related a wily story about how much Ulysses

LAOCOÖN

Now turning to the Vatican go see
Laocoön's torture dignifying pain.
— BYRON

hated him, and how he had been selected as a sacrifice to Apollo, but had escaped just in time.

With a shout the people laid hold of the great wooden horse and dragged it toward the walls of the city. There busy hands already hewed and hacked at the wall, in order to open a space large enough for the wooden horse to enter.

TROJAN FUGITIVES

There will come a day when sacred Ilium shall be no more. — HOMER

Then the horse was dragged toward the center of the city, and toward it turned the eyes of revelers all through that noisy day of celebration.

At last came night and with it quiet. A cunningly concealed door in the wooden horse was opened by Sinon, and out stole the armed men who had lain hidden within. Quickly they ran to the gates of the city and opened them wide to the Greek hosts, who had returned from the sheltering cliffs of a near-by island. Priam and his people were awakened by the strident yells of warriors, under the leadership of Pyrrhus, son of Achilles, and arose to find their city in the hands of the Greeks.

On that night Priam and many other noble Trojans were slain. By the hand of Menelaus fell Deiphobus; and Helen, who since the death of Paris had aided the Greeks on a number of occasions, was reconciled to her husband, who forgave her disloyalty as really due to the urging of Venus. Aeneas, although his wife Creüsa died in the wreck of the city, was able to save his aged father and his young son. Many of the Trojan women were carried off as captives to Greece, and the city was left a heap of ruins.

STUDY APPLICATION

The Myths in Literature

Of all the great "matter of Greece and Rome" the deepest and most lasting impression has undoubtedly been made by the story of Helen of Troy, with all the remarkable incidents that followed in the train of her abduction by Paris.

In Greek literature itself the greatest of Greek poets, Homer, devoted to the subject his masterpieces, the *Iliad* and the *Odyssey*. The greatest of Latin poets, Virgil, took the Trojan War and its consequences for one man, Aeneas, as the theme of his *Aeneid*, the Roman national epic. Again and again the other poets of classical antiquity selected one aspect or another of the same war and its aftermath as the subject of their writings.

In the Middle Ages and during the Renaissance period the attention paid to this theme was scarcely less. The references to Helen and her contemporaries are innumerable. Chaucer, the greatest of English poets before Shakespeare, wrote a novel in verse about certain incidents of the Trojan War. The same incidents suggested to Shakespeare himself the plot of a play. Into the translation of Homer, George Chapman, a contemporary of Shakespeare, put energy and ability equal to the production of an original work; and since his time one rendering after another of Homer has appeared — several excellent ones, like those of George H. Palmer, C. A. Pease, and T. E. Lawrence, in recent years.

Upon the poets of all times Helen of Troy has exercised her fascination. Homer himself never directly describes the famous beauty, but he tells how the old men of Troy, watching her walk past them, gazed upon her beauty and declared that it was no wonder that a war had been waged for her. Since Homer the poets and dramatists of all literatures have again and again endeavored to picture her, concretely or by suggestion.

Unquestionably the most magnificent of these pictures occurs in Marlowe's play, *Dr. Faustus*. The magician, by his magic arts, has called up the shade of Helen, and looking upon her beauty he exclaims in ecstasy:

> O thou art fairer than the evening air
> Clad in the beauty of a thousand stars!

and again:

> Was this the face that launch'd a thousand ships,
> And burnt the topless towers of Ilium?
> Sweet Helen, make me immortal with a kiss!

The greatest of German poets, Goethe, in addition to writing a play, one of his finest, about Iphigenia, also made Helen one of the most important figures of the second part of *Faust*.

Edgar Allan Poe, again, reached the very height of his genius in the lyric, *To Helen*. This was addressed to a living person, Mrs. Jane Stanard, but the whole inspiration of the verses is Greek, and the memory of the Greek heroine and of Ulysses fills the opening stanza:

> Helen, thy beauty is to me
>   Like those Nicaean barks of yore
> That gently o'er a perfumed sea
>   The weary wayworn wanderer bore
>   To his own native shore.

Tennyson, in *A Dream of Fair Women*, thus describes Helen:

> A daughter of the gods, divinely tall,
>   And most divinely fair.

To Shakespeare she was

> . . . a theme of honor and renown,
> A spur to valiant and magnanimous deeds;

and he thought of her, too, as

> . . . a Grecian queen, whose youth and freshness
> Wrinkles Apollo's, and makes stale the morning.

Of the other figures of the Trojan War Ulysses has received most attention, and of what poets and dramatists have done with him, more will be said in the next chapter. Catullus and "H. D." have written of Thetis, Robert Bridges and George Santayana of Achilles, Euripides of Iphigenia and of Hecuba, Sophocles of Ajax; Ovid, Landor, and Tennyson of handsome Paris. In French literature Racine wrote two of his finest dramas on Andromache and Iphigenia.

References to Mythology in Literature

What do the following references mean? Where a word or phrase is italicized, explain only the word or phrase.

1. *Achilles* ponders in his tent. — *Arnold*
2. I've stood upon Achilles' tomb,
   And heard *Troy doubted;* time will doubt of Rome. — *Byron*
3. And, like another Helen, fires another Troy. — *Dryden*
4. So now he smiled and gazed at his boy silently, and *Andromache* stood by his side and wept. — *Homer*
5. *Helen's* lips are drifting dust;
   Ilion is consumed with rust. — *Knowles*
6. Better like Hector in the field to die,
   Than like a perfumed Paris turn and fly. — *Longfellow*
7. The tale of *Troy* divine. — *Milton*
8. And strike to dust th' imperial tow'rs of *Troy.* — *Pope*
9. Behold Pelides, with his yellow hair,
   Proud child of Thetis, hero beloved of Jove. — *Santayana*
10. There pleading might you see grave *Nestor* stand.
    — *Shakespeare*
11. Had doting *Priam* checked his son's desire,
    Troy had been bright with fame and not with fire. — *Shakespeare*

2. Her name was *Ate*, mother of debate
And all destruction. — *Spenser*

13. By trying, the Greeks got into Troy. — *Theocritus*

14. It was for thee gold-crested *Hector* tried
With *Thetis' child* that evil race to run. — *Wilde*

Exercises in Composition, Oral and Written

1. Memorize the following outline of the Trojan War:
   A. Causes of the War
       I. The marriage of Peleus and Thetis
       II. The judgment of Paris
       III. The marriage of Helen
       IV. The elopement of Helen and Paris
   B. Gathering of the Hosts
       I. The summoning of the Greek heroes
       II. Iphigenia at Aulis
       III. Important Greek leaders
       IV. Important Trojan leaders
   C. The War against Troy
       I. Early years of the war
       II. The quarrel of Achilles and Agamemnon
       III. The death of Patroclus
       IV. The death of Hector
       V. The death of Achilles and Paris
   D. The Capture of Troy
       I. The building of the wooden horse
       II. The death of Laocoön
       III. Bringing of the horse into Troy
       IV. The taking of the city

2. As one of the guests, describe the marriage feast of Peleus and Thetis.

3. One of the cousins of Achilles was present when Ulysses arrived in disguise as a peddler. She tells her father what happened.

4. You belong to the Myrmidons of Achilles. To a comrade in the Greek camp narrate the death of Patroclus.

5. In recent years excavations on the site of Troy have resulted in many interesting finds. Ask your librarian to help you secure

some facts as to these excavations, and tell about them in a talk to your class.

6. How did the Greeks dress? Prepare an essay on this subject. Any book on Greek life will help you — also *The New Larned History*, the article on costume, volume iii, page 2136.

Word Study

1. Give the correct pronunciation of the following words:

Eris, Priam, Leda, Odysseus, Menelaus, Agamemnon, Mycenae, Aulis, Penelope, Palamedes, Achilles, Iphigenia, Clytemnestra, Tauri, Patroclus, Myrmidon, Laocoön, Sinon, Deiphobus, Phthia, Simois, Protesilaüs, Laodamia, Philoctetes, Penthesilea, Thersites, Creüsa.

2. Look up in a good dictionary all the words that begin with the name *Helen* (for example, *Helena* and *Helenium*) and see if there is any connection between these words and Helen of Troy.

3. In modern English, *hector* has come to mean "to bully" or "to treat insolently." The word is derived from the name of the Trojan hero. Does it do justice to his character?

4. Explain the origin of *myrmidon* — a faithful adherent; *stentorian* — loud-voiced. There is a genus of plants called *Achillea*. See what Webster's *Dictionary* says on the origin of the name. What is a *palladium?* What other names were sometimes given to Troy?

5. What do the following expressions mean?

> "That is his Achilles' tendon."
> "As wily as Ulysses."
> "As wise as Nestor."
> "Difficult as the judgment of Paris."
> "Sulk in one's tent like Achilles."
> "To work like a Trojan."
> "An apple of discord."

6. What was the Greek word for *beauty contest?*

Rapid Quiz

Why did Jupiter not marry Thetis? Who became her husband? What deity was not invited to the marriage feast? What was her revenge? How did Paris render judgment? What was the name of his father and of his native city? What woman was promised Paris as a reward? What oath did Ulysses propose to her suitors? Whom did she marry? What happened when Paris visited Sparta? What call for help did Menelaus send out? Who failed to respond and why? How was he forced to come? Who was Achilles? What were the oracles concerning him? Who managed to find him and bring him to the Greek camp? Why was the Greek army delayed at Aulis? How was Diana appeased? What happened during the first nine years of the war? Why did Agamemnon and Achilles quarrel? What was the result? How was Patroclus killed? What was the effect on Achilles? How was Hector killed? How were Paris and Achilles slain? What was the stratagem of the wooden horse? What priest tried to save the Trojans? What was his fate? What was the fate of Troy?

FOR STUDENTS OF LATIN

1. Why did the Romans have a special interest in the Trojan War? With which side were their sympathies enlisted? Why?

2. Would the Romans have regarded the abduction of a queen as sufficient cause for a war? Why were some of their own wars fought?

3. What Latin poet continued Homer's account of the Trojan War? Did the two poets ever treat the same episodes?

4. Would Paris's choice win the approval of the average Roman?

5. What was the Greek name for Ulysses?

6. Was the art of war such in Roman times that the siege of a city like Troy could have been greatly shortened? Explain.

7. Answer in Latin two or three questions in the Rapid Quiz.

READING LIST

Poems, Plays, Stories, and Music

Baring, Maurice: *The Aulis Difficulty* [a travesty]
Bridges, Robert: *The Tale of Achilles*
Browning, Elizabeth Barrett: *Hector and Andromache*
Doolittle, Hilda ("H. D."): *Thetis*
Euripides: *Iphigenia at Aulis*
Flower, Robin: *Troy*
Gay, John: *Achilles* [play]
Gayley, Charles M.: Catullus's *Wedding of Peleus and Thetis*

Gluck, C. W.: *Iphigénie en Aulide* [opera]

Homer: The *Iliad*, translated by Lang, Leaf, and Myers

Landor, Walter Savage: *The Death of Paris*

Lang, Andrew: *Helen of Troy*

MacKaye, A. L.: *The Slave Prince* [a novel]

Marlowe, Christopher: *Dr. Faustus*

Morris, William: *The Death of Paris*

Ovid: *Paris to Helen* (in *Heroines*)

Ovid: *Helen to Paris* (in *Heroines*)

Peele, George: *The Arraignment of Paris*

Poe, Edgar Allan: *To Helen*

Putnam, Emily James: *Candaules' Wife, and Other Old Stories* (in prose)

Racine, Jean: *Andromache*

Teasdale, Sara: *Helen of Troy*

Tennyson, Lord: *Oenone*

White, Edward Lucas: *Helen* [a novel]

Wilde, Oscar: *Serenade* (to Helen)

Wordsworth, William: *Laodamia*

Gramstorff Bros.

ULYSSES AND HIS COMPANIONS GIVE WINE TO POLYPHEMUS

Cyclops, come now and try this wine, to see how tasty a drink was hidden in
our ship. — HOMER

XIV

AFTER THE TROJAN WAR

But Neptune strove still with Ulysses, till he reached his native land.
— HOMER

THE RETURN OF THE HEROES

Menelaus and Helen, after the fall of Troy, returned to
Sparta together, and lived there for many years in happiness.
According to some accounts, their homeward voyage was
delayed by storms and the ill favor of the gods, and they
visited many countries of the Mediterranean, in most of
which they were well received. When Telemachus, some
years later, visited Sparta in search of his father Ulysses, he
found the royal pair just celebrating the marriage of their
daughter Hermione to the son of Achilles, Pyrrhus (also
called Neoptolemus).

To Agamemnon came a different fate. He, it will be recalled, had incurred the deep anger of his wife Clytemnestra by getting her to send their daughter Iphigenia to Aulis on the pretext that she was to marry Achilles. She had instead been, seemingly, sacrificed to Diana. Neither of

AJAX AND CASSANDRA

But, like Cassandra, prophesies in vain. — EDWARD YOUNG

them knew that Iphigenia had been snatched away by the goddess and was still alive among the Tauri.

When Agamemnon sailed for home, he carried with him much spoil, including some Trojan slaves. Among the latter was a daughter of Priam and Hecuba, named Cassandra. Apollo had conferred upon her the gift of prophecy. But she rejected his advances, and he punished her by decreeing that although her vision of the future would always

Sargent   *Boston Museum of Fine Arts*

Orestes Pursued by the Furies

Great Nemesis!
Thou who didst call the Furies from the abyss,
And round Orestes bade them howl and hiss!
— Byron

be true, no one would believe her.   Cassandra had during
the Trojan War prophesied many dire events, but her predictions had always been received with scorn.   So now, too,
she foretold what was going to happen to Agamemnon, but he
smiled at her prophecies as absurd.

Benjamin West   Gramstorff Bros.

ORESTES AND PYLADES BEFORE IPHIGENIA

Priests, altars, victims swam before their sight.
— EDMUND SMITH

When Agamemnon reached home, he found Clytemnestra
in apparently a friendly and loving mood, but even before
he could partake of the banquet offered him, he was killed
by her minions.   Clytemnestra then hastily married Aegisthus, who had aided her in her crime.   It was the purpose
of the conspirators to get rid of all of the family of Agamem-

non, that their hold on the throne might be secure, but Electra saved the life of her brother, Orestes; and from these children of the slain king vengeance duly came. For Orestes took refuge in the palace of a kinsman; and when he grew up, he returned to his father's palace and slew his mother and Aegisthus.

Such horrifying crimes, whatever the motives back of them, could, of course, not be justified by the gods, and Orestes was consequently pursued by the Furies, those dreadful creatures who typify the conscience. He fled from land to land in madness, seeking purification and always accompanied by his friend Pylades. Finally an oracle declared that he must seek the temple of Diana in the land of the Tauri. When he arrived there, still in the company of the faithful Pylades, the savage inhabitants seized them and prepared to sacrifice them to the goddess, as was their wont with strangers. But when he was placed upon the altar, the priestess of the temple, his own sister Iphigenia, recognized him, and all three managed to escape, taking with them the statue of Diana. They returned to Mycenae, and Orestes, freed of the Furies, took possession of his father's kingdom. Pylades married Electra, and Orestes, it is said, married Hermione, daughter of Menelaus and Helen, after the death of Neoptolemus.

THE ADVENTURES OF ULYSSES

To Ulysses came the most startling adventures, recounted by Homer in the second of his masterpieces, the *Odyssey*.

Ulysses left Ithaca, as we know, most unwillingly, and for ten years he fought at Troy. Ten more years it was before he returned to Ithaca, to his wife Penelope and his son Telemachus.

1. *The Land of the Ciconians.* Laden with spoil, Ulysses set sail from Troy with twelve ships. His first landing was made at Ismarus, a city of the Ciconians. He sacked the city and took much additional spoil. Ulysses wished to leave immediately, but his men overruled him and reveled for many hours. While they lay asleep on the shore, the Ciconians attacked them. As a result, the Greeks were driven back to their ships, with the loss of seventy-two men.

2. *The Land of the Lotus-Eaters.* For nine days then they sailed on, and on the tenth day they came to the land of the lotus-eaters, who ate a flower as food. Ulysses and his men landed and partook of their own food, but he sent three of his crew as an embassy to the inhabitants of the country, to find out what manner of men they were. They mingled with the lotus-eaters, who made no attempt to do them any harm, but gave them of the lotus to eat. Straightway these men lost all their strength, and no longer wished to return home, but desired to remain forever in this pleasant land, where it always seemed like a languid afternoon. Only by force did Ulysses get them back to the ships.

3. *The Country of the Cyclopes.* Swiftly the ships hastened from this dangerous land of languor, and sailing onward they came to the land of the one-eyed monsters called Cyclopes. The land where these favorites of the gods lived yielded them food without effort, and each inhabited his own cave. The ships of Ulysses grounded on an island near this country, and for a time he and his men feasted on the flesh of the goats that they found here. But Ulysses resolved with his own ship to go closer to the mainland. He found a cave near the sea, wherein was a lofty hall; and near by many cattle, both sheep and goats, were sleeping. Taking a large goatskin filled with wine and choosing twelve men to accompany him,

Ulysses entered the cave, but failed to find its owner within.
His men begged him to seize some of the cattle and take some
of the rich cheese they found within and escape, but Ulysses
chose to remain, hoping that he would obtain fine presents
from the master of the cave.

Keystone View Co.

AN ISLAND SUPPOSED TO BE THAT OF THE CYCLOPES OFF
THE EAST COAST OF SICILY

Anything would grow well there in season, in the soft moist meadows behind
the dikes of the silvery sea. — HOMER

Shortly there was a great clamor without, as the Cyclops
called Polyphemus, a son of Neptune, returned, throwing
down a huge load of firewood from his shoulders. He
drove his flocks within the cave, and at the entrance he
placed a great stone as a door; two-and-twenty good wagons
could not have moved it from the threshold. Suddenly he
saw Ulysses and his men.

"Who are you?" he cried in his giant's voice, and thereat
the hearts of all of them trembled.

Ulysses recounted to him their voyage from Troy and

begged him for the gifts due a stranger. Then the Cyclops mocked him, and asked where his ship was. Ulysses craftily told him that it had been wrecked, and even as he spoke the Cyclops seized two of his men, dashed them on the ground, and made a meal from their bodies. Thereupon he fell asleep, and Ulysses all night long pondered ways by which he might overcome the monster.

The next morning the Cyclops ate two more of the Greeks, and then left the cave, fastening the door securely. But now Minerva inspired Ulysses and he ordered his men to sharpen a huge beam, and bade them at the word be ready to thrust it into the giant's eye when he lay asleep. That evening he came again, and again slew two of the men for food. But to him then came Ulysses bearing a present of wine, and the giant drank and was pleased. Thrice he took a huge draught, and he asked the name of Ulysses. Once more Ulysses replied to him craftily:

"Do you ask my name?" he inquired. "Give me then the gifts due to hospitality, and I will tell you. No One is my name; so they all call me."

To him replied Polyphemus the Cyclops cruelly:

"This shall be your gift: I will eat No One last of all."

Even as he spoke he fell back in drunken sleep.

Then Ulysses heated the beam, and when it began to glow and take fire, they all took hold of it, and Ulysses, standing above, whirled it round as they moved. They thrust it swiftly into the eye of Polyphemus, and blinded him. Horribly he roared with pain, so that the other Cyclopes hastened up and asked:

"Polyphemus, who is hurting you?"

And he replied:

"O my friends, No One is hurting me."

POLYPHEMUS

A monster horrifying, hideous, huge. — VIRGIL

At his words they were bewildered but returned to their caves.

The next morning Polyphemus was obliged to open his cave to let the cattle out. He stood there, however, as a guard, seeking to prevent the escape of the Greeks. But Ulysses bound each of his men under the middlemost of three rams, and he himself clung to the wool of the last three; and so they escaped the detection of Polyphemus. They returned to their ship, and once on board Ulysses called to the Cyclops and mocked him. Even in his blindness Polyphemus hurled a huge rock in the direction of his voice, and almost wrecked the ship. Then, at a safer distance, Ulysses once more reproached the Cyclops, and told him that if any one asked him who had blinded him, he might reply that it was "Ulysses, son of Laertes, of Ithaca."

At his words Polyphemus lifted up his hands to the heavens and prayed to his father Neptune:

"Hear me, O earth-shaking, blue-haired Neptune! If I am indeed your son, keep this Ulysses from his home. But if he is destined to reach his home, may he come late and in evil plight, and find calamities in his house!"

Neptune heard him, and was angered at the wrong done his son; and he answered the prayer of Polyphemus. Many years he kept Ulysses from home, and many troubles he found when he at last reached Ithaca, disguised as a beggar.

4. *The Island of Aeolus.* Not many days later they came to the home of Aeolus, king of the winds, who received them hospitably. When they were preparing to leave, Aeolus gave Ulysses a great bag made of oxhide, and told him that in it he had confined all the winds that might oppose his voyage home. So they set sail, and for nine days a steady breeze behind them propelled them toward Ithaca. They were in

sight of the shore, when Ulysses, who had watched the bag day and night, fell fast asleep, and his men, who thought he had some treasure concealed in the bag he guarded so carefully, stole the bag and opened it. Immediately the confined winds rushed out, and drove the ships back to Aeolus, who refused, however, to aid Ulysses again.

5. *The Land of the Laestrygonians.* Tempted by what seemed a friendly and safe harbor, the ships next came to the land of the Laestrygonians, Ulysses alone keeping his ship outside the haven. But this was a land of man-eating giants, even fiercer than the Cyclopes; and they destroyed all the ships within the harbor.

6. *The Island of Circe.* Next Ulysses, with his single ship, came to the island Aeaea, where dwelt the enchantress Circe, child of Apollo and of a daughter of Oceanus. For two days Ulysses lay off the shore, but at last he divided his men into two companies. By lot it fell that the company headed by his lieutenant Eurylochus was chosen to explore the island. They walked inland, and came to a beautiful palace, surrounded by wolves and lions and other animals, all of whom seemed tame. Within they heard a woman singing over the spindle. They called, and Circe came out and welcomed them. Yet she noted not that Eurylochus remained without. Food she gave them, mixed with a potent drug; and when they had eaten, she struck them with her wand, and they were forthwith changed to swine.

Now Eurylochus reported to Ulysses that none of his company had returned to him. Then Ulysses took his sword and resolved alone to explore the island. But on the way a beautiful youth, with the first down on his lips and cheeks, met him; and it was the god Mercury. He told Ulysses of the enchantments of Circe, but gave him a magic herb, called *moly*, to protect him. Then Ulysses entered the palace, and was welcomed by Circe, who set a banquet before him. But when she struck him with the wand, it had no effect, and Ulysses rushed on her with his sword. At that Circe sought to make peace with him, for she recognized him as Ulysses, but he refused until she had returned his men to human guise.

Riviére   *Gramstorff Bros.*

CIRCE AND ULYSSES' COMPANIONS

They entreated me —
till in pity
I turned each to his own self. — "H. D."

This was done. At her palace Ulysses remained month after month, and he seemed to have forgotten his native land. At last the urging of his companions recalled him to himself, and he made preparations to set sail.

7. *The Visit to Hades.* But first, Circe told him, it was necessary for him to visit the underworld and obtain further instructions. With the help of the goddess he was able to do this, and he obtained from Tiresias, a blind seer who still retained in the underworld his gift of prophecy, counsel as to

the way he should take to get home. In Hades he saw too the shades of his mother, of Agamemnon and Achilles and Ajax, and of many others.

8. *The Sirens.* First of the perils which Ulysses faced after leaving the pleasant island of Circe was that of the sirens — the dangerous maidens who sang a most sweet song

Flaxman

THE SIRENS

Then listen I
To the celestial Sirens' harmony. — MILTON

and enticed mariners to their destruction on the cruel rocks which they inhabited. As Ulysses approached the place where the sirens dwelt, he instructed his men to fill their ears with wax and to bind him firmly to the mast of their ship. He ordered them under no circumstances to free him. When the sirens sang their sweetest songs and promised Ulysses all sorts of precious boons, he struggled madly to free himself and with dire threats commanded his men to release him. But they heard neither the sirens' song nor the words of Ulysses. So he and they passed this peril safely.

9. *Scylla and Charybdis.* Between this rock and this whirlpool, each inhabited by a monster, Ulysses passed with the loss of only some of his men, where other mariners and their ships had perished utterly. For while Ulysses and his men watched Charybdis anxiously on one side, the six heads of Scylla seized from the other side six of the crew.

10. *The Cattle of the Sun.* Greater misfortune came to him when the ship reached Thrinacia, where were pastured the cattle of the Sun. Ulysses had been warned by both Tiresias and Circe not to eat these cattle. The ship was becalmed at the island for several days, and the supply of food gave out. So long as he could Ulysses kept watch, but at last in utter weariness he dozed, and while he slept his men killed some of the cattle and ate them. When Ulysses awoke and realized what sacrilege they had committed, he was horrified. A breeze sprang up and they set sail, but the sun-god, in wrath at their impiety, sent a terrible storm. The ship was wrecked and all the men were drowned, but Ulysses improvised a raft and on it floated to a near-by shore.

11. *The Island of Ogygia.* He found that he was on Ogygia, an island ruled over by a fair-haired nymph named Calypso. She received him most kindly and kept him on the island for seven years. Indeed, she wished to marry him and offered him immortality if he would become her husband. But he refused, and day by day lamented his lot and prayed the gods constantly to be allowed to return to his wife and child. Yet the gods suffered Neptune to vent his anger on Ulysses for the blinding of Polyphemus. One day, however, Neptune was absent in Ethiopia, the inhabitants of which country were favorites of his. Minerva, who was friendly to Ulysses, used the opportunity to urge the council of the gods to help the Greek hero. Jupiter hearkened to her words,

and sent Mercury as a messenger to Calypso, bidding her
free Ulysses.   Calypso demurred, but dared not disobey.   So
Ulysses built a raft, received food and wine from Calypso,
and bade farewell to the nymph.

For many days he sailed in peace and was almost in sight
of Ithaca, when Neptune, returning from his visit to the

Flaxman

NAUSICAÄ AND HER MAIDS PLAYING BALL

They began to play at ball, and white-Nausicaä led their sport. — HOMER

Ethiopians, caught sight of him.   His wrath was kindled, but
he knew that he could not much longer keep Ulysses from his
native land.   Yet for the last time he sent a storm, and
Ulysses was driven back, and just barely managed to save
himself from the wreck of his raft and swim to a strange and
rocky shore, the kingdom of Phaeacia.

12. *The Land of the Phaeacians.*   From this time on
Ulysses was under the fostering care of Minerva, and his
path was made much smoother.   He met first in this new
land the Princess Nausicaä, who came with her maidens to

wash clothes on the beach. While the clothes were drying, the maidens enjoyed lunch, after which they amused themselves on the beach with a game of ball. Their cries awakened Ulysses from his deep slumber. Nausicaä was impressed by his appearance and his wisdom in speech. She took him to her father's palace, and there for several days Ulysses was royally entertained. The king, Alcinoüs, and the queen, Arete, would have been glad to give Nausicaä in marriage to this noble stranger, but he implored their aid in returning to Ithaca. Before he left they held in his honor elaborate games, in which Ulysses displayed his strength and skill, and later related to them his adventures.

13. *The Slaying of the Suitors*. Ulysses was landed on Ithaca in secret by a ship of the Phaeacians, which on its return was changed to stone by Neptune in his anger. He set out to discover the condition of affairs in his kingdom. He was able to make himself known to his son Telemachus, who told Ulysses that Penelope was besieged by a host of suitors, feasting day and night in his palace and insisting that she must marry one of them. She put them off by saying she must first weave a shroud for Ulysses' father, an old man; but each night she unraveled what she had spun.

This was evil news for Ulysses, who saw that even in his home he must continue to endure hardships. Disguising himself as a beggar, he made his way to his palace, where none recognized him except Argus, the old dog that had been his faithful companion in his youth. Full of years, he was now blind and feeble, but as Ulysses approached he recognized him at once. He wagged his tail and lifted his ears and tried to move toward him. The effort was too much and he died.

In the palace Ulysses suffered all manner of abuse from the suitors and from the servants. At last he laid with Telem-

achus the plot that was to lead to the undoing of the evil
suitors.   To determine who should marry Penelope it was
proposed that a contest with a mighty bow owned by Ulysses
should be held, and he who should shoot best at a set mark
was to have the hand of Penelope.   The suitors agreed, and

Waterhouse, Aberdeen Art Gallery   *Ewing Galloway*

PENELOPE AND HER SUITORS

Penelope, for her Ulysses' sake,
Devised a web her wooers to deceive. — SPENSER

Telemachus carefully removed all other arms from the great
hall where the contest was to be held.

The time for the trial of the bow came.   The suitors were
in the hall, and near Telemachus stood the beggar that was
Ulysses disguised.   Unknown to the suitors the doors leading
to the hall had been locked.   Now the trial began, and the
mighty bow was brought forward.   They started with the
business of stringing it, and first Telemachus, then one after
another of the suitors tried to bend the bow, but in vain.

"Let me try," said Ulysses, and the suitors laughed in scorn at the impudent beggar.

But with skilled hands Ulysses took the bow, and without effort strung it. Consternation fell upon the suitors, and their faces grew pale. Just then thunder rumbled on the air, and all knew that Jupiter looked with favor on the strange

ULYSSES RECOGNIZED BY HIS DOG
The faithful dog alone his rightful master knew. — POPE

beggar. He picked up a swift shaft which lay beside him on the table, laid it upon the arch, drew the bow to his shoulder, and sent the arrow straight through the mark. Thereupon he gave the signal to Telemachus, and his son, clad in shining armor and girt with a sword, took his stand beside him.

Then wise Ulysses threw off his rags and sprang to the broad threshold, his bow in hand and his quiver full of arrows. Out he poured the swift shafts at his feet, and as he stood there Minerva gave him the kingly bearing that was his due.

PENELOPE

Heedful Penelope, you excel all womankind in beauty, height, and balanced
mind within. — HOMER

"Dogs!" he cried. "You have said that never should I return, and therefore you destroyed my home, wooed my wife, insulted my son, nor did you fear either the wrath of the gods or the indignation of men. Now you shall all die!"

So shaft after shaft he shot at the insolent suitors, until all but two, less guilty than the rest, were slain. Then Penelope

THE SLAYING OF THE SUITORS

Then looking sternly on him wise Ulysses said: "You shall not now avoid a shameful death." — HOMER

learned that her husband had returned, and all was well again in the palace of Ulysses.

14. *The Death of Ulysses.* The stories vary as to what came after the slaying of the suitors. For some say that Ulysses lived peacefully and died happily, after many years. But others recount that in time Ulysses grew weary of quiet and longed again for turmoil and danger. At last he could bear it no longer, and collecting a band of kindred spirits he set out once more, aiming to reach some lands, far to the west, of which he had heard. On that quest he died, and no man knows where.

STUDY APPLICATION

THE MYTHS IN LITERATURE

"The wily Ulysses" has passed into a proverb, and with Helen has become the best-known figure of the Trojan War and its succeeding events. But the tragic fate of Agamemnon has moved poets hardly less.

It is noteworthy that the story both of Ulysses and of Agamemnon has proved especially attractive to dramatists. In recent years, for example, plays about Ulysses have been written by Stephen Phillips, Robert Bridges, and Gerhart Hauptmann. In ancient times plays about the return of Agamemnon were composed by Aeschylus, Euripides, and Sophocles; in modern times by Robinson Jeffers.

In the adventures of Ulysses it is the sojourn with Circe, the passing by the dangerous rock of the sirens, and the episodes in Ithaca that have most won poets. Among those who have treated these themes are Ovid, Samuel Daniel, Matthew Arnold, Austin Dobson, "H. D.," Walter Savage Landor, James Russell Lowell, Dante Gabriel Rossetti, Edmund Clarence Stedman, Tennyson, and Stephen Phillips.

Perhaps the two finest poems are Arnold's *The Strayed Reveler* and Tennyson's *Ulysses*.

In the former Arnold tells how a youth approaches the palace of Circe and there sees the enchantress and Ulysses. He recognizes the latter:

> How shall I name him —
> This spare dark-featured,
> Quick-eyed stranger?
> Ah! and I see too
> His sailor's bonnet,
> His short coat, travel tarnished,
> With one arm bare!
> Art thou not he, whom fame
> This long time rumors
> The favored guest of Circe, brought by the waves?
> Art thou he, stranger —
> The wise Ulysses,
> Laertes' son?

Tennyson tells how Ulysses, in his old age, sickens of peace and rest and yearns again for the turmoil of adventure, the zest of danger, the quest of the unknown; and how once more he sets forth, with a few comrades, in search of new experiences.

REFERENCES TO MYTHOLOGY IN LITERATURE

What do the following references mean? Where a word or phrase is italicized, explain only the word or phrase.

A

1. Agamemnon,
   Betray'd like him, but, not like him, aveng'd. — *Arnold*
2. *Cassandra* at the gate,
   With wide eyes the vision shone in.

   — *Elizabeth Barrett Browning*
3. Then death came to old *Argus*, soon as he had lived to see Odysseus restored after twenty years. — *Homer*
4. I saw him on an island weeping, in the hall of the nymph Calypso, who holds him there by force. — *Homer*
5. To the *son of Achilles Menelaus* gave his daughter. — *Homer*
6. Black at the root is it, like milk its blossom, and the gods call it *moly*. — *Homer*
7. But Poseidon strove still with Odysseus, until he reached his native land. — *Homer*
8. Then wise Odysseus cast off his rags and sprang to the broad threshold, bow in hand. — *Homer*
9. Old Ulysses tortured from his slumbers
   The glutted *Cyclops*. — *Keats*
10. Nor pour wax into the little cells of thy ears, with self-mistrusting Ulysses. — *Lamb*

B

1. It was the mournful privilege of Ulysses to descend twice to the shades. — *Lamb*
2. As one that for a weary space has lain
   Lulled by the song of *Circe*. — *Lang*
3. Or when Ulysses on the larboard shunn'd
   Charybdis, and by th'other whirlpool steer'd. — *Milton*

4.   Who knows not *Circe*,
The daughter of the Sun? — *Milton*

5.   That moly
That Hermes once to wise Ulysses gave. — *Milton*

6. A wond'rous bag with both her hands she binds,
Like that where once Ulysses held the winds. — *Pope*

7. Lucky, if, like Ulysses, he can keep
His head above the waters of the deep. — *H. and J. Smith*

8. Not so great wonder and astonishment
Did the most chaste *Penelope* possess
To see her lord. — *Spenser*

9. In New Jersey our worst affliction is the "one-eyed car," the automobile with one headlight extinguished and the other glaring balefully like an angry *Cyclops*.
— *Newark Sunday Call*

10. A little *Cyclops*, with one eye. — *Wordsworth* (in *To the Daisy*)

Exercises in Composition, Oral and Written

1. The adventures of Ulysses are given in numbered order in this chapter. Copy the titles of the adventures in a list, memorize the list, and be able to describe each adventure in a well-constructed sentence.

2. To Telemachus Ulysses narrates his encounter with Polyphemus. Give the story in his own words. Let him emphasize the way in which the prayer of Polyphemus was fulfilled.

3. The sirens of the *Odyssey* resemble the Lorelei of Heinrich Heine's famous poem. Find the poem in some songbook and compare the Greek and the German idea.

4. Did Ulysses, do you suppose, stay peacefully and contentedly at home after the slaying of the suitors? Did he have any further adventures? Give your idea of his life after his return home.

5. Why did the Greeks esteem Ulysses so highly? What good qualities did he have? Write a character sketch of Ulysses, with references throughout to his various adventures and the traits he displayed in them.

6. Can the trail of Ulysses be followed today? Bring in a report on the entertaining book by Halliburton (see page 319).

7. In connection with Argus, tell the story of some famous dogs of fact and fiction.

WORD STUDY

1. Give the correct pronunciation of the following words:
Hermione, Neoptolemus, Cassandra, Aegisthus, Orestes, Pylades, *Odyssey*, Ciconians, Polyphemus, Laestrygonians, Circe, Eurylochus, Tiresias, Ogygia, Phaeacians, Nausicaä, Alcinoüs, Arete, Telemachus.

2. What is the meaning of the following expressions? "To go on an Odyssey," "to dally in a lotus-eaters' land," "Cassandra-like prophecies," "the spell of the sirens," "between Scylla and Charybdis."

3. What is a pun? Where in the story of Ulysses is a pun used?

4. The island of Circe was called *Aeaea*. What is odd in this word? Can you think of any others that resemble it?

5. Gene Fowler speaks of Hollywood actors "making strange antics before a three-legged Cyclops." What is this Cyclops? Why does Fowler call it so?

RAPID QUIZ

What happened to Menelaus and Helen? to Agamemnon? How did Orestes find Iphigenia? Where does Homer relate the adventures of Ulysses? How many years was he away from home? What befell him in the land of the Ciconians? in the land of the lotus-eaters? in the country of the Cyclopes? on the island of Aeolus? in the land of the Laestrygonians? on the island of Circe? on his visit to Hades? on his voyage past the sirens? on his encounter with Scylla and Charybdis? on the island of the Cattle of the Sun? on the island of Ogygia? in the land of the Phaeacians? In what condition did he return home? What situation did he find in his own palace? Who helped him in his plans? Who recognized him? What was the trial of the bow? What did Ulysses do to the suitors? What, according to the legends, became of Ulysses?

FOR STUDENTS OF LATIN

1. Whom would the Romans admire more, Achilles, hero of the *Iliad*, or Ulysses, hero of the *Odyssey?* Explain your answer.

2. Ulysses' adventures represent the Greek idea of the world in Homer's time, especially of the Mediterranean shores and islands. Why would the Romans have a more accurate idea?

3. Answer in Latin two or three of the questions in the Rapid Quiz.

Reading List

For a collection of poems dealing with Ulysses, see Stella S. Center's edition of C. A. Pease's version of the *Odyssey*.

Poems, Plays, and Music

Arnold, Edwin : *Iphigenia*
Arnold, Matthew : *The Strayed Reveler*
Bridges, Robert : *The Return of Ulysses*
Buchanan, Robert : *Penelope*
Daniel, Samuel : *Ulysses and the Sirens*
Dobson, Austin : *A Tale of Polypheme — Prayer of the Swine to Circe*
Doolittle, Hilda ("H. D.") : *At Ithaca — Odyssey*
Euripides : *Iphigenia among the Taurians*
Goethe, J. W. von : *Iphigenia in Tauris*
Landor, Walter Savage : *The Last of Ulysses*
Lang, Andrew : *A Song of Phaeacia — The Odyssey*
Lowell, James Russell : *The Sirens*
Mather, Frank Jewett : *Ulysses in Ithaca*
Ovid : *Hermione to Orestes* (in *Heroines*) — *Penelope to Ulysses* (in *Heroines*)
Phillips, Stephen : *Ulysses*
Rossetti, Dante Gabriel : *The Wine of Circe*
Strauss, Richard : *Elektra* [opera]
Tennyson, Lord : *The Lotos-Eaters and Choric Song — Ulysses*

See also in prose:

Chidsey, Alan Lake : *Odysseus, Sage of Greece*
Fénelon, François de : *Adventures of Telemachus*
Halliburton, Richard : *The Glorious Adventure*
Homer : *Odyssey*, translated by C. A. Pease
Homer : *Odyssey*, translated by T. E. Lawrence
White, Edward Lucas : *The Song of the Sirens*

AENEAS AT THE COURT OF DIDO

With his solemn tongue he did discourse
To love-sick Dido's sad attending ear,
The story of that fateful burning night. — SHAKESPEARE

XV

THE ADVENTURES OF AENEAS

One speech in it I chiefly loved: 'twas Aeneas' tale to Dido.
               — SHAKESPEARE

FROM TROY TO CARTHAGE

One of the bravest heroes of the Trojan War was Aeneas, who, it will be recalled, was the only man that dared oppose Achilles in his wrath after the death of Patroclus. He was the son of Venus by a mortal father, Anchises, and from him the Romans traced their descent; and a great Latin poet, Virgil, told in one of the master epics of all times, the *Aeneid,* how Aeneas escaped from Troy and after many adventures came to Italy and founded the state of Latium.

AENEAS AND ANCHISES

         Our great ancestor
Did from the flames of Troy upon his shoulder
The old Anchises bear.

              — SHAKESPEARE

When Ilion fell, Aeneas escaped from the conflagration. He carried Anchises out on his back, and with him went his wife and young son. But before they could get away, his wife perished. For a time Aeneas lingered, together with other refugees, at a place near by, and then set sail for some new land in which he and his fellow-Trojans might settle. He came first to Thrace, afterwards to Crete, but in neither place did the gods favor the idea of building a city; and in a dream Aeneas was told to seek a land in the west called Hesperia, where Dardanus, ancestor of the Trojans, had been born.

So westward sailed Aeneas and his companions, but before they reached Hesperia (today called Italy) many adventures befell them. First they encountered the Harpies. They had landed on an island on which roamed many fat cattle. Some of these they killed for food. Just as they were sitting down to eat, a flock of evil-appearing and evil-smelling Harpies appeared and snatched the food from the tables. In vain they beat at them with their swords; and in disgust they left the island.

Later they came to the land of the Cyclopes, and from the shore they were hailed by a man in tattered garments, who implored them to take him on board. He was a Greek, he told Aeneas, a sailor on the ship of Ulysses, who had accidentally been left behind when Ulysses had fled from Polyphemus. Even as the Greek was speaking, Polyphemus himself came stumbling along — a fear-inspiring monster, huge in bulk and with an angry red cavity where his eye had been. Hearing the voices, the terrible giant waded toward the ship of the Trojans, his immense height standing far above the waves. He shouted at them as he heard their oars fall in the water, and his voice brought the other Cyclopes to the

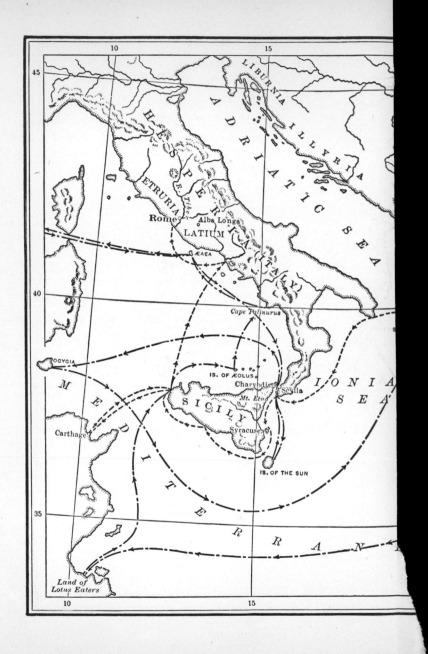

WANDERINGS OF
ULYSSES AND ÆNEAS
———————— *Track of Æneas*
—·—·—·— *Track of Ulysses*

BLACK
SEA

T H R A C E

M A C E D O N I A

PIERIA

Mt. Olympus
R. Pen.
THESSALY
Iolcus

Dodona

Ismarus   Aenos   R. Hebrus

Sestos *Hellespontus*
Abydos

Troy or Ilium

ÆGEAN
SEA

LEMNOS

ASIA MINOR

LESBOS

PHRYGIA

Mt. Tmolus

Icarian
Sea

Mt. Latmos

CIA

Mt. Parnassus   Chalcis
Delphi   Aulis
Calydon
ITHACA   Thebes

Elis Nemea Athens
Mycenæ
Argos
Olympia Trœzen

Pheræ Sparta or
Lacedaemon

NAXOS

RHODES

CYTHERA

C R E T E

A N   S E   A

shore, which they lined like a row of mighty pines. The Trojans were glad when their vessel was once more on the deep sea out of danger.

Aeneas, warned by those familiar with the dangers of Scylla and Charybdis, avoided entirely the region where these monsters dwelt and skirted the coast of Sicily. At this time his father Anchises died. Juno, looking down from heaven, felt her resentment rise again at the success with which this remnant of the Trojan people was making its way to a new land. So she induced Aeolus, king of the winds, to produce a mighty storm, promising him the most beautiful of her nymphs, Deiopea, as a reward. In the great tempest that arose the vessels of Aeneas were scattered far and wide.

NEPTUNE CALMING THE SEA

Thou frownest, and old Aeolus, thy foe,
Skulks to his cavern. — KEATS

They were all in danger of shipwreck when Neptune became aware that a storm was raging without his consent. He saw the fleet of Aeneas in the midst of the storm, and immediately guessed that Juno was at fault. He ordered the waves to cease from tumult, he sent the clouds scurrying back to their mountain homes. Such ships as had run on the rocks he pried loose with his trident.   The whole fleet, as soon as the sea had become calm, sought the nearest port in order to repair the damage that the winds and waves had done to them.   They found themselves on the shores of Carthage — a Phoenician colony which lay opposite Sicily on the coast of Africa.   Aeneas landed and explored; Venus, in the guise of a huntress, met and encouraged her adventurous and pious son.   She enveloped Aeneas in a mist to enable him to enter the city unseen.   When it dissolved, he stood revealed in heroic grace.

In Carthage reigned Queen Dido (also called Elissa), the beautiful widow of a Phoenician nobleman.   Dido, on the death of her husband, had left her home and founded a colony on this African shore.   She received Aeneas hospitably, held games in his honor, had her bard Iopas entertain the Trojans with his songs, and l:stened entranced when Aeneas told the tale of his adventures.   So attractive was the Trojan hero that Dido fell in love with him, and offered herself to him as a bride.   Aeneas might have been tempted to accept, but Jupiter sent Mercury to remind him that his destiny would not be fulfilled until he had journeyed farther.   Dido, assisted by her sister Anna, tried to dissuade Aeneas from actually setting out, but when all her allurements proved in vain and Aeneas hoisted sail, she prepared a funeral pyre, mounted it, stabbed herself, and was consumed in flames.   Aeneas, looking back, saw the flames of the pyre mounting over Carthage.

Landing in Sicily, Aeneas held funeral games in honor of Anchises, who had been buried there the year before; and in these the Sicilians joined.   There were archery competitions, foot races, and a boxing bout.   In the last, Entellus, bravest of the old Sicilian heroes, was matched with a boastful young Trojan named Dares; and the latter was defeated.

Mercury Notifies Aeneas That Jupiter Commands Him
to Leave Carthage

See where the child of heaven, with winged feet,
Runs down the slanted sunlight of the dawn.
— Shelley

Neptune, at the urging of Venus, now consented to let Aeneas reach Italy in safety, but he demanded the sacrifice of one life. The pilot of Aeneas, Palinurus, was the one

Cleveland Museum of Art

PARTING OF DIDO AND AENEAS

Even so the gentle Tyrian dame
Saw the dear object of her flame,
The ungrateful Trojan, hoist his sail. — COWLEY

whom fate selected as the victim. Neptune sent the god of sleep, Somnus, to him as he watched by the helm, and gradually slumber stole upon him. Then Somnus gently shoved him into the waves. Neptune guided the ship safely over the waves until Aeneas saw that Palinurus had disappeared. Greatly grieved at his loss, Aeneas himself took charge of the ship, and at last they reached Italy.

AENEAS IN THE UNDERWORLD

In order to obtain further counsel, he visited the Cumaean sibyl. She dwelt in a grove sacred to Apollo, and had been endowed with the gift of prophecy. No sooner did she behold Aeneas than she seemed to recognize him; and she prophesied that he would still have to undergo many hardships and perils, but in the end would conquer them.

"Yield not to misfortunes," she counseled, "but press onward ever more boldly."

Aeneas asked her to help him enter the abode of the dead, in order to meet his father, Anchises, again and hear from him what the future of the Trojans in their new home would be. The sibyl warned him that the descent to Avernus was easy, but that to retrace one's steps and come to the upper air again was very difficult. First he must seek a certain tree on which grew a golden bough. This bough he was to pluck and to carry along with him as a gift to Proserpina. Aeneas, with the help of Venus, found the tree, plucked the branch, and sought the sibyl once more.

Near Mount Vesuvius Aeneas found the cavern of Avernus, and, guided by the sibyl, descended into the underworld. There, in deep terror, he beheld the Furies, he saw the dread forms of Death and Hunger and Fear stalk past him, he heard hydras hiss frightfully and shrank back as chimeras breathed fire. At the sight of the Golden Bough Charon relaxed his sternness and consented to ferry Aeneas across the Styx.

On the opposite shore Cerberus came to meet them, his three heads growling, but when he had devoured a drugged sop that the sibyl threw him, he fell fast asleep. Through the regions of the underworld Aeneas then passed, sometimes with great sadness as he beheld persons whom he had known.   Among others whom he encountered was Dido, and Aeneas realized that the flames that he had seen when he left Carthage were those of her funeral pyre.   He asked her to forgive him and to bid him a last farewell, but with eyes averted she vouchsafed him no word.

Cleveland Museum of Art

DIDO ON FUNERAL PYRE

Yet let me die: thus, thus I go
Exulting to the shades below. — VIRGIL

He saw, too, the warriors in whose company he had fought and those others against whom his spear had many times been cast. The Trojans thronged around him, but the Greeks, as aforetime on the plains of Troy, fled when they beheld his glittering armor. He saw and recognized Palinurus, and heard from him how he had been thrust into the sea and drowned. The pilot begged Aeneas to take him back with him to the land of the living, but the sibyl told him that this was impossible, although the place where his body had been washed ashore should ever after be called Cape Palinurus. He saw Ixion and Tantalus; wandering through the Elysian Fields he heard Orpheus playing his lyre, and he gazed on heroes and bards feasting merrily or listening to strains of music. Here an ether covered the fields with a purple hue; and here another and lovelier sun was perpetually bright.

At last he found Anchises, who showed him the Valley of Oblivion, where dwell the souls of those yet to be born. He enumerated to his son what heroes and statesmen would proceed from among these to establish the glory of the Trojan — later the Roman — state. Then Aeneas and the sibyl made their way back to the mortal world.

AENEAS IN ITALY

Aeneas parted from the sibyl, to whom he promised eternal reverence, and continued to sail along the coast of Italy (called *Hesperia*, "the western land") until he came to the mouth of the Tiber. The land of Latium, situated around this river, was ruled by King Latinus, who traced his descent from Saturn. He had no son, but his beautiful daughter Lavinia had many suitors for her hand. Of them all her parents favored Turnus, king of the Rutulians, although Latinus had been warned in a dream that the man whom Lavinia was destined to marry would come from another land, and that their offspring would one day rule the world.

When Aeneas appeared in the land of Latium, he was hospitably received by Latinus, who immediately recognized in the Trojan hero the son-in-law destined for him. But Juno once more stirred up trouble for the Trojans, chiefly by arousing the wrath of Turnus against this possible rival. Finally King Latinus himself was persuaded to dismiss the strangers from his country; and Juno, descending from

AENEAS' LANDING AT LATIUM

An ample realm for thee the Fates ordain,
A town that o'er the conquered world shall reign. — VIRGIL

heaven, burst open the gates of the Temple of Janus — the sign of war.

To help Turnus, who was recognized as leader of the party opposed to Aeneas, came Camilla, a favorite of Diana. She was a huntress and a warrior; and she had taken a resolution never to marry.

Other allies ranged themselves with Turnus. Aeneas was troubled at the forces arrayed against him, but in a dream Father Tiber appeared to him and encouraged him. He told him, too, that he must seek Evander, chief of the Arcadians, who was an old enemy of Turnus, and win his alliance. Aeneas awoke and immediately sought out King Evander, whose capital was situated where later Rome arose. Evander and his son, Pallas, welcomed Aeneas and were glad to ally themselves with him; but Evander told Aeneas that his own power was very slight. He proposed, however, that Aeneas seek out the Etruscans, who had just ejected their king, Mezentius, for cruelty. Mezentius had taken refuge with Turnus, and the Etruscans would naturally be willing to join Aeneas. The latter immediately set out for the Etruscan camp, and found that the Etruscan leaders rejoiced at the opportunity to conclude an alliance with him.

While Aeneas was away on this business of winning allies for himself, Juno sent Iris to Turnus and urged him to take advantage of the fact that the leader of the Trojans was absent. Turnus accordingly attacked the Trojan camp, but the Trojans defended themselves skillfully and refused to be drawn out of their entrenchments. Night came on, and the army of Turnus withdrew in seeming triumph. Two Trojans, Nisus and Euryalus, offered to steal through the camp of their enemies and carry word of their situation to Aeneas. They set out on their mission, and had actually passed through the army of besiegers when they were intercepted by a troop coming to join Turnus. Even then Nisus might have escaped, but seeing his friend in the hands of their foes, he slew as many as he could before he and Euryalus were killed.

Soon Aeneas arrived on the scene with his Etruscan allies, and then the war raged in earnest. The two armies were pretty well matched, and for a time the advantage lay with neither. In a personal combat Aeneas killed the tyrant

Mezentius and his son Lausus, while in the same battle Turnus overcame Pallas. In another battle Camilla greatly distinguished herself, but while she pursued one foeman too ardently, she was slain by a javelin hurled by an Etruscan warrior named Aruns. Diana was angered at the death of her follower, and as Aruns stole away from the field in secret triumph, he was struck and killed by an arrow from the bow of a nymph in Diana's train.

Gradually Aeneas seemed to be getting the upper hand, and when Turnus could no longer resist the murmurings and reproaches of his followers, he was obliged to seek out Aeneas in single combat. The Trojan hero was assisted by his divine mother and by the Fates, and to protect himself he wore an armor specially fashioned for him by Vulcan. Turnus, on the other hand, was quite without the aid of the gods, for Jupiter, in obedience to the decrees of destiny, forbade Juno to interfere in his behalf against the might of Aeneas. The spear of Turnus fell harmless from the shield of Aeneas, but the spear of Aeneas pierced the shield of Turnus and wounded the latter in the thigh. Turnus begged for mercy, and Aeneas would have granted it to him gladly. But even as Turnus spoke the eye of the Trojan fell upon the belt of Pallas, a trophy of the dead prince that Turnus had taken from him when he slew him. Then Aeneas was again filled with wrath and in the name of Pallas he killed Turnus.

Juturna, the sister of Turnus, had been dowered with immortal life by Jove. When her brother died, she sorrowed greatly; and in her grief, she finally threw herself into the Tiber. In the waves of that river the awed villagers sometimes caught sight of her sad and lovely form, as she moved through the moonlit waters. In later days the Romans worshiped her as goddess of wells.

Thus the war ended, Aeneas triumphed, and the Roman state began. Aeneas married Lavinia and founded a city in her name — Lavinium. His son, Ascanius, or Iulus, founded Alba Longa. After Ascanius, reigned his stepbrother Silvius.

From Ascanius Julius Caesar claimed his descent, and of course thereby traced his ancestry back to Aeneas himself and to Venus. Because of this belief of his, Caesar, when he was pursuing Pompey through Asia Minor, gave to the inhabitants of Troy (where a new city had been built) numerous privileges. He wore a signet ring with the image of Venus armed, and *Venus Victrix* was his password at Pharsalia, where he conquered Pompey. Because of his descent from the old kings of Alba Longa, Caesar sometimes wore their costume, including red shoes and a purple robe.

ROMULUS AND REMUS

In Alba Longa reigned Silvius Proca, who left his throne to his elder son, Numitor. But a younger son, Amulius, deprived his brother of power; and when Rhea Sylvia, Numitor's daughter, bore twins, named by her Romulus [1] and Remus and believed to be her children by Mars, she and her children were condemned to be drowned in the Tiber.

But the cradle in which the children were exposed was stranded on the shore before any harm had come to them. There they were found by a she-wolf, who carried them to her den and suckled them along with her own young. They were found by the king's shepherd, Faustulus, who took the infants to his own house and gave them into the care of his wife, Acca Larentia, who became their nurse.

[1] There was also a Romulus Silvius, who was killed because he presumed himself greater than Jove.

When they had grown to manhood, Romulus and Remus resolved to found a city of their own. This they did on the banks of the Tiber. But a strife arose between the brothers over the name of the city, each wishing it to be called after himself; and a combat ensued in which Remus was killed.

Rubens   *Capitoline Museum, Rome*

ROMULUS AND REMUS NURSED BY THE WOLF

The ravening she-wolf knew them,
  And lick'd them o'er and o'er,
And gave them of her own fierce milk.— MACAULAY

The numbers in Rome were so few that Romulus invited all murderers and runaway slaves to take refuge in it, and so he increased its population. But the inhabitants were mainly men, and to secure wives a large number of maidens were carried off from the neighboring tribe of the Sabines and

brought to Rome. Their kinsmen angrily attacked Rome.
Tarpeia, a Roman maiden, betrayed the citadel to the
Sabines if they would give her "what they wore on their
arms," meaning their gold bracelets. They threw their
shields on her and killed her, on what was later called "the
Tarpeian rock." In the ensuing battle the Sabine women
themselves, now reconciled to their Roman husbands, intervened and made peace. The two tribes formed one nation,

Gramstorff Bros.

THE VESTAL VIRGINS

Dread Vesta, with her holy things. — VIRGIL

over which Romulus ruled for thirty-seven years. Then he
was snatched up to heaven in a fiery chariot by his father Mars.
He was worshiped thereafter under the name of Quirinus.

EARLY KINGS OF ROME

Seven kings, including Romulus, ruled Rome until it
became a Republic. For a time after the death of the founder
no man was found fit to rule over the city. At last the
choice fell on a wise and just man named *Numa Pompilius*.

Whereas the Romans during Romulus's reign had been an exceedingly warlike people, Numa preached and practiced peace. He it was who erected a temple in Rome to Janus, the gates of which were closed during times of peace; during the forty-three years of the reign of Numa these gates were

ROME TODAY

A thousand roads lead men forever to Rome. — ALAIN DE LILLE

never open a single day. He made laws regarding religion and its practice; he instituted the order of the Vestal Virgins, whose task it was to see that the sacred flame of Vesta was kept eternally burning. He reformed the calendar, and divided conquered lands among the poor. Even the surrounding nations were influenced by Numa's wisdom and sense of justice; and when he died, more than eighty years old, the neighboring states did him honor at his funeral.

He was succeeded by a king of totally different character,
Tullus Hostilius, who sought everywhere a pretext for war.
A quarrel was easily made with Alba Longa, the inhabitants
of which claimed, like the Romans, descent from Aeneas and
his Trojans.   Both sides prepared for war, but the suggestion

Louvre

OATH OF THE HORATII

Let's do it after the high Roman fashion. — SHAKESPEARE

was made and accepted that three champions from each side
meet and decide the issue.

As it happened, there were three brothers in each army —
the Horatii in the Roman, the Curiatii in the Alban.   The
combatants met, and shortly two of the Romans were slain.
But the third brother, still unwounded, feigned flight and
drew after him the three wounded Albans.   He managed to
slay them one by one, and great was the triumph of the

Romans. It is said that Horatia, sister of the three champions, had been betrothed to one of the Curiatii. When she saw her brother returning with the cloak of her betrothed among the spoils, she wept bitterly. In anger, Horatius slew her, but on the plea of their father Tullus acquitted him of murder.

The Albans submitted grumblingly to Roman rule, and after a while Tullus destroyed their city. He reigned, always making war, for thirty-two years, and at last died when a thunderbolt struck his palace and all within were destroyed.

Then the people chose Ancus Martius, grandson of Numa, to be king. He preferred the path of peace, but when some of his neighbors made unjust war on Rome, he fought bravely and conquered them. In his reign of twenty-four years Rome was greatly expanded, and the condition of the city improved. He built the port of Ostia at the mouth of the Tiber and bridges across that river.

Ancus died while his sons were still too young to ascend the throne, and in his place the people chose a wealthy Etruscan who had only recently settled in Rome — Lucius Tarquinius Priscus. Tarquin ruled on a magnificent scale. He waged successful wars, and brought back much plunder to Rome. In his reign was first marked out the site of the Circus Maximus, and here magnificent games were held, particularly contests in horse racing and boxing. The city itself was greatly improved during Tarquin's reign. New buildings went up everywhere, the Forum and other parts of the city were drained, and a great temple to Jupiter was erected on the Capitoline Hill. His queen was Tanaquil.

When the time came for Tarquin to die, the sons of Ancus conspired against him in a vain attempt to seize the throne, but Tarquin himself had already trained a former slave, Servius Tullius, to take his place. Servius first set himself the task of dividing the people according to the wealth each man possessed; he imposed on the various groups certain requirements as to the number of soldiers they would be expected to furnish in time of war. He, too, enlarged the city, and gradually extended its power so as to include all of

CHARIOT RACE

The madding wheels
Of brazen chariots. — MILTON

Latium [land of the Latins]. He reigned well and wisely for forty-two years, but at last died basely. For his daughter Tullia, a woman of wicked character, was married to Lucius Tarquin, son of the preceding monarch; and the pair conspired against Servius and had him killed.

Lucius Tarquin, nicknamed Superbus, or "the Proud," began his reign with an act of murder, and for twenty-five years ruled in tyranny and oppression. Yet he was successful in war. It is said that one day a strange and aged woman mysteriously appeared before Tarquin and offered to sell him nine books at a great sum. She told him that in these books were oracles that deeply concerned Rome. Tarquin scorn-

fully refused her offer, and she left in silence. Shortly she
returned with six, and offered them at the same sum, saying
the other three had been burnt. Again the king refused her
offer. Once more she went away and returned with three of
the books, and this time the king bought them at her price.
It was believed that the old woman was the sibyl of Cumae

Elihu Vedder

THE CUMAEAN SIBYL

She utters mysteries shrouded in terrors. — VIRGIL

with whom Aeneas had spoken. The books were called the
Sibylline Books and were greatly revered.

Lucretia (or Lucrece) was the wife of Tarquinius Collatinus. She was dishonored by Sextus, son of Lucius Tarquin ;
and having informed her father, her husband, and their friend
Lucius Junius Brutus of his misdeed, she stabbed herself.
Brutus, ancestor of the Brutus in Shakespeare's *Julius Caesar*,
led a revolt against the tyrannical Tarquins, and banished
them forever. A republic was established, but for a number
of years the exiled Tarquins waged war against Rome.

It was during one of these wars that the Tarquins obtained the aid of Lars Porsena, a neighboring king; and he summoned his army and allies to help restore them:

> Lars Porsena of Clusium,
>   By the Nine Gods he swore
> That the great house of Tarquin
>   Should suffer wrong no more.
> By the Nine Gods he swore it,
>   And named a trysting day,
> And bade his messengers ride forth,
> East and west and south and north,
>   To summon his array.[1]

To save the town from the army of Lars, it became necessary to cut down the bridge over the Tiber. But the foe was approaching too fast, and the Roman general called for a volunteer to hold the bridge.

> Then out spake brave Horatius,
>   The Captain of the Gate:
> "To every man upon this earth
>   Death cometh soon or late.
> And how can man die better
>   Than facing fearful odds,
> For the ashes of his fathers,
>   And the temples of his Gods?
> Hew down the bridge, Sir Consul,
>   With all the speed ye may;
> I, with two more to help me,
>   Will hold the foe in play.
> In yon strait path a thousand
>   May well be stopped by three.
> Now who will stand on either hand
>   And keep the bridge with me?"

Horatius kept the bridge and even managed to escape alive through the waves of the Tiber, and for ages after mothers

[1] Macaulay's *Lays of Ancient Rome.*

HORATIUS AT THE BRIDGE

How well Horatius kept the bridge
In the brave days of old.

— MACAULAY

prayed to Juno that they might bear sons as brave as Horatius, and sitting by the fireside men told

> How well Horatius kept the bridge
> In the brave days of old.

It was at this time that Caius Mucius Scaevola sought to assassinate Porsena, but by mistake killed the king's scribe. Threatened with death, he laid his right hand on an altar of burning coals to prove his contempt of pain, and told the king that three hundred other Roman youths had sworn to take his life. Porsena, in admiration, freed him. Cloelia, a Roman girl who was being held as hostage, escaped by swimming the Tiber.

The Tarquins persisted in their efforts to regain the throne at Rome. At one time they joined forces with an army of Latins, and there was fought the Battle of Lake Regillus, a long and fierce conflict. Victory for a while was doubtful, but at the very crisis of the battle two horsemen, all in white armor and on magnificent white horses, suddenly appeared among the Romans and gave them victory. Hardly was the battle over when they disappeared, and then they were seen in Rome itself, cooling their horses at a fountain in the Forum. To a citizen who spoke to them they gave the first news of the victory at Lake Regillus. Then they vanished. The Romans, in awe, always believed that it was the Gemini, the twin brethren Castor and Pollux, who had given them such timely assistance; and they erected a temple to them in the Forum, and as long as Rome lasted gave them due honor.

Under the Republic, legends clustered around favorite Roman heroes. Marcus Manlius Capitolinus, consul in 392 B.C., was awakened by the cackling of geese when the Gauls tried to surprise the Capitol. With a few warriors he repelled the attack. Later, he tried to seize power, and was sentenced to be thrown from the Tarpeian Rock.

Titus Manlius Torquatus killed a Gaul, took from him a golden chain (*torques*), and placed it around his own neck. This same Manlius had his own son executed for engaging without permission in single combat with an enemy.

A year later a chasm suddenly appeared in the Forum. Soothsayers declared it could be filled only if Rome's greatest treasure were cast into it. Mettius Curtius, crying that Rome could have no greater treasure than a brave citizen, leaped into the chasm in full armor and on horseback; it closed over him.

A noble figure was the centurion Lucius Virginius. Sooner than see his lovely daughter Virginia fall into the power of Appius Claudius, a corrupt magistrate, he plunged a dagger into her heart. He then rushed to camp with the bloody weapon in his hand, and successfully roused his fellow-soldiers against the tyrant, who committed suicide in prison; with him fell others who had ruled evilly with him, and the rule of the common people was reëstablished.

Spartacus, a Thracian sold into slavery, became a gladiator and in 71 B.C. led an insurrection of slaves against Rome. He proclaimed the end of all slavery, but was defeated in battle and slain.

Another gladiator figures in the story of Androcles and the lion. Androcles was a runaway slave who took refuge in a dark cavern. A lion entered, and instead of tearing Androcles to pieces, showed him his forepaw, swollen with a huge thorn. Androcles extracted the thorn, and the lion allowed him to leave the cavern unharmed. Later the slave was captured and brought into the arena to fight a fierce lion. But the lion was the one he had befriended, and to

the amazement of all the beast bestowed on Androcles signs
of affection that won him his freedom.

STUDY APPLICATION

REFERENCES TO MYTHOLOGY IN LITERATURE

What do the following references mean? Where a word or phrase is
italicized, explain only the word or phrase.

1. What though I outlive Nestor, and what though
    You in your turn a *sibyl's* years shall know? — *Ausonius*
2. *Sibylla* tells *Aeneas* in Virgil, the thin habit [clothing] of spirits
    was beyond the force of weapons. — *Sir Thomas Browne*
3. Not great Aeneas stood in plainer day,
    When, the dark mantling mist dissolved away,
    He to the Tyrians [Carthaginians] showed his sudden face,
    Shining with all his goddess mother's grace;
    For she herself had made his countenance bright,
    Breathed honor on his eyes, and her own purple light. — *Dryden*
4. The word by seers or *sibyls* told,
    In groves of oak or fanes of gold,
    Still floats upon the morning wind,
    Still whispers to the willing mind. — *Emerson*
5. It was like *the golden branch* that gained Aeneas and the sibyl
    admittance into Hades. — *Hawthorne*
6. They do not willingly seek *Lavinian shores*. — *Lamb*
7. Softer than the lap where Venus lulled *Ascanius*. — *Lamb*
8.   Long is the way
    And hard, that out of Hell leads up to light. — *Milton*
9. Not half so fixed the Trojan could remain,
    While Anna begged and Dido raged in vain. — *Pope*
10. One speech in it I chiefly love: 'twas *Aeneas' tale to Dido*.
                                           — *Shakespeare*
11.   In such a night
    Stood *Dido*, with a willow in her hand,
    Upon the wild sea-banks, and waved her love
    To come again to *Carthage*. — *Shakespeare*
12. *Ilion's* lofty temples robed in fire. — *Tennyson*

13. *Golden branch* amid the shadows. — *Tennyson*
14. *Dido*, with the driven hair
    And with the salt-sea spray
    Upon those undesired lips. — *Winslow*

EXERCISES IN COMPOSITION, ORAL AND WRITTEN

1. When Aeneas takes on board the sailor of Ulysses who was left in the land of the Cyclopes, the Greek has an interesting story to tell. Describe how Aeneas questions him, and what replies he receives.

2. Aeneas is telling Dido how Troy fell as a result of the stratagem of the wooden horse. Give the story as he tells it.

3. You have an opportunity to interview Aeneas in the Elysian Fields. Tell him about Rome and Italy of today, and report his comments.

4. Write a description of the city of Carthage as it was in the days of Queen Dido; or give a brief account of the Punic Wars waged between Rome and Carthage; or tell what recent excavations on the site of Carthage have revealed.

5. Invent an adventure in which Camilla played a part, in the days before the coming of Aeneas.

6. Give a number of suggestions for effective scenes in a motion-picture play to be based on the story of Aeneas.

7. Read Kipling's *Jungle Books* and compare Mowgli with Romulus and Remus.

8. Make a table of similarities between the story Homer tells (Chapters XIII and XIV) and that told by Virgil.

WORD STUDY

1. Tell something about the origin of the following words:

> sibylline — prophetic, mysterious
> Hesperian — western
> harpy — a greedy, grasping person

2. Give the correct pronunciation of the following words:

Latium, Anchises, Phoenician, Dido, Palinurus, Cumaean, sibyl, Latinus, Lavinia, Rutulians, Camilla, Evander, Mezentius, Etruscans, Nisus, Euryalus, Iulus.

3. Which names of characters in the story of Aeneas are still used today as given names? Do any others attract you so that you would like to see them revived and used today — as your own name, for example?

4. What names of places are explained by the story of Aeneas? How did Rome derive its name? What is meant by the expression "to cut up didoes"?

5. Students of Latin will enjoy this old jingle of Richard Porson, a famous classical scholar:

On the Latin Gerunds

When Dido found Aeneas would not come,
She mourned in silence, and was Dido-dum.

Rapid Quiz

Who was Aeneas? Describe his parentage. How did he escape from Troy? Where was Hesperia? What adventure did Aeneas and his companions have with the Harpies? in the land of the Cyclopes? How did Aeneas escape Scylla and Charybdis? Who was the enemy of Aeneas among the gods? What trouble did she cause as he was approaching his future home? How did Neptune help him? Where did Aeneas find himself at the end of the storm? Who was the ruler of the land? Was she attracted to Aeneas? What happened when Aeneas rejected her proposals and set sail? What sacrifice did Juno demand before Aeneas was allowed to reach Italy? What prophetess did Aeneas visit? What land did he visit with her assistance? What did Aeneas see on his trip to the underworld? What figures of the future did Anchises show him? What was the "Lavinian shore," and who was Lavinia? Who was the rival of Aeneas for the hand of the latter? What war ensued? Who was Camilla? Who were Evander and Pallas? Why did the Etruscans help Aeneas? How did Nisus and Euryalus die? How was Camilla slain? Who was the victor in the combat between Aeneas and Turnus? Who were the descendants of Aeneas, and how did they become the founders of the Roman state? Who was the father of Romulus and Remus? What happened to them? What city did they found? Why did they quarrel? Give an incident from the history of the later kings of Rome.

For Students of Latin

1. Give some facts concerning Virgil.

2. For what qualities is Virgil's *Aeneid* so highly regarded? Why would the ancient Romans hold it in particular esteem?

3. What was the relation of Latium to Rome?

4. What long-enduring antagonism between two nations does the *Aeneid* seek to explain? What wars did this antagonism produce? What, according to historians, was the cause of these wars?

5. How did Virgil in the *Aeneid* flatter the Romans?

6. What do these Latin words mean: *somnus, victrix, longa, superbus?*

7. Answer in Latin two or three questions in the Rapid Quiz.

Reading List

Atherton, Gertrude: *Dido* [novel]
Brooks, Edward: *The Story of the "Aeneid"*
Chidsey, Alan Lake: *Romulus, Builder of Rome* [fiction]
Church, A. J.: *Virgil's "Aeneid" Retold*
Clarke, M.: *The Story of Aeneas*
Dryden, John: *Virgil's "Aeneid" in English Verse*
Howell, H. L.: *Stories from the "Aeneid"*
Knowles, Sheridan: *Virginius*
Macaulay, Thomas Babington: *Lays of Ancient Rome*
Marlowe, Christopher, and Thomas Nash: *Dido* [play]
Miller, Frank J.: *Two Dramatizations from Virgil*
Mills, Dorothy: *The Book of the Ancient Romans*
Purcell, Henry: *Lament of Dido* [music]
Shaw, George Bernard: *Androcles and the Lion*
Slaughter, M.: *The Story of Turnus*
Webster, John: *Appius and Virginius*
Wyatt, Sir Thomas: *The Song of Iopas*

A SACRIFICE

Vatican Museum

From fires of sacrifice, —
Sacred incense to the dead!
— GOODALE

XVI

THE DIVINITIES OF ROME

Long ere Rome had gathered slowly
Round the sacred fane of Saturn. — SHARP

ROMAN RELIGION

The Roman religion, like the Roman people, was practical in character. The imagination of the Romans was not rich and poetic as was that of the Greeks; it did not people hill-side and glen, stream and ocean-wave, mountain top and shadowy cave with strange and beautiful and terrifying figures. Such gods and goddesses as the Romans created

349

were somewhat vague in outline, often the direct outgrowth
of the life of the farmer or the needs of daily life.

Every village settlement was haunted by its own local
spirits: of the wood, of the spring, of the hill, of the household. They were grouped together under the general name
of *numen*, which means "will" or "divine will." These
spirits often had no sex, and one tablet is dedicated to a deity
"sive deo sive deae" (whether god or goddess). These
deities were homely ones. There was a goddess whose
function was to guard the door hinge, a god who stood watch
over the threshold, a whole group who regulated the life of an
infant — its feeding, its motions, its sleep.

Gradually, under Greek influence, the Roman gods and
goddesses became more definite and more stately. Gladly
the Romans took over the store of legends that the fertile
Greek imagination had invented, and gladly they identified
their own deities with those of Greece. But it is largely with
the Roman coloring of them and under their Latin names
that we know these ancient deities today.

JANUS, SATURN, AND VESTA

Just as some deities are found only in Hellenic worship,
so others are found only among the Romans.

One such god was *Janus*. He was usually represented
with two faces, and originally, it is said, this god was really
two deities, representing the sun and the moon. Janus
occupied an important place in the Roman religion. He
presided over the beginning of everything, and his name was
always invoked first in every undertaking, taking precedence
even over Jupiter. He opened the year, and hence the first
month was named after him. He was the porter of heaven,

and was called the "opener" and the "shutter," and he was therefore also the guardian of gates — which of course look two ways. In Rome there was a covered passage dedicated to him. This was opened in time of war and closed in time of peace; during the great days of the Roman state it was rarely closed. On New Year's Day, which was the principal festival of Janus, people exchanged presents. These usually consisted of sweetmeats and of copper coins, which showed the double head of Janus on one side and a ship on the other.

Another Roman god was *Saturn*, whom some connect with Cronus, the Greek god of the beginning. But in his functions Saturn (whose name means "the Sower") is much more closely connected with Demeter

JANUS

Janus am I, oldest of potentates.
— LONGFELLOW

(Ceres) than with Cronus, and his worship continued at Rome along with that of Zeus or Jupiter. He was believed to be the deity who had introduced agriculture and with it civilization and government. He carried a sickle as his symbol. Some legends identified him with an ancient king of Italy, and it was believed that during his reign, as in that of Cronus, had occurred a Golden Age, when all was well with mankind; we still speak of the "Golden Age of Saturn." His wife was *Ops*, the goddess of plenty; her temple was used as a state treasury.

The statues of Saturn were hollow, and were filled with olive oil, to denote the fertility of Italy in this product. The god was usually represented as holding in his hands a crooked pruning knife, and his feet were wrapped up in woolen ribbon. His temple at Rome was used as a treasury of the state, and in it were deposited copies of many laws. The chief festival of this god was called the "Saturnalia," and it was celebrated toward the end of December.

A fresco at Perugia

SATURN

All the gods
Gave from their hollow throats the name of
"Saturn!" — KEATS

Vesta, identified with Hestia of Greek mythology, had special functions and a particular reverence in Rome. She was the symbol of family life; the food in the larder, destined for the heat of the hearth-flame, was under her care, and the matron was her priestess. So, similarly, the House of Vesta in the Roman Forum. This was the home, the fireside of the state, where the sacred fire was kept perpetually burning, where there was a sacred larder that furnished food for the state sacrifices. Herein the purity of Vesta and her Virgins typified the integrity of the state and the home. To Vesta was given the gracious title of *Mater*, "mother."

Treaties and wills were often left for safekeeping in the House of Vesta; for example, Caesar left his testament with the Vestal Virgins, and Antony and Octavius deposited with them a treaty of friendship they had concluded.

OTHER ROMAN DEITIES

The Greek deities Castor and Pollux were enthusiastically adopted by the Romans, who revered them for their interest in sports, in war, and in horses. On them they depended for help in time of dire need, and soldiers in battle often appealed to them, the great Gemini or Dioscuri. It is recorded in Roman legend that at

Torlonia Museum

VESTA

Bright-haired Vesta. — MILTON

least three times the Twins appeared personally to help the Roman cause — at the battles of Lake Regillus, Pydna, and Verona. They were honored with a temple in the

Forum, and were made the patrons of Roman knighthood. Each year the knights, robed in purple and wearing wreaths, marched in solemn procession to honor the Twin Brethren.

Similarly, Hercules was adopted in Rome; but rather strangely he was at the beginning a god of commerce rather than of heroic deeds. The Romans liked to believe that in the course of his wanderings Hercules had often come to Italy. To him was attributed the building of a great dam for an Italian lake. It was said, too, that when he was going home with the oxen of Geryon (see page 240), an Italian shepherd stole some of them, and drove them backward into a cave. Hercules was at first puzzled by the inverted tracks, but soon located the cattle and killed the thief.

The *Camenae* were nymphs endowed with the gift of prophecy, and in some legends they were identified with the Muses. The most famous of them was *Egeria*, who was also the goddess of fountains. She became the wife of the great Roman king, Numa Pompilius, and imparted to him such wisdom that he became the real founder of the religious system of the Romans. He built the passage dedicated to Janus which has been mentioned, but during his reign, which lasted for forty-three years, its gate remained shut, for he cherished peace.

To the goddess *Fortuna* great reverence was paid in Italy. She was represented in different ways. Sometimes she was shown with a rudder, as the divinity who guides the affairs of the world. Again, she was shown with a ball, to indicate how unsteady and slippery fortune is. Occasionally she carried a horn of plenty. There was also at Rome a Temple of *Felicitas*, or Good Fortune.

Vatican Museum

FORTUNA

Thou wouldst have no divine power if we were prudent. It is we, O
Fortune, we who make thee a goddess and place thee in the heavens.

— JUVENAL

Bellona was a goddess of war; she is sometimes spoken of as the sister or the wife of Mars. *Libitina*, originally among the Italians a goddess of the earth, came in time to be regarded as the goddess of death; and it was she rather than Proserpina whom the Romans revered as such.

Sargent   Boston Museum of Fine Arts

FAMA

Fame, a fleet evil, than which is swifter none;
That moving grows, and flying gathers strength. — BEN JONSON

The Romans, who largely lacked the genius for drama and story of the Greek, loved to take mere abstract qualities and turn them into deities. Thus one finds worshiped among them such beings as Fear and Poverty, Old Age and Disease, Grief and Discord, Faith and Anger and Concord, Piety and Fame. Of the last Virgil has a noted description in the *Aeneid*, which Ben Jonson paraphrased as follows:

> Fame, a fleet evil, than which is swifter none;
> That moving grows, and flying gathers strength;
> Little at first, and fearful; but at length
> She dares attempt the skies, and stalking proud
> With feet on ground, her head doth pierce a cloud!

Two other deities that remind us of revered figures of our own day are *Roma* and *Italia* (compare them with our familiar symbol, Columbia). Roma appears again and again on Roman coins, as representing the Republic; occasionally the figure of Italia is seen.

ROMA

Roma aeterna [eternal Rome]. — TIBULLUS

Terminus, as his name indicates, presided over boundaries. His worship is said to have been instituted by Numa, who ordered that everyone should mark the limits and bounds of his landed property by placing stones sacred to Jupiter, and that every year, at these boundary stones, sacrifices should be offered in the festival of the Terminalia. This festival took place on the twenty-first of February, and on that day the owners of the adjoining pieces of land met at the stones or posts of Terminus and placed garlands on them. Then they raised rude altars, on which were offered gifts of grain, honey, and wine. They concluded by singing a hymn in praise of the god. The roof over the altar of Terminus in the Capitoline temple at Rome was kept open, to indicate that this god can be worshiped only in the open air.

Silvanus was a Roman god who in some ways resembled Pan. His name is connected with the Latin word *silva*, or "woods." He was the god of fields and forests, and, like Terminus, he also protected the boundaries of fields. He delighted in trees that grew wild, and was sometimes shown as carrying the trunk of a cypress. At other times he was represented as joyously bestriding a wineskin. To the care of Silvanus flocks were entrusted; he made them fertile and protected them from wolves. The sacrifices offered to him consisted of grapes, ears of corn, milk, meat, wine, and pigs. A somewhat similar deity was *Pales*, goddess of shepherds.

Another Latin deity who resembled Pan was *Faunus*, the protecting deity of agriculture, the god of shepherds, also a giver of oracles. He represented the kindly spirit of out-of-doors. Yet there was a mischievous side to his nature, since it was he who sent *Incubo*, the nightmare. Like Pan he was shown with horns and the feet of a goat.

Later the idea arose of many *fauns*, usually represented as

POMONA

Pomona loves the orchard. — MACAULAY

beautiful young men with tiny horns hardly visible. They lived joyous lives, haunting the woods with music and speaking with unearthly voices in mountain recesses.

Vatican Museum

THE GENIUS OF AUGUSTUS

The Genius and the mortal instruments
Are then in council. — SHAKESPEARE

There was also a deity who was sometimes called *Fauna*, sometimes *Bona Dea* (the Good Goddess), and sometimes *Maia* (as the last, identified with the mother of Mercury). She presided over the fruitfulness of the earth, as well as over the purity and faithfulness of women. She was worshiped at Rome as an austere virgin, men being forbidden to enter her temple. Her rites were celebrated by the Vestal Virgins and by matrons.

Lupercus and *Luperca* were worshiped as the protectors of flocks from wolves and as deities of fertility. Their festival was called the Lupercalia, and was held on the fifteenth of February.

Pomona presided over fruit trees. *Vertumnus*, god of the seasons and giver of fruits, fell in love with her, pursued her in various shapes, and finally, as a beautiful youth, won her. *Flora* (Greek: *Chloris*), on the other hand, was the goddess of flowers and of the springtime. She gave fragrance to blossoms, sweetness to honey, aroma to wine, and charm to youth. Her festival, the Floralia, was celebrated at the end of April and the beginning of May. The poets said of Flora that she was the bride of Zephyr, the West Wind.

Louvre

FATHER TIBER

The troubled river knew them,
    And smoothed his yellow foam,
And gently rocked the cradle
    That bore the fate of Rome. — MACAULAY

It was believed that each person and each place alike had a presiding spirit — a *genius* that was his or its guardian. A person's genius watched over him throughout life and bestowed blessings on him. The genius of a woman was called her *juno;* of a place, its *genius loci.* To genius and juno, each Roman paid worship on birthdays.

Hymen (supposedly descended from Urania) was the god of marriage, a winged youth, carrying a bridal veil and a torch.

Among the most striking of the purely Roman deities were their domestic gods, the *Lares* and *Penates*. The former presided over the house, fields, and roads. They were in reality the souls of the dead, who still hovered over the places in which they had dwelt. The public Penates were housed in the Temple of Vesta.

But only the spirits of good men were honored as Lares. Head of each family group was the *Lar familiaris*, regarded as the founder of the family. Images of the Lares stood in Roman houses, and upon joyful family occasions these images were crowned with wreaths. The Penates were gods of the whole house, but especially of the storeroom. They had their images at the hearth of every house, and the table was sacred to them. On the table the saltcellar and the firstlings of fruits were regarded as connected with them. Collectively, the Lares and Penates of a man represented his family through all the generations and typified the family spirit and traditions, his property and his possessions.

The *Manes* were shades that presided over places of burial.

A familiar deity of the Romans was *Father Tiber*, spirit of the important river that flowed through Rome.

HUMAN AND DIVINE

The Greeks and the Romans did not distinguish so nicely as we do between human and divine. The gods possessed human qualities, and were distinguished from human beings only by their greater power and their immortality. But human beings, on the other hand, could become gods or demi-gods, as did Hercules, Aesculapius, Orpheus, and others. Even in their lifetime mortals sometimes assumed the name and, so far as they could, the functions of the gods. Thus

THE APOTHEOSIS OF THE EMPRESS OF MARCUS
AURELIUS

And after death for deities were held. — DRYDEN

Cleopatra was worshiped as Aphrodite and went forth to meet Mark Antony under that name; and even earlier Julius Caesar had paid her divine honors, placing her bust in the temple of Venus.

The Romans in general were fond of regarding mortals as gods — or of allowing such mortals to assume divine airs. This process of deification (*apotheosis* is the technical word) occurred with special frequency after the time of Caesar, and what happened in his case may be taken as a good example of how the Romans confused Rome with Mt. Olympus.

In May 45 B.C. (while Caesar was still alive) it was decided to set up a statue of him as "the Unvanquished God" in the Temple of Quirinus. At the Sacred Games his statue in ivory was carried in the procession next to the images of the gods. In the following year orders were issued to erect a statue of Caesar in every city of the Roman Empire, and sacrifices, with full ceremonials, were offered to him on his birthday, the 12th day of the month of Quintilis. Moreover, this month was renamed July in his honor; and inasmuch as we still use the name, we too are still paying honor to the Roman hero. An oath in Caesar's name was introduced into the ancient formula for swearing by the gods, and he was included among the gods of the city with the title of Jupiter Julius.

Other Roman emperors followed his example and deified themselves liberally. One Roman emperor, however, Vespasian, who had a keen sense of humor, called out on his deathbed, "Woe's me! Methinks I'm turning into a god!" There was also a Latin satire which told, in burlesque form, how the Emperor Claudian was considered for *pumpkinification* rather than deification.

Gramstorff Bros.

COUNCIL OF THE GODS

Now Zeus whose joy is in the thunder let call an assembly of the gods upon
the topmost peak of many-ridged Olympus. — HOMER

THE OLYMPIC COUNCIL

	Greek	Latin	Realm	Symbols
1.	Zeus	Jupiter (Jove)	King of the gods and ruler of mankind.	Eagle, thunderbolts and oak.
2.	Poseidon	Neptune	God of sea, horses, and earthquakes.	Trident,[1] dolphins, and horses.
3.	Phoebus Apollo	(Same)	God of sun, music, poetry, and medicine.	Lyre,[2] arrows, and sun chariot.
4.	Hermes	Mercury	Messenger of the gods, god of commerce and theft.	Winged cap, winged sandals, and caduceus.[3]
5.	Ares	Mars	God of war.	Sword, shield, dogs, and vultures.
6.	Hephaestus	Vulcan	God of fire and of workers in metal.	Anvil and forge.
7.	Hera	Juno	Queen of the gods, wife of Jove, and patroness of married women.	Pomegranate, peacock, and cuckoo.
8.	Demeter	Ceres	Goddess of agriculture.	Sheaf of wheat, poppies, and cornucopia.[4]
9.	Artemis	Diana	Goddess of moon and hunting, patroness of maidens.	Crescent, stag, and arrows.
10.	Pallas Athena	Minerva	Goddess of wisdom, war, and weaving.	Aegis,[5] owl, olive tree.
11.	Aphrodite	Venus	Goddess of love and beauty.	Doves and sparrows.
12.	Hestia	Vesta	Goddess of hearth and home.	Hearth fire.

OTHER IMPORTANT GODS

1.	Cronus[6]	Saturn	Father of Jupiter; among the Romans, god of agriculture.	Sickle.

---

[1] A three-pronged spear.   [2] A musical instrument resembling a harp.

[3] A winged staff with two serpents twined around it.

[4] The horn of peace and plenty.

[5] A shield on which was fixed the head of Medusa, a woman with snaky locks, whose look was supposed to turn beholders to stone.

[6] Not to be confused with Chronos, the god of time.

Greek	Latin	Realm	Symbols
2. Bacchus } Dionysus }	Liber	God of wine, drama, and revelry.	Ivy, grapes, and leopards or panthers.
3. Hades } Pluto }	Dis	God of the underworld, minerals, and wealth.	Cerberus, the bident,[1] and cypress.
4. Eros	Cupid	God of love.	Heart pierced with arrow.
5. Pan	Faunus	God of nature.	Goats and satyrs.
6. Eos	Aurora	Goddess of the dawn.	

GROUPS OF DEITIES

The three Graces
The three Fates
The three Furies
The nine Muses
The dryads
The naiads
The Nereids
The Oceanids

The oreads
The four Winds
The Hours
The fauns
The satyrs
The sirens
The Hesperides
The Pleiades

ENGLISH DERIVATIVES

jovial
mercurial
martial
March
volcano
vulcanize
June
cereal
vestal
saturnine

Saturday
Bacchic
plutocrat
panic
satire
satirical
music
museum
auroral
chronology

ROMAN FESTIVALS

The Romans had many holidays, and these were really, in accordance with the origin of the word, *holydays;* for they were almost always in some way associated with religion.

Generally, these festivals were accompanied by *ludi* (games): plays, sports, races, and gladiatorial exhibitions.

[1] A two-pronged spear.

On these days no legal business could be transacted, and work of every kind was suspended. First would come, as a rule, sacrifices and prayers, and then the day or days would be given up to all kinds of merrymaking.

GLADIATORIAL COMBAT

The arena swims around him — he is gone,
Ere ceased the inhuman shout which hailed the wretch who won.
— BYRON

What with one festival or another, the Romans spent a large amount of time each year in paying due reverence to the gods and at the same time enjoying themselves. It has been calculated that at about the beginning of our era 64 days were given over to festivals. In the reign of Tiberius the number had increased to 87. It was 135 in the reign of Marcus Aurelius, and it is said that 175 days were devoted to festivals by the middle of the fourth century. Sometimes, in addition, there were special *ludi*. When Titus took Jerusalem in A.D. 70, 100 days were devoted to a celebration, and when Trajan conquered the Dacians, the gods were thanked for 123 days.

The Roman year began in March, and we may follow its cycle to indicate what some of the chief festivals were that the Romans celebrated. Honor was paid to Mars himself at the beginning of the month named after him, not only as a war god but as the quickening spirit of the springtime. Later there were horse races, and on the Ides, or 15th, of March was held the popular festival of Anna Perenna, the sister of Dido, who according to an ancient legend had wandered in her later years into the territory governed by Aeneas. The 17th was sacred to Liber, god of the vine.

An important festival in March was the Matronalia, said to be the forerunner of our Mother's Day. On this occasion husbands and wives offered sacrifices to Juno, as typifying the mother and matron. On the Liberalia, March 17, the Roman boy put on the toga of manhood.

April was rich in holydays. The *ludi Megalenses* were instituted in honor of the Great Mother. They were celebrated in the Temple of Cybele, but there were also shows in the Circus and other events. Ceres was a goddess especially dear to the common people of ancient Rome, and in April they paid her particular reverence. One curious custom was observed, for which no explanation has been found: foxes, with firebrands tied to their tails, were let loose in the Circus. Still another festival was held in honor of Flora. But the most important festival of April was the *Parilia* for Pales, the divinity of shepherds. At that time flocks and herds were solemnly purified, and men and women leaped through blazing bonfires.

In May occurred the *Lemuria*, when midnight offerings were made to placate certain evil spirits called *Lemures;*

and the *Argei*, when puppets of straw were solemnly cast into the Tiber by the Vestal Virgins, apparently as a charm to bring rain. Vesta was the goddess chiefly honored in June, when during the *Vestalia* her storehouse was thrown open for eight days, and on the last day the temple and sacred hearth were swept out and the refuse thrown into the Tiber. It was, in other words, a house-cleaning festival.

TEMPLE OF VESTA, ROME

There's nothing ill can dwell in such a temple. — SHAKESPEARE

During July the *ludi Apollinares* were celebrated for eight days; in this month, too, Neptune was honored. The festivals of August mainly marked the gathering in of harvests. But Vulcan, too, was honored — some have conjectured that the idea was chiefly to beg him not to burn granaries, at this time full of grain. During September reverence was paid to Jupiter at the *ludi magni* or *Romani*, established after the victory at Lake Regillus.

October was the vintage month, and its principal festival was the *Meditrinalia*, when the wine of the old vintage and the must of the new were tasted and compared. During November occurred the *Plebeii*, celebrated for fourteen days as a tribute to the common people (*plebs*) of ancient Rome.

SPRING — AN ANCIENT FESTIVAL

No Roman festival has had a greater influence on our own times than the *Saturnalia*, already mentioned. Originally this holiday was celebrated only for one day, December 17, but by Cicero's time the celebration had extended to seven

Alma-Tadema

VINTAGE FESTIVAL

What were revel without wine?
What were wine without a song?—STEPHEN PHILLIPS

days. It was a season of unrestrained merrymaking, a good deal of the spirit and some of the customs of which have been taken over for our Christmas and New Year's celebrations. Friends made presents to one another; schools were closed, and the Senate did not sit; no war was proclaimed; no criminals were executed; slaves were permitted to jest with their masters, and the latter even waited on them at table. A public sacrifice was made in the Temple of Saturn, which was followed by a banquet ending with cries of "Io Saturnalia!" by the banqueters. During December occurred, too, the *Faunalia*, in honor of the woodland spirits of *Fauni*, and the *Laurentalia*, sacred to the nurse of Romulus and Remus.

In January were celebrated the *Compitalia*, in which the

Lares were invoked at crossroads, and the *Paganalia*, when offerings were made to the spirits of earth on behalf of seed lately sown.

The *Lupercalia*, at the Ides of February, was a festival in honor of Faunus, who as Lupercus (wolf-scarer) protected the cattle and imparted fertility. On the famous occasion of the Lupercalia in 44 B.C. the crown was offered to Caesar by Mark Antony, who represented Lupercus. The year closed this month with the festivals of *Quirinus* (Romulus) and *Terminus*. In February occurred also the *Parentalia*, when Romans visited the graves of their dead and made offerings of wine, milk, and honey.

STUDY APPLICATION

The Myths in Literature

The great contribution of the Romans to mythology as embodied in modern literature has been in the matter of *names*. The Greek deities are more familiar to us by the titles of their Latin equivalents than in the original Hellenic form. We are more likely to think of Jupiter or Jove than of Zeus, of Juno than of Hera, of Minerva than of Pallas Athena, of Vulcan than of Hephaestus, of Hercules than of Herakles, of Cupid than of Eros.

This is true despite the fact that it is generally admitted that the Greek names are frequently both more beautiful in themselves and more significant in their associations. The Romans would have been the first to confess this, and it was the chief duty of an educated Roman to become well acquainted with Greek literature and with the stories of the gods as told by the Greeks. Latin has, however, been the mediator and interpreter for Greek literature and for Greek ideas; and of course for many centuries Greek was practically unknown, whereas Latin was the familiar second tongue of every educated person. It became very natural, therefore, to use the Latin rather than the Greek names of gods. In recent years, as the Hellenic influence has increased, the tendency of poets has, however, been in the opposite direction; and many writers today go back to the Greek forms. It is quite necessary that all of us know both forms — Latin and Hellenic.

The fauns of Latin myth have impressed the modern imagination greatly, and have been joined with Pan and the satyrs to symbolize the forces of nature. The idea of the Lares, Penates, and Manes, the conception of Janus and of Saturn's Golden Age, and the belief in Pomona and in Flora have all found their place in later literature. Of the Roman way of thinking a spirited representation is given in Macaulay's excellent *Lays of Ancient Rome*.

References to Mythology in Literature

What do the following references mean? Where a word or phrase is italicized, explain only the word or phrase.

A

1. Oft do the *fauns* and *satyrs*, flushed with play,
   Come to my coolness in the hot noonday. — *Buchanan*
2. I shall not altogether die; the greater part of me
   From *Libitina* will escape. — *Horace*
3. O, for a draught of vintage! that hath been
   Cool'd a long age in the deep-delved earth,
   Tasting of *Flora* and the country green. — *Keats*
4. Allan Cunningham vowed a memoir to his *manes*. — *Lamb*
5. When all the Tuscans and their *lars*
   Shouted, and shook the towers of *Mars*. — *Landor*
6. The *Saturnalia* will not last forever. — *Latin proverb*
7. O Tiber! *Father Tiber!*
   To whom the Romans pray,
   A Roman's life, a Roman's arms,
   Take thou in charge this day! — *Macaulay*
8. There let *Hymen* oft appear,
   In saffron robe, with taper clear. — *Milton*
9. And shadows brown that *Silvan* loves. — *Milton*
10. Long ere Rome had gathered slowly
    Round the sacred fane of *Saturn*. — *Sharp*
11. Like as *Bellona*, being late returned
    From slaughter of the giants conqueréd. — *Spenser*
12. *Faunus*, lover of the woods. — *Virgil*

B

1. Here didst thou dwell, *Egeria!* — *Byron*
2. Since so our fathers willed it,
   Let us December's freedom [Saturnalia] well enjoy. — *Horace*
3. Far from the fiery noon, and eve's one star,
   Sat gray-hair'd *Saturn*, quiet as a stone. — *Keats*
4.   At the feet
   Of *Ops* the queen, all clouded round from sight. — *Keats*
5. Those *Saturnalia* of two or three brief hours. — *Lamb*
6. *Janus* am I: Oldest of potentates!
   Forward I look and backward. — *Longfellow*
7.   When *Bellona* storms,
   With all her battering engines bent to raze
   Some capital city. — *Milton*
8. How happy is the blameless Vestal's lot!
   The world forgetting, by the world forgot. — *Pope*
9. Since love our hearts and *Hymen* did our hands
                       Unite. — *Shakespeare*
10. Beware the Ides of March! [Soothsayer to Julius Caesar.]
                        — *Shakespeare*
11. Bear me, *Pomona*, to thy citron groves. — *Thomson*
12.   Came *Silvanus* too,
    With rural glory crowned, and brandishing
    Fennels and giant lilies in his hand. — *Virgil*

EXERCISES IN COMPOSITION, ORAL AND WRITTEN

1. Write from memory the table of the twelve chief gods, giving their Greek and Latin names, their realms, and symbols.

2. Write from memory a similar table of other important gods.

3. Compose ten sentences in which you use ten of the derivatives listed on page 367.

4. You meet a faun while wandering in the wood, and he tells you of the joys of living close to the heart of nature and of knowing the ways of the little creatures of the wild. Give an account of your meeting.

5. Go to the front of the room. Say: "I am a god (or goddess)," but do not mention your name. Then go on and describe your realm.

See how many in the class can guess what your name is. Let others do the same with other deities. Go through the same process with the symbols of the gods.

WORD STUDY

1. Explain how the following words came to have their present meanings:

saturnalian — marking a period of riot and indulgence

Saturnian — distinguished for peacefulness, happiness, content

January — March — July

terminal — the end or boundary

silvan — woodlike

hymeneal — pertaining to marriage

floral — pertaining to flowers

janitor — a doorkeeper

opulent — rich, luxuriant

pomology — the science and practice of fruit-growing

2. What is the correct pronunciation of the following words?

Ares, Janus, Saturnalia, Camenae, Egeria, Fortuna, Bellona, Terminus, Silvanus, Pomona, Penates, Lar familiaris, Manes, Ascanius, Quirinus, apotheosis.

3. Give the Latin equivalents for Zeus, Ares, Artemis, Pallas Athena, Cronus, Hermes, Demeter, Hera, Herakles.

4. What is meant when a woman is called an "Egeria"? What are "flora and fauna"?

5. Which names of gods and ancient heroes have been more used in our literature and language, the Greek or Roman? Is there any reason for this fact?

6. Show that the names of September and the months that follow prove that the Roman year began in March.

7. *Genius* has two plurals in English. Tell what each one of these plurals means.

8. What is the difference between *Juno* and *juno?*

RAPID QUIZ

Do the Roman gods resemble those of Greece? What was the attitude of the Romans toward the Greeks? Who was Janus? Saturn? What were the characteristics of the rule of Saturn? What was the

Saturnalia? Who was the wife of Saturn? How did the Romans regard Vesta? Who was the most famous of the Camenae? Who was Fortuna? Bellona? Terminus? Silvanus? What Greek god did the last-named deity resemble? What other Roman deity resembled this Greek god? Who were the fauns? What gods protected flocks from wolves? Which one presided over fruit trees? Who was the god of marriage? Who were the Lares and Penates? the Manes? To what river did the Romans pay reverence? Name some Roman festivals.

For Students of Latin

1. Translate: *numen, sive deo sive deae, mater, felicitas, terminus, silva, genius loci, ludi, plebs.*

2. Name some deities found only among the Romans.

3. Give the Roman idea of mortals and immortals.

4. How was Caesar deified? Explain how we still pay honor to him.

5. Compare the Latin with the Greek influence on our knowledge of mythology.

Reading List

Poems, Plays, and Music

Corbin, Alice: *What Dim Arcadian Pastures*
Debussy, Claude: *L'Après-Midi D'Un Faune* [music]
Doolittle, Hilda ("H. D."): *Hymen*
Long, Haniel: *The Faun*
Pope, Alexander: *Vertumnus and Pomona*

Novels and Descriptive Works

Bailey, C.: *The Legacy of Rome*
Davis, W. S.: *A Day in Old Rome*
Fowler, W. W.: *Roman Ideas of Deity*
Fox, W. S.: *Greek and Roman Mythology*
Hawthorne, Nathaniel: *The Marble Faun*
Lamprey, Louise: *Children of Ancient Rome*
Showerman, Grant: *Eternal Rome*
Showerman, Grant: *Rome and the Romans*
Shumway, E. S.: *A Day in Ancient Rome*
White, Edward Lucas: *Anduvius Hedulio*
White, Edward Lucas: *The Unwilling Vestal*

Thorwaldsen   *Copenhagen Museum*

HOMER SINGING TO THE PEOPLE

Deep-brow'd Homer. — KEATS

XVII

MYTHS IN HOMER, VIRGIL, AND OVID

Oft of one wide expanse had I been told
That deep-brow'd Homer ruled as his demesne. — KEATS

THE GREEKS AND THEIR GODS

To understand the Greek attitude towards the gods of whom we have been speaking, we must go back in imagination to ancient Hellas.   William Stearns Davis, in his vivid book called *A Day in Old Athens*, writes thus :

"Gods are everywhere in Athens.   You cannot take the briefest walk without being reminded that the world is full of deities.   There is a *herm* by the main door of every house, as well as a row of them across the Agora.   At many of the street crossings are little shrines to Hecate, or statues of Apollo Agyieus, the street guardian ; or else a bay-tree stands there, a graceful reminder of this same god, to which it is

377

sacred. In every house there is the small altar whereon garlands and fruit offerings are laid daily for Zeus, and another altar to Hestia. On one or both of these altars a little food and a little wine are cast at every meal. All public meetings or court sessions open with sacrifice; in short, to attempt any semi-important public or private act without inviting the friendly attention of the deity is unthinkable.

"To a well-bred Athenian this is second instinct; he considers it as inevitable as the common courtesies of speech among gentlemen. Plato sums up the current opinion well, 'All men who have any decency, in the attempting of matters great or small, always invoke divine aid.'"

How noble the ancient conception of the gods was is evident in an old saying current at Delphi. It was customary for worshipers to sprinkle themselves with running water before invoking the gods. The saying ran:

Only when pure in thy heart canst thou enter the god's holy temple,
After thy form has been wet with the flowing of sacred water.
For the good pilgrim a drop is enough; but oh! from the wicked
Not all the floods of the ocean could wash away his transgression.

THE GROWTH OF GREEK MYTHS

Among the ancient Greeks, as among most other peoples, there was no definite body of myths to which anyone could go as an authority on the form and spirit of a particular story. Myths began among the people. They grew and changed with the ages. In different parts of Greece the same god was worshiped under different names, the same myths told with variations.

The poets who told and retold the Greek myths through the course of the centuries came to play a very important part in giving a story a particular form. From the very earliest

Puvis de Chavannes

HOMER RECEIVES INSPIRATION FROM THE MUSE

Μῆνιν ἄειδε, θεά, Πηληϊάδεω Ἀχιλῆος [Sing, O Goddess, the
wrath of the son of Peleus, Achilles]. — HOMER

times the Greeks, like most other races, regarded the poet as a sacred person, one directly inspired by the gods and under their constant protection.   The poet, according to the Greek belief, composed his songs in a kind of divine madness.   The Muse entered into him, and it was the gods and not he that spoke in his poems.   The poet was only an instrument of heaven — a pipe on whom the gods played.   One of the most highly regarded of the Greek gods was Apollo, deity of song and music; and no greater compliment could be paid to the other gods than to record of them that they had invented a musical instrument and composed songs.

Such being the attitude of the Greeks toward their poets, it is easily understandable that to poets' versions of stories of the gods great respect was paid.   In the misty beginnings of Greek literature certain of these poets were thought of as the sons of one or another of the gods — Orpheus was, for example, the son of Apollo; Musaeus was the son of Orpheus; and Amphion was the son of Jupiter.   Naturally such bards would be especially endowed by the gods with vision of the truth of things, the nature of the universe, and the experiences of the deities.

But, although fragments of hymns were attributed to Orpheus, these first poets left no definite compositions to which later generations could turn.   It remained for two later poets to provide a body of facts to which the Greeks went reverently for information about their gods.   These poets were Homer and Hesiod.

It may be that neither of these poets really existed, but around their names gathered a great mass of literature of a very significant kind.

In Homer's two great epics, the *Iliad* and the *Odyssey*, and in certain hymns attributed to him, were told with surpassing skill many stories of the gods; and from Homer's allusions and references still other stories can be built up.

Hesiod, supposed to have lived not very much later than Homer, was a shepherd and poet to whom are attributed two

long poems — *Works and Days* and *The Origin of the Gods*. In these writings Hesiod organized what is almost a definite system of the gods and their history.

In later Greek literature the most important poet, so far as the development of myths is concerned, was Pindar, of the sixth century B.C. Pindar was the most popular and the greatest of the poets who were engaged to celebrate the victors in the various athletic contests held in Greece. No matter what other honors were paid

Raphael Massard

HOMER

The blind old man of Scio's rocky isle.
— BYRON

such a victor, his glory was felt to be incomplete unless a poem of praise was written in his honor. In writing such poems Pindar quite often concentrated on the victor's ancestors or on the glory of his city rather than on the athlete himself. While so doing he took occasion to relate or to suggest many exploits of early Greek heroes.

Greek drama frequently took as its subject the adventures of the gods, the events of the Trojan War or those that fol-

lowed it, and other mythical subjects.   The dramatist treated
his themes freely, and developed the story according to his
own conception.   It frequently happens, therefore, that the
story as told by Aeschylus and the story as told by Sophocles
are by no means the same; and then Euripides may add
his own variation.   The great comic dramatist of Greece,
Aristophanes, moreover, had his own viewpoint; and some
of his remarks and some of the adventures in which he
makes the gods engage must have seemed very irreverent
to many of his listeners.

THE MYTHS IN VIRGIL

The genius of the Romans was not an inventive, original
genius.   Their strength lay rather in their ability to seize
and comprehend what others had done, and to give it a more
practical form.   Through the Romans the ideas of other
nations have often reached the rest of the world; and this
is particularly true with reference to their adoption of Greek
ideas.   But the Romans gave many ingenious turns to the
myths of the gods.

When the Romans became acquainted with the Greek gods
and with Greek myths they perceived at once the remarkable
similarities that existed between these and their own gods and
myths.   The more educated among the Romans were very
proud of being as familiar with Greek literature and philosophy as with their own literature and philosophy; and they
adopted the Greek *pantheon*, or system of gods, wholesale.

When we come to the Latin poets, especially to Virgil and to
Ovid, the two writers who did most for the growth of myths,
we find that they were thoroughly familiar with the stores
and treasures of Greek myth.   Whether they called the

Greek gods by their own names or by the names of their Latin counterparts, these poets made constant use of them. But they did more than merely adopt Greek mythology in a mechanical way. Both poets were endowed with fine imagination, with a gift for beautiful phrasing, and with genius for telling a story.

It frequently happens, consequently, that the modern world is acquainted with a particular legend or with the career of a particular god rather through Virgil or Ovid than through some version to be found in a Greek poet. We think of the gods by the names that these poets gave them; their descriptions of them occur first to us; and we accept their version of the details of a myth.

Virgil, as has already been stated, is the author of the *Aeneid*, a twelve-book account of the adventures of Aeneas, as well as of other works. In general Virgil follows Homer's scheme of narrative and treatment. His first six books, relating the journey of Aeneas from Troy to Italy, correspond to the *Odyssey*. His last six books, relating the struggle of Aeneas to found a state, correspond to the *Iliad*.

But although, as a writer, Virgil followed the Greek Homer, as a man he was an ardent Roman patriot, one deeply interested in the success of the empire newly founded by his patron Augustus Caesar. This patriotism is reflected in his treatment of mythology. Most frequently he uses Latin rather than Greek names, and his purpose throughout is to show that Italy and the Roman state had always been under the protection of the gods. He seeks, moreover, to awaken in his reader a new reverence toward these gods, a new devotion to them. He stresses at all times Roman *virtus* and *pietas*, the sense of duty to family, state, and gods as against selfishness. Aeneas is sorely tried and bears many misfortunes, but it is Jupiter, king of the gods, who rescues him, and thus emphasis is laid on the divine care for Rome.

In general, one may express the changes which Virgil made in the Greek myths by saying that he refined them and made them more plausible and less childlike, less primitive. He

VIRGIL

Roman Virgil, thou that singest
Ilion's lofty temples robed in fire,
Ilion falling, Rome arising,
wars, and filial faith, and Dido's pyre. — TENNYSON

had, too, a gift for picturesque language, and often our memory of a mythical character or place comes from his vivid descriptions — Venus revealing herself a goddess by her gait, the blind and shapeless monster Polyphemus, the horrid sights of the underworld. He has, moreover, bound up the myths in history; he explains, for example, the long and bitter enmity between Rome and Carthage by telling the story of Aeneas's rejection of Dido.   The places mentioned in the *Aeneid* are definitely fixed : unlike those in Homer, they have a "local habitation" in modern geography.

In his narrative Juno is endowed with that same too human spirit of implacable vengeance toward Aeneas which Homer shows Neptune as displaying toward Ulysses.   The most pleasing aspect of Juno is, perhaps, her messenger Iris, who makes her way back and forth from heaven on the rainbow.   Of Minerva a full-length picture is drawn, and it is from Virgil that one gets the best account of the stratagem of the wooden horse, which the goddess of wisdom assists the Greeks to make as a means of taking Troy.   In connection with the episode of the wooden horse occurs one of the most famous phrases in Virgil, spoken by a Trojan :

Timeo Danaos et dona ferentes.

"I fear the Greeks, even though they come bearing gifts," exclaims the priest Laocoön ; and then Virgil describes, with powerful vividness, how the serpents came and killed the priest and his children.

Venus is an important character in the *Aeneid*, inasmuch as Aeneas is her son.   She helps him on many important occasions.   Apollo figures in Virgil particularly as a giver of oracles and as a prophet, but one likes the glimpse of him in Book IV as a god of war — the arms rattling on his shoulders as he walks along.   Diana is called "brightest glory of the star land."   Vulcan makes a shield for Aeneas, just as in the *Iliad* he made armor for Achilles.   Neptune is shown calming a storm as an orator calms a mob.

A host of minor deities appear in the *Aeneid* — Triton, for example, blowing with skill his snail-shaped horn ; many

nymphs, Saturnus, Faunus, the two-headed Janus, hoar-
headed Vesta (thought of as the oldest of the Roman deities),
the friendly Penates, the familiar Lar who presides over the
fortunes of the house, and others.   When the Trojans come
to Italy they invoke the gods in prayer and pay special
tribute to the *genius loci* — the presiding spirit of the place.

VENUS GIVING ADVICE TO AENEAS
[Achates in the Background]

By her gait she was revealed as truly a goddess. — VIRGIL

Aeneas's visit to the underworld, although an imitation of
that of Ulysses in Homer, is beautifully done.   The "sop
to Cerberus" which he prepares so that the three-headed
dog may not harm him has become famous as a symbol
for placating monsters, physical and mental; and the lines
which the sibyl, or prophetess, who assists Aeneas uses to
describe the journey are a favorite quotation :

. . . facilis descensus Averno;
sed revocare gradum superasque evadere ad auras,
hoc opus, hic labor est.

"Easy is the descent to the underworld," she explains, " but to retrace one's steps, to escape once more to the upper air, that is difficult, that is a task."

Upon the fortunes of Aeneas three deities exert an influence — Jupiter, Venus, and Juno. But back of these three deities lurks a mysterious force to which these gods are themselves subject — the power of fate, to which Virgil refers sometimes as Fata, again as Parcae, elsewhere as Fortuna. The gods recognize this force, as when Juno resolves to make Carthage a world power, "if the Fates permit" (I, 18). But, somewhat oddly, it appears that the gods, even if unable to thwart fate, are sometimes able to delay it. Just as Homer, for example, describes Neptune as holding back Ulysses from Ithaca for many years, so Juno places obstacles in the path of Aeneas.

The gods in Virgil have communication with mankind in various ways. They sometimes appear directly, as when Venus, in the disguise of a huntress, talks to Aeneas, and he does not recognize his mother until she turns to go : then her gait reveals her as a goddess. Again, the gods make their will known by signs, as when the serpents are sent to destroy Laocoön. Or mortals may consult oracles, such as that of Apollo at Delos which Aeneas consults. Finally, the gods speak to mortals by means of dreams; and Virgil has the allegory of the two gates by which dreams issue to the living world : the one of horn, through which truthful visions come; the other of ivory, through which come false and misleading apparitions. Mercury appears in a dream to Aeneas, and bids him quit Carthage immediately.

That Virgil had somewhat more than a vague foreshadowing of the idea of a one and just God that comes to us from Palestine and the Bible is evident in a famous passage in *Aeneid I*.   There Aeneas exclaims to Dido :

"May the gods — if there be any divinities that look upon the good, if justice is of any account anywhere, and if there is a mind conscious of right — may they bring you worthy rewards."

His phrase about the "mens sibi conscia recti" shows how far Roman thought had progressed.

Reference must be made to the famous "Golden Bough." In Book VI Aeneas consults a sibyl, as already mentioned, in order to discover ways and means of reaching the underworld and there visiting his father Anchises.   The sibyl tells him that if he is resolved to make the attempt, he must first find and pluck the Golden Bough, as a gift to Proserpina. Later two doves of Venus guide him to the mystic tree, and Aeneas easily plucks the bough and bears it back to the sibyl. What was this tree?   It was a tree guarded by a grim priest with sword in hand, ready to slay all comers.   But anyone who slew him became in turn guardian of the tree.   The legend was such an odd one that it immediately attracted attention and has continued to do so.   In 1890, however, appeared a famous book — *The Golden Bough*, by Sir James G. Frazer;   and in recent years other editions of this work have been printed, until it has reached the bulk of twelve volumes.   (There is, however, an abridgment in one volume.) Frazer has taken this legend and traced parallels to it in the mythology and folklore of all nations.   He has used his exposition of the mystery of the Golden Bough to cast light upon the growth and nature of mythology and magic everywhere.   His book, thus suggested by a passage in Virgil, is

AENEAS AND THE GOLDEN BOUGH

So the doves of Venus alighted upon the tree, whence shone forth the
contrasting radiance of the Golden Bough. — VIRGIL

the most famous work in any language on the subject of the early beliefs of mankind.

THE MYTHS IN OVID

Ovid was a contemporary of Virgil. He early devoted himself to poetry. When he was more than fifty years old, he

OVID

To the rude Sarmatians he left his ashes, and his glory to Rome. — LAMARTINE

offended Augustus Caesar in some way no longer known and was banished to a desolate town on the Black Sea. There he continued to write, although in sad strain, for Ovid loved the gay life and gaudy pleasures of Rome.

Of Ovid's works those that are most important from the viewpoint of mythology are his *Metamorphoses*, or *Transformations;* his *Fasti*, a calendar of religious festivals; and his twenty-one *Epistolae Herodium* — *Letters of Heroines* of mythical times to their absent husbands or their faithless lovers — from Penelope to Ulysses, for example, and from Dido to Aeneas.

The *Metamorphoses*, in fifteen books, contains more than two hundred stories of changes chronicled in myth, of Hyacinthus to a flower, for example. But Ovid does not adhere strictly to this theme and relates other stories in which transformations play no particular part, as in the story of Deucalion and Pyrrha and of Aeneas's voyage from Troy. He begins by telling how from chaos arose an ordered universe. He describes the sins of man and the great flood which Jove sent; and he tells how from this flood Deucalion and Pyrrha escaped.

The slaying of the Python, the birth of the laurel, the slaying of Argus, the death of Phaëthon, the abduction of Europa, the carrying off of Proserpina, the vengeance of Niobe, the hospitality of Baucis and Philemon, the love of Orpheus and Eurydice, the greediness of Midas, and episodes of the Trojan War are among the subjects of other stories told by Ovid.

Ovid had a knack for story-telling. Frequently his tales are true short stories, such as would at the present time be told in prose, but with the details otherwise little altered. Very famous, particularly, was his story of Pyramus and Thisbe. Often there are sly touches of humor which show he did not take the themes too seriously.

Ovid immediately became popular with the Romans. They read his tales, and when they came to decorate their houses, they often employed suggestions from the *Metamorphoses* in their frescoes and works of art. During the Renaissance Ovid was the favorite Latin author of most readers, and the great Italian writers of this period were deeply influenced by him. We can, moreover, easily trace his influence on most English authors of this same period — on Spenser, on Shakespeare, and on Milton, among others. John Macy, in his *Story of the World's Literature*, says of Ovid:

"His imagination is at its best in the *Metamorphoses*, in which he put together many of the Greek and Graeco-Roman myths.   This was the great source book of ancient legend for modern poets, the Italians of the Renaissance, Shakespeare and his contemporaries, and English poets of the eighteenth and nineteenth centuries.   His work as a whole had an incalculable influence on the literature of modern countries, unsurpassed even by the influence of Virgil."

STUDY APPLICATION

REFERENCES TO THESE AUTHORS IN LITERATURE

What do the following references mean?   Where a word or phrase is italicized, explain only the word or phrase.

1. *Pindar* sang horse races. — *Byron*
2. Greece, sound thy *Homer's*, Rome thy *Virgil's* name. — *Cowper*
3. Greece, taken captive, captured her conqueror, and carried her arts into Latium [the district in which Rome was situated].
   — *Horace*
4. Oft of one wide expanse had I been told
   That deep-brow'd *Homer* ruled as his demesne. — *Keats*
5. We fall by course of Nature's law, not force
   Of thunder, or of Jove. — *Keats*
6. They hear, like Ocean on a western beach,
   The surge and thunder of the *Odyssey*. — *Lang*
7. Zeus, himself in toils of fate. — *Ledoux*
8.   My murmuring rhyme
   Beats with light wing against the *ivory gate*. — *Morris*
9.   *Iris* bright,
   When her discolored bow she spreads through heaven's height.
   — *Spenser*
10. Roman *Virgil*, thou that singest
    Ilion's lofty temples robed in fire,
    Ilion falling, Rome arising,
    wars, and filial faith, and *Dido's* pyre. — *Tennyson*
11. He had not the slightest inkling of why the district attorney should have sent for him, and *he feared the Greeks bearing gifts*, particularly one who looked so wily a *Ulysses*. — *Train*
12. What had Achilles been without his Homer? — *John Wolcot*

Exercises in Composition, Oral and Written

1. Write an essay called "Who Was Homer?" With the help of a good encyclopedia or of *The New Larned History*, see if you can find out what scholars today believe as to the author of the *Iliad* and the *Odyssey*. A book by Samuel Butler argues in favor of the view that the *Odyssey* was written by a woman.

2. Read any Greek play in an English translation and bring to class a report on the way in which the gods are regarded in this play.   Begin by making a list of references to the gods as they occur in your reading.

3. Write a supposed letter from Penelope to Ulysses, and then compare it with a translation of the letter that Ovid thought Penelope wrote (in the *Heroines*).

Word Study

1. What is the connection between the words *music* and *Muse?*

2. Is there any relation between *inspiration* and *spirit?* between *inspiration* and *respiration?* (But Thomas A. Edison thought that *inspiration* was ninety-eight per cent *perspiration.*)

3. Give the correct pronunciation of the following words:
Hesiod, Pindar, Aeschylus, Sophocles, Euripides, Aristophanes, *Aeneid, Metamorphoses.*

4. Explain the following expressions:

> The great battle of the pitchers was Homeric.
> His ode, unrestrained and wild, was truly Pindaric.
> His smooth, happy style was Virgilian.

5. What are some famous phrases that come from Virgil?

6. Is it *Virgil* or *Vergil?*   Interview a Latin teacher on this subject.

7. How many synonyms can you find for *metamorphosis?*

Rapid Quiz

Was there a definite form for any particular myth among the Greeks? What part did poets play in their development and transmission? What was the Greek idea as to the way in which poetry was composed? What two early poets are especially important in the history of Greek mythology? Name two works by each of these. Why is Pindar important?   How did Greek dramatists treat themes from mythology? What was the rôle of the Romans in the development of myths?   What

two Latin writers did most for the growth of myths? Name one work
by each. In what ways is Virgil thoroughly Roman? How did he
treat the Greek myths? What deities appear in his work? What are
some famous passages from his pen? How do the gods in Virgil com-
municate with mankind? What was the Golden Bough? What is the
reason for calling Ovid's chief work by the name given it? How many
stories does it contain? Why is Ovid important?

FOR STUDENTS OF LATIN

1. Translate: *virtus, pietas, metamorphoses, epistolae.*
2. Quote from memory and translate two famous passages from
Virgil.
3. Compare Virgil and Ovid.
4. Answer in Latin two or three questions in the Rapid Quiz.

READING LIST

Poems and Descriptive Works

Agard, Walter R.: *The Glory That Was Greece*
Conway, R. S.: *The Vergilian Age*
Duff, J. W.: *A Literary History of Rome* (two volumes)
Fowler, W. W.: *Roman Festivals*
Fowler, W. W.: *The Religious Experience of the Roman People*
Gibson, William Hamilton: *Virgil's Tomb*
Jebb, R. C.: *Homer*
Keats, John: *On First Looking into Chapman's Homer*
Kelsey, F. W., and Scudder, J. W.: Introduction to *Selections from
   Ovid*
Lang, Andrew: *Homeric Unity — The Odyssey* (sonnets)
Murray, Gilbert: *The Rise of the Greek Epic*
Pindar: *To Hiero the Aetnaean, Victor in the Chariot Race* (Pythian I)
   — *To Hiero the Syracusan, Victor in the Horse Race* (Olympian I)
Royds, T. F.: *Virgil and Isaiah*
Tennyson, Lord: *To Virgil*

XVIII

GODS OF THE NORTHLAND

Where are in circle ranged twelve golden chairs,
And in the midst one higher, Odin's throne. — ARNOLD

THE CREATION OF THE WORLD

The peoples of the northland were allied in blood and language to those of the peninsulas of Greece and Rome; and consequently there are numerous resemblances between the myths of the North and of the South.

Yet, although the resemblances are striking, the gods of the North in a good many respects differed from those of the South. The latter were more joyous and sunny; the former reflected the gloom and the hard conditions of life in the forests and waters of northern Europe. The stories told about them likewise differed.

For the Northmen believed that at the beginning for long ages existed *Niflheim*, a world of mist and ice. In the midst of Niflheim was a deep well, and from this well flowed ten rivers. To the south lay *Muspellsheim*, which glowed with fire. Gradually, in the course of time, the warmer airs from Muspellsheim melted the frost of the North, and out of the clouds that resulted sprang the giant *Ymir* and a whole race of other giants. The ground became visible, and on it lay masses of stones. From the frost itself sprang the cow *Audhumla*, and her milk nourished Ymir. The cow herself, by licking the salt, frost-covered stones, created the gods. On the first day she licked the stones a man's hair came forth, on the next day a man's head, and on the third day a whole man came forth. He was named *Buri*, and he was fair and tall. Then a female being was created, and from her and Buri came *Bor* and a number of goddesses. Bor's sons were the gods *Odin, Vili*, and *Ve;* and from them were descended the other gods.

These three gods slew the giant Ymir, and out of his body formed the heavens and the earth : from his flesh the earth, from his blood the sea, from his bones the mountains, from his hair the trees, and from his skull the sky. *Midgard* was the name given the earth, and over it the sky was made fast at its four corners. At each corner sat a dwarf.

From the sparks that Muspellsheim sent forth the three gods made stars to illumine the earth, and set them in the sky ; and there too they placed the sun and the moon and set a course for them. Around the earth flowed the great sea, and on its coast lived the giants, at *Jotunnheim*. Among the giants was *Nor*, with his daughter *Nat* and his grandson *Dag*. Nat was dark and swarthy, Dag was light and handsome, and them Odin took into the heavens to rule over the night

ODIN

Mightiest of a mighty line. — GRAY

and the day.   Nat or Night drives first the horse *Hrimfaxi*,
from whose bit the foam flies down over the earth and becomes dew.   In her wake comes Dag or Day with his steed
Skinfaxi, and his mane throws radiance over land and water.

Toward the north, at the end of the heavens, sat *Hraesvelg*,
a giant in eagle's form.   With the violent strokes of his wings
he sent forth gales over the earth.   Between the land and
the sky stretched the bridge of three hues, the rainbow,
called *Bifrost*.   Over this rode the gods to their places in
heaven.   At the end of the bridge dwelt *Heimdall*, who
guarded the bridge against the mountain dwarfs.   These
were small, ugly, and surly creatures, endowed, however, with
great wisdom and skill.   They were supposed to have sprung
from the blood and bones of two giants whom the gods had
slain.   Quite different were the elves, handsome and well
disposed toward gods and men.

In the midst of the world stood a gigantic tree, *Yggdrasill*,
at the foot of which the gods held their assemblies.   It was
an ash, the largest and best of trees : its branches spread
over the whole world and rose high into the heavens.   This
tree had three immense roots : one extended toward the race
of men ; the other toward Niflheim or *Hel*, the underworld ;
the third toward Jotunnheim, abode of the frost giants.

The root that extended into Midgard was guarded by the
Norns, three sisters who had control over fate.   Of them one
was called *Urth* or *Wyrd*, the past ; the second, *Verthandi*, the
present ; and the third *Skuld*, the future.   Sometimes they
are called the *Wyrd*, or *Weird*, *Sisters*.

Once the three gods were walking along the beaches of the
world, and saw two trees lying on the ground before them.
Then the fancy came upon them to create human beings, and
from the one they created a man, from the other a woman ;

The Norns

Now rend, ye Norns, your rope of runes! — Wagner

and they called them *Ask* and *Embla*. The first of the gods
gave them soul and life, the second endowed them with
speech and the five senses, and the third bestowed on them
understanding and the power of motion. From them are
descended all the inhabitants of Midgard.

THE GODS OF THE NORTH

Originally there were three chief gods, but in time all the
power came into the hands of Odin, king of gods and men.
He and the other gods dwelt in *Asgard*, which lay at the end
of Bifrost, the rainbow. Asgard was divided into two realms
— *Gladsheim* for the gods, *Vingolf* for the goddesses. Here
were many palaces of gold and silver, but the most beautiful
of them was *Valhalla*, the dwelling place of Odin. Before
Odin had made his rulership secure, he had had to contend
with another race of gods far to the north, but between them
at last peace was effected, and they too came to live in Asgard.
From among them Odin chose a wife, named *Frigg*.

Upon the shoulders of Odin, the All-Father, sat the ravens
Hugin and *Munin* — Thought and Memory. They flew
each day over the whole world, and brought back to him
reports of all that was happening. At his feet lay two wolves,
and to them Odin gave the meat that was set before him,
since he himself needed no food; and he drank only *mead*, a
drink made of honey. He was the fountainhead of wisdom,
the founder of civilization, the patron of poetry, the watcher
over kings, the lord of battle. To him was ascribed the
invention of the runes, the alphabet of the Northmen; he
set forth the decrees of fate, which were then inscribed by the
Norns upon a shield. Sometimes his name was spelled
Woden; and in his honor Wednesday was named.

Gramstorff Bros.

ONE OF THE VALKYRIES

And the Valkyries on their steeds went forth
Toward earth and fights of men. — ARNOLD

When a hero died in battle his soul was carried off to Valhalla by the *Valkyries*, martial maidens clad in armor and mounted on winged steeds. In Valhalla all such heroes feasted perpetually with Odin, and the roasted boars on which they fed each day were at night miraculously renewed, and the mead which they quaffed was ever replenished. Sometimes, for amusement, the heroes fought one another with savage fervor, but their wounds were immediately healed.

Next to Odin on his throne sat his wife Frigg, queen of the gods, who knew all things.

Thor, son of Odin and Frigg, was the thunderer, the god of war. He was the strongest of gods and men. In the palace wherein he dwelt were five hundred and forty rooms, and it was the largest house that was ever built in those days. Two goats drew the wagon of Thor. He had three wonderful treasures in his keeping. One was the hammer *Mjollnir*, of which even the frost giants lived in dread, for with it he had slain many a one of them. The second was the *girdle of strength*. When Thor put this round his body, his great strength was at once doubled. The third was a pair of *iron mittens* with which to grasp the hammer handle. With these weapons Thor engaged in perpetual battle with the enemies of the gods and of mankind, for he was a good friend to human beings. He was a blunt, somewhat hot-tempered god, without fraud or guile, using few words and preferring actions to speech. In his honor was named Thursday.

Another son of Odin was *Balder*. He was the best of the gods, and in him all was perfect. He was a radiant being, from whom light seemed to shine. He was the wisest, most eloquent, most gracious of the gods, and in his dwelling was nothing impure. He was the god of sunlight, of spring and gladness. Yet of him it was prophesied that he should die.

G. E. Fagelberg

Stockholm National Gallery

THOR

I am the God Thor,
I am the War God,
I am the Thunderer! — Longfellow

Frey governed the rain and the sunshine, and made all the things of the earth to grow. Men called upon him to obtain prosperity and times of peace and happiness. His sister, *Freya*, was the goddess of love and music and flowers, and she ruled over the fairies in Alfheim. Her wagon was drawn

FREYA AND FREY

The gods held talk together, grouped in knots. — ARNOLD

by two cats. Half of those that fell in battle belonged to her, the other half to Odin. She owned a costly necklace, called *Brisingamen*, and she was called "she that shines over the sea." To her Friday was dedicated.

Tyr or *Tiu* was the most courageous of the gods and delighted in war. Upon his name brave men called in battle. His day was Tuesday.

Bragi was the god of poetry and himself the best of the skalds or minstrels. His wife was *Ithunn*, goddess of the early spring. She was the guardian of certain golden apples, of which the gods ate when they felt themselves growing old, and immediately youth returned to them.

Among other gods were *Höthr*, or *Hoder*, who presided over winter, and who was blind; *Ull*, unrivaled as an archer and ice skater, whose favor was invoked by those who engaged in single combats; and *Forseti*, god of justice.

Of a different sort was *Loki*, the god of evil. He was a god who liked to bring about quarrels, who originated all frauds and deceits, and who was the disgrace of the gods. He was handsome to look upon, but malicious in disposition and most fickle. He was very ingenious, and again and again by his cleverness he managed to escape the punishment that was due him. He was the father of the wolf *Fenrir*, of the *Midgard Serpent*, which encircled the earth, and of the goddess *Hel*, or Death. The latter was confined in Niflheim, and her home was called Sleet-Den. Among her followers were Hunger, Care, and Stumbling-Stone.

ADVENTURES OF THE GODS

For a time the wolf Fenrir dwelt in Asgard. But as he increased in size the gods perceived his evil nature, and they resolved to bind him. No bands that they could place around him, however, held fast; twice he broke forth from their strongest fetters. Finally, the mountain spirits made for the gods a chain that would hold Fenrir. This was strangely contrived out of the noise of a cat's paw, the beard of a woman, the roots of a mountain, the sinews of a bear, the breath of a fish, and the spittle of a bird. This chain looked so slender and worthless that the wolf would not let the gods place it upon him, for he suspected some fraud, some hidden power in it. At last he consented to have it placed around

THOR CHAINING FENRIR

Now did the dwarfs fashion a fetter shaped of the footfall of a cat, the spittle of a bird, the breath of a fish, the roots of a mountain, the beard of a woman, and the sinews of a bear. — KATHARINE PYLE

him if one of the gods would place his hand inside the wolf's mouth as a pledge. The gods feared to do this, but at last Tyr carried out the wolf's condition. Then the fetter was placed upon Fenrir. It held fast, but in revenge the wolf bit off the hand of the god.

Once a mountain giant assumed the form of a man and came to the gods with the suggestion that he build for them a wall that would protect them forever against the frost giants. But he asked in return that Freya be given to him as a bride and the sun and moon as a dowry. The gods consented to these conditions, provided he finish the whole work in one winter without assistance. The giant agreed, but asked that he be allowed the use of his horse, Svadilfari. Again the gods, on the advice of Loki, consented and he began work. Then the gods saw that it was really the horse, capable of drawing stones of immense size, which was doing the greater part of the work. Soon the fortification approached completion, and the gods in despair looked forward to the time when Freya would no longer give them love and music and flowers, and when the world would be darkened without sun or moon. So they laid hands upon Loki, and told him that unless he could prevent the giant from completing his work, he himself would be killed. Loki promised to use his wits against the giant. That night he managed to entice the steed into the forest and to keep him from assisting the giant. The giant did his best to work alone, but it was in vain. Just then Thor returned from an expedition, and he slew the giant and hurled him to the underworld.

Thor himself not long afterward by mischance lost his hammer, which fell into the possession of the frost giants. Their king would not return it unless Freya became his bride. She refused his proposal, but Loki persuaded Thor to dress himself in women's clothes and to accompany him to Jotunn-heim, as if he were Freya. In Jotunnheim a splendid feast was prepared for the supposed bride, but the king of the giants was amazed at the huge quantity of food which the coy goddess consumed — a whole ox roasted, eight great salmon, three tuns of mead, thirty hams, besides an immense quantity of sweetmeats. When he lifted up the veil to kiss the bride, he was terrified by her eyes shining like fire. But Loki reassured him. The bride, he said, had been so anxious to see him that for eight days she had neither eaten nor slept. At last the favorable moment arrived. Thor seized his magical hammer, slew the king and his followers, and returned to Asgard.

At another time Thor, accompanied by his servant Thialfi and Loki, set out for the land of the giants. On the way they passed through an endless forest, and came at last to a great but deserted hall, in which they lay down to rest. In the night the ground shook as if from an earthquake, and in the morning when they crawled out they found a giant of mountainous size sleeping near by, whose snoring still made the ground tremble. He awoke, and told Thor that his name was Skrymir.

"Where is my glove?" he cried, and looking around he picked it up. It was the hall in which Thor, Loki, and the servant had slept. The giant suggested that they all travel together, but Thor was hard put to it to keep up with him. At nightfall the giant lay down to sleep, but handed Thor his wallet and bade him take food from it. Thor could not open the wallet, and after struggling in vexation with the strings, he lost his temper and hit the giant a terrific blow with his hammer. The giant yawned and opened his eyes.

ODIN'S BATTLE WITH THE FROST GIANTS

There are giants to slay. — GEORGE MEREDITH

"Did a leaf fall on my head?" he asked, and fell asleep again. Again Thor struck him, and once more he awoke.

"Did some birds perch on my head?" he inquired, and again he fell asleep. Thor resolved that the third time he would slay the giant, and struck his skull with all his might, but the giant merely roused himself uneasily and grumbled at the acorn that had dropped on his head.

The giant told Thor that he himself was but a small person among the giants that lived in Jotunnheim, and he advised him to be careful when he reached that city. Then he left them and departed on a way of his own.

At last Thor, Loki, and the servant reached the city of the giants, over which Utgard-Loki ruled. This king looked at them scornfully, and bade them say in what feats they were skilled.

"I can eat," rejoined Loki, "faster than anyone else can, and I am ready to compete with your heartiest gourmands."

The king bade one of his followers named Logi come forward, and between him and Loki was placed an immense trough filled with food. Loki began at one end, Logi at the other; and they ate their way toward each other. In the exact middle of the trough they met, but inasmuch as Logi had eaten everything, whereas Loki had left the bones, Logi was called the victor.

Then the king asked Thor's servant what he could do. Thialfi replied that he could outrun anyone who might compete with him. Thereupon they all adjourned to a farspreading plain, and there a young man named Hugi was matched against Thialfi. Three times they ran, and always Hugi far outstripped Thor's servant.

Finally the king turned to Thor and inquired of him what feat he would perform. Thor claimed he could drink as no one else could.   So the king bade them bring forward a horn, which seemed of moderate size.

"A good drinker," said Utgard-Loki, "can empty this in a single draft, but a moderate one may need two.   Anyone can empty it in three."

So Thor lifted up the horn, and he drank and drank until every bit of breath had left his body.   He looked in the horn, and the liquid seemed scarcely to have been touched.   Again he drank deeply, and still it seemed not to be diminished.   A third attempt brought no better results, and in sullen anger Thor handed the horn back to the king.

Now the king proposed another test to Thor — to lift his cat from the ground.   Thor tugged and tugged, but was just able to stir one of the animal's legs.   When Thor angrily proposed that someone wrestle with him, the king smiled and called forward an old woman.

"Wrestle with my old nurse Elli," he bade Thor.

But the stronger the grip of Thor upon Elli, the more she resisted; and she was even able to bring him down upon one knee.   At that moment the king commanded that they cease.

The next morning Thor and his companions departed, and Utgard-Loki accompanied them to the gates of the city.   As they were about to set forth on their journey, he stayed them, and said to Thor:

"Now I will tell you the truth, because I know that never again shall you enter my city.   Mighty and marvelous is your strength, and throughout all these trials I have deceived you.   I was the giant in the forest.   The wallet was tied with iron wires, that you could not tear.   The three blows of your hammer never touched me: I skillfully evaded them, and if you will look on the mountain side, you will find three glens that your blows created.   Logi, whom Loki competed with, was Fire; and who can consume more than Fire? Hugi was Thought; and what is swifter than Thought? The end of the horn wherefrom you drank reached into the sea, and almost you emptied it, to my marvel. The cat was not really a cat, but the Midgard Serpent, and when you lifted its leg, it was almost loosened from the earth. As for Elli, she is Old Age; and what man or god is there whom Old Age will not, sooner or later, overcome?"

So saying Utgard-Loki disappeared, and the city with him.

THE DEATH OF BALDER

The death of Balder came about in this wise. It was known that sooner or later he would be killed, and to avert his doom his mother Frigg went around to all things on heaven and earth and made them swear that never would they harm Balder. But one thing she overlooked, the mistletoe, hidden in the oak leaves.

Now the gods, knowing what had happened, amused themselves by hurling at Balder their swords and battle-axes, stones and limbs of trees, huge masses of earth and metal. But nothing would touch him, and he remained unharmed. Loki was vexed at this, and he searched everywhere for something wherewith he might inflict harm on Balder. At last he came to an insignificant plant, the mistletoe, from which Frigg had exacted no oath. He cut a sprig of it eagerly, and then persuaded Höthr, the blind god, to hurl it at Balder. He did so, and the beautiful god fell to the ground dead. All mourned for him, as men mourn for the departed springtime. One of the gods even sought Balder in the underworld, and was told there that if all things lamented for Balder, he would return. But this could not be. Loki was punished by being

BALDER

Of all the twelve round Odin's throne
Balder the beautiful alone,
The Sun-God, good and pure and bright,
Was loved by all, as all love light. — J. C. Jones

bound in chains, and above his head was a serpent whose venom fell on him continually.

According to these Northern legends, there was to come a time when all the world would be destroyed — when the rulers of heavens would themselves be brought to judgment. This age was called *Ragnarok*, the judgment of the gods or the twilight of the gods. First would come three years that would be all winter, month after month of continuous snow and tempest. Then would come disastrous earthquakes. Men would die in hordes. The wolf Fenrir would snap his chains, the Midgard Serpent arise from his bed. Then Loki would escape and join the enemies of the gods. Over the twilight bridge the hostile hosts would advance against heaven, and a great combat would ensue in which all would perish. The sun would sink from the sky, flames would consume the earth, time would come to an end. But the Father of All, greater than Odin or his enemies, would make a new heaven and a new earth, set in a Golden Age.

STUDY APPLICATION

REFERENCES TO MYTHOLOGY IN LITERATURE

What do the following references mean? Where a word or phrase is italicized, explain only the word or phrase.

A

1.   And the stars came out in heaven,
   High over *Asgard*. — *Arnold*
2. Of *Frigga*, honored mother of the gods. — *Arnold*
3. But in his breast stood fixt the fatal bough
   Of *Mistletoe*. — *Arnold*
4. Thou camest near the next, O warrior *Thor*,
   Shouldering thy hammer. — *Arnold*

5. But in *Valhalla* all the gods went back
   From around *Balder*, all the heroes went;
   And left his body stretched upon the floor. — *Arnold*
6. For this thing also had been appointed by *Urd* and *Verdandi*
   and *Skuld* as they sat weaving under Ygg-drasil. — *Cabell*
7. *Balder* the Beautiful
   God of the summer sun! — *Longfellow*
8. But *Odin* spoke in answer, and his voice was awful and cold.
   — *Morris*
9. The *Weird Sisters*, hand in hand,
   Posters of the sea and land,
   Thus do go about, about. — *Shakespeare*
10. Their radiant palace is *Valhalla* called. — *Wagner*

B

1. And *Freya* next came nigh, with golden tears;
   The loveliest goddess she in heaven. — *Arnold*
2. And he beheld spread round him *Hela's* realm,
   The plains of *Nifleheim*. — *Arnold*
3. Where are in circle ranged twelve golden chairs,
   And in the midst one higher, *Odin's* throne. — *Arnold*
4. And in *Valhalla Odin* laid him down. — *Arnold*
5. And the *Valkyries* on their steeds went forth
   Toward earth and fights of men. — *Arnold*
6. There goes *Thor's* own Hammer,
   Cracking the dark in two! — *Kipling*
7. *Hoeder* the blind old god,
   Whose feet are shod with silence. — *Longfellow*
8. When the *Norn* mother saw the whirlwind hour
   Greatening and darkening as it hurried on,
   She left the Heaven of Heroes. — *Markham*
9. The *Norns*, the terrible maidens. — *Scott*
10. When they who built the burg *Freya* for meed demanded.
    — *Wagner*

Exercises in Composition, Oral and Written

1. Draw up a table of the gods of the Northland similar to that of the Greek and Roman gods, pages 366–367.

2. Conduct a guessing contest as to these gods, following the directions given in exercise 5, page 374.

3. Which set of gods do you find more interesting, those of the Greeks and Romans or those of the Northland? Why?

4. Invent another adventure of Thor, in imitation of those given in this chapter.

5. As one of the gods who was present at the time, tell how Balder was killed.

Word Study

1. Give the origin of the following names: Tuesday, Wednesday, Thursday, Friday.

2. Give the correct pronunciation of the following names.
Ymir, Hraesvelg, Mjollnir, Valkyries.

3. Look up in Webster's *Dictionary* the word *weird*, both the noun and the adjective, and note how its present meaning is connected with that of *wyrd*, fate.

4. What place did the old Norsemen call "middle garden"? The Norsemen had a drinking salutation, "Skoal!" (See Longfellow's *The Skeleton in Armor*.) With the name of which of the Norns is this salutation connected? Would *Valhalla* be an appropriate name for a "Hall of Fame" for heroes? (See Webster's definition of the word.) What were the runes? How many synonyms can you find for *skald*?

Rapid Quiz

How do the gods of the North differ from those of the South? What, according to the men of the Northland, was the way the world originated? How did the stars and the sun and the moon come into existence? At the foot of what tree did the gods hold their assemblies? Where did its three roots extend? Who were the Norns? Who was the king of gods and men? What was the name of his dwelling place? Who was his wife? What was his food? Who were the Valkyries? Who was the strongest of gods and men? What three wonderful treasures did he possess? Who was Balder? Frey? Freya? Tyr? Bragi? Ithunn? Höthr? Ull? Forseti? Who was the god of evil? of death? How was the wolf Fenrir bound? How was the giant outwitted who was promised Freya as a wife? How did Thor contend with the frost giants? How did the death of Balder come about? What was the belief of the Norsemen as to the final destiny of the gods? What was Ragnarok?

READING LIST

Poems, Prose Epics, and Music

Arnold, Matthew: *Balder Dead*
Bellows, H. A.: *The Poetic Edda*
Brodeur, A. G.: *The Prose Edda*
Buchanan, Robert: *Balder the Beautiful*
Gray, Thomas: *Ode on the Descent of Odin — Ode on the Fatal Sisters*
Kipling, *Song of the Red War-Boat*
Longfellow, Henry Wadsworth: *Tagner's Drapa — The Saga of King Olaf*
Scott, W. B.: *The Norns Watering Ygg-drasil*
Wagner, Richard: *Ride of the Valkyries* (in the opera, *Die Walküre*)

Novels and Descriptive Works

Anderson, R. B.: *Norse Mythology*
Asbjörnsen, P. C.: *Popular Tales from the North*
Colum, Padraic: *The Children of Odin*
Dahn, Felix: *A Captive of the Roman Eagles*
Mabie, H. W.: *Norse Stories*

SIEGFRIED AND THE DWARF AT THE FORGE

So the dwarf set to work and with his wonderful smith-craft he fashioned a
sword that he believed no blow could break. — AMY CRUSE

XIX

HEROES OF THE NORTH

Stout in battle, he slew the dragon. — BEOWULF

THE STORY OF SIEGFRIED

Near Xanten on the Rhine lived a king and a queen named
Siegmund and Sieglinde, to whom was born a fair prince
named Siegfried.   As Siegfried grew older, the Netherlands,
the kingdom over which his parents ruled, was threatened by
invaders, and the young prince was sent away from the castle,
for fear that he might fall into the hands of the foe.   His
parents entrusted him to the care of a blacksmith named
Mimer, who lived in the secret thickets of a great forest.

SIEGFRIED

Mighty Siegfried! — NIBELUNGENLIED

Now Mimer was a dwarf or troll, and belonged to a strange race of the little people, called Nibelungs. These Nibelungs dwelt for most part underground, in a dark little town which they had built. This town was named Nibelheim. The great majority of the Nibelungs were very skillful smiths, who would hammer all day at their tiny anvils. But at night the Nibelungs, men and women, would make merry with dance and music. Mimer was a Nibelung who lived on the surface of the earth, and he had built his forge under the trees of the forest.

Siegfried was delighted to join Mimer and his apprentices, and he learned in a little while how to swing the heavy hammer. Indeed, his strength soon became too great, for so resounding and powerful were the blows he struck that often the anvil would be shattered to pieces. Then Mimer would scold him sarcastically, and Siegfried, angrily leaving the smithy, would stride off into the woods and listen to the cheerful caroling of the birds.

One day, while Siegfried was wandering through the forest, the whim came upon him to blow his mighty silver horn. He did so, and before the sound had died away, he saw suddenly before him a huge shaggy bear. He was not in the least frightened. Rather it occurred to him that here was a good chance to pay Mimer back for his numerous rebukes. He rushed at the great beast, seized it in his arms, and in the twinkling of an eye had muzzled the animal with his belt. Then he led the bear quickly and quietly back to the forge.

There Mimer was sharpening a sword at the anvil. As he heard the laughter of the prince, he turned around and saw the bear. Instantly he dropped the sword with a clang and ran off to the darkest corner of the smithy, trembling with fear. For a time Siegfried continued to tease the little man, then he unmuzzled the bear and set him free in the forest again.

This was but one of the many pranks which the young prince played upon Mimer, for he did not care very much for the cunning and ill-tempered troll. Finally, the latter grew tired of the trouble that Siegfried was causing him, and determined to get rid of him.

One day, therefore, he sent him deep into the forest to bring home some charcoal for the forge from a certain storehouse. He did not tell the lad that on the road he would have to pass a terrifying dragon, named Fafnir. Siegfried strode merrily along. Once more the impulse came on him to blow a few notes on his beloved horn, and as he did so, once more danger appeared. At the sound of the blast the dragon roused himself in his lair and began to spout fire. The trees swayed and trembled as the dragon made his way underneath them toward Siegfried, and the little birds and beasts of the forest scurried away in fear.

Yet when Siegfried beheld the dragon he was not at all frightened. In fact, after a few moments, he began to laugh, for he welcomed the break in his too peaceful life that the dragon was bringing him. The dragon sat down on a hill and glared at Siegfried. But Siegfried remarked cheerfully:

"I am going to kill you, for you are too ugly to live."

At these bold words Fafnir opened his huge jaws and showed his teeth, extending in triple rows like a forest. But again Siegfried laughed. Then Fafnir, wild with anger, crept nearer and nearer and lashed his tail furiously. But Siegfried drew his sword, that he himself had forged with care at the anvil of Mimer. Leaping upon the dragon's back, he plunged the blade into his heart. In dreadful convulsions the dragon fell dead.

SIEGFRIED AND THE DRAGON

As Fafnir glided toward the water, Siegfried straightway thrust his sword through him, and that was his end. — THE PROSE EDDA

Siegfried was not yet done with the dragon, however. As the dragon lay at his feet, he remembered that while working in Mimer's smithy he had heard some of the Nibelungs talk of this very dragon. He recalled that they had said that whoever bathed in the blood of the dragon would be forever after invulnerable. For his skin would grow so tough and horny that no sword or arrow could pierce it. So Siegfried flung aside his dress of deerskins and plunged into his dragon bath. From top to toe he laved himself with the magical red fluid. Yet, as he bathed, a linden leaf dropped unseen right between his shoulders, and there alone the dragon blood did not touch him, and there alone, consequently, he was vulnerable.

SIEGFRIED BATHING IN THE BLOOD OF THE DRAGON

He had slain a dragon and bathed in its blood, so that he was invulnerable — save where a linden leaf had stuck between his shoulders. — JOHN DRINKWATER

This duty performed, Siegfried returned swiftly to the forge. He realized that Mimer had wished to kill him, so without more ado he slew the treacherous dwarf.

Afterward Siegfried wandered to many places, and after a while he came to a country called Iceland, over which reigned a queen named Brunhild, who was both beautiful and warlike. Her castle stood by the sea, and was guarded by seven gates; and her marble palace glittered in the sun. He inquired of passers-by who might dwell here, and they not only told him her name, but also spoke to him of her strange refusal to marry anyone unless he could vanquish her in the tests she set him.

When Siegfried entered the castle, Brunhild, who marveled at his handsome face and his mighty muscles, received him favorably and even allowed him to see her magic horse, Gana. Yet Siegfried somehow had no love for Brunhild, and refused to undertake the tests she set. But to prove to her that it was no lack of skill or strength that made him decline her proffers, Siegfried calmly threw down the seven gates of her castle and even enticed the horse Gana to accompany him. For his scorn of her, Brunhild never forgave Siegfried.

Siegfried, continuing on his travels, came to an immense cavern where lay outspread the treasure of the Nibelungs: gold and silver, jewels of all kinds, most marvelous riches. Quarreling over the treasure were two Nibelung princes, surrounded by twelve foolish giants, their counselors. For the king of the Nibelungs had died, and now his sons could not divide their heritage peacefully. When the little princes saw Siegfried, they asked him to act as arbitrator, promising him as a reward the sword Balmung, which could overcome the strongest warriors. He consented, and began to make a division, but soon the dwarfs in dissatisfaction began to mock at him and scold him in their harsh voices. At last Siegfried in anger slew both of them, and likewise the giants, and laid the treasure aside in a secret place.

Now seven hundred knights came to bar his way, but Siegfried conquered them, and made them swear to be his liegemen thereafter. In a little while he had need of them, for the dwarfs of Nibelheim, under the leadership of a chieftian named Alberich, took the field against him, anxious not only to avenge the death of their princes but also to recover the lost treasure of the Nibelungs. But Siegfried had little trouble with them. He chased them all into a great cave on the mountain side, and from Alberich himself he stripped his Cloak of Darkness, which rendered the wearer invisible and invincible. He made Alberich and his army of dwarfs likewise swear allegiance to him, and then he placed them in charge of his treasure.

When Siegfried returned to his own country he was most warmly welcomed. Great feasts were held in his honor, and he received knighthood from the hands of the king. But he could not rest in quiet, and shortly he set forth on a new quest. For he had heard of a beautiful princess named Kriemhild, who dwelt at the Court of Worms in Burgundy, and from her description she seemed to him the ideal maiden of his dreams. He journeyed to Burgundy, accompanied only by eleven stalwart knights, and he was graciously welcomed by King Gunther, brother of Kriemhild, and by the latter's uncle and chief councilor Hagen, who was a cunning and cruel man. Not long after Siegfried arrived, two kings threatened Burgundy, but largely by Siegfried's valor they were overcome and conquered.

Then a great feast was held, and to it Kriemhild lent her presence. For the first time Siegfried gazed upon her, and thought her more lovely even than her fame. But when Siegfried sought to have her as a bride, King Gunther, at the advice of Hagen, would by no means grant him her hand unless Siegfried first went with Gunther to Iceland and helped him win Brunhild for wife. Siegfried consented, and accompanied only by a small band they set out for the country of Brunhild.

They were gayly welcomed, although Brunhild was angry that Siegfried came to assist Gunther and not to win her himself. With the help of Siegfried, who was clad in his Cloak of Darkness, Gunther passed the three trials — to overcome Brunhild in combat, to cast a stone farther than her cast, and to jump a greater distance than the queen did. Then did Brunhild yield to Gunther and wed him, and Siegfried was given Kriemhild as his bride.

SIEGFRIED IS SLAIN

Then, as to drink, Sir Siegfried down kneeling there he found,
He pierced him through the corselet. — NIBELUNGENLIED

But the story does not end there. Siegfried and Kriemhild in time became rulers of the Netherlands, and after a while were invited to Worms to take part in a tournament and its accompanying festivals. As the two queens sat together and watched their husbands in the combat, each began to boast of the prowess of her spouse. By a slip of the tongue Kriemhild revealed that in one place her husband was vulnerable. Later, goaded to anger by Brunhild's remarks, Kriemhild revealed the stratagem by which Siegfried had aided Gunther to win Brunhild, and the latter determined on revenge. With the aid of Hagen, Kriemhild was persuaded to make a garment for Siegfried in which a silken cross was embroidered above the spot on which the linden leaf had fallen; and there one day, as he was bending over a brook to drink, Hagen thrust his spear and killed him.

The Burgundians then came into possession of the treasure of the Nibelungs, but always Kriemhild plotted vengeance. In the course of time she married again, and her husband, King Etzel, was willing to aid her schemes. She invited her brothers and Hagen to visit her. Quarreling arose, and a fierce battle took place, in which many were killed, Hagen dying by the hand of Kriemhild and she herself being slain by the knight Hildebrand.

THE STORY OF BEOWULF

In Denmark ruled at one time a king named Hrothgar, who built for himself a magnificent hall, and therein his warriors feasted by day and slept by night. For a time the monarch and his subjects rejoiced in their fine dwelling place, but suddenly their rejoicing was turned to lamentation. For in a dreary and noxious fen near by lived a monstrous creature named Grendel, and each night Grendel entered the hall and seized some of the warriors, whom he carried off to his home in the fen and devoured.

Night after night this slaying continued, and nothing seemed of any avail to check the monster. The tidings of what was happening went, however, far and wide, and at last came to the land of the Goths toward the north, where lived a young hero named Beowulf. He resolved to go to Denmark and to rid King Hrothgar of the monster who troubled him. He set sail and in a few days reached Denmark. When King Hrothgar heard of the purpose of the hero, his heart was glad. That night Beowulf and his men went to the great hall, and his comrades slept but Beowulf kept watch. At midnight the monster crawled into the hall and, before Beowulf could stop him, he had seized and killed one of the Goths. But then Beowulf grasped him in his mighty arms, and a terrible struggle took place. Grendel managed to tear himself free, leaving his arm in Beowulf's irresistible grip. Mortally wounded, the monster plunged into the waters of the fen and died.

Great was the rejoicing on the following morning in the heart of Hrothgar and his people, and Beowulf was loaded with thanks and gifts. But still the Danes could not sleep in peace in the great hall they had built, for that very night the mother of Grendel came forth and, full of wrath, seized some of the best of the king's warriors and carried them off to the fen. Now once more Beowulf steeled himself to the combat, and when Grendel's mother took refuge in the waters of the fen, the hero plunged in and dived, dived, dived until he came to the cave of the monster. He fought with her fiercely and at last slew her. In the cave, too, he found the body of Grendel, and cutting off his head, he rose with it to the surface and returned to the hall of the Danes.

Then Beowulf prepared to return to his own land and to report to his ruler, King Hygelac, what he had accomplished. Hrothgar thanked him again and again, and gave him many presents to carry back with him. In Gothland Beowulf did valiant service for his king year after year, and when that monarch died, he became ruler of the land. For fifty years

BEOWULF IS WELCOMED AT THE COURT OF HROTHGAR

Hrothgar, helm of the Scyldings, spoke, "To be a bulwark of defense hast
thou sought us, my friend Beowulf." — BEOWULF

he governed with wisdom and courage, beloved by his people, and he looked forward to closing his years in peace and honor.

Such was not, however, to be his fate. For now it happened that a runaway slave came upon a great hoard of treasure, guarded by a fearsome dragon. The slave's eyes were dazzled by the vast wealth that he saw before him, and he knew that if he could but bring some proof to his master of what he had seen, the fact that he had run away would be forgiven. Fortunately for him, the dragon was asleep; and stealthily he took a great golden cup from the hoard and stole away with it.

His master, as he had foreseen, was pleased. But the dragon awoke and missed the cup, and resolved to exact immediate punishment. He followed the track of the slave, lashing his tail in fury. He came at last to a stream and lost the trail. Then, because he could not take vengeance on the thief himself, he resolved to punish the slave's fellow men. High over the town he flew; and spitting forth flame, he set fire to many a home and slew many a man and woman.

News of this raid of the dragon was carried to King Beowulf, and he immediately made preparations to fight the monster. Of all his followers only one young man, named Wiglaf, dared to accompany the aged king. They sought the cave where the dragon brooded. At the sound of their approach the dragon rushed forth in wrath. Beowulf met him with a blow of his trusty sword. Back and forth wavered the fortune of battle, and Beowulf, fatally scorched by the flames of the monster, knew that his last hour had come. But with a final mighty effort he pierced the dragon to the heart.

There, as Beowulf lay dying on the ground, his other warriors came to him, and to them he entrusted the great treasure the dragon had guarded, bidding them use it for the welfare of the kingdom. Wiglaf he appointed as his successor. Having spoken these commands Beowulf died. His followers erected a huge funeral pyre, and placed upon it the body of their king, and burned it; and mariners far off at sea saw the leaping flames and marveled.

STUDY APPLICATION

The Myths in Literature

It is a singular tribute to the power of the classical — Greek and Latin — mythology that it has exerted a much more definite and pervading influence on literature in English than has the mythology of the ancient Norsemen. References to the ancient Teutonic gods and heroes in our writers are few and far between, and only a few authors in English have gone back to the fine old stories told by their forefathers in the primitive forest or when they first formed settlements, before their conversion to Christianity. William Morris, among others, has excellently retold some of the old tales, particularly in *Sigurd the Volsung* and in parts of *The Earthly Paradise*.

The influence of *Beowulf* can be seen in what is without question the finest of all renderings of the old Teutonic myths in modern literature — Matthew Arnold's *Balder Dead*. Arnold was so imbued with the spirit of ancient Germanic mythology that his poem is almost a manual to that mythology. In his poem one sees the gods vividly : their power, their weakness, the eerie surroundings amid which are transacted the slaying of Balder and the vain efforts to bring him back.

Thomas Gray and Henry Wadsworth Longfellow have likewise retold some of these ancient tales, and the "Three Weird Sisters" of Shakespeare's *Macbeth* are an interesting survival of the three Norns or Fates of Teuton myth. A famous German musical composer, who displayed considerable literary ability in the composition of the librettos of his operas, has perhaps given the modern world the most brilliant version of the Siegfried story — Richard Wagner in *The Ring of the Nibelung*.

REFERENCES TO MYTHOLOGY IN LITERATURE

What do the following references mean? Where a word or phrase is italicized, explain only the word or phrase.

1. Now will I, O *Beowulf*,
   Best of warriors, even as a son
   Love thee in my heart! — *Beowulf*
2. Stout in battle, he slew the dragon, keeper of the treasure-hoard. — *Beowulf*
3. Grendel's mother kept thought of her sorrow. — *Beowulf*
4. The wolfish water-hag wallowed no more;
   The mere-wife had yielded her miserable life. — *Beowulf*
5. Wiglaf in wrath upbraided his comrades. — *Beowulf*
6. Then uprose the king of the *Nibelungs*, and was clad in purple and pall. — *Morris*
7. With what joy and gladness welcomed were they there!
   It seemed when came dame *Brunhild* to Burgundy whilere.
   — *Nibelungenlied*
8. Now, as he spake, came Siegfried rushing in,
   In wanton merriment he urged along
   A great bear he had bridled for his sport. — *Wagner*
9. With one blow Siegfried quickly plunged his sword
   Into the dragon's breast. — *Wagner*
10. Hey! Siegfried doth hold now the Nibelung's hoard. — *Wagner*

EXERCISES IN COMPOSITION, ORAL AND WRITTEN

1. In what way or ways do the stories of Siegfried and of Beowulf resemble each other? How do both remind you of ancient Greek or Roman tales? Do the Germanic heroes display qualities not to be found in the heroes of Greece and Rome?

2. Siegfried, in later days, relates to a comrade his exploit with the bear. Give it in his words.

3. When Beowulf returns home, he makes a report to his king. What would he say? Would he boast, or would he be modest? Try to give an old-fashioned flavor to his remarks.

4. Give an account of Wagner's famous group of music dramas, *The Ring of the Nibelung;* and if you can do so, play one or two pieces of

the music from these dramas, or have them rendered on a phonograph
or a reproducing piano.

WORD STUDY

1. Give the correct pronunciation of the following words.

Sieglinde, Siegfried, Mimer, Brunhild, Alberich, Kriemhild, Hrothgar, Beowulf, Hygelac.

2. Ask an instructor in German to let you copy three or four lines of
the medieval German in which the epic of the *Nibelungenlied* is composed and to tell you what they mean. Does the language resemble
English in any way?

3. Similarly, try to get a fragment of the Old English epic of *Beowulf*.
How close does this come to modern English?

4. The word *dragon*, you will find on consulting the dictionary, is an
interesting one. Webster's *Dictionary* devotes more than a column to
dragon and to words connected with it. Look up the following: dragon
(especially the derivation), dragon fly, dragoon, dragonnade, dragon's
blood.

RAPID QUIZ

Of what country were the parents of Siegfried the rulers? Into
whose care was he entrusted? Who were the Nibelungs? What
qualities did Siegfried develop? What was his adventure with a bear?
How did he incur Mimer's ill will? How did Mimer determine to get
rid of him? What creature did he slay? How did he make himself
invulnerable? What revenge did he take on Mimer? Who was
Brunhild? What was Siegfried's attitude toward Brunhild? How did
he win the treasure of the Nibelungs? What condition was laid upon
him when he sought Kriemhild as a bride? How did he fulfill it? How
did Siegfried meet his death? What revenge did Kriemhild take?
Whose subjects did the monster Grendel harry? From what land did
Beowulf come to help Hrothgar? What was the issue of the battle
between him and Grendel? How did Beowulf overcome Grendel's
mother? How did Hrothgar reward him? What monster did Beowulf
fight in later years? What was the result of the battle?

READING LIST

Baldwin, James: *Story of Siegfried*
Child, C. F.: *Beowulf*

Hackel, Oliver: Wagner's *Siegfried*
Lawrence, W. W.: *Beowulf and Epic Tradition*
McSpadden, Walter F.: *Stories from Wagner*
Morris, William: *The Fostering of Aslaug* (in *Sigurd the Volsung*)
Motherwell, William: *The Battle-Flag of Sigurd*
Shumway, D. B.: *The Nibelungenlied*
Wagner, Richard: *The Ring of the Nibelung*
Whittier, John Greenleaf: *The Norsemen*

THE DRUIDS' CIRCLE
(English Lake Region)

In yonder grave a Druid lies. — WILLIAM COLLINS

XX

THE CELTIC FAIRYLAND

Sage beneath a spreading oak
Sat the druid, hoary chief. — COWPER

THE ANCIENT CELTS

Once a great empire stretched across the whole northern part of Europe, from the Black Sea to the British Isles. At one time the inhabitants of this empire were powerful enough to sack Rome itself; they conquered Spain from the Carthaginians and waged other great wars; and often they were in alliance with the Greeks and with the Romans. This empire was the empire of the Celts.

Today of this mighty empire but little visible trace remains. The Celts left no written records of their own, and our direct literary knowledge of them comes only from the histories of their foes and their allies. A few coins of the Celts have survived, a few ornaments and weapons in bronze. The names of many places, moreover, bear testimony to the fact that once the Celts possessed them, and in oral tradition and legend may be found definite traces of the stories and the myths of this ancient people.

Where are the Celts themselves today? Just as they, when they conquered the various sections of Europe, mingled with the peoples whom they overcame, so in turn the Celts have in many sections completely mingled with those that conquered them. In France, in Spain, and in England, for example, the Celtic intermixture is marked; and as to the last country in particular some historians argue that its people ought to be called, not "Anglo-Saxon," but "Anglo-Celtic."

There exists, moreover, what is known as the "Celtic fringe." As the Germanic peoples conquered the Celtic empire, the Celts retreated to the edges of various lands. Thus in France Brittany is predominantly Celtic; and in the British Isles one may find an almost unmixed Celtic population in Wales, in the Highlands of Scotland, in certain islands, and in Ireland. Ireland was never even visited by the Roman legionaries, and it has retained, under whatever domination, its marked Celtic characteristics almost unchanged through the ages. Today, in the Irish Free State, it has adopted again Gaelic, the ancient Celtic tongue.

In such Celtic countries of today one finds that many of the ancient Celtic traits, as recorded in history, are still typical of their modern inhabitants. Physically, the Celts were of old a tall, fair, possibly almost altogether red-haired

race.   By much intermixture with those who conquered them
and those whom they conquered, these traits of appearance
have somewhat changed, and one finds dark as well as light
Celts.   They were a warlike, masterful race, eager for battle,
says Caesar, but easily dashed by reverses.   Another Roman
remarked that there were two things to which the Gauls (or
Celts) were devoted — the art of war and craft in speech.
They were always eager to hear news, besieging merchants
and travelers for gossip ; easily influenced, optimistic, waver-
ing in their opinions, fond of change.   They were at the same
time very quick and intelligent.   They loved display.   Their
weapons were richly ornamented, their horse trappings were
wrought in bronze and enamel, their raiment was embroidered
with gold.   They had great respect for their poets and learned
men, and (to judge by what has come down to us through
tradition) they were rich in fancy, delighted in color and in the
beauty of nature, and created stories that have deeply influenced all later literature.

THE CELTIC GODS

Our direct knowledge of the old Celtic gods is very scanty,
and for information concerning them we must depend chiefly
on Roman chroniclers and on some recent excavations.
Probably their beliefs in many ways resembled those of the
Romans, the Greeks, and the Teutons ; and Caesar, indeed,
speaking of the five chief divinities of the Gauls, gives them
Roman names.   He says that these divinities were Mercury,
Apollo, Minerva, Jupiter, and Mars ; and of them the Gauls
regarded the first most highly.

Modern excavations, showing temples and statues dedicated to these gods, have borne out what Caesar says.
Lucan, another ancient writer, mentions a triad of gods, all

cruel in character — Teutates, Esus, and Taranis; and here, once more, excavations have been found to verify his statement. Pluto, too, according to Caesar, was worshiped among the Celts; and elsewhere one finds mention of Lugh, a god of light. Traces of other deities have survived in the legends of Celtic lands.

STONEHENGE

Stonehenge may be regarded as a monument of the Bronze Age.
— SIR JOHN LUBBOCK

One very important feature in ancient Celtic religion was *stone worship*, although the veneration of rivers, trees, mountains, and other natural objects was also common. Everywhere in the countries once part of the Celtic empire may be found inscribed stones, arranged in certain mystical forms. Some stones had, the Celts believed, magical powers; for example, a certain "coronation stone" among

AN ARCHDRUID IN FULL JUDICIAL ROBES

According to Julius Caesar the Druids believed in the immortality and
the transmigration of souls. — SIR PAUL HARVEY

the Irish. Stones were associated too with the holy places of the dead. Most famous of such surviving groups of stones is Stonehenge in England.

The priests of the ancient Celts were called *druids*. The druids ruled their people with tyrannical power, and to the misuse of this power some writers have attributed the downfall of the Celtic empire. Caesar tells of them that they had power of excommunication and were therefore greatly feared. All affairs, public and private, were subject to their authority. They were free from military service and paid no taxes. Great schools were maintained by them, and in these schools their disciples learned by heart a great number of verses, for it was not lawful to commit any of their doctrines to writing. The principal point in their teaching, according to Caesar, was that the soul does not perish, but that after death it passes from one body into another. All through history, one finds, the Celt has had an intense faith in another world.

The druids also taught many things regarding the stars and their motions, the extent of the universe and the earth, the nature of things, and the power and might of the immortal gods. They were supposed to have magical powers and to be able to give or withhold sunshine, to cause storms, to make fields fertile, to exercise invisibility, and to produce sleep. According to some, they regarded the mistletoe as sacred, especially when it grew on an oak ; and they often performed their rites in oak groves.

THE CELTIC CYCLES OF LEGENDS

When the Celtic empire was swept away, when the power of this ancient people crashed in ruin, their orderly worship of their gods naturally fell into confusion. In different parts of the old Celtic world, and especially in Ireland and Wales, new legends were born, new gods were worshiped. As to these legends and these gods our knowledge is very full, for some of this material was ultimately written down in old manuscripts, and some of it continued to be handed down from generation to generation on the lips of the people until in our own day it, too, was duly recorded.

These stories fall, to a large extent, into cycles or groups. Of them the principal ones are, first, the *Cycle of the Invasions of Ireland;* second, the *Ultonian* or *Conorian Cycle;* and third, the *Ossianic* or *Fenian Cycle.* To these must be added the account of the *Voyage of Maelduin* and, most famous of all, the *King Arthur Saga.* From Wales come the beautiful stories of the *Mabinogion.* Many of these tales of the gods and heroes are current not only in Ireland or Wales, but also in Scotland; and some of the King Arthur stories penetrated all over the European world. In addition, there are many miscellaneous legends, some of great beauty.

In these Celtic tales we come to a new realm of the imagination, and to a certain extent we of today find ourselves more at home there than in any other group of national legends. For these ancient Celts loved nature and spoke of it lovingly and gracefully. They displayed, too, a chivalry and tenderness toward women that are very modern. They had a keen sense of words and their shades of meaning, and often their phrases have an unsurpassed delicacy that makes one understand why many critics have tried to find Celtic ancestors for such masters of style as Shakespeare and Keats.

THE CYCLE OF THE INVASIONS

The invasions of Ireland are divided in the legends into several sections: the coming of Partholan, of Nemed, of the

Fomorians, of the Firbolg, of the Tuatha De Danann, and of the Milesians.

Of these the Tuatha De Danann, the people of the goddess *Dana*, were most important.

Among the ancient Celts, Dana (whose name appears in other forms — *Don, Ana, Danu*) was regarded as the mother of the gods. Sometimes, too, she is called *Brigit*. She was an earth goddess, a goddess of plenty. As Brigit she was a goddess of knowledge and presided over poetry; she was particularly a patron of women.

The *Dagda* (called too the *Dagda Mor*) was the father and chief of the people of Dana. He was conceived of as huge and mighty; to feed him a pit was dug in the ground and filled with porridge, and the spoon he used was big enough for a bed. He called the seasons into being with his harp, and from the caldron of his plenty, called *Undry*, he fed the whole earth. He was usually represented as wielding a large club or a fork, symbol of his dominion over food. He owned a harp, which came flying through the air at his call.

His son *Angus* was the god of love. Four bright birds hovered forever around his head, and they were supposed to be his kisses taking shape in this lovely form; and at their singing love sprang up in the hearts of mortals.

Midir the Proud was another son of Dagda, renowned for his splendor and his personal beauty. *Lir* was god of the sea, but his son *Manannan* in later times was regarded as the deity of the waves and was one of the most popular of Celtic gods. Beyond his ocean lay the Land of Youth, the Island of the Dead; and to that land he guided the spirits. He was a master of tricks and illusions and owned many strange objects: a boat which obeyed the thought of those who sailed in it and went without oar or sail, a steed which could travel alike on sea or land, a sword (called *Answerer*) which no armor could resist. White-crested waves were called the horses of Manannan (just as Neptune was god of the sea and of horses). He wore a great cloak which was capable of taking on every kind of color, even as the sea does when

ISLE OF MAN

The Ancient Celts believed that here Manannan, god of the waves, made his home.

looked on from a height. The Isle of Man was supposed to be his home and to take its name from him.

The *Morrigu* was an extraordinary goddess, who embodied all that was perverse and horrible. It was her delight to set men at war, and she fought in battles herself, often taking the shape of a crow hovering over the dead.

Bran (or Bron) was represented as of gigantic size. No house or ship which was ever made could contain him in it, and when he laid himself across a river, an army could march over him as if over a bridge. He was the patron of minstrels and bards and himself claimed to be a skillful musician on many kinds of instruments. He was a king of the underworld, and there guarded the treasures of Dana against aggressors.

In many stories appears the god *Gwydion*, a son of Dana, who was a teacher of the arts and a giver of great gifts. He was skilled in war and in poetry and suffered many strange experiences. He was kind-hearted, for when on *Lleu* was laid the punishment that he should never have a wife of the people of the earth, Gwydion "enchanted a woman out of blossoms" for him. This Lleu or Lug is identified with Lugh, the god of light, mentioned earlier. Such was the radiance of his face that it seemed like the sun, and none could gaze steadily at it. He was a master of all the arts of war and peace. Among his possessions was a sword that slew of itself, and his sling was seen in heaven as the rainbow, and the Milky Way was called "Lug's Chain."

In four great fairy cities — Falias, Gorias, Finias, and Murias — were reared the people of Dana, and sages taught them science and craft. To the invasion of Ireland they brought four great treasures : the Stone of Destiny, on which kings were crowned, and which today is England's Coronation Stone ; the invincible sword of Lugh, a magic spear, and the Caldron of the Dagda. They were wafted into the land on a magic cloud. But for a time the fortunes of the Tuatha De Danann wavered, and the Firbolg and the Fomorians even ruled over them for a while. To the aid of the Tuatha De Danann came Lug the sun-god, and a great battle took place, in which the people of Dana were victorious.

For a long time they ruled in Ireland, but at length they

too were overthrown by a race of men who, it was fabled, came from Spain — the Milesians. The three kings of the people of Dana were defeated and slain by them, and the children of Miled became the rulers of the land.

But although many of the Tuatha De Danann were slain, they did not withdraw from the Green Island. They exercised their magic arts but were thenceforth invisible; and in Ireland may be found two peoples: the earthly and the elvin. Over the latter still rules the Dagda, and to each of his subjects he assigns a place. On green mounds and ramparts, among the broken stones of ruined fortresses and sepulchers, in lonely woods, or by deserted pools, there the fairy divinities dwell and there their palaces rise. In eternal sunshine they hold their revels, and they feast forever on magic meat and magic ale and draw therefrom everlasting youth and beauty. Sometimes they mingle with mortal men, and of their mingling we shall speak later.

THE ULTONIAN OR CONORIAN CYCLE

Many tales are told of the Milesians at Tara and especially of their High King Conary, but in time the scene of the story shifts to Ulster, to King *Conor*, and to his great vassal *Cuchulain*.[1]

In three manuscripts are told the deeds of Conor and Cuchulain — *The Book of the Dun Cow*, *The Book of Leinster*, and *The Yellow Book of Lecan*. In these volumes it is related how Conor, by a wile of his mother, was granted the throne of Ulster for a year, but so wise and prosperous was his reign that at the year's end the people insisted that he remain their king.

---

[1] Pronounced kŏŏ-hōō′lĭn.

Now there was at this time an order of knights called the "Red Branch," noted for their daring and their chivalry. Greatest of these knights was Cuchulain, whose father was Lug and whose mother was a mortal maiden. It was prophesied of him during his infancy by the druid Morann:

Courtesy Thomas Y. Crowell Co.

CUCHULAIN [SETANTA] SETS OUT

So the boy set off by himself, full of hope and excitement. — AMY CRUSE

"His praise will be in the mouths of all men. Charioteers and warriors, kings and sages will recount his deeds. He will win the love of many. This child will avenge all your wrongs. He will give combat at the fords. He will decide all your quarrels."

Originally he was called Setanta, but at a very early age he slew, in self-defense, a huge and ferocious dog that guarded the home of a wealthy smith named Cullan. To soothe the sorrow of Cullan at the loss of his faithful dog the boy promised to guard the home until a whelp of the hound had grown up; and he was thereafter called Cuchulain — the "Hound of Cullan."

At the age of seven Cuchulain assumed the arms of a man and slew three champions who had set all the warriors of Ulster at defiance. He traveled to Scotland to learn skill in arms from a warrior witch. When at his full strength no man could look him in the face without blinking. The heat of his body melted snow. He was a champion without equal.

Now over Connaught ruled a queen named Maev, and her heart was bitter against Ulster. Among other things she coveted for her own a famous Brown Bull of Quelgny, the mightiest in all Ireland. His back was broad enough for fifty children to play on; he was like a savage lion, like a dragon.

So all the mighty men of Connaught were gathered together in a host, and in Ulster was despair, for upon the warriors of Ulster lay a curse, and no hand in all that realm could lift up a spear; only Cuchulain was free from the curse. All alone he withstood the great army of the enemy. In single combat he met their doughtiest champions, and for three months he defended the marches against them. Every day he fought a bitter duel, and often he had to combat not only the natural strength of his foes but magic arts as well. His father came at night to heal his wounds, and the fierce goddess of war, the Morrigu, was so enchanted with his deeds that she wished to marry him.

Once, with much reluctance, Cuchulain was compelled to fight his old friend, Ferdiad, who had been lured while overcome with wine into a rash pledge to fight the Ultonian champion. For three days they engaged in combat, always treating each other with knightly courtesy, and at last Cuchulain gave his friend the death wound. The hero burst into passionate lament:

"It was all a game and a sport until Ferdiad came. Now the memory of this day will be like a cloud hanging over me forever."

Finally the curse was lifted from the men of Ulster, and joyfully they hastened into battle. They drove back the men of Connaught, and Maev herself cowered under her chariot as Cuchulain came upon her, and she entreated grace.

"I am not wont to slay women," said Cuchulain scornfully, and protected her until she had crossed the Shannon at Athlone. The famous Brown Bull had been seized by Maev and sent into Connaught. There it met the white-horned Bull of Ailell, and the two beasts fought. The Brown Bull was victorious, but it ran about madly until at last it too fell dead.

Though Maev made peace with Ulster, she vowed the death of Cuchulain, and in order to bring it about the more readily she sent her minions far and wide over the earth to learn evil magic. Then they attacked Cuchulain in every possible way — deceived his eyes and lured his mind and deprived him of his weapons. Still he fought desperately, and even when he was wounded to the death, he bound himself with his belt to a pillar, so that he might die standing. After he had drawn his last breath, his sword, falling from his grasp, cut off the hand of an enemy about to seize his body.

Not long after the passing of Cuchulain his master, King Conor, was likewise slain; and with them passed the glory of the Red Branch.

Also joined with Ulster is the fame of Deirdre,[1] heroine of one of the *Three Sorrowful Stories of Erin* and as much a favorite with the Irish poets and dramatists as was Helen of Troy with those of Greece. She was daughter of the harper to King Conchobar, and he was so entranced by her beauty as a child that he destined her for his wife, even though Cathbad the Druid prophesied that her beauty would bring

[1] Pronounced dâr′drä.

ruin and death to many heroes. She was brought up in solitude, at the king's command, but the youth Naoise saw her and fell in love with her and she with him. A week before she was to be proclaimed queen, Naoise and his two devoted brothers spirited her away to Scotland, and there for seven years they lived, happy and free if often cold and hungry. But then they were lured back to Ireland by Conchobar, the three brothers were treacherously slain, and Deirdre in despair took her own life.

THE OSSIANIC OR FENIAN CYCLE

With the Ossianic cycle of stories we go back to an earlier age of history. Whereas the knights of Conor, like the warriors of Homer, dwell in fortified cities and drive forth in chariots, the followers of Finn live the lives of nomad hunters in primitive forests. The deeds of Finn's heroes are still a living reality to the peasants of Scotland and Ireland, and there is a proverb that if the Fenians found that they had not been spoken of for a day, they would rise in wrath from the dead.

This cycle deals with the adventures of a band of warriors who formed a Fianna or a standing army, in the pay of King Cormac of Tara, to protect Ireland from foes internal and external. At their head was *Finn* (also called *Fionn*), whose name means the "white" or "fair."

Under Finn the Fianna of Erin reached its highest glory. He ruled them wisely and strongly, but bore no grudges. Even his enemies sometimes came into his service and were loyal and valiant. Chief of his friends was Dermot of the Love Spot, who was so fair and noble to look on that all women fell in love with him.

Finn's son *Ossian* (called also Oisin) was both warrior and bard, and it is his songs of the deeds of the Fianna that are said to have been handed down.   Ossian's own son was *Oscar*, the fiercest of all the fighters of the Fenians.   He slew three kings in his maiden battle, and thereafter through his

FINGAL LISTENS TO THE BARD OSSIAN

"The sons of song are gone to rest.   My voice remains, like a blast that roars, lonely, on a sea-surrounded rock after the winds are laid."
— JAMES MACPHERSON

short life he fought with intense bravery.   Ossian himself, it was fabled, escaped the fate of mortals by being taken to the Land of Youth by the fairy Niam of the Golden Hair, daughter of Manannan.   He went with her to this Celtic paradise, and there enjoyed three hundred years of divine youth.   But then there came upon him the longing to see again his own country. Niam set him upon a magic horse, but warned him not to set foot on the soil. As he rode, a saddle-girth broke suddenly, and Ossian fell to the ground. When he rose up, he was a pitiably blind and decrepit old man, stripped of all the gifts of the gods. Soon thereafter he passed away.

Yet another tradition says that Finn and Ossian and Oscar and all their great clan never have died, but lie spell-bound in a magic cave, awaiting the appointed time when they shall awaken and redeem their land from all tyranny and shame.

What tests did a man have to undergo to be permitted to join the Fianna? The candidate had to be versed in the *Twelve Books of Poetry* and had to be skilled in the making of original verse in rhyme and meter. Then he was buried to his middle in the earth, and with a shield and a hazel stick he defended himself against nine warriors who cast spears at him. He had to leap over a lath level with his brow and to run at full speed under a lath level with his knee. A thorn was placed in his foot, and he had to pull it out while running and never slacken speed. He was permitted to take no dowry with his wife. Here were some of the maxims which were impressed on the Fianna :

"So long as thou shalt live, thy lord forsake not; neither for gold nor for any other reward in the world abandon one whom thou art pledged to protect.

"Be more apt to give than to deny, and follow after gentleness. Be especially gentle with women and with them that creep on the floor and with poets, and be not violent to the common people.

"Be no tale-bearer, nor utterer of falsehoods; be not talkative."

THE VOYAGE OF MAELDUIN

Maelduin was the son of a great hero, who was slain in battle by plunderers from over the sea. His mother fled with her babe, and took refuge with a neighboring queen, and with the sons of this queen Maelduin was reared. He grew up as a tall and fair youth, well skilled in the use of weapons. Then there came one who reproached him because he did not avenge the death of his father, and so Maelduin resolved to set out across the sea and find the pirates who had slain his sire.

But first he sought counsel from Nuca the wizard. Nuca instructed Maelduin what kind of boat to build and when to begin, and at what time he must put to sea. And Nuca charged him strictly that there should be seventeen men in his crew, no more or less.

So the boat was built and the voyage began. But as they moved away from the shore and the wind filled their many-colored sails, Maelduin's three foster brothers came running down to the shore and implored him to take them along; and as he paid no heed to their entreaty, they threw themselves into the water and swam after the boat. So Maelduin could not do otherwise than take them aboard, although he remembered the injunction of the wizard with foreboding.

Soon they came to the two islands whence had sailed the pirates, but a great wind drove them far away. Many days they drifted, and then one day at dawn they heard the sound of waves breaking against the shore. They were about to land when they saw before them huge ants, each the size of a small horse; and they swarmed on the beach ready to seize whatever men should land. So in great fright they hoisted sail and speeded forth.

Then for many more days they voyaged on, until they came to another island, and on the shore gamboled a great beast, in shape like a horse but with the legs of a hound and with long, sharp talons on its feet.

"I do not like this beast," said Maelduin, so they turned the boat away once more toward the ocean. Shortly they came to another land, where they seemed to hear the fierce shouting of demons, and dared not stay. A little later they came to a house on an island which had two entrances — one from the sea and one on the land. And into the former swam great salmon and were captured. Maelduin and his men went into the house by way of the island, and took of the salmon and ate, but the inmates of the house did not make themselves known. Once more they sailed on, and hunger came upon them. As they passed another shore, Maelduin seized a huge branch from a tree. He held it upright for many days, and at last it bloomed and the blossoms turned to fruit like apples, and on these apples Maelduin and his men feasted for many days.

Many other adventures they had. In some places there were strange monsters. In others the ground was hot beneath their feet. Elsewhere they found a wondrous feast made ready for them in a house rich with jewelry and precious things, and only a cat guarded the mansion. But when one of the foster-brothers of Maelduin attempted to carry off a necklace, he was forthwith consumed to ashes. Once they came to a region of the underworld, where frightful creatures and terrible ogres confronted them. In one place all the inhabitants mourned wailingly, and when the second of the foster-brothers landed on the island he too began to wail and knew not why; and on this island he remained forever.

On another island there was eternal laughter and rejoicing. The last of Maelduin's foster-brothers could not be induced to leave this place of laughter. The dweller on one lofty island entertained them well. She gave them of a sweet wine to drink, and they slept for three days and then found themselves on their own boat, far from sight of land. In similar fashion a fortress in which dwelt a fairy lady suddenly disappeared from their ken, and once they saw beneath them in the sea a beautiful country wherein lived a dreadful beast that devoured whomever it could lay its claws upon.

Many other marvels they beheld, and at the last came back to the place wherein dwelt the slayers of Maelduin's father. But the inhabitants welcomed them, and Maelduin took no vengeance. He returned to his own district again and there related the wonders he had seen. And Aed, the chief poet of Ireland, wrote down the adventures of Maelduin, that men might wonder at them forever.

THE KING ARTHUR SAGA

Of all the heroes of the Celtic race none has won renown so great as has King Arthur, who (so the legends tell us) ruled over Britain. He was the son of Uther Pendragon, and for a time lived unknown; yet when the appointed day arrived, he pulled forth a great sword from a stone wherein it seemed fixed immovably. So he proved himself worthy and destined to be king.

He took as wife the beautiful Guinevere, and around him he gathered many brave and noble knights. Each day they assembled at the Table Round, whereat might be seated fifty knights sworn and true, and all the seats were assigned to warriors saving only one — the Siege Perilous. On that was

A KNIGHT RIDING FORTH ON A QUEST

When every chance brought out a noble knight. — TENNYSON

written the warning that none should sit in it except a knight altogether pure in heart; and in time Sir Galahad dared seat himself there.

Day by day King Arthur held court, and to him came many with boons that they sought or with wrongs that they wished to have righted. Then Arthur would listen to their plea, and if it seemed just to him, he would send forth a knight with the petitioner and the knight would continue on his task until all was well again. So fared forth the greatest of King Arthur's knights — Sir Lancelot; and so too went forth on quests Sir Gareth, Sir Percival, Sir Gawain, and many another.

Greatest of the quests of King Arthur's knights was the quest for the Holy Grail. This was a chalice from which Jesus was said to have drunk at the last supper, and the legend said that only to the eyes of the wholly pure would it ever be revealed. Many knights went in quest of it, although Arthur opposed their journeyings, for he felt that only to a few of them could the sight of the Grail be vouchsafed, and the rest only wasted their time. Galahad indeed beheld it, but to most of the others the quest was a vain one, and meanwhile the kingdom of Arthur and its affairs fell into disorder.

At last, after many brave wars and after many great and noble deeds, the rule of Arthur came to an end. By the treachery of his own nephew, Sir Modred, and by the disloyalty of Lancelot, came ruin; and in a mighty battle at Lyonnesse all the Round Table fell save one knight, Sir Bedivere; and King Arthur himself was severely wounded. He bade Sir Bedivere cast his famous sword, Excalibur, into a lake near by; and a fairy hand came forth and grasped it; and shortly afterwards a wonderful barge, with three queens sitting silent on the deck, came and took Arthur away. It was believed that he dwelt in the paradise called Avalon (or Avilion), and that some day he would come and rule once more.

THE *MABINOGION*

Most of the stories that have just been told are current chiefly in Ireland, although that of Ossian may be heard even today in Scotland and that of Arthur is to be found all over the Celtic world. Variations of these tales occur also in Wales; and from this district of England comes the *Mabinogion* — a great storehouse of legends. A "mabinogi" was a story which every apprentice bard was required to know. This particular volume contains the "four branches of the mabinogi" — that is, four such tales.

The first of the stories tells how Pwyll became a king in Annwn (ăn'nōōn), the land of chaos, the Other World of the Welsh; how, by a clever trick, he won his bride; how their son, Pryderi, was born, and how he was mysteriously stolen; how his mother was falsely punished for having brought about his disappearance, and how he was recovered and restored on the night of the first of May. In the second "branch" Pryderi is grown up and married. He joins himself to Bran at Harlech and assists that god and the king in an attack upon Ireland, at the close of which the Irish are defeated, although only a few of the Welsh remain alive. Bran himself is wounded with a poisoned spear, and in his agony orders the others to cut off his head and bury it under a tower in London. It is interred with the eyes facing France, that no foreign foe may come unobserved to Britain. Arthur in later years, however, removes it, scorning to hold the island other than by valor.

In the third division a friend of Pryderi marries the latter's mother, apparently ever youthful. Then they and Pryderi himself and his wife become fugitives, for their kingdom has been taken from them by the Children of Don (Dana). They live a nomadic life, and Pryderi and his mother are spirited away by magic, but they are brought back by the craft of Manawyddan (Manannan).

The fourth "branch" deals chiefly with the Children of Don, who are ruled by Math, the brother of Don. Gwydion, who has already been mentioned, plays an important part in the story. He is a kindly character who helps his friend and his people, yet at the end it is he that is responsible for the death of Pryderi, in a war waged to secure a gift of pigs sent to Wales.

In other portions of the *Mabinogion* tales of King Arthur and his court are told, with many variations from those that are related elsewhere.

THE LITTLE PEOPLE

When one people is conquered by another, a curious phenomenon sometimes is found to take place. As the conquered people shrink into the background they take their gods with them. Instead, however, of being mighty and powerful, as once they were in their prime, these deities shrink in glory even as their worshipers shrink — and they become the "Little People," as the Irish speak of them. In other words, they diminish from gods dwelling on high mountains or in great palaces and dwindle into the fairy folk, so minute as not to be visible at all, except to eyes specially endowed with vision to see them; and so retiring that their home is a tiny mound in a meadow, a hollow in a green glen.

Almost all lands have their fairy folk, but nowhere do they dwell in greater numbers and variety than in Ireland, where the imagination of the people has always lovingly cherished them. The special name they have in Gaelic is *sheehogue*, a diminutive of *shee* in the more familiar term, *banshee*. One hears of them under other skies as elves, brownies, gnomes, goblins, kobolds, kelpies, nixies, peris, pixies, sylphs, and trolls. One special kind of Irish fairy is the *leprechaun*, or fairy shoemaker, who has by his trade grown very rich. Occasionally one may catch a glimpse of him in a cellar or out on the fields. If you can manage to steal up on him and snatch away his cap, he will grant you any wish to get it back. But he is very sly, and has often been known to fool mortals who have stolen his cap and to get away without granting a wish.

Seumas O'Brien

LEPRECHAUN

Busy click of an elfin hammer,
Voice of the Leprechaun singing shrill
As he merrily plies his trade.

— ALLINGHAM

Sometimes a circle of withered grass may be seen on a lawn. There, the night before, the fairies probably danced merrily. Sometimes bright sparks are seen in the woods by night. It is only the fairies lighting up their revels.   The fairies have three great festivals during the year — May Eve, Midsummer Eve, and November Eve.   The first two are gay holidays for them; the last is a time of gloom, and then they dance only with ghosts.   It is in Shakespeare's *A Midsummer Night's Dream* that one meets that entrancing pair, King Oberon and Queen Titania, monarchs of the little people; and there too is their son Puck (sometimes called Robin Goodfellow), the merry wanderer of the night and lover of practical jokes![1]

Sometimes mortals may associate with the Wee Folk, but usually only at great peril.   Once in a while, according to legend, the fairies steal a mortal child and substitute one of their own infants for it — a "fairy changeling," who may at any time return to his own people.

STUDY APPLICATION

THE MYTHS IN LITERATURE

The myths of the Celts have fared much more fortunately in English and American literature than have the myths of the Germans.   Their influence has been more powerful, more apparent.   One portion of Celtic mythology, that dealing with King Arthur and with the quest of the Grail, has figured in English literature since the time of Geoffrey of Monmouth, whose book on the kings of Britain in the twelfth century was the first of a still unclosed series of works to handle this theme. Since his time Spenser, Tennyson, William Morris, Lowell, Swinburne, Richard Hovey, Edwin Arlington Robinson, and many others have treated it; and at one time Milton meditated writing an epic on King Arthur, and even made an outline for the proposed poem.   So "mystic Uther's son" is in many ways the most important single theme in English literature.

Celtic myth may be regarded as fortunate in another respect.   For more than a century there has been taking place a Celtic renaissance or revival.   In large part this is due to the fact that in the eighteenth cen-

[1] Some scholars hold that Puck is really Bacchus made small.

tury an extraordinary book by James Macpherson appeared — his account of Ossian. This deeply influenced not only English literature, but all the literatures of Europe, even though it has been shown that Macpherson himself invented stories that he attributed to ancient bards.

The attention which Macpherson directed to Celtic literature has resulted in a remarkable series of historical studies, in the writing down of many stories hitherto handed on from generation to generation only by word of mouth, and in the composition of innumerable poems, dramas, and romances.

Among the most illuminating of the studies were Matthew Arnold's lectures *On the Study of Celtic Literature.* Arnold showed that English literature owed to Celtic influence much of its gift for style, considerable of the melancholy spirit that pervades it, and nearly all of what he called the "natural magic" of its poetry. This last quality is to be found particularly in the ability to render with wonderful felicity the magical and weird charm of nature. He contrasted Saxon names of places with the pleasant wholesome smack of the soil to be found in them (Weathersfield, Shalford), with the penetrating, lofty beauty of Celtic names, Velindra, Tintagel, Carnarvon. He contrasted, too, the gift that Shakespeare had of being, sometimes, Greek in his clear realism, and his gift, at other times, of Celtic aerialness and magic and charm.

More recently Ireland has witnessed a truly extraordinary rebirth of this Celtic spirit, and Irish poets have gone back eagerly to the old myths of their race and have retold them in English (some of them in Gaelic) in a beautiful way. Among the leaders in this revival William Butler Yeats may especially be mentioned.

English poets, too, have been inspired by thought of the Celtic past; for example, Siegfried Sassoon in *Stonehenge*, which begins:

> What is Stonehenge? It is the roofless past;
>   Man's ruinous myth; his uninterred adoring
> Of the unknown in sunrise cold and red;
>   His quest of stars that arch his doomed exploring.

As has been suggested, nowhere are the fairy folk more enticing and delectable than in Ireland and in Irish poetry, but the storytellers and poets of many other lands have written excellently of the Little People. In our own literature, for example, we have had quaint fancies from Joseph Rodman Drake and William Cullen Bryant. In English literature Shakespeare created sprites that dance forever in his *A Midsummer Night's Dream* and *The Tempest*, and Milton has references to the fairy people in *L'Allegro* and *Il Penseroso*. An odd use of tiny spirits of the air and water, the fire and earth was made by Alexander Pope in *The Rape of the Lock*. In a number of poems by Robert Herrick a most amusing and in many ways beautiful set of details as to fairies has been gathered.

REFERENCES TO MYTHOLOGY IN LITERATURE

What do the following references mean? Where a word or phrase is italicized, explain only the word or phrase.

A

1. Lay your ear close to the hill.
   Do you not catch the tiny clamor,
   Busy click of an elfin hammer,
   Voice of the *leprechaun* singing shrill
   As he merrily plies his trade? — *Allingham*

2. Sage beneath a spreading oak
   Sat the *druid*, hoary chief. — *Cowper*

3. Sir *Lancelot* beside the mere
   Rode at the golden close of day. — *Gould*

4. Over the graves of the *druids* and under the wreck of Rome.
   — *Kipling*

5. They are a piece of stubborn antiquity, compared with which
   Stonehenge is in its nonage. — *Lamb*

6.   Round
   A rough-hewn altar on the ground
   Weird *druid* priests are gathered. — *Sharp*

7. To the island-valley of *Avilion*,
   Where falls not hail, or rain or any snow,
   Nor ever wind blows loudly. — *Tennyson*

8. The sun came dazzling thro' the leaves
   And flamed upon the brazen greaves
   Of bold Sir *Lancelot*. — *Tennyson*

9.   *Lancelot* came,
   Reputed the best knight and goodliest man. — *Tennyson*

10. Arm'd knights go forth to redress wrongs; some in quest of the
    Holy Grail. — *Whitman*

B

1. Altar-fires twinkle at *Stonehenge*. — *Allen*
2. Up the airy mountain
   Down the rushy glen,
   We daren't go a-hunting
   For fear of *Little Men*. — *Allingham*
3. Before the first of *druids* was a child. — *Keats*
4. They have sought him high, they have sought him low,
   They have sought him over down and lea;
   They have found him by the milk-white thorn
   That guards the gates o' *Faerie*. — *Kipling*
5. For tomorrow I go over land and sea
   In search of the *Holy Grail*. — *Lowell*
6. Ye *elves* of hills, brooks, standing lakes, and groves,
   And ye that on the sands with printless foot
   Do chase the ebbing Neptune. — *Shakespeare*
7. A thousand years! The grass is still the same,
   The clouds as lovely as they were that time
   When *Deirdre* was alive. — *James Stephens*
8. So all day long the noise of battle roll'd
   Among the mountains by the winter sea;
   Until *King Arthur's Table*, man by man,
   Had fall'n in Lyonnesse about their lord,
   King Arthur. — *Tennyson*
9. A gentle sound! an awful light!
   Three angels bear the *Holy Grail*! — *Tennyson*
10. It was before the time of the great war
    Over the *White-Horned Bull* and the *Brown Bull*. — *Yeats*

Exercises in Composition, Oral and Written

1. Which of the cycles summarized in this chapter do you like best?
Why? Tell the episode that particularly pleased you.

2. How does Celtic mythology compare with the Greek and the
Roman? with the German? List comparisons and contrasts.

3. Select a hero of Celtic myth and imagine him visiting the world
of today. Of what things would he approve? Of what disapprove?
What aspect of our life would astonish him most, in your opinion?

4. Write another incident for the voyage of Maelduin, some wonder that he beheld in his journeyings.

5. In three paragraphs, sketch the character of Achilles and that of Cuchulain; then compare and contrast the two heroes.

6. Compare King Arthur's knights and the state troopers of our own day.

Word Study

1. Give the correct pronunciation of the following words:

Teutates, Esus, Taranis, Ossian, Ossianic, Fenian, Tuatha De Danann, Midir, Manannan, Gwydion, Falias, Conary, Cuchulain, Setanta, Maev, Connaught, Guinevere, Gawain, Modred, *Mabinogion*, Annwn, Pryderi, Deirdre, leprechaun.

2. Authorities vary as to whether *Celtic* ought to be pronounced with a hard or soft *c*. Consult your dictionary and see what it says.

3. The "Siege Perilous" in which Galahad sat is obviously an odd term. Look up *siege* in the dictionary; or, if you know some French, give the meaning of the word as it is used here.

4. *Titan* and *Titaness* in Greek mythology refer to gigantic, super-human beings; and that is how the adjective *Titanic* gets its meaning. But Titania, in Shakespeare's *A Midsummer Night's Dream*, was a tiny creature, queen of the fairies. What passage in this chapter explains the change in size?

5. Explain this statement by G. K. Chesterton: "I am very fond of the grotesque, and in some ways I much prefer Puck to Apollo."

6. What does *cycle* mean when applied to stories? What is the meaning of *saga*? What is the meaning of *Mabinogion*?

Rapid Quiz

Who were the Celts? Where may their descendants be found today? What were the traits of the ancient Celts? How has information as to their gods come down to us? What is stone worship? Who were the druids? What did they teach? Name the six groups of Celtic legends that still survive. Why do modern readers enjoy these legends? Who were some of the gods and heroes that appear in the *Cycle of the Invasions*? Who were the Tuatha De Danann? How do they still survive? In which cycle appears the hero Cuchulain? To what order did he belong? Why was he so called? Who was Queen Maev?

What possession of Ulster did she desire? What great deeds did Cuchulain perform? How was he slain? Who was Finn? What was the name of his son? of his grandson? What were the latter's great achievements? What were the tests set a man who wished to join the Fianna? Who was Maelduin? Why did he set out on his voyage? What were some of the marvels he beheld? Where did King Arthur reign? Who was his wife? What was the Table Round? Who was the greatest of his knights? the purest? On what quest did his knights set forth? How did the rule of Arthur come to an end? To what land does the *Mabinogion* belong? Who are some of the characters in its stories? How is the existence of fairies sometimes explained? What is a leprechaun? By what signs may one know where the little people have been? What are their three great festivals?

Reading List
Descriptive Works

Arnold, Matthew: *On the Study of Celtic Literature*
Caesar, Julius: *The Gallic War*, book v, 11-20
Curtin, Jeremiah: *Myths and Folklore of Ireland*
Guest, Lady Charlotte: *Mabinogion*
MacCulloch, John A.: *Celtic Mythology*
Rolleston, T. W.: *Myths and Legends of the Celtic Race*
Squire, Charles: *The Mythology of Ancient Britain and Ireland*
Yeats, W. B.: *The Celtic Twilight*

Poems and Plays

Ferguson, Samuel: *Lays of the Western Gael*
Ledwidge, Francis: *The Wife of Lew*
Macpherson, James: *Fingal — Temora*
O'Sheel, Shaemas: *They Went Forth to Battle, But They Always Fell*
Robinson, Lennox: *The Golden Treasury of Irish Verse*
Russell, G. W. ("AE"): *Deirdre* [play]
Synge, J. M.: *Deirdre of the Sorrows* [play]
Tennyson, Lord: *The Voyage of Maeldune*
Wordsworth, William: *Glen-Almain*
Yeats, W. B.: *Baile and Aillinn — On Baile's Strand* [play] — *The Old Age of Queen Maev — The Song of Wandering Aengus — The Wanderings of Oisin — Under the Moon — Deirdre* [play]

Novels and Tales

Bishop, Farnham, and A. G. Brodeur: *The Altar of the Legion*
Colum, Padraic: *The Voyagers*
Gregory, Lady Augusta: *Cuchulain of Muirthemne — Gods and Fighting Men*
Jacobs, Joseph: *The Book of Wonder Voyages*
Kipling, Rudyard: *Puck o' Pook's Hill — Rewards and Fairies*
Lamprey, Louise: *Children of Ancient Britain*
Mundy, Talbot: *Tros of Samothrace*
O'Duffy, Eimar: *King Goshawk and the Biros*
Stephens, James: *The Crock of Gold — Deirdre*
Yeats, W. B.: *Irish Fairy and Folk Tales*

The Arthurian Cycle

Emerson, Ralph Waldo: *Merlin*
French, Allen: *Sir Marrok*
Hovey, Richard: *The Birth of Galahad*
Lowell, James Russell: *The Vision of Sir Launfal*
MacDowell, Edward: *Eroica* [music]
Malory, Sir Thomas: *Morte d'Arthur*
Millay, Edna St. Vincent: *Elaine*
Morris, William: *The Defense of Guinevere*
Robinson, Edwin Arlington: *Lancelot*
Swinburne, Algernon Charles: *The Tale of Balen*
Tennyson, Lord: *Gareth and Lynette — Morte d'Arthur*

Fairy Lore

Bryant, William Cullen: *The Little People of the Snow*
Drake, Joseph Rodman: *The Culprit Fay*
Herrick, Robert: *Oberon's Feast*
Hopper, Nora: *The Fairy Fiddler*
Pope, Alexander: *The Rape of the Lock*
Shakespeare, William: *A Midsummer Night's Dream — The Tempest*
Weber, C. M. von: *Oberon* [opera]
Yeats, W. B.: *The Land of Heart's Desire*

THE PROMETHEUS FOUNTAIN IN THE SUNKEN PLAZA,
ROCKEFELLER CENTER, NEW YORK CITY

An inscription above the fountain reads: Prometheus, Teacher in every art,
brought the fire that hath proved to mortals a means to mighty ends.

XXI

SOME ASPECTS OF MYTHOLOGY

*The gods, the goddesses, and the demigods, the heroes, Titans, and spirits
of good and evil are the pageant of eternity.* — HANIEL LONG

EXPLANATION OF MYTHS

Although we know that myths were the attempts of
primitive peoples to explain the world around them, scientists
have been trying to find a more specific explanation of mythmaking and to classify the myths of all nations according to
the themes they treat and the germs of their plots. The
ancient Greeks, the first people to develop a true sense of
science, in very early times began to investigate the origin of
the myths which were their religion. As far back as the
fourth century B.C. a Greek named Euhemerus, a native of
Messene, arrived at some conclusions concerning the nature
of the gods, but did not dare express them directly. So he
invented a story. He said that in the course of a voyage he
had discovered in the Indian Ocean an island called Pan-

chaia.   Here he had found a number of inscriptions which showed that the principal gods of Greece were really only earthborn beings, who had performed such heroic deeds that they had been deified after death.   This theory of Euhemerus brought down upon him many reproaches and accusations from those who still piously worshiped the old gods.

But his theory has persisted through the ages, and is some- times called "euhemerism."   It was adopted in ancient times by many eminent men, among whom were the historian Polybius and the great church father St. Augustine.   Fol- lowing the thought of Euhemerus, Greek writers said that Aeolus was an ancient mariner, the Cyclopes were savages inhabiting Sicily, Atlas was an astronomer, and Scylla a fast- sailing pirate.   During the eighteenth century French writers made similar applications of euhemerism.   In the nineteenth century Gladstone employed it in his treatment of Greek mythology.

Another theory was advanced by the famous philologist and Orientalist, Friedrich Max Müller; namely, that mythology was only a disease of language.   That is, the gender or sex of words in time created in the mind of primitive peoples an idea of personality, which was gradually extended into the notion of godhood.   Thus *der Mond* in German is masculine, *luna* in Latin is feminine.   A moon masculine in gender would give in time an idea of a male deity of the moon; a moon feminine in gender would suggest a female deity.   He also showed that there was a close connection among the Greeks and Romans, the Germans, the Celts, and the Hin- dus, whose languages and whose mythologies resembled one another, though there was little racial connection.

In more recent years mythology has been explained largely in the light of what is called *anthropology:* the study of man in all his relations and aspects. The anthropologist makes a detailed study of savage life today, to help him learn what the beginnings of mankind were. Anthropology has shown that the myths of the Greeks, the Romans, and many other peoples that have attained a high state of culture are not essentially different from those of savage folks, and that all mythologies arise out of the same needs and often employ similar plots and explanations.

It is generally thought today that myths go back to the time when early man, looking around his universe with awe, endowed trees, stones, mountains, and clouds with the same sort of life which he himself possessed. This earliest faith is called *animism*, and was found in many parts of the world. Another early belief was *fetishism*: the notion that certain inanimate objects are inhabited by spirits who have a magic power to ward off evil, to destroy enemies, and to produce prosperity. Fetishism, in the worship of stones, of wooden figures, and of beads, still exists today among the tribes of Africa.

A TOTEM POLE

Totemism has a very wide distribution, being found in America, Australia, Melanesia, Africa, and parts of Asia.

— ROBERT H. LOWE

Totemism is also widely spread among primitive peoples. A totem is an animal or bird or plant worshiped by a family or clan and regarded by it as its original ancestor. Many peoples all over the surface of the earth show the influence of totem-worship, although it is best known at the present time in connection with the American Indian, from whose language the word *totem* is derived.

These various ideas — hero-worship, gender in language, the belief in spirits, the worship of inanimate objects, and the deification of totems — probably account for the existence of the gods and goddesses of most mythologies. Possibly another element is deliberate invention by poets, whose imagination enlarged upon the mythical stories, and by moralists, who found lessons and allegories in such myths.

CLASSES OF MYTHS

Scientists have classified myths. Among almost all peoples are found myths to explain the creation and the origin of man, myths which tell of a place of reward and of a place of punishment, myths concerning a great flood, the sun, the moon, important heroes, beasts, the soul, and death, and myths of journeys through the underworld. There is a similarity, too, in the myths which account for arts and inventions, customs and rites.

There are, too, well-defined groups of deities. In almost all mythologies we find war gods, weather gods, wind gods, thunder gods, gods of agriculture, gods of the chase, and gods of death. Often one set of deities is described as being displaced by another set, and the displacement is perhaps to be accounted for in various ways — by one nation's conquering another, by the change from the hunting stage to the agricultural stage, and by a general advance in the power to reason.

MODERN MYTHMAKING

The mythmaking faculty did not cease after primitive or ancient times. Poets still love to make myths, and often create figures equal to the best of the ancient world.

No poet, for example, has made more beautiful figures of a mythical sort than did Shelley in *Prometheus Unbound*. He mingled in this great drama deities of the Greeks and some of his own imagining. Another mind strongly endowed with the mythmaking faculty was that of William Blake, who with mystic fervor created a whole pantheon of superhuman persons — and seemed to believe in them, too. Some fanciful moderns have endowed this or that city, this or that river with a presiding deity. Milton, in his *Comus*, tells how a gentle nymph, named Sabrina, fleeing the mad pursuit of her enraged stepmother, sought refuge in the Severn River, and how the god Nereus transformed her in pity into a goddess of the stream. She often helps the herds that stray along her banks, and she is filled with kindly thoughts for maidens such as she herself was. To her the Good Spirit sings:

> Sabrina fair,
> Listen where thou art sitting,
> Under the glassy, cool, translucent wave,
> In twisted braids of lilies knitting
> The loose train of thy amber-dropping hair;
> Listen for dear honor's sake,
> Goddess of the silver lake,
> Listen and save!

With Sabrina may perhaps be contrasted a mythical figure that is thoroughly American: the Ol' Man River of the Mississippi.

A myth of a city is to be attributed to Washington Irving, whose character Diedrich Knickerbocker (appearing in *The*

Sketch-Book and in *Diedrich Knickerbocker's History of New York*) is the original of *Father Knickerbocker*, that well-known figure who typifies the metropolis of America, and who has been the model for many similar patron saints of other American cities. Irving, moreover, is responsible for still another myth, that of Rip Van Winkle, the old Dutchman

RIP VAN WINKLE ARRIVES HOME AFTER TWENTY YEARS

"My very dog," sighed poor Rip, "has forgotten me."

— WASHINGTON IRVING

who sleeps twenty years at a stretch and awakens to find the world altogether changed. Maeterlinck has created the myth of the *Bluebird of Happiness*, Sir James M. Barrie the appealing figure of *Peter Pan;* and there is a hamadryad in P. L. Travers' *Mary Poppins*. There is no more beautiful mythical figure than Rima in W. H. Hudson's *Green Mansions*.

Among other myths that are very widely known two more may be mentioned: that of the *Fountain of Youth*, which Ponce de León and many another has sought through the ages; and that of Santa Claus or Kris Kringle, who was brought over from "the old country," and who has become the patron saint of children.

Just one other author may be described here — Lord Dunsany, who has shown an astonishing gift for creating a whole company of gods, all most plausibly pictured. For the most part these gods belong to a group which Dunsany calls the "Gods of Pegana." It is thus, for example, that his tale of *When the Gods Slept* begins:

All the gods were sitting in Pegana, and Their slave, Time, lay idle at Pegana's gate with nothing to destroy, when They thought of worlds, worlds large and round and gleaming, and little silver moons. Then (who knoweth when?), as the gods raised their hands making the sign of the gods, the thoughts of the gods became worlds and silver moons. And the worlds swam to Pegana's gate to take their places in the sky, to ride at anchor forever, each where the gods had bidden. And because they were round and big and gleamed all over the sky, the gods laughed and shouted and all clapped their hands. Then upon earth the gods played out the game of the gods, the game of life and death, and on the other worlds They did a secret thing, playing a game that is hidden.

In the realm of the photoplay Walt Disney has several times made amusing use of mythology, as in the *Silly Symphonies* dealing with King Midas and with Neptune.

MYTHOLOGY AND SCIENTIFIC TERMS

To scientists, always in need of good descriptive terms for the new things they are constantly discovering, mythology has been a gold mine. Again and again they have gone to these old legends for the names of birds, butterflies, insects, fishes, minerals, animals. To make clear the extent of the tribute they have levied, the following table, in which only a small part of the field is covered, is presented :

Amazon.   (1) Amazon ant — a kind of ant.   (2) Amazon stone — a bright green feldspar, used as a gem.

Apollo.   A variety of butterfly found in Europe.

Argonaut.   A cuttlefish (paper nautilus) found in the Mediterranean.

Balder.   Balder's-blood — the name of a flower found in Norway.

Cadmus.   Cadmium — one of the elements, sometimes used in an amalgam for filling teeth.

Calliope.   A humming bird of the western United States and Mexico.

Cyclops.   Cyclopidae — a family of crustaceans, with a large eye.

Diana.   (1) A West-African monkey, with a white mark across the forehead.   (2) A variety of butterfly, found in North America.

Europa.   One of the satellites of the planet Jupiter.

Freya.   Freyalite — the name of a mineral found in Norway.

Hamadryad.   Another name for the king cobra.

Helen.   (1) Helenium — a genus of the aster family, bearing yellow flowers.   (2) Helenin — a drug obtained from elecampane root.

Hercules.   (1) A large northern constellation.   (2) Hercules beetle — found in America.   (3) Hercules'-club — another name for the pepper-wood tree.

Juno.   (1) Juno's-tears — name of a European flower.   (2) Junonia — a genus of butterfly, found in the United States.

Jupiter.   (1) One of the planets.   (2) Jupiter fish — the gibbar.   (3) Jupiter's flower — the columbine.

Medusa.   (1) A jellyfish.   (2) Medusa's head — a cluster of stars.   (3) Medusa's-head — a species of fungus.

Mercury.   (1) One of the planets.   (2) A silver-white liquid metal, often used in thermometers.   (3) Dog's mercury — the name of a plant.

Odin.   Odinite — the name of a mineral.

Penelope.   Penelopinae — a subfamily of birds, related to the curassows.

Phaëthon.   The genus of tropic birds.

Tantalus.   Tantalum — a white metallic element, which was isolated only after great difficulty ; hence the name.

Thor.   Thorium — a gray metallic element, used in the manufacture of gas mantles.

Titan. (1) Titanic acid. (2) Titanite — a mineral used sometimes as a gem. (3) Titanium — a gray metallic element, used in making certain kinds of steel.

MYTHS AND THE CONSTELLATIONS

All peoples on the face of the earth, filled with wonder at the stars and seeking to explain their existence and their curious groupings, have told mythical stories about the heavenly bodies, and have by various legends attempted to account for the presence of the sun by day, of the moon and the stars by night.

Most numerous, of course, are the stories of the sun and the moon, some of which have already been referred to — in particular, the legends told of Phoebus Apollo, of Diana, and Hesper. The magnificent constellation Orion, for example, with the three blazing stars that make a belt, will be recalled as connected with the giant whom Diana unwittingly slew.

THE CONSTELLATION ORION

Many a night from yonder ivied casement,
ere I went to rest,
Did I look on great Orion, sloping slowly
to the west. — TENNYSON

The legend of Perseus was used by the Greeks to account for several constellations and stars. The hero was so loved by the gods that on his death they transported him and

Andromeda and the latter's mother Cassiopeia to the heavens as stars.   Cassiopeia appears in a group which is supposed to be her chair.   It is of her that Milton speaks in *Il Penseroso* when he refers to

That starred Ethiop queen
    that strove
To set her beauty's praise
    above
The sea nymphs, and their
    powers offended.

Often the twelve labors of Hercules, like the great achievements of other heroes, are explained as really representing the traveling of the sun through the year: one thinks of the twelve signs of the Zodiac.   There is a constellation, incidentally, named after Hercules.   Pegasus, too, is in the skies; and so, too, are Castor and Pollux, the twin brothers who accompanied Jason on his quest — they are called by the Latin word for "twins," *gemini*, which has continued to be a mild expletive today as it was in ancient times.   Sagittarius, a southern constellation, is sometimes called *The Archer*, and is pictured as a centaur shooting an arrow.   According to the

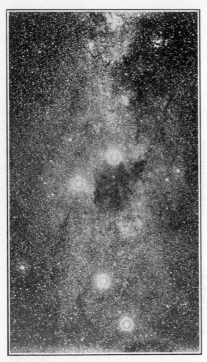

THE MILKY WAY

The antique gods a new Olympus find
In the vast starry heavens.
                — JOHN HEARTHILL

Greeks, he was Chiron, placed by Jove among the stars. Orpheus' lyre, Europa's bull, and the ship *Argo* are, too, remembered in the names of heavenly bodies. The Pleiades were the seven daughters of Atlas. Four of the moons of Jupiter are called Io, Callisto, Europa, and Ganymede.

In ancient times the Milky Way was believed to lead directly to the throne of Zeus-Jupiter. One legend accounted for this bright pathway in the heavens by saying it was the road along which Phaëthon had traveled in his mad course over the sky. Both the Chinese and the Japanese regard the Milky Way as a silver celestial river. The ancient Norsemen believed that the Milky Way was the path along which the souls of the departed went to Valhalla. To the Algonquin Indians it was "the path of souls," leading to the villages in the sun — the stars were bright lights and campfires guiding the spirits on their journey to the Happy Hunting Grounds. In northern India it was the "path of the snake," and in ancient Wales it was the "silver street leading to Caer Groyden," the castle where dwelt the king of the fairies.

MYTHOLOGY IN ADVERTISING

Examples have already been given to show that it is not only the poets and other authors who have made use of the ancient myths of Greece and Rome or the tales of the Teutons and Celts. The modern advertising man has frequently found in these narratives a stimulus to his imagination, an impetus to invention, and a storehouse of apt reference and allusions. The advertising copy writer of big business firms realizes that all educated persons are familiar with such myths and stories, and he has often used them to point a business moral or drive home a selling-point. It is very instructive to glance over the advertisements in a newspaper or a magazine, and to see how numerous such references to mythology are.

NEPTUNE

An advertisement of the Canadian Pacific Steamship Company.

Thus an advertisement for the Atlas Portland Cement Company opens with these words:

A thousand years before Helen brought disaster to Troy, a Sea King of Crete built himself a lordly palace at Knossos. The architect, in a moment of sentiment, forgot the procession of warriors and scenes from the arena with which the stucco walls were decorated and, in a panel of the great hall, he painted a picture of a little Minoan boy gathering flowers. The colors are as fresh as if laid on yesterday; the stucco is smooth and unbroken, although the hand which smoothed its surface has been dust for three thousand years.

So, too, the Harriman National Bank of New York makes clear a question of international finance by retelling the story of Midas and showing thereby that it is possible to have too much gold. The man who writes the pointed little advertisements of Childs' restaurants likes to illustrate his homilies on food by references to mythology. Thus he speaks of one character:

ATALANTA — the fairest and fleetest runner in all the world — would marry only him who could outdistance her in a race. The cunning Hippomenes won her by dropping three golden-hued apples as he ran. The maid stopped to pick them up. Anyone who has enjoyed the deliciousness of the baked apples at CHILDS will understand the temptation of Atalanta.

Or again, somewhat modifying the ancient story:

HESPERIAN APPLES: In Greek mythology the Garden of Hesperides was the abode of the setting sun. There golden apples grew on a tree guarded by a sleepless dragon. To secure the coveted fruit Herakles risked his life in mortal combat with the monster. This was a risk worth taking if the apples were as delicious as those served at CHILDS.

The Colonial Fireplace Company pleasingly uses the Greek tale of the origin of fire to make its implements for the hearth more attractive:

MERCURY

Official emblem of the Florists' Telegraph Delivery Association.

In the beginning only the Immortals had Fire. Prometheus looked with compassion on the cheerless creatures of earth. In defiance of the gods he stole Fire from the heavens and brought it to earth in the pith of a reed.

"Now will man overthrow us," said the Immortals. And they chained Prometheus to Mount Caucasus and sent a vulture to feed forever on his liver. But man from that day has treasured this miracle that lifted him above the shivering brutes.

Postage stamps, those couriers of business, are often adorned with mythological figures. Mercury (Hermes) appears again and again, especially on Greek stamps, but one may also find Apollo, Penelope, Ulysses, Ceres, and many others. (See the list below.)

One frequent use of mythology has been in the realm of names. Seeking to give a new product a title that will attract attention, manufacturers have placed on the market the Minerva automobile, Ajax tires, Apollo candies and pianos, Argo starch, Hercules oil-burner and powder, Vulcan springs, Vesta batteries, Atlas cement, and used many more such names reminiscent of old myths. *Mercury* is a frequent name for periodicals, as in *The American Mercury*.

GODS ON POSTAGE STAMPS

Apollo: Greece: 1906: Olympic Games issue: 1 lepton, 2 lepta
Ariadne: Crete: 1905: 50 lepta
Artemis: Crete: 1905: 2 lepta
Athena: Greece: 1896: 20 lepta, 40 lepta
   U. S. A.: 1875: Newspaper stamp: $9.00
Atlas: Greece: 1906: 3 lepta, 5 lepta
Clio: U. S. A.: 1875: Newspaper stamp: $6.00
Demeter: Argentine: Corrientes: all issues
   France: 1849–62 (First Republic): all values
   France: 1870–75 (Second Republic): all values
   U. S. A.: 1875: Newspaper stamp: $1.92
   Uruguay: 1895: 10 centesimos
Europa: Crete: 1905: 5 lepta
   U. S. A.: 1875: Newspaper stamp: $48.00
Hera: Crete: 1900: 5 lepta, 20 lepta
   Crete: 1901: 20 lepta
Heracles: Greece: 1906: 20 lepta, 50 lepta
Hermes: Austria: Various newspaper stamps
   Bosnia: 1916: Express stamps: 2 heller, 5 heller
   Bolivia: 1925: 2 bols.
   Brazil: 1920–21: 300, 400, and 500 reis
   Canada: 1930: Airmail: 5 cents

Crete: 1900–1: 1, 5, and 50 lepta
Greece: 1861–82: all values
Greece: 1886–89: all values
Greece: 1896: Olympic Games issue: 2 drachmas
Greece: 1901: all values
Greece: 1902: 5, 25, and 50 lepta, 1 and 2 drachmas
Greece: 1906: 40 lepta
Greece: 1911–20: 1, 3, 10, 30, and 50 lepta
Greece: 1911–20: 1, 2, 3, 5, 10, and 25 drachmas
Greece: 1921: 3, 5, and 10 drachmas
Greece: Samos: 1912: 5, 10, 25, and 50 lepta
Liberia: 1906: 20 cents
Liberia: 1918: 20 cents
Newfoundland: 1897: 30 cents
Newfoundland: 1911: 15 cents
Uruguay: 1889: 50 centesimos
Uruguay: 1894: 50 centesimos
Uruguay: 1895: 50 centesimos
Uruguay: 1897: 50 centesimos
Uruguay: 1901: 50 centesimos
Uruguay: 1921: 1, 2, 4, and 5 centesimos
Uruguay: 1922: Parcel Post: all values
Uruguay: 1926: all values
Uruguay: 1927: all values
Uruguay: 1928: all values (Staff of Hermes)
Uruguay: 1923: Water mark of that issue
Uruguay: 1923–29: Special Delivery: all values
Hebe: U. S. A.: 1875: Newspaper stamp: $48.00
Hestia: U. S. A.: 1875: Newspaper stamp: $12.00
Hope: Cape of Good Hope: 1853–1902: all issues
   South Africa: 1926: 4 pence
Iris: Greece: 1911: 2, 20, 25, and 40 lepta
   Greece: 1916: 1, 5, 10, 25, and 50 lepta
   Greece: 1916: 1, 2, 3, 5, 10 , and 25 drachmas
Justice: U. S. A.: Newspaper stamp: 1875: 96 cents
Medusa: Austria: 1922–24: 20, 25, 50, 100, 200, 500, etc., kronen
Minos: Crete: 1900: 2 drachmas
Pegasus: Uruguay: 1929–31: Air mail: all issues

Italy: 1930–32: 50 centesimos, 5 and 10 lire
Peace: U. S. A.: Newspaper stamp: $24.00
She-Wolf Suckling Romulus and Remus: Italy: 1929: various de-
    nominations
Fiume: 1918: various denominations
Triton: Crete: 1905: 25 lepta
Victory: U. S. A.: Newspaper stamp: $3.00
Zeus: Crete: 1905: Newspaper stamp: 1 drachma
    Greece: 1906: Olympic Games: 5 drachmas

STUDY APPLICATION

REFERENCES TO MYTHOLOGY IN LITERATURE

What do the following references mean? Where a word or phrase is
italicized, explain only the word or phrase.

1. Or keeping watch among those starry Seven,
   Old Atlas's children. — *Keats*
2. A dignity equivalent to Cassiopeia's chair. — *Lamb*
3. The centaur, Sagittarius, am I. . . .
   With sounding hoofs across the earth I fly. — *Longfellow*
4. These be the great Twin Brethren,
   To whom the Dorians pray. — *Macaulay*
5. Those three stars of the airy giant's zone
   That glitter burnished by the frosty dark. — *Tennyson*

EXERCISES IN COMPOSITION, ORAL AND WRITTEN

1. Give a talk on "Explanations of Myths."
2. Invent a "modern myth," dealing, for example, with the origin of
some invention, the name of a country, or some allegorical figure like
Uncle Sam or John Bull.
3. Select some group of stars, try to think of some object (like an
automobile or a steam engine) the group resembles, and then devise a
myth to account for its presence in the skies.
4. Rewrite an advertisement in your favorite magazine so as to
introduce an effective reference to mythology.
5. Prepare a talk on the use of myths by musical composers, or on
the use of myths in art.

6. Examine the list of scientific terms on pages 474–475, and explain the significance of five of the names.

7. Bring to class specimens of postage stamps showing figures of mythology.

Word Study

1. Give the correct pronunciation of the following words:

Euhemerus, Messene, Panchaia, euhemerism, Polybius, anthropology, fetishism, Sabrina, Maeterlinck, Ponce de León, Dunsany, Pegana, Gemini.

2. Tell what *euhemerism* is.

3. Look up in the dictionary the word *mythopoeic* and bring the definition to class. See if you can then explain this sentence by Fiona Macleod: "The mythopoeic faculty is not only a primitive instinct, but a spiritual necessity." Does it mean that people ought still to make up myths?

4. What is an *expletive?* Have you ever heard *Gemini* so used? Do people still swear "by Jove"?

Rapid Quiz

How did Euhemerus endeavor to explain myths? How did Max Müller explain myths? What science has recently studied mythology? What has it shown? What is animism? fetishism? totemism? What are some classes of myths? of gods? Who are some modern authors who have created myths? How is mythology employed in advertising? How are the stars connected with mythology?

Reading List

Bacon, Francis: *The Wisdom of the Ancients*
Barrie, Sir James M.: *Peter Pan and Wendy*
Butterworth, Hezekiah: *The Fountain of Youth*
Dunsany, Lord: *Book of Wonder*
France, Anatole: *Putois*
Grahame, Kenneth: *The Wind in the Willows*
Harris, H. Gordon: *Postage Stamps and Greek Mythology*
Hudson, W. H.: *Green Mansions*
Irving, Washington: *Rip Van Winkle*

Kellett, E. E. : *The Story of Myths*
Olcott, W. T. : *The Star Lore of All Ages*
O'Neill, Eugene : *The Fountain*
Procter, Mary : *The Young Folks' Book of the Heavens*
Ruskin, John : *The Queen of the Air*
Thomas, Edith M. : *Ponce de León*
Travers, P. L. : *Mary Poppins*

APPENDIX

APPENDIX

REVIEW REFERENCES TO MYTHOLOGY IN LITERATURE

What do the following references mean? Where a word or phrase is italicized, explain only the word or phrase.

1. 'Tis Apollo comes leading
   His choir, the *Nine*. — *Arnold*
2. They see the *centaurs* . . .
   Reared proudly, snuffing
   The mountain wind. — *Arnold*
3. But in my helpless cradle I
   Was breathed on by the rural *Pan*. — *Arnold*
4. Pagan and homely, but *Pan* —
   Pan of the sap and the soil! — *Chalmers*
5. Hans Sachs, in describing *Chaos*, said it was so pitchy dark that even the very cats ran against each other! — *Coleridge*
6. She heaved a sigh — indeed, her breast was a very cave of *Aeolus* that morning — and stepped across the room on tiptoe.
   — *Hawthorne*
7. The springtime, fresh and green,
   And sweet as Flora. — *Herrick*
8. O'er the long hills of folded Arcady
   Fleets *Artemis*, a-hunting of the deer. — *Hewlett*
9. In gulfs enchanted, where the *siren* sings,
   And coral reefs lie bare,
   Where the cold sea maids rise to sun their streaming hair.
   — *Holmes*
10. Speak to me, *Muse*, of the *long-wanderer*. — *Homer*
11. Meanwhile before the palace of *Odysseus* the suitors were making merry. — *Homer*

12. *Zeus* that rolls the clouds of heaven. — *Homer*
13. I will not have the mad Clytie,
    Whose head is turn'd by the sun. — *Hood*
14. Nor does *Apollo* keep his bow continually drawn. — *Horace*
15. Of *Pan* we sing, the best of leaders Pan,
    That leads the *naiads* and the *dryads* forth. — *Jonson*
16. Within his car, aloft, young *Bacchus* stood. — *Keats*
17. Like a *Silenus* on an antique vase. — *Keats*
18. Ah, *Zephyrus*, art here, and *Flora* too! — *Keats*
19. Dame *Helen* caused a grievous fray. — *Kilmer*
20. Silence stiller than the shore
    Swept by *Charon's* stealthy oar. — *Knowles*
21. *Gorgons*, and *hydras*, and *chimeras* dire may reproduce themselves
    in the brain of superstition, but they were there before.   The
    archetypes are in us, and eternal. — *Lamb*
22. Visions of love, of *Cupids*, of *Hymens!* — *Lamb*
23. Had he asked of me, what song the *sirens* sang, or what name
    Achilles assumed when he hid himself among women, I might
    have hazarded a "wide solution." — *Lamb*
24. We occasionally caught glimpses of *Tartarus*. — *Lamb*
25. *Cerberus* held agape his triple jaws. — *Landor*
26. To the two powers that soften virgin hearts,
    Eros and *Aphrodite*. — *Landor*
27. [Hermes to Pluto :]
    From Zeus who rules with you the threefold realm I come.
    — *Ledoux*
28. Let not our town be large, remembering
    That little Athens was the *Muses' home*. — *Lindsay*
29. *Fauns* with youthful *Bacchus* follow. — *Longfellow*
30. The old classic superstition
    Of the theft and the transmission
    Of the fire of the Immortals. — *Longfellow*
31. *Pomona* loves the orchard,
    And *Liber* loves the vine. — *Macaulay*
32. Apollo hunted Daphne so
    Only that she might laurel grow ;
    And Pan did after Syrinx speed
    Not as a nymph, but for a reed. — *Marvell*

33. With all the grisly legions that troop
    Under the sooty flag of *Acheron,*
    Harpies and *hydras.* — *Milton*

34. *Bacchus,* that first from out the purple grape
    Crushed the sweet poison of misused wine. — *Milton*

35.   I have oft heard
    My mother *Circe* with the *sirens* three,
    Amidst the flowers-kirtled *naiades,*
    Culling their potent herbs and baleful drugs,
    Who, as they sang, would take the prison'd soul,
    And lap it in *Elysium: Scylla* wept,
    And chid her barking waves into attention,
    And fell *Charybdis* murmur'd soft applause. — *Milton*

36. Rough *satyrs* danced, and *fauns* with cloven heel
    From the glad sound would not be absent long. — *Milton*

37. Or the unseen *genius* of the wood. — *Milton*

38.   Nature breeds,
    Perverse, all monstrous, all prodigious things,
    Gorgons, and *hydras,* and *chimeras* dire. — *Milton*

39. As when the wrath of *Jove*
    Speaks thunder and the chains of Erebus
    To some of *Saturn's* crew. — *Milton*

40.   Hovering dreams,
    The fickle pensioners of *Morpheus'* train. — *Milton*

41. What the sage poets, taught by the heavenly *Muse,*
    Storied of old in high immortal verse,
    Of dire *chimeras* and enchanted isles. — *Milton*

42. With flower-inwoven tresses torn
    The *nymphs* in twilight shade of tangled thickets mourn. — *Milton*

43. That *Orpheus'* self may heave his head
    From golden slumber on a bed
    Of heap'd *Elysian* flowers, and hear
    Such strains as would have won the ear
    Of *Pluto* to have quite set free
    His half-regain'd *Eurydice.* — *Milton*

44. When the gray-hooded Even,
    Like a sad votarist in palmer's weed,
    Rose from the hindmost wheels of *Phoebus'* wain. — *Milton*

45. An announcement was made today that there will be a dance during the present meeting, organized by the scientists themselves, on which festive occasion many of the most learned professors intend to abandon the altars of *Pallas Athena*, to pay homage to *Terpsichore.* — *The New York Times*

46. Straightway he shuts the north wind up in the cave of *Aeolus.*
— *Ovid*

47. Her hair was changed to leaves, her arms to branches. — *Ovid*

48. Then Pallas assumed the form of an old woman. — *Ovid*

49. The sea holds the dark-hued gods: tuneful *Triton* and changeful *Proteus.* — *Ovid*

50. I was wont to behold Queen Elizabeth riding like Alexander, hunting like *Diana*, walking like *Venus*, the gentle wind blowing her fair hair about her pure cheeks, like a *nymph;* sometimes singing like an angel, sometimes playing like *Orpheus.*
— *Raleigh*

51.   Through the glow
The goddess *Flora* moved in sudden flight. — *Sharp*

52.   Now, by *two-headed Janus*,
Nature hath framed strange fellows in her time;
Some that will evermore peep through their eyes,
And laugh, like parrots, at a bagpiper;
And others, of such vinegar aspect,
That they'll not show their teeth in way of smile,
Though *Nestor* swear the jest be laughable. — *Shakespeare*

53.   Highest queen of state,
Great Juno, comes: I know her by her gait. — *Shakespeare*

54. As huge as high Olympus. — *Shakespeare*

55. O Phoebus! hadst thou never given consent
That Phaëthon should check thy fiery steeds,
Thy burning car never had scorched the earth. — *Shakespeare*

56. To *Phoebus* was not *Hyacinth* so dear,
Nor to himself *Narcissus*, as to both
Thou, Adonais. — *Shelley*

57. Dan Perseus, born of heavenly seed,
The fair Andromeda from peril freed. — *Spenser*

58.   *Bellona*, in that warlike wise
To them appeared, with shield and armor fit. — *Spenser*

59. Foolhardy as th' *Earth's children*, the which made
Battle against the gods. — *Spenser*
60. Foolish *Narcisse*, that likest the wat'ry shore. — *Spenser*
61. The evening light came level across the land, making the new
grass look like heavenly pasturage, fit for *Pegasus*.

— *Howard Spring*

62. You cannot shut the windows of the sky,
Through which *Aurora* shows her brightening face.

— *James Thomson*

BRIEF DESCRIPTIONS

Write a sentence of about twenty-five to thirty-five words concerning
ten terms in each of the following groups.

1. Zeus, Hermes, Poseidon, Pluto, Minerva, Daphne, Calypso,
Cupid, Venus, Proserpina, Odysseus, Helen.

2. Menelaus, Hyacinthus, Arachne, Atalanta (describe both),
Meleager, Ceres, Narcissus, Hero, Agamemnon, Argus, Aeneas.

3. Charybdis, sirens, Baucis, Phaëthon, Hephaestus, Eumaeus,
Achilles, Patroclus, Hera, Ganymede, Iris, Dido.

4. Pan, satyr, faun, Pomona, Ares, Jupiter, Liber, Telemachus,
lotus-eaters, Aeolus, Anchises, Polyphemus.

5. Circe, Scylla, Penelope, Ithaca, Troy, Phaeacia, Neptune, naiad,
Graces, Muses, Niobe, Jason

6. Pallas Athena, Artemis, Psyche, Pluto, Rhadamanthus, Icarus,
Meleager, Mount Olympus, Elysium, Clytie, Aesculapius, Theseus.

7. Tithonus, Orpheus, Herakles, Perseus, Minotaur, Pygmalion,
Eros, Leander, Thisbe, Hades, Menelaus, Thetis.

8. Cassandra, Clytemnestra, Medea, Europa, Admetus, Hesperides,
Bacchus, Saturn, Father Tiber, Marpessa, Hestia, Echo.

9. Eros, Pyramus, Minos, Cadmus, Diana, Chaos, Epimetheus,
Cyclops, Apollo, *Argo*, Nemean lion, Eos.

10. Tantalus, Hebe, Anchises, Hecuba, Nestor, Medusa, Andromache, Andromeda, Romulus, Lares, wooden horse, Python.

11. Balder, Thor, Niflheim, Odin, Freya, Loki, Norns, Yggdrasill,
Asgard, Valhalla, Siegfried, Beowulf.

12. Druids, King Arthur, Holy Grail, leprechaun, Tuatha De
Danann, Manannan, the Dagda, Cuchulain, Ossian, Queen Maev,
Oscar, Maelduin.

SOME QUESTIONS AS TO MATTERS OF FACT AND FANCY

1. What story explains the coming of spring? Which explains the origin of a flower? of a star? of diseases? of an insect? of the color of skin of the Ethiopians? of the echo? of a tree?

2. What were some ideas that prevailed among ancient peoples as to the origin of the world?

3. Give examples of some strange transformations described in myths.

4. In what stories were gods friendly with mortals? In what other stories did they try to harm them?

5. What caused the death of Meleager? Why did Echo speak the last word? What were the Olympic Games? What sons of Apollo were slain by Jove? Who saved Alcestis from death? What were the twelve labors of Hercules? How did Theseus cause his father's death? How did Perseus save Andromeda? Who was the slave of Admetus? How did Orpheus twice lose his wife?

6. Mention five kinds of nymphs. What other deities appear in groups?

7. From what names of gods are the following English words derived? Jovial, mercurial, vulcanize, cereal, Herculean, vestal, volcano, martial.

8. What gods fought on the side of the Greeks? of the Trojans? Who rendered the greatest service to Ulysses — a god, a goddess, or a mortal? What happened to Agamemnon after the war? to Helen? Who was Telemachus?

9. What are some differences between Greek and Northern mythology? What gods were especially worshiped in Rome?

10. What poets were especially fond of Greek and Roman myths?

11. Against whom did Apollo have a grudge? Against whom did Apollo and Diana have a grudge? Neptune? Mars? Juno? Venus?

12. What is meant by the following expressions: "An Adonis," "the Midas-touch," "halcyon days," "a sop to Cerberus," "an Elysium," "the riddle of the Sphinx"?

13. In what stories in this volume does a dragon appear?

14. What heroes go on long voyages or quests?

15. What heroes visit the underworld while still alive?

16. In what stories does the influence of women play an important part?

17. In how many stories do the Golden Apples of the Hesperides appear?

18. Why would Argus make a good traffic policeman? What character in mythology was able to change his appearance at will, and therefore might have made a good actor? Which exploit of Hercules shows that he might have been put in charge of health work?

19. What ancient deity would you pick out to preside over radio? bicycle riding? motion pictures? Why?

20. Tuesday, Wednesday, Thursday, and Friday were named after old Teutonic deities. What Greek or Roman gods correspond to these deities? Name the days after them, and see if they sound as well.

21. The ancient Greeks had nine Muses, each presiding over her own realm. What new Muses would the present day need for realms the Greeks knew nothing about?

22. What athletic games of the Greeks are still celebrated today?

23. Find in Greek or Latin mythology names suitable for the following: a rowing club, a debating society, a dramatic society, a literary club, an athletic club, a polo team, a new high school, an outdoors club, a park, a swimming pool, a dog, a cat.

24. Find similar names taken from other mythologies.

SUGGESTIONS FOR COMPOSITIONS, ORAL AND WRITTEN

A. See how well you can tell, in not more than three minutes, *one* of the following stories:

1. The Theft of Fire and the Coming of Pandora
2. The Disappearance of Proserpina
3. A Visit to Mount Olympus
4. A Visit to the Underworld
5. Aurora and Tithonus
6. The Great Flood
7. Zeus Visits the Earth
8. A Story of Apollo
9. Admetus and Alcestis
10. The Golden Apples
11. The Calydonian Hunt

12. The Slaying of a Monster
13. One Labor of Hercules
14. The Marriage Feast of Thetis
15. The Judgment of Paris
16. The Trojan War
17. The Stratagem of the Wooden Horse
18. An Adventure of Ulysses
19. The Golden Fleece
20. The Wanderings of Aeneas
21. Romulus and Remus
22. An Ancient Romance
23. A Tale from Northern Mythology
24. A Tale from Celtic Mythology

B. Prepare a talk on *one* of the following subjects:

1. The Origin of Myths
2. Myths and the Stars
3. Myths and Modern Advertising
4. Myths in Art (Use examples from this book.)
5. Myths in Literature
6. Do We Make Myths Today?
7. Customs of the Ancient Greeks
8. Customs of the Ancient Romans
9. The *Aeneid* of Virgil
10. The Poems of Ovid
11. The Ancient Germans
12. The Ancient Celts
13. Myths in Music
14. The Meaning of Myths
15. The Story in This Book I Like Best

C. Compose one of the following, using your imagination freely:

1. The Diary of Pandora
2. A Speech of Prometheus to Zeus
3. A Monologue of Tantalus
4. A Ghost Is Brought before the Three Judges of the Underworld
5. A Letter from Telemachus to Menelaus, after the Slaughter of the Suitors

6. A Thirteenth Labor of Hercules

7. An Adventure of Ulysses That Homer Did Not Chronicle

8. A Conversation of the Sailors about the Bag of Winds — While Ulysses Is Asleep

9. If Pan (or some other god or some goddess) Came to Earth Today

10. A Mythology of My City (a god *Motionpictures*, for example; or *Chicago*, or *Electricity*)

DRAMA PROJECTS

1. Prepare a "Symposium of the Gods." Imagine that you are on Mount Olympus, and that each member of the class represents a deity. Zeus speaks first, and tells who he is — what powers he has, what his symbols are. Then in turn he calls on each of the others to give a brief soliloquy of description. Perhaps the three Graces will dance, the Muses sing.

2. Similarly, tableaux or living pictures can be prepared, with well-known pictures (like those in this volume) as models. Try, for example, Niobe and a kneeling daughter, or "The Three Fates."

3. If talent of the terpsichorean order is present in the class, a ballet of the ancient gods of Greece may be performed. Enlist the help of the music teacher, and give your performance before the school. "Echo and Narcissus," for example, would make a fine subject.

4. Pageants of Greek mythology are very effective, and have often been given in schools. In one school the material for such a pageant was found in George Peele's old play, *The Arraignment of Paris*. In another school, a play composed by Miss Ethel E. Holmes, of the Wyman School of Denver, was performed. In this the teacher's only contribution was the prologue and epilogue (which were written in blank verse and which explained that true immortality was remembrance, thus accounting for the return of the gods and goddesses who appeared) and the rhyming couplets which introduced the characters. The speeches of these characters were the result of the oral composition study of the class. Individuals were chosen in competition; the unsuccessful members of the class assisted in securing the desired effects on the stage, a dance being given in which a Greek frieze was twice reproduced.

5. Many of the old stories, of Greek and other mythologies, offer excellent material for original plays — as writers through the centuries have been well aware. A one-act play (or a good short story) may readily be based on this material. Puppet shows likewise may deal with themes from mythology. Try writing a simple play on *one* of these themes:

   a. Alcestis and Admetus
   b. Apollo and Marpessa
   c. Pallas Athena and Arachne
   d. The Slaying of the Suitors
   e. Pygmalion and Galatea
   f. Thor in the Home of the Giants

SOME MISCELLANEOUS EXERCISES

1. Make up the following lists:

   a. American towns named after mythical persons or places.
   b. Persons part of whose names is that of some mythical person.
   c. Ships named after classical persons, places, or objects.
   d. Advertisements that refer to mythology.

2. Explain the following expressions, all common in modern speaking and writing:

   a. Cleansing the Augean stables.
   b. The heel of Achilles.
   c. In the arms of Morpheus.
   d. Between Scylla and Charybdis.
   e. Rich as Midas.
   f. She was an Amazon.
   g. A follower of Aesculapius.
   h. Fair as Helen.
   i. Sly as Ulysses.
   j. Strong as Hercules.

3. Prepare a scrapbook in which you paste pictures of the gods, each with a line of verse underneath. You might also copy in this book useful facts of all kinds that you wish to remember, advertisements containing references to myths, and so on.

4. If you have any talent in verse writing, compose a poem on a subject selected from mythology — an ode to Mercury, a sonnet to Psyche, a narrative of the adventures of Jason, a monologue of Eurydice, an elegy for Adonis.

5. See if you can work out the following cross-word puzzle. Do not write the words on the page, but place them on a separate slip of paper. The definitions are on page 496. The answers will be found on page 504.

GRECIAN [1]

By Marion Louise Foster

Not all of the terms and references are Grecian, and not enough of them are so difficult that any one may say that the puzzle is "all Greek" to him. Yet there is an Hellenic tinge to the whole and something of an Hellenic wiliness to some of the definitions.

[1] Courtesy of the *Boston Evening Transcript*.

Definitions

Horizontal	*Vertical*
1. Father of Hector	1. A Trojan who had a hard choice to make
5. City round which waged a ten-year war	2. The sun god (Egypt)
9. Lava whose surface is rough	3. Science of husbandry (abbr.)
10. Urges on; spurs on	4. One of the six Sedarim of the Mishna
12. Personal pronoun	5. Idle (obs. spelling)
13. Native of Greece	6. Latin School graduates
15. An artificial language	7. Not wed (abbr.)
17. 650	8. A metal disk often thought sufficient reward for loss of limb
18. Wrath (Lat.); a man's name	
20. Gentlemen	
22. Name "I am strong" (Prov. XXX, 1)	11. Organic growth
23. Brother of Menelaus and commander-in-chief of an army	13. Three sisters with serpentine locks
	14. "My lady ——" of tobacco
24. Enough (obs. spelling)	16. Goddess of the chase
25. Pertaining to the ear	19. Hindu queens
27. God of shepherds, half goat, half man	21. A maxim
	22. One (Lat.)
28. To be ill	24. The builder of a huge wooden horse
30. Greek prefix indicating same-ness	
31. To dwell	26. Poetic for a defunct person
34. Skywards	28. A hero in one of Homer's epics
36. Many such are issued in June	29. A large, beautiful moth; moon (Lat.)
37. Because	
38. A tribe of American Indians	32. One Big Union (abbr.)
39. Cause of the war in No. 5 and all the rest of the world's troubles	33. Royal Society of Printers (abbr.)
	35. Mixed type
	37. Aluminum (symbol)

6. In the game called "Categories," sometimes "Guggenheim," one is required to fill in blank spaces with names beginning with a certain letter. These names cover persons, objects, institutions, ideas, and the like. "Guggenheim A," on page 497, is a sample, properly filled in.

See whether you can find the names that belong in "Guggenheim B," on the same page.   Do not write your answers on the page ; take a sheet of paper, rule it off properly, and make your own chart.

GUGGENHEIM A

LETTER	PLACES IN GREECE	PLACES IN ITALY	PLACES IN GERMANY
C	Crete	Capua	Carlsbad
A	Athens	Ancona	Augsburg
P	Parnassus	Palermo	Posen

GUGGENHEIM B

LETTER	NAMES OF GREEK AND ROMAN GODS	NAMES OF GREEK AND ROMAN GODDESSES	MORTALS IN GREEK AND ROMAN MYTHS	MORTALS BELOVED OF GODS AND MORTALS METAMORPHOSED	PRODIGIES, MONSTERS, GIANTS, AND SYMBOLS
C					
A					
S					
T					
E					

7. Explain the italicized words in the following passage :

"In the palm room of that hotel is a ceiling of painted mythology. While you wait for any one who may be coming to have tea with you, you can examine a series of episodes gracefully conjectured from the life of a famous family.   First there is *Aphrodite*, rising alluringly from the foam of a blue sea whose crumbling surf is pink with sunrise. Then there is the marriage, if one calls it so, of Aphrodite and *Hephaestus — Vulcan*, if you prefer, the fellow the Swedes name their matches for. It was a queer marriage for so handsome a goddess when Aphrodite became *the first Mrs. Smith;* but handsome women so often choose odd-looking men. Then there's their small boy, *Eros*, with the toy bow and arrows his father made for him, asking Vulcan to sharpen the darts for him, and his father, busy about thunderbolts, replying that the toys are quite sharp enough. In the last scene Eros, grown to a braw laddie, is trying a chance shot at *Psyche*. You generally have plenty of time to study all four scenes."—From *The Arrow* by Christopher Morley.

READING LIST FOR TEACHERS

Browne, Lewis : *This Believing World*
Cabell, James Branch : *The Silver Stallion*
Disraeli, Benjamin : *Ixion in Heaven*
Erskine, John : *Galahad*
Erskine, John : *The Private Life of Helen of Troy*
Farnell, L. R. : *Value of Methods of Mythologic Study*
Firestone, C. B. : *The Coasts of Illusion*
Fiske, John : *Myths and Myth-Makers*
Frazer, Sir James G. : *The Golden Bough* (abridged)
Gardiner, E. N. : *Greek Athletic Sports and Festivals*
Harrison, Jane : *Mythology*
Harrison, Jane : *The Religion of Ancient Greece*
Long, Haniel : *Notes for a New Mythology*
Merezhkovski, D. S. : *The Birth of the Gods*
Merritt, A. : *The Ship of Ishtar*
Norris, Orland O. : *Myths and the Teaching of Myths*

A TRUE–FALSE TEST

Copy on a slip of paper the numbers 1 to 20, in a column. Alongside each number place the answer *true* or *false*, making your answer depend on whether the statement corresponding to the number is true or false, in your judgment. Do not write your answer in this book.

1. Prometheus was glad to receive Pandora as his wife.
2. Minerva was the goddess of weaving.

3. As a symbol of his authority, Apollo carried the caduceus.

4. From the very beginning, Venus favored the idea of Cupid's marriage to Psyche.

5. The children of Latona were twins: Apollo and Diana.

6. Prosperpina was the goddess of the springtime.

7. It was Juno who changed Io into a heifer.

8. Narcissus rejected the advances of Echo.

9. Sisyphus was tormented in Hades by being chained perpetually to a wheel.

10. Jupiter placed Orpheus among the stars.

11. The mother of Perseus was named Danaë.

12. Ariadne helped Theseus when he set out to battle with the Minotaur.

13. Minerva helped both Jason and Ulysses.

14. Achilles was the son of Thesis and Jupiter.

15. Ulysses proposed an oath to the suitors of Helen.

16. Iphigenia died as a sacrifice on Diana's altar.

17. Patroclus was slain in battle by Aeneas.

18. Ulysses reached Ithaca two years after leaving Troy.

19. The father of Aeneas died on the journey to Italy.

20. Aeneas married the princess Lavinia.

A MULTIPLE-CHOICE TEST

Copy each of the following sentences on a slip of paper, but omit all but one of the words or groups of words in parentheses in each sentence. Keep that *one* which, in your opinion, is correct.

1. The maenads were followers of (Apollo, Pan, Bacchus, Neptune).

2. Pan was the son of (Jove, Mercury, Mars, Vulcan).

3. The satyrs had some of the characteristics of a (goat, horse, lion, bird).

4. During her stay in the underworld Proserpina ate (of a golden apple, of a pomegranate, of nectar, of grapes).

5. Daphne was changed into (an oak, a birch, a beech, a laurel).

6. (The Acheron, the Cocytus, the Styx, the Lethe) was the river of forgetfulness.

7. Perseus rescued Andromeda from (a sea monster, a dragon, a lion, a giant).

8. Pegasus was in the service (of Apollo, the Muses, Neptune, the wood nymphs).

9. The ancients called (Sicily, Gibraltar, Crete, Sparta) by the name of Hercules.

10. Boreas was the ruler of (east, west, north, south) wind.

11. Pelias gave up the throne to Jason (willingly, by force, on Jason's return with the fleece, because of the wiles of Medea).

12. Paris gave the Golden Apple to (Juno, Venus, Minerva).

13. Achilles quarreled with (Ajax, Ulysses, Agamemnon, Patroclus).

14. Ulysses tarried seven years with (the lotus-eaters, Circe, Calypso, King Aeolus).

15. An ally of Aeneas was (Turnus, Camilla, Evander, Mezentius).

QUESTIONS INVOLVING MYTHOLOGICAL REFERENCES IN RECENT COLLEGE BOARD AND REGENTS ENGLISH EXAMINATIONS

1. Answer the following questions with reference to the poem given below:

   a. What three persons are described in these lines?
   b. In what respect are these persons similar?
   c. How does each show his imagination?

   The lunatic, the lover, and the poet
   Are of imagination all compact:
   One sees more devils than vast hell can hold,
   That is the madman: the lover, all as frantic,
   Sees Helen's beauty in a brow of Egypt:
   The poet's eye, in a fine frenzy rolling,
   Doth glance from heaven to earth, from earth to heaven;
   And as imagination bodies forth
   The forms of things unknown, the poet's pen
   Turns them to shapes, and gives to airy nothing
   A local habitation and a name.

2. What is the underlying idea in these lines?

   Hence, loathéd Melancholy,
       Of Cerberus and blackest Midnight born

In Stygian cave forlorn
  'Mongst horrid shapes, and shrieks, and sights unholy!
Find out some uncouth cell,
  Where brooding darkness spreads his jealous wings,
And the night-raven sings;
  There, under ebon shades and low-browed rocks,
As ragged as thy locks,
  In dark Cimmerian desert ever dwell.

3. Tell in the first person, from the point of view of one of the characters, a story from the Bible, the *Odyssey,* or the *Aeneid.*

4. Discuss the two sides of the character of Achilles as shown in the *Iliad.* Illustrate each and tell whether we find anything like this contrast in the character of Hector. (Two or more pages)

5. Describe the parting of Hector and Andromache. (150 words or more)

6. Describe Helen watching the combat between Menelaus and Paris. (150)

7. Tell about Odysseus among the Phaeacians. (150 words or more)

8. Narrate the slaying of the suitors. (150 words or more)

9. Was the desertion of Dido by Aeneas justified? (150 words or more)

10. Describe the performance of *Pyramus and Thisbe* before Duke Theseus. (150 words or more)

11. Write very brief explanatory notes for *Apollo* and *Ulysses.*

12. Write brief explanatory notes, of not more than a few sentences each, for *Dido, Achilles,* and the *sirens.*

13. State in a few sentences what you know about Medusa, Parnassus, and Pegasus.

14. Write a theme entitled "Riding Pegasus."

15. Contrasts between ancient battles (in the *Iliad,* etc.) and modern. (150 words or more)

16. The ancient idea of a hero. (150 words or more)

17. Have you, in your reading from the Greek and Latin classics, found any story that you think especially suitable for modern literary treatment? If you have, explain your choice and suggest how the story might be treated by a modern author. If you have not, tell what differences you see between ancient and modern life that make it hard for you to understand the ancients.

18. What interest do you find in the ancient Greek narratives as compared with the modern fiction that you have read? Answer in one or two well-constructed paragraphs, referring to specific narratives.

19. The military, family, or business life of today as contrasted with that depicted in the *Iliad*, the *Odyssey*, or the *Aeneid*. (One or more paragraphs; 400 words)

20. Tell in the first person, from the point of view of one of the characters, a story from the *Odyssey* or the *Aeneid*.

21. What effect did the presence of sin among Arthur's knights have upon the quest for the Holy Grail? What was Arthur's attitude toward the quest?

Whose quest is referred to in the following lines?

> And but for all my madness and my sin,
> And then my swooning, I had sworn I saw
> That which I saw; but what I saw was veil'd
> And cover'd; and this quest was not for me.

22. Do you regard Milton's use of allusion as a grace or as an encumbrance to his verse? Illustrate your answer by references to particular passages in *L'Allegro*, *Il Penseroso*, or *Comus* in which he employs allusions of a mythological, a pastoral, or a literary nature.

QUESTIONS FROM COLLEGE ENTRANCE BOARD EXAMINATIONS IN LATIN

ILLUSTRATING MYTHOLOGY

I.
> "O soror, O coniunx, O femina sola superstes,
> quam commune mihi genus et patruelis origo,
> deinde torus iunxit, nunc ipsa pericula iungunt:
> nos duo turba sumus: possedit cetera pontus.
> Quis tibi, si sine me fatis erepta fuisses,
> nunc animus, miseranda, foret? Quo sola timorem
> ferre modo posses? Quo consolante doleres?
> Namque ego, crede mihi, si te quoque pontus haberet,
> te sequerer, coniunx, et me quoque pontus haberet.
> O utinam possem populos reparare paternis
> artibus atque animas formatae infundere terrae!"
> — Ovid, *Metamorphoses*, i, 351–364.

a. Who is speaking in this passage? To whom? Under what circumstances?

b. What mythological tale is referred to in *populos reparare paternis artibus* (verses 363, 364)?

II. Give three causes of Juno's attitude toward the Trojans.

III.   "Iam solitos poscunt cursus populusque paterque,
cum me sollicita proles Neptunia voce
invocat Hippomenes, 'Cytherea' que, 'comprecor, ausis
adsit,' ait, 'nostris et quos dedit adiuvet ignes.'
Detulit aura preces ad me non invida blandas :
motaque sum, fateor.   Nec opis mora longa dabatur.
Est ager (indigenae Tamasenum nomine dicunt),
telluris Cypriae pars optima, quam mihi prisci
sacravere senes, templisque accedere dotem
hanc iussere meis.   Medio nitet arbor in arvo,
fulva comam, fulvo ramis crepitantibus auro."
— Ovid, *Metamorphoses*, x, 638–648.

Who is meant by Cytherea (640), and why was she so called?

IV. Translate into Latin :

After Troy was captured and burned, Aeneas set out to find a new home for himself and his companions.   But at the very first place he reached he was warned to flee.   So when he again landed, he consulted the oracle of Apollo to learn where he was to go, and was bidden to seek his ancient mother, which his father Anchises said was surely Crete. But arriving there, he again had to leave, for the gods informed him that not Crete but Italy was the ancient mother.   And so after this, although he delayed in many places where he would have been willing to stay, he believed the oracle and proceeded on until he should reach Italy.

V. Discuss the statement : "The real keynote to the *Aeneid* is not '*arma virumque*' but the '*Tantae molis erat Romanam condere gentem.*'"

VI. Translate into Latin :

As Phaëthon wished to prove that he was really the child of the Sun, he made his way to the palace where his father was about to drive his famous horses through the sky.

"Let me, dear father, drive the chariot today," said Phaëthon.

But his father answered, "Do not ask me such a favor !   No mortal is sufficiently strong or worthy to restrain these sacred animals."

"That is just the reason why I beg you," cried Phaëthon. "If I should be able to drive them from sea to sea, no one would hereafter doubt that I too am immortal."

With such words, Phaëthon, unconscious of his fate, persuaded his father to grant his request.

VII. A certain scholar maintains that the *Aeneid* is, in its main intention, a religious poem. Discuss this opinion.

VIII. Translate into Latin:

At Syracuse, not far from the harbor, is an extremely beautiful fountain of great size. A Roman poet tells us why it is called Arethusa. The story is that a certain nymph, Arethusa by name, who lived on the other shore of the Adriatic, tried to escape from the river god, Alpheus, who was pursuing her. Fearing that he would overtake her, she prayed to Diana to help her. So, before the god could seize her, the goddess changed her into a stream of water which flowed under the sea toward Sicily and emerged on an island near Syracuse. The ancients believed that if anything should be thrown into the river Alpheus, it would later appear in this fountain.

IX. Why is Juno called Saturnia? What part does she play in the story of Aeneas? Who was Iris?

X. Describe the part that Iulus plays in the *Aeneid*.

ILLUSTRATIVE MATERIAL

This is an age of interest in pictures. Textbooks today are bright with illustrations. Motion-pictures are the world's favorite amusement. Even conservative newspapers pride themselves on their use of photographs taken in the very midst of important events. The radio is hastening towards television. It is no wonder that our pupils are emphatically *picture-minded*, and that pictures have become a potent source of motivation in education.

No richer field for pictures — fine artistic pictures, moreover — exists than in the field of mythology, and pupils scan with enjoyment the numerous illustrations with which most textbooks in mythology are provided. Many of them, furthermore, wish to go on from the illustrated textbook to the making of scrapbooks and albums of their own, with good pictures to brighten notes, outlines, creative compositions, reproductions, and the like. On pages 505 and 506 is a list of suggestions as to sources from which pictorial material may be obtained to illustrate the study of Greek and other mythologies.

Such material as that to be obtained from these sources may be employed to illustrate talks by teachers or pupils, to furnish material for classroom or library exhibits, to suggest creative activities in art, to provide illustrations for miniature anthologies and scrapbooks, to adorn classroom and home walls, and to enliven class procedure generally. The writing of letters of inquiry, especially to foreign dealers, is a useful by-product.

SOURCES FOR PICTORIAL MATERIAL DEALING WITH MYTHOLOGY

Alinari Prints, 8 Via Nazionale, Florence, Italy.
  Many photographs of statues, paintings, and other art objects.
Anderson, Via Salaria, Rome, Italy.
Art Institute of Chicago.
British Museum.
  Reproductions may be obtained through G. E. Stechert, 33 East 10th Street, New York City.
Brogi, Giacomo, Via Tornabuoni, 1 ; Florence, Italy.
Brooklyn Museum of Arts and Sciences.
  Helpful to students of ancient legends.

Chauffourier, Tourist Shop, Piazza di Spagna, Rome, Italy.
Inexpensive photographs on postal cards.

Gramstorff Brothers, Malden, Massachusetts.

Hellenic Society, 50 Bedford Square, London, England.

Keystone View Company, Meadville, Pennsylvania.
This firm issues a useful brochure called *Keystone English Literature*, prepared by Clarence S. Dike and giving lists of stereographs and lantern slides. In connection with Milton, pages 21–23, mythological subjects are listed. The same firm has, in its *Keystone Catalogue No. 26 for the Social Sciences*, a list of stereographs and lantern slides on Greece and on Rome (see pages 89–92 and 101–103).

Louvre Museum, Paris, France.

Metropolitan Museum, New York City.
This institution is most generous in its willingness to lend material for small fees. It issues several pamphlets listing reproductions that are on sale and describing the Museum's extension service with lantern slides, cinema films, color prints, and other collections. .

Museum of Fine Arts, Boston, Massachusetts.
This Museum has issued a valuable paper-bound book, *Greek Gods and Heroes*, by Arthur Fairbanks. Herein are described, with numerous illustrations, the classical collections of the Museum.

Thomas Nelson and Sons, 381 Fourth Avenue, New York City.
This firm issues a set of sixteen pictures by Helen Stratton, illustrating great world myths. The set is priced at 50¢.

Ny Carlsberg Glyptothek, Copenhagen, Denmark.

Nystrom, 3333 Elston Avenue, Chicago, Illinois.

Papagionnopoulos, B., Place de la Constitution, Athens, Greece.

Perry Pictures, Malden, Massachusetts.
A number of pictures reproducing ancient sculpture.

Service Educatif, Musées Royaux, Bruxelles, Belgium.

Swain, George, Ann Arbor, Michigan.

Thompson Company, Syracuse, New York.

University Prints, Newton, Massachusetts.
This firm issues a set of seventy-five prints (at $1.13, or separately at 1½¢) dealing with mythology.

Any stamp-dealer will have stamps (especially those of Greece) on which mythological subjects appear.

Advertisements should be watched for use of classical themes, names, and subjects.

The following bulletins, published by the Service Bureau for Classical Teachers, New York University, Washington Square, New York City, are likely to prove suggestive:

Photographs for the Classical Teacher, No. 12 and No. 13;

Illustrations Sold by the Metropolitan Museum, No. 174;

Latin Notes Supplement, No. 31.

Note also the following publications:

Wheeling, K. E., and Hilson, J. A., *Illustrative Material for Junior and Senior High-School Literature*. H. W. Wilson, New York, 1930.

Penoyer, John, *Ante Oculos*. Oxford University Press, New York, 1929.

Woodring, M. N., Jewett, Ida, and Benson, R. T., *Enriched English Teaching in the High School*. Bureau of Publications, Teachers College, Columbia University, New York, 1935.

Woodring, M. N., and Sabin, F. E., *Enriched Teaching of Latin in the High School*. Bureau of Publications, Teachers College, Columbia University, New York.

GLOSSARY OF IMPORTANT NAMES
AND TERMS

Fuller information can be obtained by consulting the index, in which help as to pronunciation is also given. When a term in this glossary appears in italics, an explanation of the term marked in this way appears elsewhere in the glossary.

Achilles, the outstanding Greek leader in the *Trojan War* and hero of Homer's "Iliad."

Adonis, a handsome youth, beloved of *Venus* and slain by a boar.

aegis, Minerva's shield, to which was attached the head of *Medusa.*

Aeneas, the son of *Venus* and the Trojan Anchises, hero of Virgil's "Aeneid," and the reputed ancestor of the Roman state.

Aeolus, the keeper of the winds.

Aesculapius, the son of *Apollo* and the god of medicine.

Agamemnon, a Grecian king, commander-in-chief of the Greek troops in the *Trojan War.*

Alcinoüs, king of the Phaeacians in the "Odyssey."

Amazons, a band of fierce women warriors.

ambrosia, the food of the gods. It was supposed to give immortality.

Aphrodite, literally "sea foam." (Roman: *Venus.*)

Apollo, god of the sun, of poetry, and of music.

Ares, the god of war. (Roman: *Mars.*)

Argonauts, those who sailed with *Jason* in the "Argo," on his quest of the Golden Fleece.

Artemis, the goddess of the moon, of maidens, and of hunting. (Roman: *Diana.*)

Arthur, King, a British chieftain. With his knights he formed the *Round Table.*

Asgard, the heaven to which the Norse heroes, slain in battle, went.

Athena. See *Pallas Athena.*

Atlas, a *Titan* who held the world on his shoulders.

Atropos, one of the Three Fates. She cuts the thread of life at the destined moment.

Aurora, goddess of the dawn. (Greek: *Eos*.)

Avalon, the Celtic paradise or *Elysium*. To it *King Arthur* retired when fatally wounded.

Avernus, a lake at the entrance of *Hades*, sometimes a synonym for the infernal regions.

Bacchus, also called *Liber*, the god of wine. (Greek: Dionysus.)

Balder, a Norse god, the son of *Odin* and god of spring and sunlight.

Bellona, goddess of war, called the sister or sometimes the wife of *Mars*.

Beowulf, hero of the Old English epic which is named after him, and which tells how he rescued mankind from a sea-monster and from a dragon.

Boreas, the North Wind.

Brunhild, heroine of the various Norse myths which deal with *Siegfried*. One version of these myths is given in the "Nibelungenlied."

Cadmus, the brother of *Europa*, who set off to find her, but founded Thebes instead and brought the alphabet to Greece.

caduceus, *Mercury's* staff, about which two serpents twined. In modern times, the symbol of physicians.

Calliope, *Muse* of epic poetry.

Cassandra, to whom *Apollo* gave the powers of prophecy, but whose predictions were doomed never to be believed.

Castor, the twin brother of *Pollux*. The constellation *Gemini* (the Twins) is named after them.

centaur, a fabulous creature, half-man, half-horse. The best-known centaur was *Chiron*.

Cerberus, a three-headed dog who guarded the gates of the infernal regions.

Ceres, the goddess of sowing and reaping. (Greek: *Demeter*.) *Proserpina* was her daughter.

Charon, the ferryman who carried souls over the *Styx* to *Hades*.

Charybdis, a monster that was a whirlpool, which only *Ulysses* was able to avoid. Opposite was *Scylla*.

Chimera, a monster, one-third lion, one-third goat, and one-third dragon. She was killed by Bellerophon.

Chiron, a *centaur*, the instructor of *Achilles* and *Aesculapius*.

Circe, a beautiful enchantress, daughter of *Apollo*, who turned Ulysses' companions to swine when they landed on her island, but who later yielded to the power of *Ulysses* and restored them to human form.

Clio, the *Muse* of history.

Clotho, one of the Three Fates. She spins the thread of destiny.

cornucopia, the horn of plenty, carried by *Ceres*.

Cupid, son of *Venus* and god of love. (Greek : *Eros*.)

Cyclopes, giant one-eyed shepherds. One of them, Polyphemus, was blinded by *Ulysses*. Also, a race of giants, sons of Uranus and Gaea.

Daphne, beloved and pursued by *Apollo*, she escaped him when her father, a river god, changed her into the laurel-tree.

Deirdre, the beautiful and tragic heroine of the Irish tale, " The Sons of Usnach."

Demeter, the goddess of sowing and reaping. (Roman : *Ceres*.)

Diana, the goddess of the moon, of maidens, and of hunting. Twin sister of *Apollo*. (Greek : *Artemis*.)

Dido, the Queen of Carthage, one of the principal characters in Virgil's " Aeneid." She killed herself because *Aeneas*, fulfilling his destiny, deserted her and sailed for Italy.

dryads, nymphs who inhabited trees.

Elysium, the Greek heaven in which dwelt heroes and sages.

Endymion, a youth whom *Diana* loved. *Jupiter*, forbidding their marriage, granted him eternal youth and sleep.

Eos, goddess of the dawn. (Roman : *Aurora*.)

Erato, the *Muse* of love poetry.

Eros, son of *Venus* and god of love. (Roman : *Cupid*.)

Eumenides, the Furies, who pursued those who had committed crimes.

Europa, whom *Jupiter* in the form of a bull carried from Phoenicia to Crete. Her son Minos became king of that land.

Euterpe, the *Muse* of music and lyric poetry.

Excalibur, *King Arthur's* sword.

fauns, beautiful and divine young men, with tiny horns barely visible, who lived joyously in the woods.

Frey, the Norse god of fertility, the dispenser of rain and sunlight.

Freya, the Norse goddess of love and music and flowers, corresponding to *Venus*.

Ganymede, cup-bearer to *Jupiter*. He was carried off to *Mt. Olympus* by *Jove's* eagle.

Gemini, the Twins, *Castor* and *Pollux*, gods of wrestling and boxing.

Grendel, a sea-monster whom *Beowulf* slew.

Guinevere, the wife of *King Arthur*, loved by Sir Lancelot.

Hades, originally another name for *Pluto*, later the name of Pluto's place of abode in the underworld.

Hagen, a character in the "Nibelungenlied," enemy of *Siegfried*.

hamadryads, *dryads*, nymphs who lived in trees.

Harpies, women with claws and wings, horrible to look at, who were sent to punish offenders.

Hebe, daughter of *Jupiter* and *Juno*, goddess of youth and cup-bearer to the gods.

Hecate, goddess of darkness, of ghosts, and of barking dogs.

Hector, the great hero of the Trojans in Homer's "Iliad."

Helen of Troy, the beautiful wife of *Menelaus*, whom *Venus* promised to *Paris*. Her elopement with the latter caused the *Trojan War*.

Hephaestus, blacksmith of the gods and husband of *Venus*. (Roman: *Vulcan*.)

Hera, literally "splendor," the Queen of the Heavens, wife of *Jupiter*, and goddess of marriage. (Roman: *Juno*.)

Hercules, the powerful son of *Jupiter*, performer of the "Twelve Labors," and greatest hero of the Greeks and Romans. (Greek: Herakles.)

Hermes, the messenger of the gods, and the escort of dead souls on their way to *Hades*. God of merchants and eloquence. (Roman: *Mercury*.)

Hestia, the goddess of the hearth. (Roman: *Vesta*.)

Holy Grail, the cup used by Jesus in the Last Supper. It was the object of a quest by the Knights of the "Round Table."

Hymen, the god of marriage.

Hypnos, the god of sleep.

Iris, the goddess of the rainbow.

Janus, the god with two faces, one looking forward, the other backward. He presided over the New Year.

Jason, a Greek hero, who successfully sought the Golden Fleece, taken from a sacred ram and guarded by a dragon in a temple at Colchis.

Jove, shortened form of *Jupiter.*

Juno, the Queen of the Heavens, wife of *Jupiter*, and goddess of marriage. (Greek : *Hera.*)

Jupiter, the King of the Heavens and father of gods and men. The supreme ruler of all beings, he sent rain, snow, thunder, and lightning. (Greek : *Zeus.*)

Kriemhild, heroine of the "Nibelungenlied" and wife of *Siegfried.*

Lachesis, the Fate who tells *Atropos* when to cut the thread of life.

Lares, gods of the house, fields, and roads.

Lavinia, daughter of King Latinus, who, though betrothed to Turnus, was given in marriage to *Aeneas.*

Liber, the god of wine. (Roman : *Bacchus.*)

Loki, the Norse god of strife.

Manannan, the god of sailors and merchants in Celtic mythology.

Mars, the god of war. (Greek : *Ares.*)

Medusa, one of three women of dreadful aspect called Gorgons, whose appearance was believed to freeze beholders to stone.

Melpomene, the *Muse* of tragedy.

Menelaus, husband of Helen and a leader of the Greeks in the *Trojan War.*

Mercury, the messenger of the gods and the escort of dead souls on their way to *Hades.* God of merchants and eloquence. (Greek : *Hermes.*)

Minerva, the goddess of wisdom and weaving, who sprang full-grown from the forehead of *Jupiter.* She carried the *aegis.* (Greek : *Athena.*)

Minotaur, the huge monster, half-bull, half-man, who fed on seven Athenian youths and seven Athenian maidens sent as a tribute to Crete each year. He was finally slain by *Theseus.*

Mnemosyne, the goddess of memory and the mother of the *Muses.*

Morpheus, the son of *Somnus*, god of sleep, and himself god of dreams.

Muses, the daughters of *Jupiter* and *Mnemosyne*, who presided over the arts and sciences.

Myrmidons, the soldiers of *Achilles* in the *Trojan War.*

myth, an account of the deeds of a god or of a being of supernatural powers. It gives, frequently, an explanation of some practice, belief, institution, or natural phenomenon.

naiads, nymphs who inhabited springs, brooks, fountains, and rivers.

Nausicaä, the daughter of *Alcinoüs,* king of the Phaeacians, who, in the "Odyssey," discovered *Ulysses* shipwrecked on the shores of her father's kingdom and was willing to marry him.

nectar, the drink of the gods.

Neptune, god of the sea, brother of *Jupiter.* (Greek : *Poseidon.*)

Nereids, the fifty sea-nymphs who waited on *Neptune.*

Nestor, the oldest of the Greek leaders in the *Trojan War.* He was noted for his wisdom.

Nibelungs, the supernatural beings who guarded the Nibelung hoard until *Siegfried* wrested it from them.

Norns, the three Fates of Norse literature.

Odin, the supreme god of the Norsemen, corresponding to *Jupiter.*

Odysseus, the Greek name for *Ulysses.*

Oedipus, son of King Laius and Queen Jocasta of Thebes, who was fated to kill his father and marry his mother.

Olympus, Mt., the home of the gods.

oreads, nymphs who lived in the hills and valleys. One of these nymphs was Echo.

Ossian, the son of Finn, a hero in Celtic mythology. He was also a famous bard.

Pallas Athena, the goddess of wisdom and weaving. (Roman : *Minerva.*) Athens was named after her.

Pan, the good-natured musician with horns and hoofs whose name signifies "all." He was the god of nature.

Pandora, the first woman in Greek mythology. She received as a wedding gift from the gods a box wherein were contained all evils and diseases ; when she opened the box, they flew out to torment mankind, leaving only Hope behind.

Paris, the son of *Priam,* who judged *Venus* the most beautiful of the goddesses, awarded to her the Apple of Discord, obtained *Helen* as a reward, and thus started the *Trojan War.*

Parnassus, Mt., the favorite haunt of *Apollo* and the *Muses.*

Pegasus, a winged horse, whom *Minerva* tamed and gave to the *Muses.* He was the mount of Bellerophon when that hero killed *Chimera.*

Penates, gods of the house, especially of the storeroom.

Phoebus Apollo. See *Apollo.*

Pluto, the god of the underworld and of riches, brother of *Neptune* and *Jupiter*. (Greek: *Hades* or *Dis*.)

Pollux, twin brother of *Castor*.

Polyhymnia, the *Muse* of sacred poetry.

Pomona, goddess of gardens and fruit-trees.

Poseidon, god of the sea. (Roman: *Neptune*.)

Priam, King of Troy and father of *Hector, Paris*, and *Cassandra*.

Prometheus, the *Titan* who created man and stole fire for him. For the latter offense, *Jupiter* chained him to a rock, where a vulture ate part of his liver, which constantly grew whole again. He was finally released by *Hercules*.

Proserpina, the daughter of *Ceres*, whom *Pluto* loved and kidnaped while her mother was away. She became queen of the underworld. (Also called *Persephone*.)

Psyche, the wife of *Cupid*, who almost surpassed *Venus* in beauty.

Puck, a mischievous sprite in Celtic belief, also known as Robin Goodfellow and Hobgoblin.

Ragnarok, a day, according to Norse mythology, when the powers of good and evil will wage a great battle for supremacy. Also explained as the *"twilight of the gods."*

Romulus, son of *Mars* and Sylvia Rhea, the mythical founder of Rome.

Round Table, an association of knights, headed by *King Arthur* and sworn to deeds of chivalry.

Saturn, the ruler of the universe before *Jupiter*, his son, wrested his power from him. Also the god of agriculture.

satyrs, clownish deities of the woods and fields, half-goats, half-men. Attendants of *Bacchus*.

Scylla, a six-headed monster who lived in a cave opposite the whirl-pool *Charybdis*. She seized six of Ulysses' crew.

sibyl, a prophetess.

Siegfried, the hero of the "Nibelungenlied." He slew a dragon and became invulnerable (save for one spot) in its blood, won the treasure of the *Nibelungs*, married *Kriemhild*, and was killed by the treachery of *Hagen*.

sirens, maidens who enticed sailors to destruction by their enchanting songs.

Somnus, god of sleep.

Styx River, the dark stream which wound seven times around *Hades.*

Telemachus, the faithful son of *Ulysses.*

Terpsichore, the *Muse* of dancing.

Thalia, the *Muse* of comedy.

Thanatos, the god of death, twin-brother of *Somnus.*

Themis, goddess of law and equity, the mother of the Fates.

Theseus, an Athenian hero, slayer of the *Minotaur.*

Thor, the Norse god of thunder.

Titans, children of Uranus and Gaea. Larger than men, they were not so big as were their brothers, the *Cyclopes.* They were overthrown by the gods.

totem, the sign of an animal held sacred by the American Indians and other primitive peoples.

trident, the three-pronged spear (originally a fish-hook) used by *Neptune* to stir up storms.

Trojan War, the battles involved in the siege of Troy, which lasted ten years, caused by Helen's elopement with Paris. The "Iliad," the "Odyssey," and the "Aeneid" all tell stories of this siege.

twilight of the gods, the final destruction of the Norse deities in a great struggle between them and the forces of evil. See *Ragnarok.*

Ulysses, king of Ithaca, a Greek hero in the Trojan War.

Urania, the *Muse* of astronomy.

Valhalla, the castle of *Odin,* where dead warriors were received, and where they feasted and fought perpetually.

Valkyries, beautiful maidens who searched on battlefields for slain heroes to escort to *Valhalla.*

Venus, a daughter of *Jupiter,* the goddess of love and beauty. (Greek : *Aphrodite.*)

Vertumnus, god of the changing year and the giver of fruits.

Vesta, the goddess of the hearth. Her temple in Rome was tended by the Vestal Virgins. (Greek : *Hestia.*)

Vulcan, the lame blacksmith of the gods and husband of *Venus.* (Greek : *Hephaestus.*)

Weird Sisters, the three Fates of the Norsemen. One told of the past, another of the present, the third of the future. The "witches" in "Macbeth" are these three sisters.

wooden horse, the strategy by which the Greeks entered Troy: a huge wooden horse, in which some Greeks hid while the rest of the Greek army pretended defeat and withdrew. The Trojans broke down part of their walls to get it into the city, and that night were wiped out by the Greek warriors who came into the city.

Yggdrasill, a tree in Norse mythology, representing the whole universe.

Zephyrus, the west wind.

Zeus, the King of the Heavens, and father of gods and men. The supreme ruler of all beings. (Roman: *Jupiter*.)

INDEX OF AUTHORS, ARTISTS, AND COMPOSERS

Aeschylus, 26, 121, 212, 315, 382

Agard, Walter R., 394

Allen, Hervey, 463

Allingham, William, 459, 462, 463

Alma-Tadema, Sir Lawrence, *illustration* 371

Anderson, R. B., 417

Apollonius of Rhodes, 261, 264

Apuleius, 44, 81, 88, 98

Aristophanes, 188, 382

Arnold, Sir Edwin, 319

Arnold, Matthew, 57, 74, 77, 124, 202, 247, 264, 266, 290, 315, 316, 319, 395, 401, 404, 414, 415, 417, 431, 461, 465, 485

Asbjörnsen, P. C., 417

Atherton, Gertrude, 347

Augustine, Saint, 468

Aurelius, Marcus, 363, 368

Ausonius, 343

Bacchylides, 50

Bacon, Francis, 483

Bailey, C., 376

Baldwin, James, 433

Bangs, J. K., 206

Baring, Maurice, 294

Barrie, Sir James M., 10, 12, 472, 483

Bates, Fred, *illustration* 25

Beddoes, T. L., 159

Belloc, Hilaire, 202

Bellows, H. A., 417

Benet, William Rose, 57

Benson, Rachel T., 506

Bernini, Giovanni, *illustration* 174

Binyon, Laurence, 159

Bion, 81, 99

Bishop, Farnham, 466

Blake, William, 57, 471

Bodenhausen, *illustration* 95

Boecklin, Arnold von, *illustration* 161

Boswell, James, 247, 265

Bridges, Robert, 27, 188, 290, 293, 315, 319

Brodeur, A. G., 417, 466

Brooks, Edward, 347

Browne, Lewis, 498

Browne, Sir Thomas, 63, 343

Browning, E. B., 102, 159, 184, 293, 316

Browning, Robert, 102, 123, 124, 155

Bryant, W. C., 228, 231, 461, 466

Buchanan, Robert, 159, 205, 319, 373, 417

Bunner, H. C., 102

Burne-Jones, Sir Edward, *illustrations* 97, 210, 212

Burroughs, Bryson, *illustration* 164

Butler, Samuel, 393

Butterworth, Hezekiah, 483

Byron, Lord, 16, 23, 26, 27, 28, 30, 58, 74, 95, 99, 102, 125, 139, 265, 286, 290, 297, 368, 374, 381, 392

Cabell, J. B., 415, 498

Campion, Thomas, 159

I

Carlyle, Thomas, 27
Catullus, 141, 144, 155, 184, 202, 220, 228, 290
Center, Stella S., 319
Chalmers, 485
Chapman, George, 98, 102, 288
Chaucer, Geoffrey, 51, 228, 231, 288
Chavannes, Puvis de, *illustration* 379
Cheney, J. V., 124
Chesterton, G. K., 464
Chidsey, Alan Lake, 319, 347
Child, C. F., 433
Church, A. J., 30, 347
Cicero, 371
Clarke, M., 347
Clodd, Edward, 76
Coates, F. E., 74, 125
Coleridge, S. T., 485
Collins, William, 435
Colum, Padraic, 264, 417, 466
Coluthus, 268
Conway, R. S., 394
Corbin, Alice, 376
Corneille, Pierre, 231
Correggio, *illustrations* 38, 42
Cosmio, *illustration* 207
Cowley, Abraham, 326
Cowper, William, 392, 435, 462
Cruse, Amy, 418, 446
Curtin, Jeremiah, 465

Dahn, Felix, 417
Daniel, Samuel, 184, 315, 319
Dante, 9, 200, 205, 257
Darwin, Erasmus, 232, 233
David, 230
Davis, W. S., 30, 376, 377–378
Debussy, Claude, 159, 376
De Lille, Alain, 336
Deutsch, *illustration* 273

De Vere, Aubrey, 77, 182
Disney, Walt, 15, 473
Disraeli, Benjamin, 7, 74, 498
Dobson, Austin, 202, 315, 319
Doolittle, Hilda ("H. D."), 57, 102, 127, 159, 162, 188, 275; 290, 293, 306, 315, 319, 376
Dowden, Edward, 74, 205, 228, 231
Drake, J. R., 461, 466
Drayton, Michael, 27
Drinkwater, John, 423
Drummond, William, 127, 228
Dryden, John, 74, 184, 185, 290, 343–344, 347, 363
Duff, J. W., 394
Dunsany, Lord, 12, 473, 483
Dyer, John, 250, 264

Eliot, George, 55, 205
Emerson, R. W., 54, 77, 159, 344, 466
Erskine, John, 498
Euripides, 123, 127, 246, 249, 264, 266, 290, 293, 315, 319, 382

Fagelberg, G. E., *illustration* 403
Farnell, L. R., 498
Fenelon, François de, 319
Ferguson, Sir Samuel, 465
Fielding, Henry, 205
Firestone, C. B., 498
Fiske, John, 498
Flaccus, Valerius, 234, 263
Flaxman, John, *illustrations* 31, 32, 104, 267, 307, 309
Flecker, J. E., 185
Fletcher, John, 159, 188
Flower, Robin, 293
Forman, S. E., 75
Foster, Marion Louise, 495
Fowler, Gene, 318
Fowler, W. W., 376, 394

Fox, W. S., 376
France, Anatole, 483
Franck, Cesar, 102
Frank, Florence K., 188
Frazer, Sir James G., 388-390, 498
Fremiet, Emmanuel, *illustration* 160
French, Allen, 466

Gardiner, E. N., 498
Garrick, David, 77
Gay, John, 74, 293
Gayley, C. M., 293
Geoffrey of Monmouth, 9, 460
Gerwig, Henrietta, 189
Gibson, W. H., 394
Gilbert, Sir W. S., 98
Gladstone, W. E., 468
Gluck, C. W. von, 127, 205, 294
Goethe, J. W. von, 9, 289, 319
Gosse, Sir Edmund, 141, 147, 159, 184, 205
Gould, Gerald, 462
Grahame, Kenneth, 483
Graves, C. L., 265
Gray, Thomas, 155, 164, 397, 417, 431
Gregory, Lady Augusta, 466
Guercino, *illustration* 131
Guerin, Jules, *illustration* 320
Guest, Lady Charlotte, 465

Hackel, Oliver, 434
Hake, T. G., 228
Hall, Jennie, 30
Halliburton, Richard, 317, 319
Handel, G. F., 249
Harris, H. Gordon, 483
Harris, Joel Chandler, 11
Harrison, Jane, 498
Harvey, Sir Paul, 439
Hauptmann, Gerhart, 315

Hawthorne, Nathaniel, 185, 344, 376, 485
" H. D." See *Doolittle, Hilda.*
Hearthill, John, 476
Heine, Heinrich, 317
Hemans, Felicia, 132
Henderson, Daniel, 30
Herrick, Robert, 102, 156, 462, 466, 485
Hewlett, Maurice, 52, 139, 485
Hilson, J. A., 506
Holmes, Ethel E., 493
Holmes, O. W., 156, 485
Homer, 3, 8, 9, 27, 33, 34, 47, 51, 52, 53, 54, 57, 75, 151, 184, 186, 200, 228, 245, 267, 274, 278, 279, 280, 282, 287, 288, 289, 290, 294, 295, 299, 301, 310, 313, 314, 316, 319, 345, 365, 377-381, 383, 384, 386, 387, 392, 393, 394, 485, 486
Hood, Thomas, 127, 150, 186, 486
Hopper, Nora, 466
Horace, 54, 61, 78, 125, 190, 349, 373, 374, 392, 486
Horne, R. H., 156
Hovey, Richard, 460, 466
Howell, H. L., 347
Hudson, W. H., 472, 483
Hughes, Rupert, 28
Hunt, Leigh, 102

Idrac, *illustration* 47
Iles, George, 75
Ingelow, Jean, 188
Ingres, J. A. D., *illustration* 65
Irving, Washington, 471, 472, 483

Jacobs, Joseph, 466
Jebb, R. C., 394
Jeffers, Robinson, 315
Jewett, Ida A., 506

Johnson, Samuel, 265
Jones, J. C., 413
Jonson, Ben, 52, 54, 102, 128, 141, 356, 486
Joyce, James, 205
Juvenal, 355

Keats, John, 1, 27, 30, 51, 52, 53, 54, 57, 75, 83, 85, 99, 102, 104, 124, 127, 129, 131, 139, 141, 155, 156, 159, 186, 202, 207, 247, 265, 316, 323, 352, 373, 374, 377, 392, 394, 441, 463, 482, 486
Keller, Martha, 155
Kellett, E. E., 484
Kelsey, F. W., 394
Kilmer, Aline, 102
Kilmer, Joyce, 486
Kingsley, Charles, 214, 228, 231
Kipling, Rudyard, 345, 415, 417, 462, 463, 466
Knowles, F. L., 290, 486

Lamb, Charles, 11, 28, 53, 99, 247, 265, 316, 344, 373, 374, 462, 482, 486
Lamprey, Louise, 30, 376, 466
Landor, W. S., 74, 77, 99, 102, 123, 127, 156, 159, 202, 205, 231, 290, 294, 315, 319, 373, 486
Lang, Andrew, 99, 102, 141, 184, 206, 249, 294, 316, 319, 392, 394
Langhorne, C. H., 139
Lawrence, T. E., 289, 319
Lawrence, W. W., 434
Lazarus, Emma, 103, 123, 127
Leaf, Walter, 294
Ledoux, Louis V., 75, 188, 392, 486
Ledwidge, Francis, 465
Lindsay, Vachel, 486
Lodge, G. C., 246, 249
Long, Haniel, 376, 467, 498

Longfellow, H. W., 1, 26, 30, 139, 156, 159, 184, 202, 231, 265, 290, 351, 374, 403, 415, 417, 431, 482, 486
Lorrain, Claude, illustrations 41, 59
Low, Will H., illustration 179
Lowe, Robert H., 469
Lowell, J. R., 26, 54, 57, 123, 127, 141, 174, 184, 185, 206, 315, 319, 460, 463, 466
Lubbock, Sir John, 438
Lucan, 49, 58, 437
Lully, G. B., 127
Lyly, John, 103, 141

Mabie, H. W., 417
Macaulay, Lord, 334, 341–343, 347, 359, 361, 373, 482, 486
MacCulloch, J. A., 465
MacDowell, Edward, 466
MacKaye, A. L., 294
MacKaye, Percy, 28
MacLeod, Fiona, 483
MacPherson, James, 450, 461, 465
Macy, John, 391–392
Maeterlinck, Maurice, 472
Maignan, illustration 279
Malory, Sir Thomas, 466
Manship, Paul, illustration 467
Markham, Edwin, 415
Marlowe, Christopher, 98, 99, 103, 247, 267, 271, 289, 294, 347
Marvell, Andrew, 486
Massard, Raphael, illustration 381
Massenet, Jules, 6
Mather, F. J., 319
McEwen, illustrations 232, 251
McSpadden, W. F., 434
Meleager of Gadara, 134
Meredith, George, 409
Merezhkovski, D. S., 498
Merritt, A., 498

Michelangelo, *illustration* 113
Millay, Edna St. Vincent, 466
Miller, F. J., 348
Mills, Dorothy, 30, 348
Milton, John, 19, 25, 27, 28, 31, 42,
53, 54, 67, 69, 89, 92, 100, 105,
124, 125, 148, 150, 155, 156,
159, 176, 184, 186, 194, 197, 200,
201, 203, 207, 229, 243, 247, 290,
307, 316, 317, 339, 345, 353, 373,
374, 391, 460, 462, 471, 476, 487
Mitchison, Naomi, 30
Moody, W. V., 26, 30
Moore, Thomas, 90, 103
Morley, Christopher, 497–498
Morris, Lewis, 182, 206
Morris, William, 9, 98, 100, 103,
123, 127, 184, 210, 219, 228, 229,
231, 249, 264, 266, 294, 392, 415,
431, 432, 434, 460, 466
Moschus, 59, 156
Motherwell, William, 434
Motte, *illustration* 285
Moulton, L. C., 103
Mozart, W. A., 57
Müller, Friedrich Max von, 468
Mundy, Talbot, 466
Murray, Gilbert, 394
Musaeus, 98, 103, 201, 380
Myers, Ernest, 294
Myron, *illustration* 122

Nash, Thomas, 348
Neide, *illustration* 88
Norris, Orland O., 498
Noyes, Alfred, 103, 127, 141, 206

O'Brien, Seumas, *illustration* 459
O'Duffy, Eimar, 466
Offenbach, Jacques, 6
Olcott, W. T., 484
O'Neill, Eugene, 484

O'Sheel, Shaemas, 465
Ovid, 9, 36, 53, 75, 103, 111, 115,
125, 139, 145, 155, 156, 186, 208,
231, 249, 264, 266, 290, 294, 315,
319, 382, 383, 390–392, 393, 394,
488, 502, 503

Palmer, G. H., 289
Pater, Walter, 98, 103
Peabody, J. P., 247
Peacock, T. L., 184
Pease, C. A., 289, 319
Peattie, D. C., 186
Peele, George, 294, 493
Penoyer, John, 506
Petronius, 156
Phillips, Stephen, 123, 124, 127,
200, 206, 315, 319, 370
Pindar, 48, 122, 124, 250, 381, 392,
394
Plato, 210, 378
Pliny the Younger, 53
Plutarch, 231
Poe, E. A., 75, 289, 294
Polybius, 468
Pope, Alexander, 119, 155, 170,
199, 203, 214, 290, 312, 317, 345,
374, 376, 462, 466
Porson, Richard, 347
Poussin, Nicholas, *illustrations* 6,
219
Poynter, Sir Edward J., *illustration* 90
Procter, B. W., 141, 184
Procter, Mary, 484
Purcell, Henry, 6, 348
Putnam, E. J., 294
Pyle, Katherine, 406

Racine, Jean, 294
Raleigh, Sir Walter, 488
Regnault, A. G. H., *illustration* 283

Reni, Guido, *illustration* 150
Respighi, Ottorino, 159
Rivière, Briton, *illustration* 306
Robinson, E. A., 460, 466
Robinson, Lennox, 465
Rolleston, T. W., 465
Rosa, Salvatore, *illustration* 170
Rossetti, D. G., 30, 184, 188, 228,
    231, 315, 319
Royds, T. F., 394
Rubens, Peter Paul, *illustrations*
    67, 166, 334
Ruskin, John, 11, 52, 484
Russell, G. W., 465

Sabin, F. E., 506
Saint-Saëns, Camille, 127, 249
Santayana, George, 290
Sappho, 103
Sargent, John S., *illustrations* 1, 5,
    19, 40, 111, 121, 144, 168, 189,
    211, 237, 275, 297, 356
Sassoon, Siegfried, 461
Saxe, J. G., 127
Schiller, Friedrich von, 57
Scott, W. B., 415, 417
Scriabine, Alexander, 30
Scudder, J. W., 394
Scudder, Janet, *illustration* 148
Seneca, 232, 246
Shakespeare, 6, 9, 28, 31, 37, 51,
    53, 54, 97, 98, 99, 100, 101, 103,
    124, 139, 155, 156, 172, 186,
    201–202, 203, 204, 228, 231, 239,
    246, 247, 250, 288, 290, 320, 321,
    337, 340, 345, 360, 370, 374, 391,
    392, 415, 431, 441, 460, 462, 463,
    466, 488
Sharp, William, 348, 373, 462, 488
Shaw, George Bernard, 348
Sheepshanks, Richard, 30
Shelley, P. B., 26, 40, 46, 51, 57, 73,
    124, 125, 127, 155, 156, 159, 166,
    183, 184, 188, 203, 217, 231, 325
Sherman, Frank Dempster, 188
Showerman, Grant, 376
Shumway, D. B., 434
Shumway, E. S., 376
Sichel, *illustration* 261
Sill, Edward Rowland, 103
Simonides, 160, 228, 231
Sitwell, Edith, 229
Slaughter, M., 348
Smith, Edmund, 298
Smith, Horatio, 41, 317
Snedecker, C. D., 30, 127
Sophocles, 72, 77, 246, 290, 315, 382
Southey, Robert, 104
Spenser, Edmund, 28, 54, 100, 152,
    168, 186, 190, 229, 291, 311, 317,
    373, 391, 392, 460, 488, 489
Spring, Howard, 489
Squire, Charles, 465
Stedman, E. C., 159, 315
Stephens, James, 127, 463, 466
Stoddard, R. H., 182, 188
Story, W. W., 188
Strauss, Richard, 319
Stravinsky, Igor, 77
Swift, Jonathan, 51, 74, 203
Swinburne, A. C., 51, 78, 137, 138–
    139, 141, 159, 182, 188, 200–201,
    460, 466
Synge, J. M., 465

Taylor, Bayard, 30, 57, 77, 188, 266
Teasdale, Sara, 294
Tennyson, Frederick, 188
Tennyson, Lord, 38, 54, 57, 74,
    103, 140, 182, 186, 188, 203, 229,
    231, 276, 289, 290, 294, 315, 319,
    345, 346, 384, 392, 394, 455, 460,
    462, 463, 464, 465, 466, 478, 482
Terence, 75

Theocritus, 155, 255, 265, 291
Theognis, 32
Thomas, Edith M., 484
Thompson, Francis, 229
Thomson, James, 54, 374, 489
Thorwaldsen, A. B., *illustrations* 23, 245, 255, 377
Thumann, Paul, *illustrations* 49, 83, 85, 89
Tibullus, 356
Tietjens, Eunice, 159
Train, Arthur, 392
Travers, P. L., 472, 484
Trumbull, John, 47
Twain, Mark, 53

Vedder, Elihu, *illustrations* 46, 217, 340
Veronese, Paul, *illustration* 208
Virgil, 8, 9, 16, 28, 53, 114, 144, 149, 156, 161, 178, 184, 189, 191, 195, 200, 203, 221, 224, 228, 29, 237, 285, 288, 303, 320, 328, 330, 335, 340, 345, 346, 373, 374, 382–390, 392, 393, 394

Wagner, Richard, 6, 395, 399, 415, 417, 431, 432, 434

Waterhouse, John William, *illustration* 311
Watts, George Frederick, *illustration* 221
Weber, C. M. von, 466
Webster, John, 348
West, Benjamin, *illustration* 298
Wheeling, K. E., 506
White, E. L., 30, 184, 294, 319, 376
Whitman, Walt, 462
Whittier, J. G., 29, 155, 434
Wilde, Oscar, 71, 103, 140, 141, 156, 177, 186, 203, 211, 229, 265, 291, 294
Winslow, A. G., 346
Wodehouse, P. G., 100
Wolcot, John, 392
Wolfe, Thomas, 11
Woodberry, G. E., 182
Woodring, Maxie N., 506
Wordsworth, William, 13–14, 127, 156, 184, 226, 294, 317, 465
Wyatt, Sir Thomas, 348
Wylie, Elinor, 54

Yeats, W. B., 461, 463, 465, 466

GENERAL INDEX

abstractions, 356

Absyrtus, 263

Abydos (*a*-bī′dŏs), 94

Acastus, 264

Acca Larentia, 333, 371

Achates (*a*-kā′tēz), 386

Acheron (ăk′ēr-ŏn) River, 191, 192

Achillea (ăk′ĭ-lē′*a*), 292

Achilles (*a*-kĭl′ēz), and Patroclus, 278 f.; death of, 282; in Trojan War, 272 f.; wrath of, 281

Acidalia (ăs-ĭd-dā′lĭ-*a*), 43

Acrisius (*a*-krĭs′ĭ-*u*s), 207, 217–218

Admeta (ăd-mē′t*a*), 240

Admetus (ăd-mē′t*u*s), 115 f., 254; and Alcestis, 116–119; and Apollo, 115–119

Adonis (*a*-dō′nĭs), 78 f.; Venus and, 78 f.

Adrastea (ăd-răs-tē′*a*), 18

Adrastus (*a*-drăs′t*u*s), 65

advertising, 11; mythology in, 477 f.

Aeaea (ē-ē′*a*), 305

Aed (ä′ēd), 454

Aeëtes (e-ē′tēz), 259 f.

Aegeus (ē′j*u*s), 218–223

aegis (ē′jĭs), 45, 207, 214, 217, 366

Aegisthus (ē-jĭs′th*u*s), 298–299

Aeneas (ē-nē′*a*s), 191, 195–196, 269, 277, 288, 320–333, 337, 369, 383–390, 391; adventures of, 320–333; from Troy to Carthage, 320–326; in Italy, 329–333; in the underworld, 327–329

Aeneid (ē-nē′ĭd), Virgil's, 320, 383–390

Aeolian (ē-ō′lĭ-*a*n) Islands, 150

Aeolus (ē′ŏ-l*u*s), 150, 180–182, 304, 323; home of, 150

Aeschylus (ĕs′kĭ-l*u*s), 382

Aesculapius (ĕs′k*u*-lā′pĭ-*u*s), 40, 112–115, 362; death of, 112–115

Aeson (ē′s*u*n), 250 f.

Aethra (ē′thr*a*), 218–219

Aetna. See *Etna.*

Agamemnon (ăg′*a*-mĕm′nŏn), 270 f., 296–299; at Troy, 270 f.

Aganippe (ăg′*a*-nĭp′ē), 40

ages of man, 21–26

Ajax (ā′jăks), 244, 272, 278, 282–284, 296, 480

Alba Longa, 333, 337

Alberich (äl′bēr-ĭk), 424–425

Alcaeus (ăl-sē′*u*s), 233

Alcestis (ăl-sĕs′tĭs), 116 f.; and Admetus, 116 f.

Alcides (ăl-sī′dēz), 233

Alcinoüs (ăl-sĭn′ŏ-*u*s), 310

Alcmene (ălk-mē′nē), 232

Alecto (*a*-lĕk′tō), 17

Alfheim, 404

All-Father, 400, 414

alphabet, introduction of, 62

Alpheus (ăl-fē′*u*s), 182; and Arethusa, 182

Alpheus River, 182, 183, 236

Althaea (ăl-thē′*a*), 135 f.

Amalthaea (ăm-ăl-thē′*a*), 18

Amazons, 223–224, 238, 240, 474

ambrosia, 8, 32, 88, 215

Ammon, 33
Amphion (ăm·fī′ŏn), 133, 380
Amphitrite (ăm′fĭ-trī′tê), 153
Amphitryon (ăm-fĭt′rĭ-ŏn), 233, 235
Amulius, 333
Ana, 442
Anchises (ăn-kī′sēz), 269, 320, 321, 322, 323, 324, 327, 329, 388
Ancus Martius, 338
Androcles, 344-345
Andromache (ăn-drŏm′a-kê), 278, 279
Andromeda (ăn-drŏm′ê-da), 207, 213 f., 476, 488; rescue of, 213 f.
anemone, creation of, 81
Anger, 356
Angus (ăng′gŭs), 442
animism, 469
Anna, 324, 344
Anna Perenna, 369. See Anna.
Annwn (ăn′nōōn), 457
Answerer, the, 443
Anteaus (ăn-tē′ŭs), 244
anthropology (ăn′thrŏ-pŏl′ô-jĭ), 468-469
Antigone (ăn-tĭg′ô-nê), 65
Antony, Mark, 190, 353, 364, 372
Aphrodite (ăf′rô-dī′tê), 43. See Venus.
Apollo (a-pŏl′ô), 1, 3, 39-41, 45, 48, 62, 94, 132, 133, 174, 195, 196, 233, 241, 244, 296, 305, 308, 327, 366, 370, 380, 385, 437, 474, 475, 480; and Admetus, 115 f.; and Aesculapius, 112 f.; and Clytie, 173-175; and Daphne, 171-173; and Hyacinthus, 106 f.; and Latona, 104 f.; and Marpessa, 107 f.; and Midas, 166-167; and Niobe, 133-135, 146; and Phaëthon, 109 f.; and the Python, 119 f.

Apollo Agyieus (a-jī′ūs), 377
Apollo Paean, 40
apotheosis (ăp′ô-thē′ô-sĭs), 363, 364
Appius Claudius, 344
apple of discord, 268-269
Aquilo, 150
Arachne (a-răk′nê), 70 f.; and Athena, 70 f.
Arcadia, 22, 65, 148, 160
Arcadians, 331
Arcady (är′ka-dĭ). See Arcadia.
Arcas (är′kăs), 65 f., 254
Archer, The, 476
Ares (ā′rēz), 37. See Mars.
Arete (ăr′ê-tē), 310
Arethusa (ăr′ê-thū′sa), 182; and Alpheus, 182
Argei, 370
Argo, the, 253 f., 477
Argonauts, 254 f., 474
Argos (är′gŏs), 207, 217
Argus (är′gŭs), servant of Juno, and Io, 168-171
Argus, the shipbuilder, 253 f.
Argus, Ulysses' dog, 310, 312
Ariadne (ăr′ĭ-ăd′nê), 220-223, 480; and Bacchus, 223; and Theseus, 222-223
Arion (a-rī′ŏn), 167-168; and the dolphins, 167-168
Aristophanes (ăr′ĭs-tŏf′a-nēz), 382
Artemis (är′tê-mĭs), 41. See Diana.
Arthur, King, 9, 441, 454-457, 458; legend of, 454-457
Aruns (ā′rŭnz), 332
Ascanius (ăs-kā′nĭ-ŭs), 333. See Iulus.
Asgard (äs′gärd), 400, 405
Asia Minor, 238, 333
Ask (ăsk), 400
Assyria, 78
Astarte (äs-tär′tê), 78

astronomy, 45, 66, 133, 144–146, 475–477; myths and, 475–477

Astyanax (ăs-tī'a-năks), 278, 279

Atalanta (ăt-a-lăn'ta), of Arcadia, 135–138, 254; of Boeotia, 90 f., 479; of Calydon, 43

Ate (ā'tē), 268. See *Eris*.

Athena (a-thē'na), 69 f.; and Arachne, 70 f. See also *Minerva*.

Athens (ăth'ĕnz), 58, 69–70, 218 f.

athletic contests, Greek, 120 f. See *ludi*.

Atlas (ăt'lăs), 20, 45, 150, 212, 213, 241–242, 468, 477, 480; Hercules and, 241–242

Atropos (ăt'rŏ-pŏs), 48

Attica (ăt'tĭ-ka), 69, 178

Audhumla (ou'thōōm-lä), 396

Augean (ô-jē'an) **stables,** 236

Augeas (ô-jē'ăs), 236

Augustus, 353, 360, 383, 390

Aulis (ô'lĭs), 272, 274

Aurora (ô-rō'ra), 144, 149, 150, 180, 277, 367; and Cephalus, 178 180; and Tithonus, 178; duties of, 149

Auster, 150

Autolycus (ô-tŏl'ĭ-kŭs), 233

Avalon (ăv'a-lŏn), 457

Avernus (a-vûr'nŭs), 189, 327

Avilion (a-vĭl'yŭn), 457. See *Avalon*.

Babylon, 96

bacchanals (băk'a-nălz). See *bacchante*.

bacchante (ba-kánt'; ba-kăn'tê), 148

Bacchus (băk'ŭs), 4, 146–148, 165 f., 198, 200, 223, 367; duties of, 146–148; grapes of, 367;

ivy of, 367; leopards of, 367; wanderings of, 165 f.

Balder (bôl'dēr), 402, 474; death of, 412–414; description of, 402

ballads, 2

Balmung (bäl'mōong), 424

banshee (băn'shē), 459

Baucis (bô'sĭs) **and Philemon** (fĭ-lē'mŏn), 66 f.

Bedivere, Sir, 456

Bellerophon (bĕ-lĕr'ô-fŏn), 225–227, 279; adventures of, 225–227

Bellona (bĕ-lō'na), 356

Beowulf (bā'ô-wŏŏlf), 427 f.

Bifrost (bēf'rŏst), 398, 400

Black Sea, 255, 390, 435

boar, Erymanthian (ĕr'ĭ-măn'-thĭ-ăn), 236

Boeotia (bĕ-ō'sha), 90, 272

Bona Dea (bō'na dē'a), 360

Bor (bôr), 396

Boreas (bō'rĕ-ăs), 150, 258

Bragi (brä'jē), 404

Bran (brăn), 443–444, 457; description of, 443–444

Briareus (brī-âr'ĕ-ŭs), 17

Brigit (brĭg'ĭt), 442

Brisingamen (brē-sĕn-gä'mĕn), 404

Bron (brŏn), 443–444. See *Bran*.

Bronze, Age of, 21, 438

Brown Bull of Quelgny, 447

brownies, 459

Brunhild (brōōn'hĭlt), 423 f.

Brutus, Lucius Junius, 340

Brutus, Marcus, 340

Bull of Ailell (ī'lĕl), 448

Buri (bōō'rê), 396

Cadmus (kăd'mŭs), 62, 474

caduceus (ka-dū'sĕ-ŭs), 47, 366

Caesar (sē'zēr), **Augustus.** See *Augustus*.

Caesar, Julius, 190, 333, 353, 364, 372, 437, 438, 439, 440
Calaïs (kăl'ā-ĭs), 254, 258
Caldron of the Dagda, 444
calendar, Greek, 120; Roman, 369–372
Calliope (kă-lī'ō-pē), 48, 196, 200, 474
Callisto (kă-lĭs'tō), 65 f., 477; and Jupiter, 65 f.
Calydon (kăl'ĭ-dŏn), 135 f.
Calydonian hunt, 135–138
Calypso (kă-lĭp'sō), Ulysses and, 308–309
Camenae (kă-mē'nē), 354
Camilla (kă-mĭl'ȧ), 330–332
Care, 405
Carthage (kär'thăj), 324, 385, 386, 435
Cassandra (kă-săn'drȧ), 296–298
Cassiopeia (kăs'ĭ-ō-pē'yȧ), 213 f., 476
Castalia, 173
Castaly. See Castalia.
Castor (kȧs'tēr), 11, 233, 254, 270, 343, 353–354, 476
Cathbad the Druid, 448
Cattle of the Sun, 308
Celtic cycles of legends, 440 f.
Celtic gods, 437–440.
Celts (sĕlts), 9, 435 f.
centaurs (sĕn'tôrz), 112–113, 224, 244, 476; and Aesculapius, 112–113. See also Chiron.
Cephalus (sĕf'ȧ-lŭs) and Aurora, 178–180
Cepheus (sē'fūs), 213 f.
Cerberus (sûr'bēr-ŭs), 20, 191–192, 242, 327; sop to, 191, 327, 386
Ceres (sē'rēz), 4, 18, 145, 146, 351, 366, 369, 480; and Proserpina, 160 f., 193; description of, 146

Ceyx (sē'ĭks), 180–182
Chaos (kā'ŏs), 16, 391
Charon (kā'rŏn), 88, 189, 190, 327
Charonides, 190
Charybdis (kă-rĭb'dĭs), 154, 308, 323; Ulysses and, 308
Chimera (kĭ-mē'rȧ), 19, 20, 225; Bellerophon and, 225
Chiron (kī'rŏn), 112–113, 250, 251, 274, 275, 476; and Aesculapius, 112–113
Chloris (klō'rĭs), 151, 361
Chronos (krō'nŏs), 366
Ciconians (sĭ-kō'nĭ-ănz), 300
Circe (sûr'sē), 305–307, 308; Ulysses and, 305–307
Clashing Islands, 258–259
Clio (klī'ō), 48, 480
Cloak of Darkness, 425, 426
Cloelia, 343
Clotho (klō'thō), 48
Clymene (klĭm'ē-nē), 109
Clytemnestra (klī'tĕm-nĕs'trȧ),276, 296–299; crime of, 298–299
Clytie (klī'tē) and Apollo, 173–175
Cocytus (kō-sī'tŭs) River, 191
Colchis (kŏl'kĭs), 253 f.
Compitalia, 371–372
Conary (kŏn'ȧ-rĭ), King, 445
Conchobor (kŏng'kō-wŭr), 448–449
Concord, 356
Connaught (kŏn'ôt), 447, 448
Conor, King, 445, 448, 449
Conorian Cycle, 441, 445–449
constellations, 475–477
contests of Minerva, 69–72
Cormac (kôr'măk), King, 449
cornucopia, 146
coronation stone, 438–440, 444
Coronis (kō-rō'nĭs), 112
Council of the gods, 365, 366–367
Cretan Bull, 238, 239

Crete (krēt), 18, 60, 220 f., 322, 478

Creüsa (krē-ū′sá), 288, 322

Croesus (krē′sŭs), 50

Cronus (krō′nŭs), 17 f., 192, 351, 366; sickle of, 351

Cuchulain (kŏŏ-hŏŏ′lĭn), 445 f., 464, 466

Cullan (kŭl′ĕn), 446

Cumaean (kŭ-mē′ăn) sibyl, 327–329, 339–340; and Aeneas, 327–329; and Sibylline Books, 339–340

Cupid (kū′pĭd), 4, 37, 43, 44, 78 f., 367; and Apollo, 171–173; and Psyche, 81 f.

Curiatii (kū-rĭ-ā′shĭ-ī), 337–338

Cybele (sĭb′ê-lē), 92, 93, 369

Cycle, Conorian, 445–449; of legends, Celtic, 440 f.; of the Invasions of Ireland, 441–445; Ossianic, 449–451; Ultonian, 445–449

cyclopean, 29

Cyclopes (sī-klō′pēz), 17, 18, 115, 300–304, 322–323, 468, 474; Ulysses and, 300–304

Cymothoe (sī-mŏth′ō-ē), 149

Cynthia (sĭn′thĭ-á), 106

Cynthus (sĭn′thŭs), Mt., 106

Cyprus (sī′prŭs), 93

Cyrus, 50

Cythera (sĭth′ēr-á), 43, 51. See Venus.

Cytherean (sĭth′ēr-ē′ăn), the, 43. See Venus.

Daedalus (dĕd′á-lŭs), 60 f.

Dag (däg), 396–398

Dagda (dåg′thá), the, 442, 444, 445

Damon (dā′mŏn) and Pythias, 227–228

Dan (Cupid), 101

Dana (thàn′á), 442, 444, 445, 458

Danaë (dăn′ā-ē), 207 f.

Danaïdes (dá-nā′ĭ-dēz), 189, 195

Danaüs (dăn′ā-ŭs), 195

Danu (thàn′ŏŏ), 442. See Diana.

Daphne (dăf′nê), 171–173, 174; and Apollo, 171–173

Dardanelles (där-dá-nĕlz′), 253

Dardanus, 322

Dares, 324

dawn, gods of, 149 f.

Days, the, 109

Death, 118–119, 327. See Mors and Hel.

Deianira (dē-yá-nī′rá), 244–245

deification, 364

Deiopea (dē-ĭ-ō-pē′á), 149, 323

Deiphobus (dē-ĭf′ō-bŭs), 284

Deirdre (dâr′drá), 448–449

deities, table of, 366–367; groups of, 367

Delos (dē′lŏs), 387

Delphi (dĕl′fī), 48 f., 378

Delphic sibyl, 48 f.

Demeter (dĕ-mē′tēr), 21, 146. See Ceres.

Dermot (dûr′mŏt), 449

Deucalion (dŭ-kā′lĭ-ŏn), 26, 391

Diana (dī-ăn′á), 3, 39, 41–43, 90, 104, 105, 112, 135, 175, 178, 193, 296, 330, 332, 366, 385, 474, 475, 480; and Endymion, 128 f.; and Niobe, 133–135; and Orion, 132–133; at Aulis, 274 f.; crescent of, 43

Dido (dī′dō), 320, 324, 326, 328, 369, 384, 385, 388; and Aeneas, 324

Dike (dī′kē), 48

Diomedes (dī′ō-mē′dēz), mares of, 238; Greek Hero, 272, 284

Dione (dī-ō'nē), 43
Dionysius (dĭ'ô-nĭsh'ĭ-ŭs), 227–228
Dionysus (dī'ô-nī'sŭs), 367. See Bacchus.
Dioscuri (dī'ŏs-kū'rī), 254
Dirae (dī'rē), 17. See Erinyes.
Dis (dĭs), 160, 367. See Pluto.
Discord, 356
Dodona (dô-dō'nà), 50
Doliones (dô-lī'ŭn-ēz), 255
Dolon, 278
dolphins (dŏl'fĭnz), 153, 166, 168
Don (dŏn), 442, 458. See Dana.
Doris (dô'rĭs), 151
doves, of Venus, 43
dragons, 62, 259–263, 418, 421–423, 430–431
Dreams. See Somnus and Morpheus.
druids (drōō'ĭdz), 435, 439, 440, 446, 448
dryads (drī'ădz), 149
Dunsany (dŭn-sā'nĭ), 473
Duty, 234
dwarfs, 396 f., 420 f.

earth, Greek conception of, 144–146
Earth-Mother, 4
East Wind, 151
Echo and Narcissus, 175–177
echo, origin of, 175
Eddas (ĕd'ás), 9, 422
Egeria (ê-jē'rĭ-à), 354
Electra (ê-lĕk'trà), 299
Eleusinian mysteries, 165
Eleusis (ê-lū'sĭs), 165
Elis, 150, 182, 236
Elissa, 324. See Dido.
Elli (ĕl'lĭ), 411, 412.
elves, 459
Elysian (ê-lĭzh'ăn) Fields, 329. See Elysium.

Elysium (ê-lĭzh'ĭ-ŭm), 192, 195 f.; description of, 195 f.
Embla (ĕm'blä), 400
Endymion (ĕn-dĭm'ĭ-ŏn) and Diana, 128–132
Entellus, 324
Eos (ē'ŏs), 149. See Aurora.
Epeus (ê-pē'ŭs), 285
Epimetheus (ĕp'ĭ-mē'thūs), 20, 24–26
Erato (ĕr'à-tō), 48
Erebus (ĕr'ê-bŭs), 192. See Hades.
Erin, 449
Erinyes (ê-rĭn'ĭs), 17
Eris (ē'rĭs), 268
Eros (ēr'ŏs), 43. See Cupid.
Erymanthian (ĕr'ĭ-măn'thĭ-ăn) boar, 236
Erythea (ĕr'ĭ-thē'à), 240–241
Esus (ē'sŭs), 438
Eteocles, 65
Ethiopians (ē'thĭ-ō'pĭ-ănz), 112, 144, 213, 308, 309
Etna (ĕt'nà), Mount, 39, 115
Etruscans (ê-trŭs'kănz), 331–332, 338
Etzel (ĕt'sĕl), King, 427
Euhemerism (û-hē'mēr-ĭz'm), 468
Euhemerus (û-hē'mēr-ŭs), 467
Eumenides (û-mĕn'ĭ-dēz), 17, 193. See Erinyes.
Euripides (û-rĭp'ĭ-dēz), 382
Europa (û-rō'pà), 58 f., 474, 477, 480; and Jupiter, 58 f.; Jupiter's satellite, 76, 474
Eurus (ū'rŭs), 151
Euryalus (û-rī'à-lŭs), 331
Eurydice (û-rĭd'ĭ sē), 196 f. See also Orpheus.
Eurylochus (û-rĭl'ŏ-kŭs), 305
Eurystheus (û-rĭs'thê-ŭs), 235 f.
Eurytion (û-rĭsh'ĭ-ŏn), 240–241

Eurytus (ū'rĭ-tŭs), 233
Euterpe (ŭ-tûr'pĕ), 48
Evander (ē-văn'dēr), 331 f.
Evenus (e-vē'nŭs), 107
Excalibur (ĕks-kăl'ĭ-bēr), 456

Fafnir (fäv'nĭr), 421, 422
fairies, Celtic, 445, 450, 454, 458–
    460, 477; little people, 458–460
fairy changeling, 460
Faith, 356
Falias (făl'ĭ-ȧs), 444
Fame, 356
fasces (făs'ēz), 35
Fata, 387
fate, power of, 387
Fates, the three, 48, 49, 135 f., 242,
    332
Fauna, 360
Faunalia, 371
fauns, 148, 358, 360, 371
Faunus (fô'nŭs), 358, 367, 372
Faustulus (fôs'tŭ-lŭs), 333
Fear, 37, 327, 356
Felicitas, 354
Fenian cycle, 441
Fenians (fē'nĭ-ănz), 449, 450
Fenrir (fĕn'rĭr), 405–407, 414
Ferdiad (fâr'dĕ-ȧd), 447
festivals, Roman, 367–372
fetishism (fē'tĭsh-ĭsm), 469
Fianna (fē'ȧ-nȧ), 449, 451
Fingal, 430
Finias (fĭn'ĭ-ȧs), 444
Finn, 449–451
Fionn (fĭ'ŏn). See Finn.
Firbolg (fĭr'bŭl-ŭg), 442, 444
fire, 412
Fire-Giver, 22–24
Flood, the Great, 26
Flora (flō'rȧ), 150, 361, 369
Floralia (flō-rā'lĭ-ȧ), 361, 369

Fomorians (fō-wôr'ĭ-ănz), 442,
    444
Foresti (fôr'ĕs-tē), 405
Fortuna (fôr-tū'nȧ), 354, 355,
    387
forum, Roman, 338, 343, 352, 354
Fountain of Youth, 473
Frey (frā), 404
Freya (frā'ä), 404, 407, 474
Friday, 404
Frigg (frĭg), 400, 402, 412, 414
frogs, origin of, 106
frost giants, 398 f.
Furies, 17, 190, 192–193, 297, 299,
    327

Gaea (jē'ȧ), 16 f.
Galahad (găl'ȧ-hăd), Sir, 456
Galatea (găl'ȧ-tē'ȧ), 93–94, 153;
    and Pygmalion, 93–94
Games, Nemean, 121; Olympic,
    120–121; Pythian, 120, 121
Gana (gä'nȧ), 424
Ganymede (găn'ĭ-mēd), 38, 39, 477
Gareth (găr'ĕth), Sir, 456
Gauls, 343
Gawain (gä'wăn), Sir, 456
geese, 343
Gemini (jĕm'ĭ-nī), 11, 343, 353–
    354, 476. See Castor and Pollux.
genius, 360, 361
genius loci (jēn'yŭs lō'sī), 361, 386
Geryon (jē'rĭ-ŏn), oxen of, 240–241,
    354
giants, 17, 396 f.; frost, 398 f.
Gladsheim (gläts'hām'), 400
gnomes (nōmz), 459
goblins, 459
gods, Greek, 377–378; idea of, 388,
    414; minor, 48–51; of the air,
    149–151; of the earth, 146–149;
    of nature, 144–146, 160–182;

of the Northland, 395–414; of
Rome, 348–372; of the sky, 31–
51; of the waters, 151–154;
on Olympus, 31–32; origin of,
16–21; table of, 366–367
gold, shower of, 207, 208
Golden Age, 21, 192, 352, 414
Golden Apples, 90 f.
Golden Bough, 327, 388, 389
Golden Fleece, 250, 252 f.
Good Spirit, 471
Gorgons (gôr′gǒnz), 45, 207 f.
Gorias (gō′rĭ-ȧs), 444
Graces, the three, 48
grasshopper, origin of, 178
Gray Sisters, 209–210, 217
Great Bear, 66
Great Mother, 17, 93, 369
Greeks, 144 f.
Green Island. See *Ireland*.
Grendel (grĕn′dĕl), 427–428
Guinevere (gwĭn′ĕ-vēr), 454
Gunther (gōōn′tēr), King, 425 f.
Gwydion (gwĭd′ĭ-ŏn), 444, 458

Hades, 21, 160, 189 f., 306–307;
chief figures in, 192–193; de-
scription of, 189 f. See also
underworld.
Hagen, 425 f.
halcyon (hăl′sĭ-ŭn) days, 182
Halcyone (hăl-sī′ō-nē) and Ceyx,
180–182
hamadryads (hăm′ȧ-drī′ădz), 149,
472, 474
Happy Hunting Grounds, 477
Happy Isles, 195. See *Elysium*.
Hare, the, 133
Harlech (här′lĕk), 457
Harmonia (här-mō′nĭ-ȧ), 62
Harpies (här′pĭz), 256–258, 322
Hebe (hē′bè), 39, 245, 481

Hecate (hĕk′ȧ-tē), 41, 106, 193,
377
Hecatoncheires (hĕk′ȧ-tŏn-kī′rēz),
17, 18
Hector, 269 f.
Hecuba (hĕk′ū-bȧ), 269 f.
heifer (hĕf′ēr), 169
Heimdall (hām′däl), 398
Hel (hĕl), the goddess, 398, 405;
the place, 398
Helen of Troy, 267 f., 295, 448, 474,
478
Helicon, Mt., 40
Helios. See *Apollo*.
Helle (hĕl′lē), 253
Hellespont (hĕl′ĕs-pŏnt), 253; ori-
gin of name, 253
Hephaestus (hē-fĕs′tŭs), 24. See
Vulcan.
Hera (hē′rȧ), 21. See *Juno*.
Herakles (hĕr′ȧ-klēz), 232. See
Hercules.
Hercules (hûr′kŭ-lēz), 39, 45, 224,
232, 254, 269, 284, 362, 474, 476,
480; adventures of, 232–249;
and Alcestis, 118–119; and
Hylas, 255–256, 265; and the
Romans, 354; birth of, 232;
choice of, 234; early life of, 232–
234; first six labors of, 235–238;
last six labors of, 238–242; later
career of, 242–245; madness of,
234–235; marriage of, 234–235
Hermes (hûr′mēz), 45. See *Mer-
cury*.
Hermione (hûr-mī′ō-nē), 295, 299
herms (hûrmz), 45, 377
Hero (hēr′ō) and Leander, 94 f.
Hesiod (hē′sĭ-ŏd), 20, 380, 381
Hesione (hē-sī′ō-nē), 244
Hesper. See *Hesperus*.
Hesperia, 322, 329

Hesperides (hĕs-pĕr'ĭ-dēz), Garden of the, 150, 213, 241–242, 268, 479
Hesperus (hĕs'pēr-ŭs), 150
Hestia (hĕs'tĭ-à), 21. See *Vesta*.
Hildebrand (hĭl'dĕ-brănd), 427
Hippocrene (hĭp'ŏ-krēn), 40
Hippolyta (hĭ-pŏl'ĭ-tà), 223–224, 238, 240
Hippomenes (hĭ-pŏm'ĕ-nēz), 90 f., 479; and Atalanta, 90 f.
Hoder (hû'dēr), 405. See *Hothr*.
Holy Grail, 456
Hope, 25, 481
Horatii (hŏ-rā'shĭ-ī), 337–338
Horatius (1), 337–338
Horatius (2), 341–343
horn gate, 193, 387
Horn of Plenty, 4
Hothr (hû'th'r), 405, 412
Hound of Cullan, 446
Hours, the, 31, 32, 40
household gods, 362
Hraesvelg (hrĕs'vĕlg), 398
Hrimfaxi (hrĕm'făk-sī), 398
Hrothgar (hrōth'gär), 427 f.
Hugi (hōō'gē), 410, 412
Hugin (hōō'gēn), 400
Hunger, 327, 405
hyacinth, 107
Hyacinthus (hī'à-sĭn'thŭs), 106–107, 390; and Apollo, 106 107
Hydra (hī'drà), Lernaean (lûr-nē'ăn), 236, 237
hydras, 236, 237, 327
Hygelac (hī'gĕ-lăk), 427
Hylas (hī'làs), 255–256
Hymen (hī'mĕn), 361
Hyperboreans (hī'pēr-bō'rĕ-ănz), 144
Hyperion (hī-pē'rĭ-ŏn), 17
Hypnos (hĭp'nŏs), 193. See *Somnus*.

Iacchus (ī-ăk'ŭs), 146
Icaria (ī-kā'rĭ-à), 165
Icarian (ī-kā'rĭ-ăn) Sea, 62
Icarus (ĭk'à-rŭs), 60 f.
Ida (ī'dà), 18
Idas (ī'dàs), 108–109
Ides of March, 269
Idmon (ĭd'mŏn), 70
Ilion (ĭl'ĭ-ŏn), 269. See *Troy*.
Ilium (ĭl'ĭ-ŭm), 269. See *Troy*.
Inachus (ĭn'à-kŭs) River, 168
Incubo, 358
inspiration, 379, 380
Invasions of Ireland, Cycle of, 441 f.
Io (ī'ō), 168–171, 477; and Jupiter, 168–171
Iobates (ī-ŏb'à-tēz), 225
Iolaüs (ī'ŏ-lā'ŭs), 236
Iolcus (ī-ŏl'kŭs), 250, 251, 264
Ionian Sea, origin of name, 171
Iopas, 324
Iphicles (ĭf'ĭ-klēz), 235
Iphigenia (ĭf'ĭ-jē-nī'à), 296–299; at Aulis, 276; in Tauris, 276, 299
Iphitus (ĭf'ĭ-tŭs), 242
Ireland, 436, 441 f.
iris (ī'rĭs), 55, 107
Iris, 35, 180–181, 331, 385, 481
Iron, Age of, 21
iron mittens, Thor's, 402
Ishtar (ĭsh'tär), 78
Island of the Dead, 442
Islands of the Blest, 195. See *Elysium*.
Ismarus (ĭs-mā'rŭs), 300
Italy, 322, 326, 329 f., 352, 354, 386
Ithaca (ĭth'à-kà), 272, 299, 304, 310–314
Ithunn (ē-thōōn), 404–405
Iulus (ī-ū'lŭs), or Ascanius (ăs-kā'nĭ-ŭs), 333

ivory gate, 193, 387
Ixion (ĭk-sī'ŏn), 112, 194-195, 197, 329; in Tartarus, 194-195

Janus (jā'nŭs), 8, 330, 336, 350-351, 354; description of, 350-351
Jason (jā'sŭn), 250-264; quest of the Golden Fleece, 250-264
Jocasta (jō-kăs'tȧ), 65
Jotunnheim (yŏ'tōon-hām), 396, 398, 408, 410
Jove (jōv), eagle of, 33, 38, 39. See *Jupiter*.
judgment of Paris, 268-269
juno (jōō'nō), 35, 361
Juno, 8, 18, 21, 31, 33-34, 39, 66, 104, 149, 165, 343, 366, 369, 385, 386, 474; and Aeneas, 323 f.; and Echo, 175-177; and Halcyone, 180-181; and Hercules, 232 f.; and Io, 168-171; and Trojan War, 267 f.; children of, 37, 39; cuckoo of, 35; pomegranate of, 163
Juno Moneta, 35
Jupiter (jōō'pĭ-tēr), 3, 18-26, 31-33, 39, 50, 81, 104, 105, 108, 112, 113, 115, 116, 121, 123, 130, 133, 146, 150, 160, 163, 175, 178, 181, 254, 308, 312, 349, 350, 358, 365, 366, 370, 378, 380, 384, 387, 391, 437, 474, 477; and Aeneas, 324, 325, 332; and Baucis, 66-68; and Callisto, 65-66; and Danaë, 207 f., 225; and Europa, 58-60; and Hercules, 232 f.; and Io, 168-171; and Minerva, 43; and Trojan War, 267 f.; children of, 37-48; eagle of, 33, 38, 39
Jupiter, the planet, 52, 474
Jupiter Ammon, 33
Jupiter Fulminator, 33

Jupiter Julius, 364
Jupiter Optimus Maximus, 33
Jupiter Pluvius, 33
Jupiter Stator, 33
Jupitor Tonans, 33
Justice, 481. See also *Themis*, *Dike*, and *Nemesis*.
Juturna (jōō-tûr'nȧ), 332

kallisteion (kăl'ĭs-tī'ŏn), 269
kelpies, 459
King Arthur Saga, 441, 454-457
kingfishers, origin of, 181
kings of Rome, 335 f.
kobolds (kō'bŏldz), 459
Kriemhild (krēm'hĭld), 7, 425 f.
Kris Kringle, 473

labors of Hercules, 235 f.
labyrinth, 60, 221-223
Lachesis (lăk'ē-sĭs), 48
Laelaps (lē'lăps), 178
Laertes (lā-ûr'tēz), 304, 310
Laestrygonians (lĕs-trĭ-gō'nĭ-ȧnz), 305
Laius (lā'yŭs), 64
Lake Regillus, Battle of, 343, 353, 370
Lancelot (lăn'sĕ-lŏt), Sir, 456
Land of Youth, 442, 450
Laocoon (lā-ŏk'ō-ŏn), 284-285, 286, 385, 387
Laodamia (lā'ō-dȧ-mī'ȧ), 277
Lapithae, 112-113
Lar, 386
Lares (lā'rēz), 362, 372
Lar familiaris (lär fȧ-mĭl'ĭ-ā'rĭs), 362
Lars Porsena. See *Porsena*.
Latinus (lȧ-tī'nŭs), 329-333
Latium (lā'shĭ-ŭm), 320, 329, 330, 339, 392

Latona (là-tō'nà), 39, 104 f., 120, 133, 195; wanderings of, 104 f.
laurel, 121; origin and meaning of, 173
Laurentalia, 371
Lausus (lô'sŭs), 332
Lavinia (là-vĭn'ĭ-à), 329-333
Lavinium (là-vĭn'ĭ-ŭm), 333
Leander (lē-ăn'dēr) and Hero, 94 f.
Leda (lē'dà), 269
Lemnos (lĕm'nŏs), 39, 254
Lemures, 369
Lemuria, 369
leprechaun (lĕp'rē-ĸôn'), 459
Lernaean (lûr-nē'ăn) Hydra, 236, 237
Lesbos, 167
Lethe (lē'thē) River, 190-191
Leto (lē'tō), 39. See Latona.
libations, 47-48
Liber (lī'bēr), 146, 367. See also Bacchus.
Libera, 146
Liberalia, 369
Libitina (lĭb'ĭ-tīn'à), 356
Linus (lī'nŭs), 233
lion, Androcles and, 344-345
Lir, 442
Little Bear, 66
"Little People," 458-460
Lleu (hlĕ'ü). See Lugh.
Logi (lō'jĭ), 411, 412
Loki (lō'kĕ), 405, 407-412; and Balder, 412-414
Lotus-Eaters, 300
Lucius Tarquin, 340
Lucrece. See Lucretia.
Lucretia, 340
ludi, 367 f.
Lug (lōōĸ). See Lugh.
Lugh (lōō), 438, 444, 446
Lug's chain, 444

luna (lū'nà), 3, 468
Luna, 41
Luperca (lū'pēr-kà), 360
Lupercalia (lū'pēr-kā'lĭ-à), 360, 372
Lupercus (lū'pēr-kŭs), 360, 372
Lyaeus (lī-ē'ŭs), 146
Lycia (lĭs'ĭ-à), 225
Lyonnesse, 456
lyre, 40, 106, 116, 196, 200, 366, 477

mabinogi (măb'ĭ-nō'gĭ), 457
Mabinogion (măb'ĭ-nō'gĭ-ŏn), 441, 457, 458
Maelduin (mà-ĕl'dû-ĭn), 441, 452-454; voyage of, 445, 452-454
maenads (mē'nădz), 148, 198-200
Maeterlinck (mä'tēr-lĭŋk), 472
Maev (māv), 405, 447-448
Maia (mā'yà), 45, 360. See fauna.
Man, Isle of, 443
Manannan (măn'ă-nàn), 442-443, 450, 458
Manawyddan (măn'à-wû'thàn), 458
Manes (mā'nēz), 362
Manlius Capitolinus, Marcus, 343
Manlius Torquatus, Titus, 344
March, 37
Marcus Aurelius, 368
Marpessa (mär-pĕs'à), 107-109, 123; and Apollo, 107-109
Mars (märz), 4, 36, 37, 62, 238, 259, 277, 333, 335, 356, 366, 369, 437; dogs of, 37, 366; vultures of, 366
Math, 458
Matronalia, 369
mead, 400
Medea (mĕ-dē'à), 260 f.
Medusa (mĕ-dū'sà), 209-217, 474, 481; slaying of, 209-217

Megara (mĕg′á-rá), 17, 235
Meleager (mĕl′ē-ā′jēr), 135 f., 244
Melpomene (mĕl-pŏm′ē-nē), 48
Memnon, 277
Memory, 400
Menelaus (mĕn′ē-lā′ŭs), 270 f., 295
Mercury (mûr′kŭ-rĭ), 32, 45 f.,
    67–68, 88, 106, 148, 163, 190, 199,
    209, 210, 233, 242, 253, 277, 305,
    309, 324, 325, 360, 366, 387, 437,
    474, 479, 480; and Argus, 169–
    170; cap of, 47; description of,
    45 f.
mermaids, 153
Metamorphoses (mĕt′á-môr′fô-
    sēz), Ovid's, 390–392
Messene (mĕ-sē′nē), 467
Mettius Curtius, 344
Mezentius (mē-zĕn′shĭ-ŭs), 331,
    332
Midas (mī′dăs), 166–167, 473, 478
Midgard (mĭd′gärd), 396, 398
Midgard Serpent, 405, 412, 414
Midir (mē′dĭr), 442
Miled (mē′lád), 445
Milesians (mī-lē′shănz), 442, 445
Milky Way, 476, 477
Mimer (mē′mēr), 418–423
Minerva (mĭ-nûr′vá), 23, 32, 43 f.,
    46, 62, 207, 209, 217, 225, 235,
    238, 242, 253, 254, 264, 308, 309,
    312, 366, 385, 437, 480; and
    Athens, 69–70; and Arachne,
    70–72; and Trojan War, 267 f.;
    contests of, 69 f.; description of,
    43 f.; Jupiter and, 43; owl of,
    366
Minos (mī′nŏs), 60, 238, 481
Minotaur (mĭn′ô-tôr), 60, 221–223
mistletoe, 412
Mjollnir (myôl′nêr), 402
Mnemosyne (nē-môs′ĭ-nē), 17, 40

Modred (mō′drĕd), **Sir,** 456
moly (mō′lĭ), 305–306
Momus, 193
money, 35
moneta, 35
Morann (mō′rän), 446
Morpheus (môr′fūs), 181, 193
Morrigu (môr′ē-ōō), 443, 447
Mors (môrz), 4, 193
Mother Earth, 244
Mowgli (mou′glĭ), 345
mulberry, origin of, 98
Munin (mū′nĭn), 400
Murias (mū′rĭ-ăs), 444
Muses (mū′zĕz), 1, 5, 40, 48, 106,
    225, 227, 354, 379, 380; descrip-
    tion of, 48
music, 4, 6, 106, 116, 148, 169–170,
    196
Muspellsheim (mōōs′pĕls-hām′),
    396
Mycenae (mī-sē′nē), 270, 299
Myrmidons (mûr′mĭ-dŏnz), 267, 279
mythmaking, 1 f., 11–12; modern,
    471–473
mythology, and scientific terms,
    473–475; definition of, 12;
    explanation of, 467–470; Greek
    and Roman names in, 372; im-
    portance of, 1–4; in advertising,
    477–479
myths, 467–470; and constella-
    tions, 475–477; classes of, 470;
    definitions of, 12; explanation
    of, 467–470; growth of, among
    the Greeks, 378–382; impor-
    tance of, 1–4; in advertising,
    477–479; in astronomy, 475–
    477; in business, 482; in
    Homer, 9, 380–381; in litera-
    ture, 4, 9–12; in Ovid, 9, 390–
    392; invention of, today, 471–

473; in Virgil, 9, 382–390; meaning of, 1 f.; on postage stamps, 479–482; use of, in science, 473–475; where found, 9–12; why studied, 4–8

naiads (nā′ădz), 14, 149
Naoise, 449
Narcissus (när-sĭs′ŭs) and Echo, 175–177
narcissus, origin of, 177
Nat (nät), 396–398
nature, gods of, 144–188
Nausicaä (nô-sĭk′ä-à), 309–310
Naxos (năk′sŏs), 165, 223
nectar, 32
Nemea (nē′mĕ-à), 233
Nemean (nē′mĕ-ăn) Games, 121
Nemean lion, 232, 234, 235
Nemed (nē′mĕd), 441
Nemesis (nĕm′ĕ-sĭs), 48, 297
Neoptolemus (nē′ŏp-tŏl′ĕ-mŭs), 295. See Pyrrhus.
Nephele (nĕf′ĕ-lē), 253
Neptune (nĕp′tūn), 3, 4, 18, 21, 69–70, 108, 116, 132, 144, 149, 151–154, 180, 213, 244, 251, 264, 323, 326, 366, 370, 385, 387, 443, 473; and Aeneas, 323 f.; and Trojan War, 267 f.; and Ulysses, 295, 304 f.; contest with Minerva, 69–70; description of, 151–154
Nereids (nē′rĕ-ĭdz), 149, 151, 182, 267
Nereus (nēr′ūs), 151, 471
Nessus (nĕs′ŭs), 244–245
Nestor (nĕs′tôr), 254, 272, 278
Niam (nī′ăm), 450–451
Nibelheim (nē′bĕl-hām), 420
Nibelungenlied (nē′bē-lŏŏng′ĕn-lēt′), 419, 426

Nibelungs (nē′bĕ-lŏŏngz), 418, 424, 427
Niflheim (nĕv′′l-hām), 396, 398, 405
Night, 16
Nike (nī′kē), 48, 50
Niobe (nī′ŏ-bĕ), 133–135
Nisus (nī′sŭs), 331
nixies, 459
Nor (nôr), 396
Norns, 398, 399, 400
Northland, gods of, 395–414; heroes of, 418–431
North Wind. See Boreas.
Notus (nō′tŭs), 150
Nuca (nū′kà), 452
Numa Pompilius (nū′mà pŏm-pĭl′ĭ-ŭs), 335–336, 338, 354, 358
Numen (nū′mĕn), 350
Numitor, 333
nymphs (nĭmfs), 149, 151, 153, 171 f., 210, 255, 354; and Apollo, 171 f.; description of, 149

oak, 33
obolus (ŏb′ŏ-lŭs), 189
Oceanids (ŏ-sē′à-nĭdz), 149
Oceanus (ŏ-sē′à-nŭs), 17, 43, 109, 144, 149, 151, 168, 212, 305; description of, 151
Odin (ō′dĭn), 395, 396, 397, 400, 402, 404, 409, 413, 414, 474; description of, 400
Odysseus (ŏ-dĭs′ūs). See Ulysses.
Odyssey (ŏd′ĭ-sĭ), Homer's, 278, 299, 380, 383
Oedipus (ĕd′ĭ-pŭs), 62 f.
Oeneus (ē′nūs), 135, 244
Ogygia (ŏ-jĭj′ĭ-à), 308
Oisin, 450. See Ossian.
Old Age, 356, 412
olive tree, 69–70

Olympiads (ô-lĭm′pĭ-ădz), 120
Olympic Council, 366–367
Olympic Games, 120 f.
Olympus, Mt., 18, 21, 31, 89, 245, 364, 365, 476
Omphale (ŏm′fȧ-lē), 242, 243
Ops (ŏps), 352
oracles, 48 f., 64, 180, 207, 213, 225, 251, 267, 269, 272, 274, 277, 299, 387
Orcus, 192
oreads (ō′rê-ădz), 149, 175
Orestes (ô-rĕs′tēz), 276, 297, 298–299
Orion (ô-rī′ŏn), 132–133, 475; and Diana, 132–133
Orpheus (ôr′fūs), 4, 6, 196 f., 254, 264, 329, 362, 380, 477; and Eurydice, 196 f.
Ortygia (ôr-tĭj′ĭ-ȧ), 182
Oscar, 450–451
Ossa (ŏs′ȧ), Mt., 18, 31
Ossian (ŏsh′ȧn), 450–451, 457
Ossianic (ŏsh′ĭ-ăn′ĭk) Cycle, 441, 449–451
Ostia, 338
Overhanging Heavens. See Uranus.

Pactolus (păk-tō′lŭs) River, 167
Paean. See Apollo Paean.
Paganalia, 372
Palamedes (păl-ȧ-mē′dēz), 272
Palës, 358, 369
Palinurus (păl′ĭ-nū′rŭs), 326, 328–329
palladium (pă-lā′dĭ-ŭm), 284
Pallas (păl′ȧs), 331–332
Pallas Athena (ȧ-thē′nȧ), 43. See Minerva.
Pan (păn), 148–149, 160, 358, 367; and Midas, 166–167; and

Syrinx, 169–170; description of, 148–149
Panchaia (păn-kā′yȧ), 467–468
Pandora (păn-dō′rȧ), 24 f.
Panic, 37, 149
Panope (păn′ŏ-pê), 62
pantheon, 382
Paphos (pă′fŭs), 94
paradise. See Avalon, Elysium, and Valhalla.
Parcae (pär′sē), 387
parentalia, 372
Parilia, 369
Paris, 269 f.
Parnassus (pär-năs′sŭs), Mt., 40, 41, 120, 173
Partholan (pär′thŏ-lăn), 441
Pasiphaë, 221
Patroclus (pȧ-trō′klŭs), 278–282
Peace, 482
peacock, 35, 170
Pegana (pĕ-gä′nȧ), Gods of, 473
Pegasus (pĕg′ȧ-sŭs), 41, 210, 225–227, 476, 481; and Bellerophon, 225–227
Peleus (pē′lūs), 254, 267–268, 272, 282
Pelias (pē′lĭ-ăs), 116, 250 f.
Pelion (pē′lĭ-ŏn), Mt., 18, 264
Penates (pĕ-nā′tēz), 362, 386
Penelope (pĕ-nĕl′ŏ-pê) 272, 299, 311–314, 474, 480; and return of Ulysses, 311–314
Penelopinae (pĕ-nĕl′ŏ-pī′nē), 474
Peneus (pĕ-nē′ŭs) River, 31, 171, 236
Pentathlon (pĕn-tăth′lŏn), 121
Penthesilea (pĕn′thĕ-sĭ-lē′ȧ), 282
Percival, Sir, 456
Periphetes (pĕ-rĭf′ê-tēz), 220
Peris, 459
Perithoüs, 224

Perseus (pûr'sūs), 45, 207–218, 233, 475–476; birth of, 207; rescue of Andromeda, 213 f.; slaying of Medusa, 209 f.

Peter Pan, 10, 472

Phaeacia (fē-ā'shǐ-ǎ), 309–310

Phaeacians (fē-ā'shǎnz), 309–310

Phaedra (fē'drá), 224

Phaëthon (fā'ē-thŏn), 109–112, 474, 477

Pherae (fē'rē), 115

philately. See postage stamps.

Philemon (fǐ-lē'mŏn), 66 f.

Philoctetes (fǐl'ŏk-tē'tēz), 284

Phineus (fī'nūs), 216, 256–258

Phintias, 227

Phlegethon (flēg'ē-thŏn) River, 191

Phoebus (fē'bǔs) Apollo. See Apollo.

Phoenicia (fē-nǐsh'ǐ-á), 58, 324, 343

Phoenician (fē-nǐsh'ǎn), 324

Phosphor (fŏs'fŏr), 150

Phrixus (frǐk'sǔs), 253

Phrygia (frǐj'ǐ á), 67, 166

Phthia (thǐ'á), 267

Pieria (pī-ē'rǐ-á), 41, 106

pietas, 383

Piety, 356, 383

Pillars of Hercules, 241

Pindar (pǐn'dár), 381

Pittheus (pǐt'thūs), 218–220

pixies, 459

Pleasure, 88, 234

Plebeii, 370

Pleiades (plē'yá-dēz), 45, 132, 133, 477

Pluto (plōō'tō), 18, 21, 189 f., 242, 367, 438, 486, 487; and Proserpina, 160 f.; cypress of, 367; description of, 189 f.

poets, inspiration of, 225

Pollux (pŏl'ǔks), 254, 256, 270, 343, 353–354, 476

Polybius (pŏ-lǐb'ǐ-ǔs), 468

Polybus (pŏl'ǐ-bǔs), 64

Polydectes (pŏl'ǐ-dĕk'tēz), 208–209, 217

Polyhymnia (pŏl'ǐ-hǐm'nǐ-á), 48

Polynices (pŏl'ǐ-nī'sēz), 65

Polyphemus (pŏl'ǐ-fē'mǔs), 295, 301–304, 322–323

Pomona (pŏ-mō'ná), 359, 360

Ponce de Leon (pŏns-dē-lē'ǔn), 473

Porsena, Lars, 341–343

Poseidon (pŏ-sī'dŏn), 21. See Neptune.

postage stamps, 479 f.

Priam (prī'ǎm), 39, 269 f.

Priscus, Lucius Tarquinius, 338

Proca, Silvius, 333

Procris, 178–180

Procrustes (prŏ-krǔs'tēz), 220; bed of, 220

Prometheus (prŏ-mē'thūs), 20, 21 f., 242–244, 467, 471, 479; and fire, 22; freeing of, 242–244; punishment of, 24–26

Proserpina (prŏ-sûr'pǐ-ná), 86 f., 146, 182, 192, 197, 224, 327, 356, 388; and Pluto, 160 f.

Protesilaüs (prō-tĕs'ǐ-lā'ǔs), 277

Proteus (prō'tūs), 154

Pryderi (prǐ-dá'rǐ), 457–458

Psyche (sī'kē), 81 f.; and Cupid, 81 f.

Pwyll (puŕl), 457

Pydna, Battle of, 353

Pygmalion (pǐg-mā'lǐ-ŏn) and Galatea, 93–94

Pylades (pǐl'á-dēz), 298–299

Pyramus (pǐr'á-mǔs), 96 f., 391; and Thisbe, 96 f.

Pyrrha (pǐr'á), 26, 391

Pyrrhus (pǐr'ŭs), 288, 295, 299.
See *Neoptolemus*.
Pythia (pǐth'ǐ-à), 48 f.
Pythian (pǐth'ǐ-ăn) Games, 120, 121
Pythias (pǐth'ǐ-ăs), Damon and, 227–228
Python (pī'thŏn), 119 f.

Quirinus (kwǐ-rī'nŭs), 335, 364

Ragnarok (ràg'nà-rŏk'), 414
Red Branch, 446, 448
Regillus (rĕ-jǐl'lŭs), Battle of, 343, 353, 370
Remus (rē'mŭs), 333–334, 361, 371; Romulus and, 333–335
Rhadamanthus (răd'à-măn'thŭs), 60, 233
Rhea (rē'à), 17, 93
Rhea Sylvia, 333
Roma, 356, 357
Romans, 33, 35, 37, 320, 329, 332, 382–392; divinities of, 348–372; festivals of, 367–372; religion of, 348–367
Rome, 331, 334 f.; divinities of, 348–372; early kings of, 335–343
Romulus (rŏm'ū-lŭs), 333–335, 361, 371, 372; and Remus, 333–335
Romulus Silvius, 333
Round Table, 454–456
runes (rōōnz), 399, 400
Rutulians (rŭt-ū'lǐ-ănz), 329

Sabine women, 334–335
Sabrina (sà-brī'nà), 471
sacrifices, 48, 207, 348, 349
Sagittarius (săj'ǐ-tā'rǐ-ŭs), 476, 482
Saint Elmo's Fire, 254
Salmoneus (săl-mō'nūs), 150
Santa Claus, 473
Sarpedon (sär-pē'dŏn), 60, 279

satire, 158
Saturn (săt'ērn), 17, 329, 348, 351–352, 366, 371; description of, 351–352
Saturnalia (săt'ēr-nā'lǐ-à), 352, 371
satyrs (săt'ērz), 148, 149
Scaevola, Caius Mucius, 343
science, 467–470, 473–477
Scio, 381
Scotland, 436, 441, 446, 449, 457
Scylla (sǐl'à), 154, 308, 323, 468
sea, gods of the, 151 f.
seasons, explanation of, 81, 163
Seasons, the four, 48
Semele (sĕm'ĕ-lē), 146
Semiramis (sĕ-mǐr'à-mǐs), 96
Servius Tullius, 339
Sestos (sĕs'tŏs), 94, 93
Setanta (sĕ-tän'tà), 446. See *Cuchulain*.
Seven against Thebes, 65
Sextus, 340
sheehogue (shē'hōg), 459
sibyl (sǐb'ǐl), 48, 344, 386–387, 388, 389
Sibylline books, 340
Sicily (sǐs'ǐ-lǐ), 161, 182, 227, 301, 323, 324
Siege Perilous (sēj pĕr'ǐ-lŭs), 454–456
Siegfried (sēg'frēd), 6, 7, 418–427, 431; story of, 418–427
Sieglinde (zēk'lǐn-dē), 418
Siegmund (zēk'mŏŏnt), 418
Silenus (sī-lē'nŭs), 146, 147, 167
Silvanus (sǐl-vā'nŭs), 358
Silver Age, 21
Silvius, 333
Simois (sǐ-mō'ǐs), 269
Sinon (sī'nŏn), 285–287
sirens (sī'rĕnz), 154, 307; description of, 154; Ulysses and, 307

Sirius (sĭr'ĭ-ŭs), 133
Sisyphus (sĭs'ĭ-fŭs), 194, 195, 197
skald (skōld), 404
Skinfaxi (shĭn'fäk-sĭ), 398
Skrymir (skrē'mĕr), 408
Skuld (skŏŏld), 398
Sky, gods of the, 31 f.
Sleet-Den, 405
Somnus (sŏm'nŭs), 4, 180–181, 193, 326
Sophocles (sŏf'ŏ-klēz), 382
Sparta, 270, 295
Spartacus, 344
Sphinx (sfĭngks), 19, 20, 63 f.
spider, origin of, 72
stag, Arcadian, 236
Stentor (stĕn'tôr), 272
Stonehenge, 438, 440
Stone of Destiny, 444
stone worship, 438
Storm-Foot, 258
Stumbling-Stone, 405
Stymphalian (stĭm-fā'lĭ-ạn) birds, 238
Stymphalus (stĭm-făl'ŭs), 238
Styx (stĭks) River, 88, 189 272, 327
suitors, slaying of the, 310–314
Sun. See Apollo.
sunflower, origin of the, 175
Svadilfari (sväd'ĭl-fä'rĭ), 407
Swift-Wing, 258
sylphs (sĭlfs), 459
Symplegades (sĭm-plĕg'ạ-dēz), 258–259
Syracuse, 227
syrinx (sĭr'ĭngks), invention of the, 169–170
Syrinx, 169–170

Tanaquil, 338
Tantalus (tăn'tạ-lŭs), 133, 194, 197, 329, 474

Tara (tä'rä), 445, 449
Taranis (tăr'ạ-nĭs), 438
Tarpeia, 335
Tarpeian Rock, 335, 344
Tarquin, Lucius, 339, 340
Tarquinius Collatinus, 340
Tarquinius Priscus, 338–339
Tarquin Superbus, 339
Tarquins, the, 338–343
Tartarus (tär'tạ-rŭs), 17, 20, 192, 193 f.; dwellers in, 193 f.
Tauri (tô'rĭ), 276, 299
Telamon (tĕl'ạ-mŏn), 244, 254
Telemachus (tĕ-lĕm'ạ-kŭs), 272, 295, 299, 310–314; Ulysses and, 310–314
Tellus, 16
Tempe, Vale of, 31
Terminalia (tûr'mĭ-nā'lĭ-ạ), 358
Terminus (tûr'mĭ-nŭs), 358, 372
Terpander, 65
Terpsichore (tûrp-sĭk'ŏ-rē), 48
Terror, 37
Tethys (tē'thĭs), 17, 43, 151
Teucer (tū'sēr), 244
Teutates (tŭ-lā'tĕz), 438
Thalia (thạ-lī'ạ), 48
Thanatos (thăn'ạ-tŏs), 193. See Mors.
Thea (thē'ạ), 17
Thebes (thēbz), 62 f., 232, 233
Themis (thē'mĭs), 17
Thersites (thĕr-sī'tēz), 282
Theseus (thē'sūs), 218–225, 254; and the Minotaur, 220–223; early adventures of, 218–220; later adventures of, 223–225
Thespian lion, 233
Thessaly, 31, 112, 115, 171, 250, 267
Thetis (thē'tĭs), 153, 267 f.
Thialfi (thĭ-ăl'fĭ), 408–412

Thisbe (thĭz'bĕ) and Pyramus, 96 f.
Thor (thôr), 8, 402, 403, 406, 407–
412, 474; adventures of, 407–
412; description of, 402
Thought, 400, 412
Thrace (thrās), 196, 322
Thrinacia (thrĭ-nā'shĭ-à), 308
thunderbolt of Jupiter, 2
Thursday, 8, 402
thyrsus (thûr'sŭs), 148
Tiber River and god, 329, 330, 332,
333, 341, 361, 362, 370
Tiresias (tī-rē'shĭ-ăs), 306–307, 308
Tisiphone (ti-sĭf'ŏ-nĕ), 17
Titania (tĭ-tā'nĭ-à), 460
Titans (tī'tănz), 16 f., 475
Tithonus (tĭ-thō'nŭs), 178, 277;
and Aurora, 178
Tityus, 195
Tiu (tē'ōō), 404. See Tyr.
totemism (tō'tĕm-ĭzm), 469–470
Trachis (trā'kĭs), 180
Trembling, 37
trident, 152, 324, 366
triens, 45
Triton (trī'tŏn), 153, 385
Troezen (trē'zĕn), 218
Trojan Horse. See wooden horse.
Trojans, under Aeneas, 320 f., 369
Trojan War, 267 f., 381, 384, 392;
fall of Troy, 282 f.; narrative of,
277 f.; origin of, 267–270; re-
turn of heroes of, 295 f.
trolls (trōlz), 420, 459
Troy, 244, 269, 320, 321, 322, 333;
fall of, 282 f.; siege of, 277 f.;
war against, 267 f.
Tuatha De Danann (thōō'à-hà
dā dà'nàn), 442, 444, 445
Tuesday, 404
Tullia, 339
Tullius, Servius, 339

Tullus Hostilius, 337
Turnus (tûr'nŭs), 329 f.
twilight of the gods, 414
Twin Brethren, the. See Castor,
Pollux, and Gemini.
Typhoeus (tī-fō'ūs), 2c
Tyr (tür), 404, 407

Ull, 405
Ulster, 445 f.
Ultonian Cycle, 441, 445–449
Ulysses (ŭ-lĭs'ēz), 45, 270 f., 295 f.,
322, 385, 386, 387, 392, 480;
adventures of, 299–314; Aeolus
and, 304–305; and Ciconians,
300; and Circe, 305–306; and
Cyclopes, 300–304; death of,
314; in Hades, 306–307; and
Laestrygonians, 305; and Lotus-
Eaters, 300; madness of, 272;
in Ogygia, 308–309; and Phaea-
cians, 309–310; and Scylla and
Charybdis, 308; and sirens, 307;
and the suitors, 310–314
underworld, 189 f., 412; Aeneas
in, 327–329, 386–387; regions
of, 189–192. See also Hades.
Undry, 442
Urania (ŭ-rā'nĭ-à), 48, 361
Uranus (ū'rà-nŭs), 16 f.
Urth, 398
Utgard-Loki (ōōt'gär-lō'kĕ), 410–
412
Uther (ū'thēr) Pendragon, 454, 460

Valhalla (văl-hăl'à), 395, 400, 402,
477
Valkyries (văl-kĭr'ĭz), 401, 402
Valley of Oblivion, 329
Ve (vā), 396
Venus (vē'nŭs), 4, 43, 44, 51, 91,
93, 94, 96, 215, 326, 364, 366,

384, 385, 386, 387, 388, 389;
and Adonis, 78–81; and Aeneas,
320–333; and Psyche, 81–89;
and Trojan War, 268 f.; de-
scription of, 43; doves of, 43,
100, 388, 389; magic girdle of,
43; sparrows of, 366
Verona, Battle of, 353
Verthandi (vĕr'thän-dĕ), 398
Vertumnus (vēr-tŭm'nŭs), 360–361
Vesper (vĕs'pēr). See *Hesperus.*
Vesta (vĕs'tả), 18, 35, 335, 336,
352–353, 366, 378, 386, 480, 481;
description of, 352–353; hearth
fire of, 37; House of, 352
Vestalia, 370
Vestal Virgins, 35–36, 335, 336,
352–353, 360, 370
Vesuvius, Mt., 327
Victoria. See *Nike.*
Victory, 482. See also *Nike.*
Vili (vē'lē), 396
Vingolf (vĭn'gŏlf), 400
Virginia, 344
Virginiuo, Lucius, 344
virtus, 383
volcano, 39
Voyage of Maelduin, 445, 452–454
Vulcan (vŭl'kăn), 24, 37, 39, 41,

43, 115, 220, 280, 332, 366, 370,
385, 480; forge of, 39, 366
vultures, of Mars, 37

Wales, 436, 441, 457–458, 477
Wednesday, 400
Weird Sisters, 398, 431
West Wind, 82, 107, 150. See
Zephyrus.
White Horned Bull. See *Bull of
Ailell.*
Wiglaf, 427–428
Winds, 144
Woden (wō'd'n), 400. See *Odin.*
Wolf, and Romulus and Remus,
333
wooden horse, 282 f., 344, 385
worms, 425, 426
Wyrd (würd), 398

Xanten, 418

Yellow Book of Lecan, 445
Yggdrasill (ĭg'drả-sĭl), 398
Ymir (ü'mĭr), 396

Zephyrus (zĕf'ĭ-rŭs), 8 2, 107, 150
151, 361
Zetes (zē'tēz), 254, 258
Zeus (zūs), 20. See *Jupiter.*
Zodiac (zō'dĭ-ăk), 476